Christian faith and practice

Christian faith and practice

in the experience

of the Society of Friends

RICHMOND
INDIANA

London Yearly Meeting of the
Religious Society of Friends

'Christian faith and practice' was approved by
Yearly Meeting in November 1959.
Together with 'Church government' it forms the
'Book of Christian discipline of London Yearly Meeting
of the Society of Friends'

First printed 1960
Reprinted with minor corrections 1961
Reprinted with further minor corrections 1963
Reprinted with further minor corrections 1966
Reprinted 1972
Reprinted 1973 by permission of London Yearly Meeting

Printed in the U.S.A. by Friends United Press

Obtainable from Friends United Press
101 Quaker Hill Drive, Richmond, IN 47374

Table of contents

The numerals used in this table of contents, and elsewhere in the book, are the extract numbers (shown §). An explanation of the editorial usages in the text is given at the end of the book, and is followed by a list of the sources of the extracts. There is also a bibliographical note on the various previous editions of this book, and an index of names and subject index.

Introduction

The Society of Friends arose from a personal experience of direct encounter with God as revealed in Jesus Christ. The conviction that Christ can speak to the condition of every man spread rapidly among the seekers of the seventeenth century and has remained at the centre of the Society's faith and practice. This book, therefore, begins with extracts illustrating the spiritual experience of many Friends, from George Fox to the present time.

It is natural that Friends should try to interpret their experience, following the exhortation to 'love the Lord thy God with all thy mind'. They have, however, avoided crystallizing their thought into a creed, which they feel would be as likely to impede, as to promote, living Christian experience or enlightened interpretation of it. Instead, therefore, of requiring its members to assent to a formal creed, the Society has preferred to invite them to consider whether they are spiritually alert, and responsive to the spirit of God: 'Do you cherish that of God within you, that his power growing in you may rule your life? Do you seek to follow Jesus who shows us the Father and teaches us the Way?'

It is therefore to be expected that the thinking of Friends through the years would take many different forms. Some well-known passages from the writings of Friends were written in order to deal with special and temporary situations. George Fox's letter to the Governor of Barbados is a case in point, its object being to rebut the criticism that Friends were not Christians. Friends themselves in the seventeenth century would have regarded the language used in the letter as one way of expressing their religious experience, a way more familiar to the Governor than the interpretation which found expression in their own teaching. In the early nineteenth century many Friends, under the influence of the Evangelical Movement, came to use a religious language which other Friends felt to be extreme and un-Quakerly. This called forth, on the other side, the expression of extreme views concerning the Inner Light. The writers in such cases were interested chiefly in their differences. In the British Isles this tension did not destroy the fellowship, and the same Friends who on occasion emphasized differences, also made their own contribution to the enlargement, and deepening, of the Quaker faith. This was to be expected; as the Light of Christ within, when faithfully followed, leads into unity.

This book does not set out to be a representative anthology covering the whole field; as we look back over the Society's history there is to be discerned a developing thread of experience resulting in a positive underlying unity. The selection of extracts has been made with this in mind, and it is hoped that the reader may be drawn into this uniting and developing life.

Compared with its predecessor, this book contains more reference to the contribution of the psychologist, and of the scientist. This is an indication of the development in thinking which is taking place, and a reminder that there is much more of the love and wisdom of God to be revealed to those who seek.

The Society of Friends has always recognised that corporate worship is central to its life. Both in the past and in the present such worship lies behind the Quaker testimonies against the activities and conditions that hinder the spiritual union of mankind with God and with one another, and behind the positive concerns that favour that union. For Friends there is in united worship a sense of adventure in the consciousness that the Holy Spirit has new light and truth to reveal. The central place in this book, therefore, is concerned with the Meeting for Worship.

The spiritual experience of individual Friends, and the quickened life of the group, have awakened in the Society a concern for the spread of its message at home and abroad, and have led the Society to expressions of its faith in personal and corporate living. It is these which occupy the remainder of the book.

The contents of this part of the book reveal that, with changing climate of thought, there has come an awareness of new Christian responsibilities, and of hitherto unsuspected applications of long accepted principles, in both personal and corporate living. In personal living, for instance, many questions relating to marriage are more to the fore in the minds of Friends to-day, than at the time of the previous revision. In the Welfare State so recently established the responsibility of the Christian is only beginning to be perceived. Even now some of the extracts relating to economic responsibilities of the individual bear the stamp of a passing economic organization of life. The Light which called Friends to be among the social pioneers of the past is still present to give fresh insights in the very different world of to-day.

The same is true of the Society's corporate testimonies. They all spring from a growing understanding of the will of God; their character has developed, and they are not necessarily accepted to-day in the form in which they were originally expressed. The development of the Peace Testimony can be traced through the years, taking different shape under changing conditions. The first generation of Friends did not recognise the essential wrongness of slavery. They appealed to the slaveholder to treat his slaves humanely; but it was a later generation that entered fully into the campaign which led to abolition. With changing conditions the concern for right relations between races has now come to the fore. In the early years of the present century the Society became concerned about the evils in the social order, and in particular with their relation to war. The 'Eight Foundations of a True Social Order' adopted by Yearly Meeting in 1918 seemed to put the concern of Friends into focus. Recent doubts as to whether they are adequate to-day reveal a contemporary uneasiness in the minds of Friends which has not yet reached the stage of united positive judgment.

The Society of Friends is tolerant of varied judgments amongst its members. It does not expect acceptance of a precise definition of its faith. It does not adopt an order of service for its public worship. It leaves its members wide freedom in working out the application of its testimonies. Throughout the Society's history there have been tensions, but in practice these have proved to be fruitful, and the result has been a continuing and developing unity in both faith and practice. The book is, therefore, intended to reflect the way in which Friends have come to understand their Christian faith and how they have been led into the service of Truth. Its purpose is to make Friends aware of their inheritance, not that they should be enslaved or fettered by their past, but that they may find guidance and inspiration to-day in the faith and practice of their predecessors.

1959

To the reader

Dearly beloved Friends, these things we do not lay upon you as a rule or form to walk by, but that all, with the measure of light which is pure and holy, may be guided: and so in the light walking and abiding, these may be fulfilled in the Spirit, not from the letter, for the letter killeth, but the Spirit giveth life. *Postscript to an epistle to 'the brethren in the north' issued by a meeting of elders at Balby, 1656*

All Truth is a shadow except the last, except the utmost; yet every Truth is true in its kind. It is substance in its own place, though it be but a shadow in another place (for it is but a reflection from an intenser substance); and the shadow is a true shadow, as the substance is a true substance. *Isaac Penington (1653)*

It is not opinion, or speculation, or notions of what is true, or assent to or the subscription of articles or propositions, though never so soundly worded, that...makes a man a true believer or a true Christian. But it is a conformity of mind and practice to the will of God, in all holiness of conversation, according to the dictates of this Divine principle of Light and Life in the soul which denotes a person truly a child of God. *William Penn (1692)*

Chapter 1:   Spiritual experiences of Friends

This section of our Book of Discipline was first conceived in 1921, after a time of theological difference, by Friends who longed not to be separated by dispute, but to share an experience which men and women had reached in diverse ways. For the Society of Friends might be thought of as a prism through which the Divine Light passes, to become visible in a spectrum of many colours; many more, in their richness, than words alone can express.

George Bradshaw made railway time-tables to the glory of God, John Bellows made dictionaries, Daniel Quare made clocks; but these we cannot quote. The labourer in the fields, the housewife sweeping her room, the faithful tradesman, have left few memorials. Scholars like Thomas Hodgkin, Frederic Seebohm and Rendel Harris have their memorials elsewhere. No voice speaks here for the long line of scientists that began before John Dalton, and stretches on after Arthur S. Eddington. Let no one think, because we have omitted them, that we could forget the Quaker seamen: Robert Fowler, Thomas Chalkley, Paul Cuffee the negro captain, and all their gallant band. There is no word from the masters of industry—the Darbys of Coalbrookdale, Richard Reynolds, Joseph Rowntree or George Cadbury; or from those pioneers of social protest—John Lilburne the Leveller, John Bellers, Peter Bedford or Alfred Salter of Bermondsey. Here are no pictures of the women whom we remember for the beauty of their person as well as character— Gulielma Penn and Esther Tuke; or such glorious old men as William Tuke (who in his sixties founded York Retreat) or Theophilus Waldmeier (who in his sixties founded the Lebanon Hospital); or our children James Parnell, little Mary Samm, and those who kept the meeting while their elders lay in gaol.

Even of the ministers there are few enough: George Fox, but not Richard Farnsworth, that 'man of parts and Champion for the Truth'; John Woolman, but not Anthony Benezet; Stephen Grellet, but not his friend and travelling companion William Allen; Elizabeth Fry, but not Deborah Darby who foretold her career of mercy. We have shown persecution endured and overcome in seventeenth-century England and

New England, but not in nineteenth-century Norway or twentieth-century Germany. Though the field of Quaker concern has stretched across the world, we have had for the most part to stay at home, naming but one or two of a great company beyond seas. If we could have shown Rachel Metcalfe mothering her orphans from her invalid chair; or George Swan, the boy from the fairground, playing his concertina through the villages of India—if only we could have shown them all!

But then in honesty we should have had to reveal also the extent of our failure; the light dimmed in narrow hearts and creeds, the baptism of grace lost in timidity and torpor, the corrosion of arrogance and self-satisfaction—for we have known these, too. May the light prevail over the darkness; may those who are here speak for all the children of the Light, to the needs of other times as well as their own.   *1959*

> 'As looking over the minutes made by persons who have put off this body hath sometimes revived in me a thought how ages pass away; so this list may probably revive a like thought in some, when I and the rest of the persons named above are centred in another state of being. The Lord who was the guide of my youth hath in tender mercies helped me hitherto; He hath healed my wounds; He hath helped me out of grievous entanglements; He remains to be the strength of my life, to whom I desire to devote myself in time and in eternity.'
>
> (*Written by John Woolman at the foot of a list of Ministers and Elders of Burlington, New Jersey in 1767*)

George Fox (1624-1691) *was the son of a Leicestershire weaver, and he described his mother as 'of the stock of the martyrs'. His Journal was first published in 1694, extensively edited by Thomas Ellwood, and has been many times reprinted. Our first extract shows how, in 1643, when he was nineteen, and apprenticed to a shoe-maker and wool dealer, he was shocked by the failure of 'professors', i.e. professing Christians, to live up to their Christian standards. This disillusionment drove him from his home in search of spiritual help. The passages chosen show how he reached his own first-hand experience of Christ amid the religious confusion of the Civil War. When this experience came to him he spent himself thereafter drawing others into it, and in knitting them into an enduring fellowship. Years of his life were spent in travel, and he suffered eight imprisonments for conscience' sake. He 'settled the Monthly Meetings in the Lord's everlasting power' and his organizing ability gave our Society a structure which stands to this day.*

When I came towards nineteen years of age, I being upon business
at a fair, one of my cousins, whose name was Bradford, being a
professor and having another professor with him, came to me and
asked me to drink part of a jug of beer with them, and I, being
thirsty, went in with them, for I loved any that had a sense of good,
or that did seek after the Lord. And when we had drunk a glass
apiece, they began to drink healths and called for more drink,
agreeing together that he that would not drink should pay all. I
was grieved that any that made profession of religion should offer
to do so. They grieved me very much, having never had such a
thing put to me before by any sort of people; wherefore I rose up to
be gone, and putting my hand into my pocket, I took out a groat
and laid it down upon the table before them and said, 'If it be so,
I'll leave you'. So I went away; and when I had done what business
I had to do, I returned home, but did not go to bed that night,
nor could not sleep, but sometimes walked up and down, and sometimes prayed and cried to the Lord, who said unto me, 'Thou seest
how young people go together into vanity and old people into the
earth; and thou must forsake all, both young and old, and keep out
of all, and be as a stranger unto all'. Then, at the command of God,
on the 9th day of the Seventh Month ⟨September⟩, 1643, I left my
relations and brake off all familiarity or fellowship with young or
old.   *Journal, 1643*

Sorrow, grief and troubles...were so great upon me that I could
have wished I had never been born to see vanity and wickedness,
or that I had been born blind, that I might never have seen vanity
and wickedness, and deaf, that I might never have heard vain and
wicked words, or the Lord's name blasphemed.   *Journal, 1646*

Priest Stephens asked me a question, why Christ cried out upon the
Cross, 'My God, my God, why has thou forsaken me?' and why he
said, 'If it be possible, let this cup pass from me, yet not my will but
thine be done'? And I told him at that time the sins of all mankind
were upon him, and their iniquities and transgressions with which he
was wounded, which he was to bear, and to be an offering for them
as he was man, but died not as he was God; and so, in that he died
for all men, and tasted death for every man, he was an offering for
the sins of the whole world. This I spoke, being at that time in a

measure sensible of Christ's sufferings, and what he went through.

4   I was often under great temptations; and I fasted much, and walked abroad in solitary places many days, and often took my Bible and went and sat in hollow trees and lonesome places till night came on; and frequently in the night walked mournfully about by myself, for I was a man of sorrows in the times of the first workings of the Lord in me.   *Journal, 1647*

5   As I had forsaken all the priests, so I left the separate preachers also, and those called the most experienced people; for I saw there was none among them all that could speak to my condition. And when all my hopes in them and in all men were gone, so that I had nothing outwardly to help me, nor could tell what to do, then, oh then, I heard a voice which said, 'There is one, even Christ Jesus, that can speak to thy condition', and when I heard it my heart did leap for joy. Then the Lord did let me see why there was none upon the earth that could speak to my condition, namely, that I might give him all the glory; for all are concluded under sin, and shut up in unbelief as I had been, that Jesus Christ might have the pre-eminence who enlightens, and gives grace, and faith, and power. Thus, when God doth work who shall let it?* And this I knew experimentally.   *Journal, 1647*

6   My desires after the Lord grew stronger, and zeal in the pure knowledge of God and of Christ alone, without the help of any man, book, or writing. For though I read the Scriptures that spoke of Christ and of God, yet I knew him not but by revelation, as he who hath the key did open, and as the Father of life drew me to his Son by his spirit. And then the Lord did gently lead me along, and did let me see his love, which was endless and eternal, and surpasseth all the knowledge that men have in the natural state, or can get by history or books; and that love let me see myself as I was without him. And I was afraid of all company, for I saw them perfectly where they were, through the love of God which let me see myself. I had not fellowship with any people, priests, or professors, nor any sort of separated people, but with Christ, who hath the key, and

* 'Who shall let it?' i.e. Who shall hinder it?

opened the door of light and life unto me. And I was afraid of all carnal talk and talkers, for I could see nothing but corruptions, and the life lay under the burden of corruptions. And when I myself was in the deep, under all shut up, I could not believe that I should ever overcome; my troubles, my sorrows, and my temptations, were so great, that I thought many times I should have despaired, I was so tempted. But when Christ opened to me how he was tempted by the same Devil and had overcome him and bruised his head, and that through him and his power, light, grace and spirit, I should overcome also, I had confidence in him. So he it was that opened to me when I was shut up and had not hope nor faith. Christ it was who had enlightened me, that gave me his light to believe in, and gave me hope, which is himself, revealed himself in me, and gave me his spirit and gave me his grace, which I found sufficient in the deeps and in weakness. Thus, in the deepest miseries, and in greatest sorrows and temptations, that many times beset me, the Lord in his mercy did keep me.

And I found that there were two thirsts in me, the one after the creatures, to have gotten help and strength there, and the other after the Lord the creator and his Son Jesus Christ. And I saw all the world could do me no good. If I had had a king's diet, palace and attendance, all would have been as nothing, for nothing gave me comfort but the Lord by his power.   *Journal, 1647*

I was under great temptations sometimes, and my inward sufferings were heavy; but I could find none to open my condition to but the Lord alone, unto whom I cried night and day. And I went back into Nottinghamshire, and there the Lord shewed me that the natures of those things which were hurtful without were within, in the hearts and minds of wicked men. The natures of dogs, swine, vipers, of Sodom and Egypt, Pharaoh, Cain, Ishmael, Esau, etc. The natures of these I saw within, though people had been looking without. And I cried to the Lord, saying, 'Why should I be thus, seeing I was never addicted to commit those evils?' And the Lord answered that it was needful I should have a sense of all conditions, how else should I speak to all conditions; and in this I saw the infinite love of God. I saw also that there was an ocean of darkness and death, but an infinite ocean of light and love, which flowed

George Fox

over the ocean of darkness. And in that also I saw the infinite love of God; and I had great openings. *Journal, 1647*

8 And I saw the harvest white, and the Seed of God lying thick in the ground, as ever did wheat that was sown outwardly, and none to gather it; and for this I mourned with tears. *Journal, 1647*

9 Now was I come up in spirit through the flaming sword into the paradise of God. All things were new, and all the creation gave another smell unto me than before, beyond what words can utter. *Journal, 1647*

10 Now I was sent to turn people from darkness to the light that they might receive Christ Jesus, for to as many as should receive him in his light, I saw that he would give power to become the sons of God, which I had obtained by receiving Christ. And I was to direct people to the Spirit that gave forth the Scriptures, by which they might be led into all Truth, and so up to Christ and God, as they had been who gave them forth. And I was to turn them to the grace of God, and to the Truth in the heart, which came by Jesus. ...I was to bring people off from all their own ways to Christ, the new and living way...to know the spirit of Truth in the inward parts, and to be led thereby, that in it they might worship the Father of spirits...making melody in their hearts to the Lord who hath sent his beloved Son to be their Saviour, and caused his heavenly sun to shine upon all the world, and through them all, and his heavenly rain to fall upon the just and the unjust (as his outward rain doth fall, and his outward sun doth shine on all), which is God's unspeakable love to the world. *Journal, 1648*

11 *His dying words:* I am glad I was here. Now I am clear, I am fully clear...All is well; the Seed of God reigns over all and over death itself. And though I am weak in body, yet the power of God is over all, and the Seed reigns over all disorderly spirits. *Journal, 1691*

Testimonies concerning George Fox, by those who knew him:

12 He was indeed an heavenly-minded man, zealous for the name of the Lord, and preferred the honour of God before all things. He was

valiant for the truth, bold in asserting it, patient in suffering for it, unwearied in labouring in it, steady in his testimony to it, immovable as a rock. *Thomas Ellwood (1694)*

13 I write of my knowledge and not report; and my witness is true, having been with him for weeks and months together on divers occasions, and those of the nearest and most exercising nature, and that by night and by day, by sea and by land, in this and in foreign countries; and I can say I never saw him out of his place, or not a match for every service or occasion.

In his testimony or ministry he much laboured to open truth to people's understandings, and to bottom them upon the principle and principal, Christ Jesus the Light of the World, that by bringing them to something that was of God in themselves, they might the better know and judge of him and themselves.

He had an extraordinary gift in opening the Scriptures. He would go to the marrow of things and show the mind, harmony and fulfilling of them with much plainness and to great comfort and edification. But above all he excelled in prayer. The inwardness and weight of his spirit, the reverence and solemnity of his address and behaviour, and the fewness and fullness of his words, have often struck even strangers with admiration, as they used to reach others with consolation. The most awful, living, reverent frame I ever felt or beheld, I must say, was his in prayer. And truly it was a testimony that he knew and lived nearer to the Lord than other men; for they that know him most will see most reason to approach him with reverence and fear. *William Penn (1694)*

14 *A narrative given by an aged woman of Long Lane, Borough (London) to Isaac Pickerill, c. 1720:* Now Friends, I will tell you how I was convinced. I was a young lass at that time in Dorsetshire, when George Fox came into that country; and he having appointed a meeting to which the people generally flocked, I went among the rest; and in going along the road, this query arose in my mind: 'What is it that condemns me when I do evil, and justifies me when

I do well? What is it?' In this state I went to the meeting, which was large. George Fox rose with these words: 'Who art thou that queriest in thy mind, What is it I feel which condemneth me when I do evil, and justifieth me when I do well? I will tell thee. Lo! He that formed the mountains and created the winds, and declareth unto man what are his thoughts, that maketh the morning darkness and treadeth upon the high places of the earth; the Lord, the Lord of Hosts is his name. It is He, by his Spirit, that condemneth thee for evil, and justifieth thee when thou dost well. Keep under its dictates, and He will be thy preserver to the end.' To which she added, 'It was truth, the very truth, and I have never departed from it'.

The Westmorland Seekers and the Early Friends. *A strong Seeker community in Westmorland in 1652, with its centre at Preston Patrick, prepared the way for the success which attended the work of Fox. A large part of this community joined the new movement, which at once became furnished with a band of ardent young men and women who would carry the message to the rest of England. The glowing experience which came to them with the visit of Fox was expressed by Francis Howgill (1618-1669) and Edward Burrough (1633-1663). Howgill came from Todthorne, near Grayrigg, Westmorland, had been a preacher among the Seekers, and was among the foremost workers in London, Bristol, Ireland and elsewhere. He died in the prison on Appleby Bridge in January, 1669. Edward Burrough of Underbarrow, his intimate friend, shared his service and is called on the title-page of his works 'a son of thunder and consolation, that true prophet and faithful servant of God, and sufferer for the testimony of Jesus, who died a prisoner for the Word of God in the City of London'. 'His very strength,' says Howgill, 'was bended after God.' As Howgill's account is quoted elsewhere (§184) we give below part of Burrough's version from the beginning of his Works:*

15   It is now about seven years since the Lord raised us up in the north of England, and opened our mouths in his Spirit. What we were before, in our religious professions and practice, is well known to that part of the country; how generally we were men of the strictest sect, and of the greatest zeal in the performance of outward righteousness. We went through and tried all sorts of teachers, and ran from mountain to mountain and from man to man, and from one form to another, as many do to this day, and remain not gathered to the Lord. After

our long seeking, the Lord appeared to us and revealed his glory in us, and gave us of his Spirit, and gave us of his wisdom to guide us, whereby we saw all the world and the true state of all things, and the true condition of the church in her present estate.

By this light of Christ in us we were led out of all false ways, and false preachings and false ministers; and met together often, and waited upon the Lord in pure silence...⟨We⟩ hearkened to the voice of the Lord, and felt his word in our hearts to burn up and beat down all that was contrary to God; and we obeyed the light of Christ in us, and followed the motions of the Lord's pure Spirit and took up the cross to all earthly glories, crowns and ways, and denied ourselves, our relations, and all that stood in the way betwixt us and the Lord. We chose to suffer with and for the name of Christ, rather than ⟨enjoy⟩ all the pleasures upon earth, or all our former professions and practices in religion without the power and Spirit of God.

Being prepared of the Lord, and having received power from on high, we went forth as commanded of the Lord, leaving all relations and all things of the world behind us, that we might fulfil the work of the Lord, unto which he called us...and the word of the Lord we sounded, and did not spare; and caused the deaf to hear, the blind to see, and the heart that was hardened to be awakened.

16 *A Testimony of William Penn concerning the Early Friends:*
They were changed men themselves before they went about to change others. Their hearts were rent as well as their garments, and they knew the power and work of God upon them...And as they freely received what they had to say from the Lord, so they freely administered it to others. The bent and stress of their ministry was conversion to God, regeneration and holiness, not schemes of doctrines and verbal creeds or new forms of worship, but a leaving off in religion the superfluous and reducing the ceremonious and formal part, and pressing earnestly the substantial, the necessary and profitable part, as all upon a serious reflection must and do acknowledge.   *William Penn's Preface to Fox's Journal (1694)*

The Swarthmoor household. *Margaret Fell (1614-1702) was the wife of Judge Thomas Fell of Swarthmoor Hall, near Ulverston, Lancashire. After the meeting with George Fox in June 1652, described in her own words below, she made her house (with her husband's permission) the centre for the Quaker 'Publishers of Truth' and became the nursing-mother of the new movement. Among the members of her household who became Quaker leaders were Thomas Salthouse (1630-1690/1) who laboured chiefly in the south-west of England, and Anne Clayton, who travelled to Barbados and America. The influence of Margaret Fell and her household is described here by Anthony Pearson (1628-1666) who was a frequent visitor at the time, and William Caton (1636-1665) who was then companion to young George Fell, and later became one of the apostles of Quakerism in Holland.*

17 All my religion was but the hearing of the ear, the believing and talking of a God and Christ in heaven or a place at a distance, I knew not where. Oh, how gracious was the Lord to me in carrying me to Judge Fell's to see the wonders of His power and wisdom, *a family walking in the fear of the Lord,* conversing daily with Him, crucified to the world and living only to God. I was so confounded, all my knowledge and wisdom became folly; my mouth was stopped, my conscience convinced and the secrets of my heart were made manifest, and that Lord was discovered to be near, whom I ignorantly worshipped. *Anthony Pearson, 1653*

18 Truly willing we were to sympathise and bear one with another, to be helpful one unto another, and in true and tender love to watch over one another. And, oh the love, mercy and power of God, which abounded to us, through us and among us; who shall declare it? And hence came that worthy family to be so renowned in the nation, the fame of which spread much among Friends. And the power and presence of the Lord being so much there with us, it was as a means to induce many, even from far, to come thither, so that at one time there would have been Friends out of five or six counties...I was cherished and encouraged in the way of life by my entirely beloved friend Margaret Fell, who as a tender-hearted nursing-mother cared for me and was tender of me as if I had been one of her own children; oh, the kindness, the respect and friendship which she showed me ought never to be forgotten by me. *William Caton, 1652*

In 1669, eleven years after Judge Fell's death, Margaret Fell married George Fox, though their incessant labours, travels and imprisonments prevented them from living much together at Swarthmoor. Her account of her convincement follows:

19   I was one that sought after the best things, being desirous to serve God, so as I might be accepted of him, and was enquiring after the way of the Lord, and went often to hear the best ministers that came into our parts, whom we frequently entertained at our house... This I hoped I did well in, but often I feared was short of the right way. And after this manner I was enquiring and seeking about twenty years.

20   In the year 1652 it pleased the Lord to draw him ⟨George Fox⟩ toward us. . . . My then husband, Thomas Fell, was not at home at that time, but gone the Welsh circuit, being one of the Judges of Assize, and our house ⟨Swarthmoor Hall⟩ being a place open to entertain ministers and religious people at, one of George Fox his friends brought him hither, where he stayed all night. And the next day, being a lecture or a fast-day, he went to Ulverston steeplehouse, but came not in till people were gathered; I and my children had been a long time there before. And when they were singing before the sermon, he came in; and when they had done singing, he stood up upon a seat or form and desired that he might have liberty to speak. And he that was in the pulpit said he might. And the first words that he spoke were as followeth: 'He is not a Jew that is one outward, neither is that circumcision which is outward; but he is a Jew that is one inward, and that is circumcision which is of the heart'. And so he went on and said, How that Christ was the Light of the world and lighteth every man that cometh into the world; and that by this Light they might be gathered to God, etc. And I stood up in my pew, and I wondered at his doctrine, for I had never heard such before. And then he went on, and opened the Scriptures, and said, 'The Scriptures were the prophets' words and Christ's and the apostles' words, and what as they spoke they enjoyed and possessed and had it from the Lord'. And said, 'Then what had any to do with the Scriptures, but as they came to the Spirit that gave them forth. You will say, Christ saith this, and the apostles say this; but what canst thou say? Art thou a child of Light and hast walked in the Light, and what thou speakest is it inwardly from God?'

This opened me so that it cut me to the heart; and then I saw clearly we were all wrong. So I sat me down in my pew again, and cried bitterly. And I cried in my spirit to the Lord, 'We are all thieves, we are all thieves, we have taken the Scriptures in words and know nothing of them in ourselves'. So that served me, that I cannot well tell what he spake afterwards; but he went on in declaring against the false prophets and priests and deceivers of the people.

And there was one John Sawrey, a Justice of Peace and a professor, that bid the churchwarden 'Take him away', and he laid his hands on him several times, and took them off again and let him alone; and then after a while he ⟨George Fox⟩ gave over and came to our house again that night. And he spoke in the family amongst the servants; and they were all generally convinced, as William Caton, Thomas Salthouse, Mary Askew, Anne Clayton and several other servants. And I was stricken into such a sadness I knew not what to do, my husband being from home. I saw it was the truth, and I could not deny it; and I did as the apostle saith, I 'received the truth in the love of it'. And it was opened to me so clear that I had never a tittle in my heart against it; but I desired the Lord that I might be kept in it, and then I desired no greater portion.

Margaret Fox (1694)

21   *Of her second trial in 1664 she wrote:* So they passed sentence of Praemunire upon me which was that I should be out of the King's protection and forfeit all my estate, real and personal, to the King and imprisonment during life. But the great God of heaven and earth supported my spirit under this severe sentence, that I was not terrified but gave this answer to Judge Turner, who gave the sentence, 'Although I am out of the King's protection, I am not out of the protection of the Almighty God'. (*She was subsequently released and her estate was given back to her family.*)

James Nayler (1617?-1660), *yeoman, of West Ardsley near Wakefield, had served as quartermaster in the Parliamentary Army, and fought at Dunbar. His account of his spiritual experience, given in his evidence before the Westmorland Justices brought about the convincement of one of them, Anthony Pearson, whose* *visit to Swarthmoor Hall is described in §17 and who the following year was largely instrumental in the setting up of the earliest monthly meeting, that of men Friends in County Durham.*

22   I was at the plow, meditating on the things of God, and suddenly I heard a voice saying to me, 'Get thee out from thy kindred, and from thy father's house'. And I had a promise given with it, whereupon I did exceedingly rejoice that I had heard the voice of that God which I had professed from a child, but had never known him. . . . And when I came at home I gave up my estate, cast out my money; but not being obedient in going forth, the wrath of God was upon me, so that I was made a wonder to all, and none thought I would have lived. But after I was made willing, I began to make some preparation, as apparel and other necessaries, not knowing whither I should go. But shortly afterwards going a gate-ward with a friend from my own house, having on an old suit, without any money, having neither taken leave of wife or children, not thinking then of any journey, I was commanded to go into the west, not knowing whither I should go, nor what I was to do there. But when I had been there a little while, I had given me what I was to declare. And ever since I have remained not knowing today what I was to do tomorrow...⟨The promise was⟩ that God would be with me, which promise I find made good every day.

From the examination of James Nayler at Appleby, 1652

Nayler soon appeared to some outside observers as the ablest speaker in the new movement, and a leader not second even to Fox. Many convincements followed; but in the passionate love which filled them all, neither leaders nor followers remembered the earthly vessels in which the treasure lay. During 1656, the more sober Friends became uneasy at Nayler's exaltation. He became estranged from Fox; and at an interview in Exeter jail, dissension between the two brought credit to neither. In October, Nayler entered Bristol on horseback, while his followers as a sign of Christ's presence spread garments before him and cried, 'Holy, Holy, Holy, Lord God of Israel.' The City authorities seized the little band, and sent Nayler to London to stand trial for blasphemy. There he steadily maintained that 'he denied James Nayler to be Christ, but Christ was in him.' After long debates he was sentenced to be whipped, pilloried, branded, and have his tongue bored through. He bore his punishments with heroic courage and humility, after embracing the executioner; and lay in prison until 1659, when he was released.

*Having publicly abjured his follies in several statements he sought to be recon-
ciled with Fox, who was lying ill and exhausted at Reading. Rebuffed, he wrote
to Margaret Fell: 'My spirit was quieted, in that simplicity in which I went,
in that to return . . . and so his will is our peace.' William Dewsbury was at last
instrumental in bringing a reconciliation, and Nayler resumed his Quaker service,
'living in great self-denial and very jealous of himself.' The following are from
various written statements which he made in 1659 and 1660, after his repentance.*

23   Ere I came into the Kingdom of Christ, my pure rest, I met with
      many hardships and great travails, and many temptations and trials
      within and without; but the greatest enemies were yet within me,
      which would upon every hardship be tempting with unbelief to
      destroy this faith and hope, which was all that I had set before me
      to encourage me to endure such hardships, and to follow the Light
      in a way I had not known, and to walk in the clouds to meet the
      Lord, and to leave my former knowledge and wisdom and glory and
      riches to go into a way I had not walked...And this work was not
      wrought in me by the knowledge of Christ after the flesh but as I
      came to learn him in spirit, for spiritual wickedness had taken my
      soul captive, and by the spirit it must be sanctified and set free.
      And I came to see that if I had been in his company here on earth
      as long as his disciples were, in the flesh, and ⟨had⟩ seen as much as
      they did, and heard from his own mouth, I should have been short
      of this work as they were, in whom the Child was unborn when he
      went away in the flesh. And they knew not what spirits they were of
      until he came again to them in spirit and was revealed in them.
      'What the possession of the living faith is' (1659)

24   The lower God doth bring me, and the nearer to himself, the more
      doth Love and Tenderness spring and spread towards the poor,
      simple and despised ones, who are poor in spirit, meek and lowly
      Suffering Lambs, and with those I choose to suffer, and do suffer,
      wherever they are found.
      'To all the dearly beloved people of God' (1659)

*In 1660 he set out on foot for the North, intending to go home to his wife and
children. He was seen by a Friend of Hertford, sitting by the wayside in meditation;
and passed on through Huntingdon, where another Friend saw him 'in such an awful
frame as if he had been redeemed from the earth and a stranger on it, seeking a better*

country and inheritance'. Some miles beyond Huntingdon he was robbed and bound, and found towards evening in a field. He was taken to a Friend's house near King's Ripton, and passed away in the peace of God towards the end of October, 1660.

25 *'James Nayler's last words, spoken about two hours before his departure out of this life':*

There is a spirit which I feel that delights to do no evil, nor to revenge any wrong, but delights to endure all things, in hope to enjoy its own in the end. Its hope is to outlive all wrath and contention, and to weary out all exaltation and cruelty, or whatever is of a nature contrary to itself. It sees to the end of all temptations. As it bears no evil in itself, so it conceives none in thoughts to any other. If it be betrayed, it bears it, for its ground and spring is the mercies and for-giveness of God. Its crown is meekness, its life is everlasting love unfeigned; it takes its kingdom with entreaty and not with conten-tion, and keeps it by lowliness of mind. In God alone it can rejoice, though none else regard it, or can own its life. It's conceived in sorrow, and brought forth without any to pity it, nor doth it murmur at grief and oppression. It never rejoiceth but through sufferings; for with the world's joy it is murdered. I found it alone, being for-saken. I have fellowship therein with them who lived in dens and desolate places in the earth, who through death obtained this resur-rection and eternal holy life.

Thou wast with me when I fled from the face of mine enemies: then didst Thou warn me in the night: Thou carriedst me in Thy power into the hiding-place Thou hadst prepared for me: there Thou coveredst me with Thy Hand that in time Thou mightst bring me forth a rock before all the world. When I was weak Thou stayedst me with Thy Hand, that in Thy time Thou mightst present me to the world in Thy strength in which I stand, and cannot be moved. Praise the Lord, O my soul. Let this be written for those that come after. Praise the Lord. *J.N.*

Isaac Penington (1616-1679), *the son of a prominent Parliamentarian leader, was already a man of forty-two and a practised author when he joined the Quakers in 1658. He suffered five imprisonments at Aylesbury and one at Reading—some five years' confinement in all, often in cold, damp and unhealthy rooms that nearly*

*cost him his life. He was much occupied in writing, and in travail of soul, 'being
retired in spirit and mourning to my God, for the powerful bringing forth of his pure
life yet more perfectly both in myself and others'. His writings, though diffuse, are
often strangely beautiful, and reflect his own depth of experience and tenderness of spirit.*

26   I have been a man of sorrow and affliction from my childhood,
feeling the want of the Lord and mourning after him, separated
by him from the love, nature and spirit of this world, and turned in
spirit towards him almost ever since I could remember.

In this sense of my lost estate, I sought after the Lord, I read
Scriptures, I watched over my own heart, I cried unto the Lord
for what I felt the want of, I blessed his Name in what he mercifully
did for me and bestowed on me...

But my soul was not satisfied with what I met with, nor indeed could
be, there being further quickenings and pressings in my spirit, after a
more full, certain and satisfactory knowledge; even after the sense,
sight and enjoyment of God as was testified in the Scriptures to have
been felt and enjoyed in the former times. For I saw plainly that there
was a stop of the streams and a great falling short of the power, life
and glory which they partook of. We had not so the Spirit nor were
so in the faith nor did so walk and live in God as they did. They were
come to Mount Sion, and the heavenly Jerusalem, etc., which we had
hardly so much as the literal knowledge or apprehension what they
were. So that I saw the whole course of religion among us was,
for the most part, but a talk to what they felt, enjoyed, possessed and
lived in.   *Account of his spiritual travel written in Aylesbury Prison, 1667*

27   At that time, when I was broken and dashed to pieces in my religion,
I was in a congregational way; but soon after parted with them, yet
in great love, relating to them how the hand of the Lord was upon
me, and how I was smitten in the inward part of my religion and
could not now hold up an outward form of that which I inwardly
wanted, having lost my God, my Christ, my faith, my knowledge,
my life, my all. And so we parted very lovingly, I wishing them well,
even the presence of that God whom I wanted; promising to return
unto them again if ever I met with that which my soul wanted, and
had clearness in the Lord so to do.

28 At last, after all my distresses, wanderings and sore travels, I met
with some writings of this people called Quakers, which I cast a
slight eye upon and disdained, as falling very short of that wisdom,
light, life and power, which I had been longing for and searching
after...After a long time, I was invited to hear one of them (as I
had been often, they in tender love pitying me and feeling my want of
that which they possessed)...When I came, I felt the presence and
power of the Most High among them, and words of truth from the
Spirit of truth reaching to my heart and conscience, opening my
state as in the presence of the Lord. Yea, I did not only feel words
and demonstrations from without, but I felt the dead quickened,
the seed raised; insomuch as my heart, in the certainty of light and
clearness of true sense, said: 'This is he; this is he; there is no other;
this is he whom I have waited for and sought after from my childhood, who was always near me, and had often begotten life in my
heart, but I knew him not distinctly, nor how to receive him or
dwell with him'. And then in this sense (in the melting and break-
ings of my spirit), was I given up to the Lord, to become his, both in
waiting for the further revealing of his seed in me, and to serve him
in the life and power of his seed.

But some may desire to know what I have at last met with. I answer,
'I have met with the Seed'. Understand that word, and thou wilt be
satisfied and inquire no further. I have met with my God, I have met
with my Saviour, and he hath not been present with me without his
Salvation, but I have felt the healings drop upon my soul from under
his wings. I have met with the Seed's Father, and in the Seed I have
felt him my Father; there I have read his nature, his love, his
compassions, his tenderness, which have melted, overcome and
changed my heart before him. I have met with the Seed's faith,
which hath done and doth that which the faith of man can never do.
I have met with the true Birth, with the Birth which is Heir of the
Kingdom and inherits the Kingdom. I have met with the true spirit
of prayer and supplication, wherein the Lord is prevailed with, and
which draws from him whatever the condition needs, the soul
always looking up to him in the will and in the time and way which
is acceptable with him. What shall I say? I have met with the true
peace, the true righteousness, the true holiness, the true rest of the
soul, the everlasting habitation which the redeemed dwell in.

And I know all these to be true in him that is true, and am capable of no doubt, dispute or reasoning in my mind about them, it abiding there where it hath received the full assurance and satisfaction. And also I know very well and distinctly in spirit where the doubts and disputes are, and where the certainty and full assurance is, and, in the tender mercy of the Lord, am preserved out of the one and in the other.   *1667*

Mary Penington (c. 1625-1682), *daughter of Sir John Proude and widow of Sir William Springett, married in 1654 Isaac Penington, like herself a seeker after a true spiritual experience. After earnest search and some disillusionments she, with her husband, at length found her goal in worship with Friends, though still 'exercised against taking up the cross to the language, fashions, customs, titles, honour, and esteem in the world'.*

29   My relations made this cross very heavy; but as at length I happily gave up, divested of reasonings, not consulting how to provide for the flesh, I received strength to attend the meetings of these despised people which I never intended to meddle with, but found truly of the Lord, and my heart owned them. I longed to be one of them, and minded not the cost or pain; but judged it would be well worth my utmost cost and pain to witness such a change as I saw in them— such power over their corruptions. I had heard objected against them, that they wrought not miracles; but I said that they did great miracles, in that they turned them that were in the world and the fellowship of it, from all such things. Thus, by taking up the cross, I received strength against many things which I had thought impossible to deny; but many tears did I shed, and bitterness of soul did I experience, before I came thither; and often cried out: 'I shall one day fall by the overpowering of the enemy'. But Oh! the joy that filled my soul in the first meeting ever held in our house at Chalfont. To this day I have a fresh remembrance of it. It was then the Lord enabled me to worship him in that which was undoubtedly his own, and give up my whole strength, yea, to swim in the life which overcame me that day. Oh! long had I desired to worship him with acceptation, and lift up my hands without doubting, which I witnessed that day in that assembly. I acknowledged his great

mercy and wonderful kindness; for I could say, 'This is it which I have longed and waited for, and feared I never should have experienced'.   *Experiences in the Life of Mary Penington*

William Dewsbury (1621-1688) *who as a youth was apprenticed to a cloth-maker, and came from Allerthorpe in the East Riding of Yorkshire, was one of the sweetest and wisest of the early Quakers. He spent a great part of his life in prison, chiefly at Warwick. His undaunted faith and reconciling spirit contributed greatly to the Quaker movement.*

30 About the time when I was eight years of age, of my natural birth, the Word of the Lord came unto me. 'I created thee for my glory, an account thou must give to Me for all thy words and actions done in the body', which word enlightened my heart and opened the book of conscience in me...Then I ceased from my vain conversation ...and began to read the Scriptures and books, and mourn and pray to a God I knew not where he was...They said he was above the skies, calling it Heaven, but I felt the hand of the Lord within me, executing justice upon the wicked in me, and what way ever I turned to seek him in observations, thither the flaming sword turned...to keep the way of the tree ⟨of⟩ life and execute the righteous justice of God upon me.

Then it pleased the Lord to order my friends to put me to keep the sheep, where I was retired from company, so my mind was kept in my mournful estate, where my greatest ease was in mourning to a God I knew not...⟨But⟩ I could find no peace in that worship of God the world hath set up, as in receiving the bread and wine, which they told me was the seals of the covenant...Then much fear seized upon my soul...and Judas's condition was cast into my mind, until it were showed that the seal of the covenant was the Spirit of Christ and no outward element, and the Supper was the body and blood of Christ, which the world doth not know, nor I at that time. Then I durst join no more in their practice in singing David's conditions, which they called Psalms, for the light in my conscience let me see the evil of my heart, that I was not in David's condition.

There was much speaking of God, but I met with none who could tell me what God had done for their souls, in redeeming them from the body of sin which I groaned under, and ⟨which⟩ separated me from the presence of God.

At that time did the wars begin in this nation, and the men called ministers cried, 'Curse ye Meroz, because they went not forth to help the Lord against the mighty'. Then I was willing to give my body to death, in obedience to my God, to free my soul from sin, and I joined with that little remnant which said they fought for the gospel, but I found no rest to my soul amongst them. And the word of the Lord came unto me and said 'Put up thy sword into thy scabbard; if my kingdom were of this world, then would my children fight', which word enlightened my heart and discovered the mystery of iniquity, and that the Kingdom of Christ was within, and the enemies was within, and was spiritual, and my weapons against them must be spiritual, the power of God.

Then I could no longer fight with a carnal weapon against a carnal man, and returned to my outward calling, and my will was brought in subjection for the Lord to do with me what his will was—if he condemned me, he might: and, if he saved me, it was his free love—and in this condemned estate I lay crying in the depth of misery. And the cry of my condemned soul was great, and could not be satisfied, but breathed and thirsted after Christ, to save me freely through his blood or I perished for ever, and in this condemned estate I lay waiting for the coming of Christ Jesus, who, in the appointed time of the Father, appeared to my soul, as the lightnings from the east to the west. And my dead soul heard his voice, and by his voice was made to live, who created me to a lively hope, and sealed me up in the everlasting covenant of life with his blood. Then I witnessed the wages of sin and death, and the gift of God's eternal life, through Jesus Christ my Lord.   *1655*

31   '*From some expressions of William Dewsbury near a week before his departure out of this life*':
For this I can say, I never since played the coward, but joyfully

entered prisons as palaces, telling mine enemies to hold me there as long as they could: and in the prisonhouse I sung praises to my God, and esteemed the bolts and locks put upon me as jewels, and in the Name of the eternal God I always got the victory, for they could keep me there no longer than the determined time of my God.

If any one has received any good or benefit through this vessel, called William Dewsbury, give God the glory; I'll have none, I'll have none, I'll have none.   *1688*

The Boston martyrs. *At the end of 1658, the Massachusetts legislature enacted, by a bare majority, that every Quaker who was not an inhabitant of the colony, but was found within its jurisdiction, should be banished upon pain of death, and that every inhabitant of the colony convicted of being a Quaker should be imprisoned for a month, and if obstinate should be banished on pain of death. Some Friends were banished under this law, but in June, 1659, William Robinson, Mary Dyer and Marmaduke Stephenson, came into the colony 'Boston's bloody laws to try'. The three Friends were banished, but returned and in October Governor Endicott passed sentence of death upon them; the date of execution being fixed for Thursday, 27th October, the usual meeting day of the Church in Boston. Joseph Besse, in his 'Collection of the sufferings of the people called Quakers' (1753) describes the way in which they met this persecution.*

32   *Eight days before his martyrdom, Marmaduke Stephenson wrote the following in Boston Gaol:*

In the beginning of the year 1655, I was at the plough in the east parts of Yorkshire in Old England, near the place where my outward being was; and, as I walked after the plough, I was filled with the love and presence of the living God, which did ravish my heart when I felt it, for it did increase and abound in me like a living stream, so did the life and love of God run through me like precious ointment giving a pleasant smell, which made me to stand still. And, as I stood a little still, with my heart and mind stayed upon the Lord, the word of the Lord came to me in a still, small voice, which I did hear perfectly, saying to me in the secret of my heart and conscience, 'I have ordained thee a prophet unto the nations', and, at the hearing of the word of the Lord, I was put to a stand, seeing that I was but a child for such a weighty matter. So, at the time appointed, Barbados was set before me, unto which I was required of the Lord to go and leave my dear and loving wife and tender children; for the Lord said unto me, immediately by His Spirit, that He would be as an husband to my wife and as a father to my children, and they should not want in my absence, for He would provide for them when I was gone. And I believed the Lord would perform what He had spoken, because I was made willing to give up myself to His work and service, to leave all and follow Him, whose presence and life is with me, where I rest in peace and quietness of spirit, with my dear brother ⟨William Robinson⟩ under the shadow of His wings, who hath made us willing to lay down our lives for His name's sake, if unmerciful men be suffered to take them from us. And, if they do, we know we shall have peace and rest with the Lord for ever in His holy habitation, when they shall have torment night and day.

So, in obedience to the living God, I made preparation to pass to Barbados in the Fourth Month ⟨June⟩ 1658. So, after some time that I had been on the said island in the service of God, I heard that New England had made a law to put the servants of the living God to death if they returned after they were sentenced away, which did come near me at that time; and, as I considered the thing and pondered it in my heart, immediately came the word of the Lord unto me, saying, 'Thou knowest not but that thou mayst go thither.'

But I kept this word in my heart and did not declare it to any until the time appointed. So, after that, a vessel was made ready for Rhode Island, which I passed in. So, after a little time that I had been there, visiting the seed which the Lord had blessed, the word of the Lord came to me, saying, 'Go to Boston with thy brother William Robinson', and at His command I was obedient and gave up to His will, that so His work and service may be accomplished. For He had said unto me that He had a great work for me to do, which is now come to pass. And, for yielding obedience to and for obeying the voice and command of the everlasting God, which created heaven and earth and the fountain of waters, do I, with my dear brother, suffer outward bonds near unto death.

And this is given forth to be upon record, that all people may know who hear it, that we came not in our own wills but in the will of God. Given forth by me, who am known to men by the name of Marmaduke Stevenson, but have a new name given me, which the world knows not of, written in the book of life.

On the day appointed, when the Puritan lecture was over, the condemned Friends were taken to the gallows which were a mile distant. On the way the two young men began speaking, but the drums drowned their voices. 'Yet they went on with great cheerfulness, as going to an everlasting wedding feast.' Being come to the ladder, they tenderly took leave of one another, then Robinson stepped up and told the people it was the day of their visitation, and desired them to mind the light within them, the light of Christ, his testimony for which he was going to seal with his blood. At this the Puritan minister shouted 'Hold thy tongue, thou art going to die with a lie in thy mouth.' The rope was adjusted, and, as the executioner turned the condemned man off, he said with his dying breath, 'I suffer for Christ, in whom I live and for whom I die.' Then Stephenson stepped up the ladder and said 'Be it known unto all this day that we suffer not as evil-doers, but for conscience sake.' He was turned off the gallows, saying, 'This day shall we be at rest with the Lord.' Mary Dyer also stepped up the ladder, her face covered and the halter put round her neck, when the cry was raised, 'Stop! for she is reprieved.'

She was again banished, but returned in May 1660. Since her reprieve, others, both colonists and visiting Friends, had brought themselves within the capital penalty, but the authorities had not ventured to enforce it. After ten days, Endicott sent for her, and asked her if she were the same Mary Dyer who had been there before. On her avowing this, the death sentence was passed.

33 Then Mary Dyer was brought forth, and with a band of soldiers led through the town, the drums being beaten before and behind her, and so continued that none might hear her speak all the way to the place of execution, which was about a mile. Thus guarded, she came to the gallows, and being gone up the ladder, some said to her, that, if she would return ⟨home⟩ she might come down and save her life. To which she replied, 'Nay, I cannot, for in obedience to the will of the Lord I came, and in His will I abide faithful to death'...

Then one mentioned that she should have said, she had been in Paradise. To which she answered, 'Yea, I have been in Paradise these several days'...Thus Mary Dyer departed this life, a constant and faithful martyr of Christ, having been twice led to death, which the first time she expected with an entire resignation of mind to the will of God, and now suffered with Christian fortitude, being raised above the fear of death through a blessed hope and glorious assurance of eternal life and immortality.

After Mary Dyer's death a member of the General Court uttered one of those bitter scoffs which prove the truest of all epitaphs: 'She did hang as a flag for others to take example by.' One other Friend, William Leddra of Barbados, was martyred in March, 1661. On the day before he was put to death, he wrote in a letter these words:

34 As the flowing of the ocean doth fill every creak and branch thereof, and then retires again towards its own being and fulness, and leaves a savour behind it; so doth the life and virtue of God flow into every one of your hearts, whom he hath made partakers of his divine nature; and when it withdraws but a little, it leaves a sweet savour behind it; that many can say they are made clean thro' the word that he hath spoken to them. In which innocent condition you may see what you are in the presence of God, and what you are without him...Stand still, and cease from thine own working, and in due time thou shalt enter into the rest, and thy eyes shall behold his salvation, whose testimonies are sure, and righteous altogether.

Others lay in prison awaiting sentence, but were set at liberty, and a new law passed substituting whipping out of the colony from town to town for the death penalty. Shortly after, an order described by Whittier as the 'King's Missive' reached Boston, and showed the royal disapproval of the policy of persecution. When the last Friend to be condemned to death (Wenlock Christison, afterwards released) had received his sentence, he said 'Do not think to weary out the living God by taking away the lives of His servants. What do you gain by it? For the last man you put to death, here are five come in his room. And if you have power to take my life from me, God can raise up the same principle of life in ten of His servants and send them among you in my room.'

Thomas Ellwood (1639-1713). *The extract gives an account of the early meeting of the young Oxfordshire squire, Thomas Ellwood, with Friends about 1659. His persecution for refusing hat-honour to his father, the vivid account of his sufferings in London prisons, his intercourse with the blind poet Milton, his life-long friendship with Gulielma Springett who became Penn's first wife, are all recounted in his autobiography, published in 1714 and frequently reprinted; one of the most delightful of early Quaker journals.*

35   I had a desire to go to another meeting of the Quakers, and bid my father's man inquire if there was any in the country thereabouts. He thereupon told me he had heard at Isaac Penington's that there was to be a meeting at High Wycombe on Thursday next. Thither therefore I went, though it was seven miles from me, and, that I might be rather thought to go out a-coursing than to a meeting, I let my greyhound run by my horse-side. Being come to the house...I saw the people sitting together in an outer room, wherefore I stept in and sat down on the first void seat, the end of a bench just within the door, having my sword by my side and black clothes on, which drew some eyes upon me. It was not long ere one stood up and spake, whom I was afterwards well acquainted with (his name was Samuel Thornton), and what he spake was very suitable and of good service to me; for it reached home, as if it had been directed to me.

As soon as ever the meeting was ended and the people began to rise, I, being next the door, stept out quickly and, hastening to my inn, took horse immediately homewards; and, so far as I remember, my having been gone was not taken notice of by my father.

This latter meeting was like the clinching of a nail, confirming and fastening in my mind those good principles which had sunk into me at the former...The general trouble and confusion of mind which had for some days lain heavy upon me and pressed me down, without a distinct discovery of the particular cause for which it came, began now to wear off; and some glimmerings of light began to break forth in me, which let me see my inward state and condition towards God...And now I saw that, although I had been in a great degree preserved from the common immoralities and gross pollutions of the world, yet the spirit of the world had hitherto ruled in me and led me into pride, flattery, vanity and superfluity, all which was naught. I found there were many plants growing in me which were not of the Heavenly Father's planting, and that all these, of whatever sort or kind they were or how specious soever they might appear, must be plucked up.

Now also did I receive a new law, an inward law superadded to the outward—the law of the spirit of life in Christ Jesus—which wrought in me against all evil, not only in deed and in word, but even in thought also, so that everything was brought to judgment and judgment passed upon all. So that I could not any longer go on in my former ways and course of life, for when I did judgment took hold upon me for it.

So that here began to be a way cast up before me for me to walk in, a direct and plain way, so plain that a wayfaring man how weak and simple soever...could not err while he continued to walk in it; the error coming by his going out of it. And this way, with respect to me, I saw was that measure of Divine Light which was manifested in me, by which the evil of my doings, which I was to put away and to cease from, was discovered to me. *1659*

36   A knot of my old acquaintance ⟨at Oxford⟩, espying me, came to me. One of these was a scholar in his gown, another a surgeon of that city...When they were come up to me, they all saluted me, after the usual manner, putting off their hats and bowing, and saying, 'Your humble Servant, Sir', expecting no doubt the same from me. But when they saw me stand still, not moving my cap, nor bowing my knee, in way of congee to them, they were amazed, and looked first one upon another, then upon me, and then one upon another again for a while, without a word speaking. At length, the surgeon ...clapping his hand, in a familiar way, upon my shoulder, and smiling on me, said, 'What, Tom, a Quaker!' To which I readily, and cheerfully answered, 'Yes, a Quaker.' And as the words passed out of my mouth I felt joy spring in my heart, for I rejoyced that I had not been drawn out by them into a compliance with them, and that I had strength and boldness given me to confess myself to be one of that despised people. *1659*

William Penn (1644-1718). *His life of high adventure, which has left its mark on the history of England and America, was that of a man of commanding gifts and eager spirit vowed (as the extract shows) to 'follow the Christ, the King'. When he threw in his lot with Friends in 1667, he preferred 'the reproach of Christ' to the career at Court open before him, and he never flinched from his decision. For his inner spirit, we can turn to his writings, especially to 'No Cross, No Crown', and the two little books, called 'Fruits of solitude', written when he was under the ban of the authorities owing to his friendship with the exiled James II. Penn's other writings include his 'Essay towards the present and future peace of Europe', written in 1693 and foreshadowing a League of States.*

William Charles Braithwaite wrote of him: 'Life to Penn was an arena for adventurous service. His eagerness of mind and universal spirit made him leap from the seats of the spectators with which so many are content into the thick of action. Rapt in great designs and careless of self, he was often buffeted and baffled, deceived or mistaken, but his courage was never defeated, nor the fineness of his temper marred. ... We go to others for flawless thought and deeds of passive patience, but for the kindled vision compacted into glowing act, out of which the famous deeds of history are wrought, what other Englishman of that age can rank with the hero of our religious freedom, and of the Holy Experiment of Pennsylvania?'

37   *From a letter to the Countess of Falkenstein, 1677:*
Though unknown, yet art thou much beloved for the sake of thy desires and breathings of soul after the living God...myself having from my childhood been both a seeker after the Lord and a great sufferer for that cause, from parents, relations, companions and the magistrates of this world.

Let this that hath visited thee lead thee; this Seed of light and life, which is the Seed of the Kingdom; yea, it is Christ, the true and only Seed of God, that visited my soul even in my young years; that spread my sins in order before me, reproved me, and brought godly sorrow upon me, making me often to weep in solitary places, and say within my soul 'O that I knew the Lord as I ought to know him. O that I served him as I ought to serve him!' Yea, often was there a great concern upon my spirit about mine eternal state, mournfully desiring that the Lord would give my soul rest in the great day of trouble. Now was all the glory of the world as a bubble; yea, nothing was dear to me that I might win Christ, for the love, friendship, and pleasure of this world were a burden unto my soul.

And in this seeking state I was directed to the testimony of Jesus in mine own conscience, as the true shining light, giving me to discern the thoughts and intents of mine own heart. And no sooner was I turned unto it, but I found it to be that which from my childhood had visited me, though I distinctly knew it not, and when I received it in the love of it, it showed me all that ever I had done, and reproved all the unfruitful works of darkness, judging me as a man in the flesh, and laying judgment to the line, and righteousness to the plummet in me.

And as by the 'brightness of his coming into my soul' he discovered the man of sin there, upon his throne, so by 'the breath of his mouth', which is the two-edged sword of his Spirit, he destroyeth his power and kingdom. And so having made me a witness of the death of the cross, he hath also made me a witness of his resurrection. So that in good measure my soul can now say, 'I am justified in the Spirit, and though the state of condemnation unto death was glorious, yet justification unto life was, and is, more glorious.'

In this state of the New Man all is new; behold new heavens, and a new earth! Old things come to be done away; the old man with his deeds put off. Now new thoughts, new desires, new affections, new love, new friendship, new society, new kindred, new faith; even that which overcometh this world, through many tribulations; and new hope, even that living hope that is founded upon true experience, which holds out all storms, and can see to the glory that is invisible (to carnal eyes) in the midst of the greatest tempest.

38 *Penn's description of the rise of the Quakers:*
The glory of this day...is that blessed principle of Light and Life of Christ which we profess...we judged not after the sight of the eye, or after the hearing of the ear, but according to the Light and sense this blessed principle gave us; we judged and acted in reference to things and persons, ourselves and others, yea, towards God our Maker. For being quickened by it in our inward man, we could easily discern the difference of things, and feel what was right, and

what was wrong, and what was fit and what not, both in reference to religion and civil concerns. That being the ground of the fellowship of all saints, it was in that our fellowship stood. In this we desired to have a sense one of another, acted towards one another and all men, in love, faithfulness and fear.

In the feeling of the motions of this principle we drew near to the Lord, and waited to be prepared by it, that we might feel those drawings and movings, before we approached the Lord in prayer, or opened our mouths in ministry...Care for others was then much upon us, as well as for our selves, especially the young convinced. Often had we the burden of the Word of the Lord to our neighbours, relations, and acquaintance; and sometimes strangers also. We were in travail for one another's preservation: not seeking, but shunning occasions of any coldness or misunderstanding, treating one another as those that believed and felt God present. Which kept our conversation innocent, serious and weighty, guarding ourselves against the cares and friendships of the world. We held the Truth in the spirit of it, and not in our own spirits, or after our own wills and affections...

I cannot forget the humility and chaste zeal of that day. Oh how constant at Meetings, how retired in them, how firm to Truth's life, as well as Truth's principles; and how entire and united in our communion, as indeed became those that profess one Head, even Christ Jesus the Lord.   (*1694*)

39 *From a letter to James Harrison, 25th August, 1681:*
For my country ⟨Pennsylvania⟩, I eyed the Lord in the obtaining of it; and more was I drawn inward to look to Him and to owe it to his hand and power than to any other way. I have so obtained it, and desire that I may not be unworthy of his love, but do that which may answer his kind providence, and serve his truth and people, that an example may be set up to the nations; there may be room there, though not here, for such an Holy Experiment.

40 *The following anecdote depends on oral tradition, but it has played so large a part in Quaker thinking that it is included here:*
When William Penn was convinced of the principles of Friends, and

became a frequent attendant at their meetings, he did not immediately relinquish his gay apparel; it is even said that he wore a sword, as was then customary among men of rank and fashion. Being one day in company with George Fox, he asked his advice concerning it, saying that he might, perhaps, appear singular among Friends, but his sword had once been the means of saving his life without injuring his antagonist, and moreover, that Christ had said, 'he that hath no sword, let him sell his garment and buy one.' George Fox answered, 'I advise thee to wear it as long as thou canst.' Not long after this they met again, when William had no sword, and George said to him, 'William, where is thy sword?' 'Oh!' said he, 'I have taken thy advice; I wore it as long as I could.'

Samuel Janney, Life of William Penn (1852)

Robert Barclay (1648-1690) *had experienced the extreme narrowness and bitterness of both Protestant and Catholic in the religious disputes of his time. He was the son of David Barclay, a distinguished cavalry officer who turned Quaker, and of Catherine Gordon, granddaughter of the Earl of Sutherland. With the advantage of an education part Scottish Presbyterian and part Catholic at the Scottish College in Paris, Barclay was able at twenty-seven to write the famous 'Apology', which for the first time formulated Quakerism in a way which compelled the attention of the theologians of Europe; the first edition (in Latin) appeared in 1676. In form it was a direct challenge to much of the Westminster Confession and the Shorter Catechism (1646-1648). It forcibly attacked 'school divinity', for Barclay felt that, in his own time, God had 'chosen a few despicable and unlearned instruments, as He did fishermen of old, to publish His pure and naked Truth, and to free it of these mists and fogs wherewith the clergy had clouded it'. At the first meeting of Friends which Barclay attended, he was 'reached in the time of silence' but impressed, too, with the words of an unknown minister: 'In stillness there is fullness, in fullness there is nothingness, in nothingness there are all things.'*

41 Not by strength of arguments or by a particular disquisition of each doctrine, and convincement of my understanding thereby, came ⟨I⟩ to receive and bear witness of the Truth, but by being secretly reached by ⟨the⟩ Life. For, when I came into the silent assemblies of God's people, I felt a secret power among them, which touched my heart; and as I gave way unto it I found the evil weakening in me and the good raised up; and so I became thus knit and united unto

them, hungering more and more after the increase of this power and life whereby I might feel myself perfectly redeemed; and indeed this is the surest way to become a Christian; to whom afterwards the knowledge and understanding of principles will not be wanting, but will grow up so much as is needful as the natural fruit of this good root, and such a knowledge will not be barren nor unfruitful.

Apology for the True Christian Divinity, Prop. xi, sect. 7

Luke Cock (1657-1740), *a butcher by trade, and a noted singer, was a young man living at Staithes in North-East Yorkshire when he was convinced. He may serve as a type of many a homely and unlettered Friend, whose sincere dependence on his Divine Guide brought strength to his life and acceptance for his ministry. We are told that, at the meetings he visited through England and Ireland, Friends would speak lovingly of him and desire to see him again. The following extract reports in his own idiom a sermon he gave at York in 1721:*

42   Necessity, Friends, outstrips the law: necessity has made many people go by the Weeping Cross...I remember I was yonce travelling through Shrewsbury, and my Guide said to me: 'I'll show thee the Weeping Cross'. 'Nay', said I, 'thou need not; I have borne it a great while'. Now this place that he showed me was four lane ends.

I remember when I first met with my Guide. He led me into a very large and cross one, where I was to speak the truth from my heart— and before I used to swear and lie too for gain. 'Nay, then' said I to my Guide, 'I mun leave Thee here: if Thou leads me up that lane, I can never follow: I'se be ruined of this butchering trade, if I mun't lie for gain'. Here I left my Guide, and was filled with sorrow, and went back to the Weeping Cross: and I said, if I could find my good Guide again, I'll follow Him, lead me whither He will. So here I found my Guide again, and began to follow Him up this lane and tell the truth from my heart. I had been nought but beggary and poverty before; and now I began to thrive at my trade, and got to the end of this lane, though with some difficulty.

But now my Guide began to lead me up another lane, harder than the first, which was to bear my testimony in using the plain language. This was very hard; yet I said to my Guide, 'Take my feeble pace, and I'll follow Thee as fast as I can. Don't outstretch me, I pray Thee'. So by degrees I got up here.

But now I was led up the third lane: it was harder still, to bear my testimony against tithes—my wife not being convinced. I said to my Guide, 'Nay, I doubt I never can follow up here: but don't leave me: take my pace, I pray Thee, for I mun rest me'. So I tarried here a great while, till my wife cried 'We'se all be ruined: what is thee ganging stark mad to follow t'silly Quakers?' Here I struggled and cried, and begged of my Guide to stay and take my pace: and presently my wife was convinced. 'Well', says she, 'now follow thy Guide, let come what will. The Lord has done abundance for us: we will trust in Him'. Nay, now, I thought, I'll to my Guide again, now go on, I'll follow Thee truly; so I got to the end of this lane cheerfully...

But I mun read you a little more out of my journal. Bide my din a little, I pray, you'se not be troubled with it long; and you'se have it for nought. I'll be content with a little buttermilk and a bit of bread when the meeting is over, if you will but bide my din a little. Now to my journal again: my Guide led me up another lane, more difficult than any of the former, which was to bear testimony to that Hand that had done all this for me. This was a hard one: I thought I must never have seen the end of it. I was eleven years all but one month in it. Here I began to go on my knees and to creep under the hedges, a trade I never forgot since, nor I hope never shall. I would fain think it is unpossible for me to fall now, but let him that thinks he stands take heed lest he fall.

I thought to have had a watering: but ye struggle so I cannot get you together. We mun have no watering tonight, I mun leave you every yan to his own Guide.

Thomas Story (1662-1742) *came from the parish of Kirklinton, in Cumberland, and was an intimate friend of Penn. He spent some years in America and travelled extensively. He was a man of good education, destined by his father for a lawyer, and acquired an extensive knowledge of natural history. The extracts are from the early pages of his elaborate 'Journal', which is, however, confined* *to his very wide and varied religious experiences. After composing the 'Song of praise to the saints in Zion' (before he came into touch with Friends) he was ready to destroy it, observing in it things written in the first person, which did not belong to his own spiritual state. But since the matter had been written down as it came, and with undoubted evidence of the Divine presence, he preserved it, concluding it given by dictation from the Mind of Truth. It was true in itself, and might answer the states of many, and be his own experience in time, if he was faithful.*

43   I was silent before the Lord, as a child not yet weaned;
He put words in my mouth;
And I sang forth His praise with an audible voice.

I called unto my God out of the great deep;
He put on bowels of mercy, and had compassion on me;
Because His love was infinite,
And His power without measure.

He called for my life, and I offered it at His footstool;
But he gave it me as a prey,*
With unspeakable addition.

He called for my will, and I resigned it at His call;
But he returned me His own,
In token of His love.

He called for the world, and I laid it at His feet,
With the crowns thereof;
I withheld them not at the beckoning of His hand.

But mark the benefit of exchange:
For he gave me, instead of earth, a kingdom of eternal peace.
And, in lieu of the crowns of vanity,
A crown of glory.

He gave me joy, which no tongue can express,
And peace which passeth understanding...

I begged Himself, and He gave me all.

* 'as a prey', i.e. a reward brought from a contest cf. Jer. 21.9

He gave me power to do wonders also,
To keep His commandments, through His Holy Spirit,
And to walk in the paths of righteousness with joyful songs.

1690

44 We rode some miles together in profound silence, in which my mind enjoyed a gentle rest and consolation, from the divine and holy presence. And when we came to the meeting ⟨at Broughton, Cumberland⟩, being a little late, it was full gathered; and I went among the throng of the people on the forms, and sat still among them in that inward condition and mental retirement. And though one of their ministers, a stranger, began to speak to some points held by them, and declaim against some things held by others, and denied by them...yet I took not much notice of it...my concern was much rather to know whether they were a people gathered under a sense of the enjoyment of the presence of God in their meetings; or, in other words, whether they worshipped the true and living God, in the life and nature of Christ, the Son of God, the true and only Saviour. And the Lord answered my desire according to the integrity of my heart.

For, not long after I had sat down among them, that heavenly and watery cloud overshadowing my mind brake into a sweet abounding shower of celestial rain, and the greatest part of the meeting was broken together, dissolved and comforted in the same divine and holy presence and influence of the true, holy and heavenly Lord; which was divers times repeated before the meeting ended. And, in the same way, by the same divine and holy power, I had been often favoured with before, when alone; and when no eye but that of heaven beheld or any knew, but the Lord himself; who in infinite mercy had been pleased to bestow so great a favour.

And, as the many small springs and streams descending into a proper place and forming a river become more deep and weighty; even so thus meeting with a people gathered of the living God into a sense of the enjoyment of his divine and living presence, through that blessed and holy medium the Mind of Jesus Christ, the Son of God and Saviour of the world, I felt an increase of the same joy of the salvation of God.

The meeting being ended, the Peace of God...remained as a holy canopy over my mind in a silence out of the reach of all words; and where no idea but the Word himself can be conceived. But being invited, together with the ministering Friend, to the house of the ancient Widow Hall, I went willingly with them; but the sweet silence...still remaining I had nothing to say to any of them till he was pleased to draw the curtain and veil his presence; and then I found my mind pure and in a well-bounded liberty of innocent conversation with them. *1691*

Samuel Bownas (1676-1753). *A blacksmith's apprentice, whose widowed mother had a subsistence of less than five pounds a year, Samuel Bownas, became one of the most powerful of Quaker ministers. He had a tall, comely and manly aspect and a strong, clear voice, and, though his schooling was small, he became thoroughly versed in the Scriptures, and able 'by the force of their testimony to confront and confute gainsayers', and deliver his message to multitudes on both sides of the Atlantic.*

45 Now to return to my apprenticeship, I had a very kind, loving master and mistress, and I had meat enough and work enough but had little consideration about religion nor any taste thereof. On First-days I frequented meetings and the greater part of my time I slept, but took no account of preaching nor received any other benefit, than being there kept me out of bad company, which indeed is a very great service to youth...but one First-day, being at meeting ⟨at Brigflatts, near Sedbergh⟩, a young woman named Anne Wilson was there and preached; she was very zealous and fixing my eye upon her, she with a great zeal pointed her finger at me uttering these words with much power, viz:—'A traditional Quaker; thou comest to meeting as thou went from it, and goes from it as thou came to it but art no better for thy coming; what wilt thou do in the end?' This was so pat to my then condition that like Saul I was smitten to the ground as it might be said, but turning my thoughts inwards in secret, I cried, 'Lord, what shall I do to help it?' And a voice as it were spoke in my heart, saying 'Look unto me, and I will help thee'; and I found much comfort that made me shed abundance of tears...I went home with a heavy heart, and could neither eat nor sleep as I used to do, but my work never succeeded better in my hands than it did at this time, nor my mind never less in it; but my conduct as well as countenance was much altered, so that

several in the family were doubtful that I should fall into a kind of melancholy distraction, but I longed for the meeting day and thought it a very long week. When the time of meeting came, my mind was soon fixed and staid upon God, and I found an uncommon enjoyment, that gave me great satisfaction, my understanding being opened and all the faculties of my mind so quick that I seemed another man, a divine and spiritual sweetness abiding with me night and day for some time; and I began to see and understand the Scriptures... plainly seeing a difference between a preacher of the letter and of the Spirit... And now the Scriptures and ministry from the openings of the Spirit seemed so clear and plain to my understanding that I wondered that anybody remained unconvinced. I saw by experience wherein my shortness had been in being contented and easy with a form of truth and religion, which I had only by education, being brought up in plainness of both habit and speech; but all this though very good in its place, did not make me a true Christian; I was but a traditional Quaker, and that by education only and not from the Scriptures because they were a book sealed to me. And I now saw plainly that education though never so carefully administered would not do the work... there was no other way but this, viz. by the Spirit of Christ alone (John 10, 1-3), to attain to true faith, which works by love and gives victory over our infirmities and evil deeds, working such a change in us that we can in truth from experience say we are born from above.   *1696*

John **Woolman** (1720-1772) *of Mount Holly in New Jersey, was a man of many skills, who was called (in a pioneering community) to be by turns book-keeper, store-keeper, merchant, scrivener, notary, surveyor, schoolmaster and farmer; but when tempted by wealth, he chose the trade of tailor. Although he said, with characteristic modesty, that he had 'schooling pretty well for a planter' he was in fact, well educated and widely read, and moved in the intellectual circle of the most lively minds in America just before the Revolution. His condemnation of negro slavery was a concern which was shared by others, notably (among Friends) by Benjamin Lay and Anthony Benezet. He found time to grow apples, write school books and tracts, travel widely in the ministry, attend business meetings regularly, and visit the Indians who came to Philadelphia, as well as make his famous journey into their territory in time of war (referred to in §50). His last journey was to England, where he died of smallpox in York.*

46   I have often a motion of Love to leave some hints of my experience
of the Goodness of God; and pursuant thereto, in the 36th year of
my age, I begin this work.

I was born in Northampton, in Burlington County, in West Jersey,
in the year of our Lord 1720, & before I was seven years old, I began
to be acquainted with the operations of Divine Love. Through the
care of my parents, I was taught to read near as soon as I was capable
of it, and as I went from school one seventh-day, I remember, while
my companions went to play by the way, I went forward out of
sight, and setting down, I read the twenty second chapter of the
Revelations: 'He showed me a pure River of Water of Life, clear as
Crystal, proceeding out of the Throne of God and of the Lamb', &c.
and in the reading of it, my mind was drawn to seek after that Pure
Habitation, which I then believed God had prepared for his servants.
The place where I sat, and the sweetness that attended my mind
remain fresh in my memory.

This and the like Gracious Visitations, had that effect upon me,
that when boys used ill language, it troubled me, & through the
continued mercies of God, I was preserved from it.

Opening of the Journal, written 1755

47   I kept steady to meetings, spent first-days in the afternoon chiefly
in reading the scriptures and other good Books, and was early
convinced in my mind that true Religion consisted in an inward life,
wherein the Heart doth Love and Reverence God the Creator, and
learn to exercise true Justice and Goodness, not only toward all men,
but also toward the Brute Creatures. That as the mind was moved
by an inward Principle to love God as an invisible, Incomprehensible
Being, by the same principle it was moved to love him in all his
manifestations in the Visible World. That as by his breath the flame
of life was kindled in all Animal and Sensible Creatures, to say we
Love God as unseen, and at the same time exercise cruelty toward
the least creature moving by his life, or by life derived from Him,
was a contradiction in itself. I found no narrowness respecting Sects
and Opinions, but believed that sincere upright-hearted people in
every society who truly love God were accepted of Him.

Journal, 1740

48 My mind through the power of Truth was in a good degree weaned from the desire of outward greatness, and I was learning to be content with real conveniences that were not costly; so that a way of life free from much Entanglements, appeared best for me, tho' the income was small. I had several offers of business that appeared profitable, but saw not my way clear to accept of them, as believing the business proposed would be attended with more outward care & cumber than was required of me to engage in. I saw that a humble man, with the Blessing of the Lord, might live on a little, and that where the heart was set on greatness, success in business did not satisfie the craving; but that commonly with an increase of wealth, the desire for wealth increased. There was a care on my mind so to pass my time, as to things outward, that nothing might hinder me from the most steady attention to the voice of the True Shepherd.

Journal, 1743

49 A neighbour received a bad bruise in his body, and sent for me to bleed him; which being done, he desired me to write his will: I took notes, and, amongst other things, he told me to which of his children he gave his young negro: I considered the pain and distress he was in, and knew not how it would end, so I wrote his Will, save only that part concerning his Slave, and carrying it to his bedside, read it to him, and then told him in a friendly way, that I could not write any instruments by which my fellow-creatures were made slaves, without bringing trouble on my own mind. I let him know that I charged nothing for what I had done, and desired to be Excused from doing the other part in the way he proposed. Then we had a serious conference on the Subject, and at length, he agreeing to set her free, I finished his will. *Journal, 1756*

50 *Written on the Indian Journey, 1763:* The 12th day of the 6th month ⟨the first day⟩ of the week being a rainy day we continued in our Tent and here I was led to think on the nature of the exercise which hath attended me. Love was the first motion, and then a Concern arose to spend some time with the Indians, that I might feel and understand their life, and the Spirit they live in, if haply I might receive some Instruction from them, or they be in any degree helped forward by my following the Leadings of Truth amongst them, and as it pleased the Lord to make way for my going at a time when the troubles of war were increasing, and when by reason of much wet weather travelling was more difficult than usual at that Season, I looked upon it as a more favourable Opportunity to season my mind, and bring me into a nearer sympathy with them. And as mine eye was to the great Father of Mercies, humbly desiring to learn what his will was concerning me, I was made quiet and content.

Journal, 1763

In a time of Sickness with the pleurisy, a little upward of two years and a half ago, I was brought so near the gates of death that I forgot my name. Being then desirous to know who I was, I saw a mass of matter of a dull gloomy colour between the South and the East, and was informed that this mass was human beings in as great misery as they could be, and live, and that I was mixed with them, and that henceforth I might not consider myself as a distinct or Separate being. In this state I remained several hours. I then heard a soft, melodious voice, more pure and harmonious than any voice I had heard with my ears before; and I believed it was the voice of an angel who spake to the other angels. The words were, *John Woolman is dead.* I soon remembered that I was once John Woolman and being assured that I was alive in the body, I greatly wondered what that heavenly voice could mean. I believed beyond doubting that it was the voice of an holy Angel, but as yet it was a mystery to me.

I was then carried in Spirit to the mines where poor Oppressed people were digging rich treasures for those called Christians, and heard them blaspheme the name of Christ, at which I was grieved, for His Name to me was precious. I was then informed that these heathen were told that those who oppressed them were the followers of Christ, and they said among themselves, 'If Christ directed them to use us in this sort, then Christ is a cruel tyrant'.

All this time the Song of the Angel remained a Mystery; and in the morning my dear wife and some others coming to my bedside, I asked them if they knew who I was, and they telling me I was John Woolman, thought I was only light-headed, for I told them not what the Angel said, nor was I disposed to talk much to anyone, but was very desirous to get so deep that I might understand this Mystery.

My tongue was often so dry that I could not speak till I had moved it about and gathered some moisture, and as I lay still for a time, at length I felt Divine power prepare my mouth that I could speak, and then said, 'I am crucified with Christ, nevertheless I live, yet not I, but Christ liveth in me. And the life I now live in the flesh, is by faith in the Son of God, who loved me and gave Himself for me.' Then the mystery was opened, and I perceived there was joy in heaven over a sinner who had repented, and that that language, *John Woolman is dead,* meant no more than the death of my own will.

Journal, 1772

Job Scott (1751-1793) *of Rhode Island, a man of deep spiritual experience and an impressive speaker, was the last of the 'Quietist' leaders; he left a Journal which is beautifully written and often profound. He travelled in the ministry throughout America and Great Britain, and died at Ballitore in Ireland.*

52   I heard frequent mention in books and conversations of the Spirit of God and that good people in former times had it in them, and by it learned the will of God and were enabled to perform it...I understood that true converts in these days also have it. But like many others I overlooked its lively checks and calls in myself, had no idea that I had ever known anything of it, longed to be favoured with it, but supposed it was some extraordinary appearance, different far from anything I had yet been acquainted with.

Thus the Jews, even while they were expecting Christ's coming, knew him not when he came...Just so are thousands now mistaken as to the dignity and origin of God's Spirit in them; they think it is of *man,* a part of his nature and being; whereas it is of the very life, power and substance of God. Its descent is as truly from heaven as was that of the Lord Jesus. He came in that low mean and ordinary appearance as to outward show and accommodations, teaching us thereby not to despise the day of small things, nor to overlook the littleness of the motions of divine life in our own souls. And when he compares the kingdom of heaven, which he expressly says is within, to outward things, he very instructively inculcates to us that the beginnings of it are small—'a little leaven', 'a little seed', 'a grain of mustard seed', 'the least of all seeds' (Matt. 13. 31, 32). This is true in the inward, whatever it may be in the outward, for the seed of the kingdom is the least of all the seeds in the field or garden of the heart. *Journal, c. 1765*

53 A hope was kindled in me that now I should go forward without meeting with such besetments and withdrawings of light as hereto-fore; for though the Lord still at times withdrew from me, yet as his return was not long after, and as his presence was much more constantly with me, I was ready to conclude it would continue with increasing brightness, until I should be wholly and continually swallowed up in his love. For as such a state was sometimes permitted me, I, not clearly understanding the counsel of his divine will, was apt to wish it for my constant condition; not then seeing as I have since seen that it was far from being best for me to enjoy a constancy of sunshine and fair weather. Even the outward order and economy of divine Providence affords instruction which often beautifully applies to our inward experiences. It is not all calm and sunshine. We have cold as well as heat, darkness as well as light, and cutting frosts as well as most refreshing dews, and a variety of other changes. All this is in infinite wisdom and goodness, and displays to the dis-cerning eye the providential power and glory of the great Superin-tendent. *Journal, c. 1770*

54 *His dying words:* I feel, and I wish you to feel for and with me, after the Rock of eternal life and salvation; for as we are established there-on, we shall be in the everlasting unity, which cannot be shaken by all the changes of time, nor interrupted in a never-ending eternity. We cannot approve or disapprove by parts the works of Omni-potence rightly. We must approve the whole and say, Thy will be done in all things... The desire of my heart is the great blessing of time and the consolation of eternity... let self be of no reputation; trust in the Lord, and he will carry thee through all.

Thomas Shillitoe (1754-1836) *was the son of the librarian to the Society of Gray's Inn; he came into touch with Friends through a distant relative. In early life he gave up his position in a Bank from a scruple about selling lottery tickets, and learned from a man in the Borough the humble trade of a shoemaker. Although extremely timid by nature, he travelled widely in Great Britain and on the continent* *as far as Russia, and laboured to bring the Gospel to the poor, the vicious and the neglected. He spoke also with great ones, and with kings on several occasions, and George IV remembered the simple and piercing message of 'that Quaker' till his dying day.*

55   *The incident described below occurred on a visit to Berlin in 1824. He had already paid one visit to the convict prison at Spandau; but finding that the roughest prisoners had been kept from him, he determined to return and see them.*

Whilst walking along, I was accosted by my friend the chief magistrate of the city, saying, 'So you are about to make another visit to Spandau. I would wish you not to go again. Are you not afraid?—Don't you know some of the prisoners murdered the last governor?' Although I received his counsel as a mark of his kindness towards me, I found it safest to say as little as possible in reply, having heard of this circumstance since our last visit, and that a bowl of scalding liquor had been thrown by one of the prisoners into the present governor's face; nevertheless this caution of the chief magistrate caused me, for a time, to feel keenly on the occasion, and to consider there was not only my own life, but that of my interpreter, the governor, and perhaps other attendants, at stake... these considerations, I found, without great watchfulness, were in danger of producing such agitation of mind as would be very unprofitable for me.

I had concluded, in the course of the night previous to our proceeding to Spandau, to empty my pockets of my money, watch, pocketbook, and my penknife more particularly; for, by having my penknife about me, I might be the cause of furnishing them with the means of my own destruction: this I accordingly did. But on mature deliberation on the step I had thus taken, I was mercifully led to see that it was the effect of that departure from a full and entire reliance on God's arm of power, which the enemy was endeavouring to bring about in my mind. I sensibly felt the performance of this very act had produced weakness, causing the hands that had been made strong through the power of the mighty God of Jacob, rather to fall again. I, therefore, returned to my chamber, and replaced each of these articles as they were before, taking particular care that my penknife was not left behind...

On entering the yard where they were assembled, I observed that the number assembled far exceeded what I had met with in the chapel at my first visit, there now appearing from three to four hundred prisoners: many forbidding countenances I could not recollect to have seen before, whose legs were loaded with irons, but not their hands. Had they been disposed to have injured us, I thought, as I viewed those who were placed in front, we should only be like so many grasshoppers amongst them...

After a pause had taken place, the governor addressed the prisoners; although I could not understand a word which he expressed, yet I had a clear evidence that his manner was appropriate to the occasion, and that he was assisted by best help in doing it: his observations produced such a remarkable quiet over the whole assembly, that not the motion of a foot or the clink of a fetter was to be heard... Having been favoured with ability fully to relieve my mind towards them, I found I must propose to give each of the prisoners my hand of love before I left them; the governor then arranged them for that purpose; in this state I was led to believe the prisoners generally sympathised, for although they were not able to express themselves on the occasion in my own language, their countenances and the manner of their pressing my hand, I thought fully indicated this disposition of mind.

Daniel Wheeler (1771-1840) *joined Friends at 28, having been by turns sailor and soldier in the Napoleonic wars and then become a successful seed-merchant. Like John Woolman and others, he deliberately curtailed his trade to avoid the 'hurry and bustle of business' and so turned to agricultural pursuits. From farming in Yorkshire he was called in 1818 to be agricultural adviser to the Czar Alexander I, and with George Edmondson and Robert Worthy drained the Petersburg marshes, benefiting the health of the city and bringing thousands of acres into cultivation. After the death of his wife Jane in 1832, he sailed the South Seas on missionary service for four years in the schooner Henry Freeling bought by Friends for his use; and died on a visit to America having, as he said, 'made his soundings of that rock whose foundation is from everlasting to everlasting'.*

The passage which follows is taken from a letter written to Samuel Smith in England, shortly after his arrival with his family in Russia, after experiencing the procrastination of the Czar's officials, and in anticipation of their first winter there.

56 *Ochta, nr. Petersburg, Eighth Mo. 19th, 1818.* The greatest part of the time we have been here, it hath pleased Him, who best knows what is best for us, to dispense a season of poverty and barrenness, as far as relates to myself; and my dear wife has been pretty much in the same condition. At the same time, a ray of light hath mercifully been permitted to shine upon the path, sufficient to strengthen the belief, that our being here is in the counsel of His will, without whose knowledge a single sparrow falleth not to the ground. If it was not for a gleam now and then of this kind, tho' faint and transient, how deplorable would our prospect be—separated from those we dearly love, surrounded by many persons disposed to take advantage of us, with a dreary half-year's winter gathering round us...

Ninth mo. 4th. I have now with humble thankfulness, to acknowledge the inexpressible comfort wherewith I am comforted; which nothing short of the great and promised Comforter could administer to the drooping mind. Last First day, in our little Meeting, the Master was pleased to preside, and it was indeed a 'feast of fat things'; and the language which was in my heart was, 'Take, eat, this is my body'. I never remember being under such a covering, and my desire is, that I may never forget it; and oh! that the fear of the Lord may so prevail amongst us, as to entitle us to His Love, which can alone enable us to 'run thro' a troop, or leap over a wall': and which at this time enableth me to call every country my country, and every man my brother. *Memoirs (1842)*

Sarah Lynes Grubb (1773-1842) *one of the most powerful women preachers of her time, was born at Wapping, London. When she married John Grubb in 1803, she settled at Anner Mills, Clonmel, until 1818, when the family left Ireland and moved to East Anglia. Both before and after her marriage she travelled widely in Great Britain and Ireland in the service of the Gospel.*

57 At school I sought the Lord, feeling His power in my heart operating against the evil propensities of my nature; yet to these corrupt inclinations I many, many times gave way; and for this I was brought under great condemnation, even as early as when nine years old...I went on sinning and repenting for years; still my love for good books increased, and for good people. We had few

books. The Bible and one or two Journals of Friends are all that I can recollect reading; and I really valued them as highly as I was capable of doing in this my childhood. When I grew to about thirteen years of age, I began to discover something about me, or in my mind, like the heavenly anointing for the ministry; for the Lord had revealed His word as a hammer and had broken the rock in pieces in my living experience; and I was contrited under a sense of power and love; saying even vocally when alone, 'Lord, make me a chosen vessel unto Thee'...With respect to my first appearances ⟨in ministry, when about seventeen years old⟩...I shrunk from it exceedingly; and often have I hesitated, and felt such a reluctance to it, that I have suffered the meeting to break up without my having made the sacrifice: yea, when the word of life in a few words was like a fire within me...It pleased the Lord to call me into a path much untrodden, in my early travels as a messenger of the Gospel, having to go into markets and to declare the truth in the streets. ...No one knows the depth of my sufferings and the mortifying, yea, crucifying of my own will, which I had to endure in this service; yet I have to acknowledge to the sufficiency of divine grace herein...At Bath I had to go to the Pump Room and declare the truth to the gay people who resorted there. This was a time very relieving to my sorely exercised mind. In these days and years of my life I was seldom from under some heavy burden, so that I went greatly bowed down; sometimes ready to say, 'If it be thus with me, O Thou who hast given me a being, I pray Thee take away my life from me'...In the year 1801, I wrote thus: 'O my heavenly Father, Thou hast seen me in the depth of tribulation, in my many journeyings and travels...It was Thy power which supported me when no flesh could help, when man could not comprehend the depth of mine exercise...Be Thou only and for ever exalted in, by and through Thy poor child, and let nothing be able to pluck me out of Thy hand.'   *Address to her Children, 1832*

Stephen Grellet (1773-1855) (*Etienne de Grellet du Mabillier*)*, the preacher of Quakerism to Europe, and the inspirer of Elizabeth Fry's visits to Newgate, had an experience that is one of the most remarkable in our annals. Born at Limoges, of a noble Roman Catholic family, he grew up in frivolous society, was for a time an atheist, and during the French Revolution was for two years in the Army of the*

Princes. Made a prisoner of war, he escaped to Amsterdam, and after two years in Demerara, went to the United States and settled in Long Island. Before his contact with Friends, and before the experience in 1795 at Newtown, Long Island, given in the first extract below, he had been suddenly arrested, while walking in the fields, by what seemed to him to be an awful voice, proclaiming the words, 'Eternity, Eternity, Eternity!' It reached his soul, his whole man shook, it brought him, like Saul, to the ground. He remained almost whole days and nights in prayer that the Lord would have mercy upon him. In 1797, at the age of twenty-four, he began his wonderful work as an evangelist, carrying his living message through all grades of society and all parts of the United States and Europe.

58 It was a memorable meeting—held in silence, however, as usual, never to be forgotten. Very soon after sitting down, great was the awfulness and the reverence that came upon me. It was succeeded by such a view and sense of my sinful life, that I was like one crushed under the mill stones. My misery was great; my cry was not unlike that of Isaiah: 'Woe is me, for I am undone!' The nearer I was then favoured to approach to Him 'who dwelleth in the light', the more I saw my uncleanness and my wretchedness. But how can I set forth the fullness of heavenly joy that filled me when the hope was again raised that there was One, even He whom I had pierced, Jesus Christ, the Redeemer, that was able to save me?..On my earnest petition being put to Him, the language was proclaimed: 'Thy sins are forgiven; thy iniquities are pardoned.' Floods of tears of joy and gratitude gave vent to the fullness of my heart!

Then I thought I heard again a sweet language saying, 'Proclaim unto others what the Lord has done for thy soul'. Apprehending that this was a requisition of *present* duty, I began to plead excuses, from the consciousness of my inability to perform the service. 'Thou knowest, O Lord, that I cannot speak English so as to be understood', was my answer, 'and what am I that I should proclaim Thy name?'

There was not the least feeling then in me to flinch from doing or becoming whatever the Lord would require of me, but a sense of my inability and unworthiness. I have since seen that this was more to prepare me for a future day than a command for a present offering. My spirit continued so prostrated before the Lord and encircled with His love and presence, that I was insensible to what passed around

me. The meeting concluded and the people retired, without my
noticing it, till my brother, speaking to me, drew my attention, and
I saw that we two only were left in the house.   *1795*

59 *He returned to Philadelphia in 1798 during an epidemic of yellow fever, and
fell gravely ill with the disease, as a result of nursing some friendless Lascar
sailors. In his account of his experience he records that he had a very clear
presentiment that he would catch the fever, but felt obliged to go, without
knowing whether the outcome would be life or death.*

During the whole of that sickness I continued entirely sensible, and
whilst death seemed to be approaching, and I had turned myself on
one side, the more easily, as I thought, to breathe my last, my spirits
feeling already as encircled by the angelic host in the Heavenly
Presence, a secret but powerful language was proclaimed in this
wise: 'Thou shalt not die, but live—thy work is not yet done'. Then
the corners of the earth, over lands and seas, were opened to me,
where I should have to labour in the service of the Gospel of Christ.
O what amazement I was filled with! What a solemn and awful
prospect was set before me! Sorrow took hold of me at the words,
for it seemed to me as if I had already a foothold in the heavenly
places. I wept sore; but as it was the Divine Will, I bowed in reverence
before Him... I saw and felt that which cannot be written. Suffice
it to say, that from that very time the disorder subsided.

60 *In 1814, after visiting Europe during the Napoleonic Wars, he wrote:*
The fields in many parts I have visited are white unto harvest, so that
sometimes I have wished that I might have the life of Methuselah,
or that the sun might never go down, that I might do my share of
that great work which is to be done in these nations. There is a
most precious seed in these parts, and in places where I have not
actually visited it. O did our Society stand faithful, what a blessing
they might become! Many are ready to gather to the standard of
Truth, from among the various denominations and ranks. I have
been with rich and poor, princes and princesses, Protestant ministers
and Popish priests, all speaking but one language, not upholding
forms and ceremonies, but Christ and his Spirit... I am not able
to give them any other advice than closely to follow Him who
has begun a good work in them, and will lead them safely. They

feel very precious to me, and I know they rejoice in the visit which Gospel love has led me to pay them. My life seems interwoven with theirs. Some think I am a man of deep learning, whilst my greatest science is to know nothing—nothing but Jesus Christ, and Him crucified. It is He who is mouth and wisdom, when my mouth is laid in the dust.

61 I think I can reverently say that I very much doubt whether since the Lord by His grace brought me into the faith of His dear Son, I have ever broken bread or drunk wine, even in the ordinary course of life, without devout remembrance of, and some devout feeling regarding the broken body and the blood-shedding of my dear Lord and Saviour.

Hannah Kilham (1774-1832) *was bred in the Church of England, and married Alexander Kilham, founder of the Methodist New Connexion, but after his death became a Friend, and opened a successful school for girls in Sheffield. Through her interest in the movement to end negro slavery, she became concerned for African education, led three expeditions to West Africa to establish schools and reduce African languages to writing, and died at sea in 1832 between Sierra Leone and Liberia when on her way to England. A woman of brilliant mind and enlightened views, she longed to see a 'College of African Languages' and missionary settlements which should study farming, weaving and crafts as part of their service. Her name is not forgotten in the Gambia, where a street has recently been named after her.*

62 An apprehension has seized upon my mind this morning, that after having finished the little books I am preparing for the children of Sierra Leone, it will be my duty to attempt the introduction of them myself into that country and the neighbourhood, and even to attempt the reduction of unwritten languages. I would not go merely under a profession of opening a school or schools, but to proceed to the religious instruction of the children, for my heart feels an engagement towards them that cannot possibly be fulfilled without going there...

I am ready to tremble at what I have written with regard to a visit to Sierra Leone, and to doubt whether such an encounter with an element which I fear, and in so distant and wild a scene, is

required. But wherefore should we expect to choose our employment? I have been ready to say, were it in Russia or even Siberia,
how much easier would it be than Sierra Leone. I remember the
shrinking feelings I had in looking at the wide sea in the dusk of the
evening at Scarborough, and in remembering a dear Friend who had
committed himself to the waves, and was now far from the land.
But he is now returned, and a protecting power was with him;
why, if duty only appears plain, should I recoil or draw back? I
will try to be still, and hope clearly to know what is best, and not
give way to any apprehension of my own creating.   *1817*

*The 'dear Friend' referred to in this extract was Daniel Wheeler, at that
time in Russia preparing for the service described in §56. Hannah Kilham's
'shrinking' was accentuated by a life-long fear of water, which the 'life' of
her concern enabled her to overcome.*

63 It is 'life' only that can lead to life, and no forms are available without it. Seek the life in all things, and cherish it by all authorized
means.   *Written at sea, 1831*

William Dent (**1778-1861**). *This notice of William Dent, of Marr, is given
to show the transforming power that comes from one quiet life. In the Testimony of
Yorkshire Quarterly Meeting it was said of him that 'entertaining a very humble
estimate of himself, we believe that he was "quick of understanding in the fear of the
Lord"; and in all his transactions he was a conspicuous example of unswerving
conscientiousness. This led him to regard the holding of the farm at Marr as involving far more than mere gain or loss... With a heart full of love for the brethren
with whom he was united in religious fellowship, he nevertheless loved "all who loved
the Lord Jesus Christ in sincerity"'.*

64 The writer recalls in his school days the tall spare figure of a venerable
Friend who regularly attended Yorkshire Quarterly Meetings. It
was evident that he lived in the wholesome deliberate air of the
country. His Quaker garb was spotlessly neat. His face spoke of
indwelling light and peace with all mankind. When words came
they were few and weighty. It is told how he would drive fourteen
miles to a Friends' Meeting to worship. On one such occasion he
rose, and said, 'God is love', and then sat down again. It is believed

no listener forgot that sermon. He and his family were known to be of the salt of the earth; but what could a plain tenant farmer accomplish in a small village aloof from the life of the world? At the time when he settled in it, several of the houses were in an insanitary condition; the labourers had no gardens to speak of, the children had no school, but there was a public house for the parents. When at four score years his call came to go up higher, he left a village where every cottage was a healthy home, where all able bodied labourers wishing for an allotment could have one. The public house had gone, and a good village school had been established. For many years the schoolmistress had lived in his house. A Bible Society anniversary in his big barn was the annual festival and Eirenicon of the district. It may fairly be said that the whole neighbourhood was slowly uplifted by the coming of one quiet life into its midst.

Joshua Rowntree; Swarthmore Lecture (1913)

Elizabeth Fry (1780-1845) *is well known for her great work in prison reform and other causes. She was one of the seven daughters of John Gurney of Earlham, near Norwich, and was known to her sisters as Betsy. The change in her life came when she was seventeen, through a visit to Norwich of William Savery (1750-1845) of Philadelphia. Savery in his 'Journal' says, 'I thought it the gayest meeting of Friends I ever sat in, and was grieved to see it. I expected to pass the meeting in silent suffering, but at length believed it most for my peace to express a little, and through gracious condescension was favoured to relieve my mind, and many were tendered.'*

Elizabeth's sister, Richenda Gurney, wrote of this occasion: 'Betsy was generally rather restless at meeting, and on this day I remember her very smart boots were a great amusement to me; they were purple, laced with scarlet. At last William Savery began to preach. His voice and manner were arresting and we all liked the sound. Her attention became fixed; at last I saw her begin to weep, and she became a good deal agitated.'

65 *Sunday, 4th Feb. 1798.* Today much has passed in my mind of a very serious nature. I have had a faint light spread over my mind; at least I believe it is something of that kind, owing to having been much with and heard much excellence from one who appears to me a true Christian. It has caused me to feel a *little* religion. I wish the

state of enthusiasm I am now in may last, for today I *felt* there is a
God. I have been devotional and my mind has been led away from
the follies that it is mostly wrapped up in...

Sunday, 17th March 1798. May I never lose the little religion I now
have, but if I cannot feel religion and devotion I must not despair,
for if I am truly warm and earnest in the cause it will come one day.
In my idea true humility and lowness of heart is the *first grand step
towards true religion.*

66 *20th April 1798. Commenting on a letter from William Savery she writes:*
I do not know the course I am to run, all is hid in mystery, but I try
to do right in everything. I feel he gives me a stimulant to virtue,
but...I hate that he should estimate me falsely. I must remember
that on the foundations of the doctrine I believe we agree. I must
look to One higher than he; and if I feel my own mind satisfied I need
not fear. Look up to true religion as the very first of blessings, cherish
it, nourish and let it flourish and bloom in my heart; it wants taking
care of, it is difficult to obtain. I must not despair or grow sceptical
if I do not always feel religious. I felt God as it were, and I must seek
to find Him again. '*Memoir*' (*1847*)

67 *In 1843, when suffering acutely in an illness, Elizabeth Fry remarked to one
of her daughters:* 'My dear Rachel—I can say one thing: since my
heart was touched at seventeen years old, I believe I never have
awakened from sleep, in sickness or in health, by day or by night,
without my first waking thought being how best I might serve my
Lord'. '*Memoir*' (*1847*)

68 *Of her prison work she wrote:* 'Much depends on the spirit in which the
visitor enters upon her work. It must be in the spirit, not of judgment, but of mercy. She must not say in her heart *I am more holy
than thou*, but must rather keep in perpetual remembrance that "*all*
have sinned and come short of the Glory of God".'
'*Observations on the visiting of female prisoners*' (*1827*)

69 *1844.* My life has been one of great vicissitude: mine has been a hidden
path, hidden from every *human* eye. I have had deep humiliations

and sorrows to pass through. I can truly say I have 'wandered in the wilderness in a solitary way, and found no city to dwell in'; and yet how wonderfully I have been sustained. I have passed through many and great dangers, many ways—I have been tried with the applause of the world, and none know how great a trial *that* has been, and the deep *humiliations* of it; and yet I fully believe it is not nearly so dangerous as being made much of in religious society. There is a snare even in religious unity, if we are not on the watch. I have sometimes felt that it was not so dangerous to be made much of in the world, as by those whom we think highly of in our own Society: the more I have been made much of by the world, the more I have been inwardly humbled. I could often adopt the words of Sir Francis Bacon—'When I have ascended before men, I have descended in humiliation before God.'   *Annual Monitor for 1846*

John Greenleaf Whittier (1807-1892) *passed his early years working on the farm at Haverhill, Massachusetts, where he was born, earning the money for his school fees by making slippers. Taking up work as a newspaper editor, he had thoughts of entering political life, but felt the call to devote himself to the cause of the abolition of slavery, though his strenuous advocacy of it involved unpopularity and sometimes great personal risk. In later life, when giving counsel to a fifteen-year-old lad, he said: 'My lad, if thou wouldst win success, join thyself to some unpopular but noble cause.' His deep love of humanity found expression in his poems. The strength of his appeal to the religious instinct of men, far beyond the boundaries of his own religious Society, is shown by the place which is held by his poetry in modern hymn-books.*

70   They fail to read clearly the signs of the times who do not see that the hour is coming when, under the searching eye of philosophy and the terrible analysis of science, the letter and the outward evidence will not altogether avail us; when the surest dependence must be upon the Light of Christ within, disclosing the law and the prophets in our own souls, and confirming the truth of outward Scripture by inward experience; when smooth stones from the brook of present revelation shall prove mightier than the weapons of Saul; when the doctrine of the Holy Spirit, as proclaimed by George Fox and lived by John Woolman, shall be recognized as the only efficient solvent of doubts raised by an age of restless inquiry.
                    Letter in 'The Friends review', 1870

71   In calm and cool and silence, once again
            I find my old accustomed place among
            My brethren, where, perchance, no human tongue
            Shall utter words; where never hymn is sung,
            Nor deep-toned organ blown, nor censer swung;
      Nor dim light falling through the pictured pane!
      There, syllabled by silence, let me hear
      The still, small voice which reached the prophet's ear;
            Read in my heart a still diviner law
            Than Israel's leader on his tables saw!

      There let me strive with each besetting sin,
            Recall my wandering fancies, and restrain
            The sore disquiet of a restless brain;
            And, as the path of duty is made plain,
      May grace be given that I may walk therein,
            Not like the hireling, for his selfish gain,
            With backward glances and reluctant tread,
            Making a merit of his coward dread,
            But cheerful, in the light around me thrown,
      Walking as one to pleasant service led;
            Doing God's Will as if it were my own,
            Yet trusting not in mine, but in His strength alone!

                                        First-day thoughts, 1852

John Bright (1811-1889). *In a speech at Birmingham at the end of 1865, he said: 'To the outward eye, monarchs and Parliaments seem to rule with an absolute and unquestioned sway, but—and I quote the words which one of our Puritan poets has left for us—*

> *There is on earth a yet auguster thing,*
> *Veiled though it be, than Parliament or King.*

That auguster thing is the tribunal which God has set up in the consciences of men. It is before that tribunal that I am now permitted humbly to plead, and there is something in my heart—a small but exultant voice—which tells me I shall not plead in vain.' It was this inward law he was always seeking to obey. Of the depth of his personal religion Lord Morley has said that the most impressive and pure piece of religion that he ever witnessed was John Bright reading a chapter of the Bible to his maidservants shortly after his wife's death, in his beautiful and feeling voice, followed by the Quaker silence. The way in which the calm strength of John Bright's religious faith was carried into his political life is illustrated by the extract given, part of the testimony of Marsden Monthly Meeting concerning him.

72 His deep sense of responsibility in the sight of God, and his intense human sympathy were the most powerful influences in drawing him from business into public life; and his natural nervousness was thus overcome by his sympathetic nature taking up the cause of the poor and the wronged. Of his public speeches it might be said, *he believed and therefore he spoke*. His aim was not popularity or party triumph, but the hope of advancing the cause of Truth and Right so far as he saw it.

Although at one time there were grave doubts in the minds of many Friends as to whether it was desirable for members of our Society to engage in active political life...it has been evident in John Bright's case that he entered upon it under a deep sense of duty, and that he endeavoured to carry his Christianity with him into all his public life.

The consideration of his life and work, his reverence and his humility; his devotion to duty and his practical faith; his constant and active sympathy with the poor, the distressed, and the downtrodden, may well incite all of us more fully to grasp the truth that...there is a place for each one of us to occupy, wherein opportunities will present themselves for us to glorify God and benefit our fellow-men. ...In his earlier years, it was not usual with Friends to give much expression to their personal religious experiences and opinions— and our late friend fully shared in such reticence, which his own feelings of reverence and humility doubtless increased. But we feel assured that John Bright's simple, consistent life plainly indicated that his desire was to be a 'good soldier of Jesus Christ', and to live under a reverent sense of Divine guidance. Of him we believe it may be truly said, *that he served and he endured as seeing Him who is invisible.*

Joseph Bevan Braithwaite (1818-1905) *was a prominent leader of the Society of Friends in the latter part of the nineteenth century. Yet in youth he had been* *at the point, shortly after his arrival in London, of undergoing the rite of baptism and resigning his membership. Before doing so he thought it right to attend the Yearly Meeting of 1840 throughout and form his own independent judgment. The extract shows how it was the record of the lives of ministers who had finished their earthly course that won him to a life of loyal service to the Society of Friends, after he had been estranged by the bitter spirit which divided the 'conservative' and 'evangelical' wings of the Society in the 'Beaconite' controversy.*

73 'I well remember sitting with my cousin, George Stacey Gibson, on the further upper forms to the left of the Clerk's table. I listened with an open mind to all that passed, whilst I was at the same time writing a pamphlet explaining my views in opposition to Friends. The attendance of the Yearly Meeting deeply impressed me, and I was gradually brought to the conclusion that I must cast in my lot amongst Friends'.

In a letter written to intimate friends at that time, he states, 'I had been afraid that the scriptural doctrine of justification by faith in the blood of Jesus was not in deed and in truth recognized by the body of Friends... But I heard the testimonies ⟨concerning⟩ deceased ministers and was ashamed and self-condemned for my harsh judgment... The enlarged and extended view which opened before me of the true Christian doctrine of the communication of the Holy Spirit to the mind of man, and of the accordance of Friends' views on worship and the ministry therewith, was the principal circumstance that weighed with me. I had been enabled, through unutterable mercy, to accept the Lord Jesus Christ as my Saviour: now I saw somewhat of His unspeakable preciousness as "the Good Shepherd" and "Counsellor" of His people, "always, even unto the end of the world".'

At the last sitting of the Yearly Meeting, J. B. Braithwaite made a public avowal of the change that had come over him, stating that he had been mistaken in the conception he had formed of the views of Friends, and he wished to express his deep regret at the part he had taken in the late (Beaconite) controversy. 'Sweet was the peace' he writes, 'that flowed into my soul' after this avowal. Thus was it after several years of conflict that our friend's convictions became unalterably established, so that he could render unwavering allegiance and service for more than sixty years to the Society of which he was a member.

Testimony of Westminster and Longford Monthly Meeting, 1906

Although his work as a conveyancing barrister and the claims of a large family occupied much of his energy, yet he made time for wide service in Europe and America as a minister. Concerned for the right study of the Bible as a preparation for Christian service, he wrote to his mother in 1855: 'I have been increasingly impressed of late with the importance of a sound, comprehensive and intelligent acquaintance with Holy Scripture... I am not sure that we who are called into the blessed work of the ministry are altogether clear in the matter.' He had taught himself Latin and Greek, and later Hebrew, and he became a biblical scholar of some repute. For many years visitors at Sunday lunch joined the family in the Bible reading that came after, each member following in a different language or in one of the six different English translations printed in parallel columns in the Hexapla, while J. B. Braithwaite produced a seventh extemporaneous one direct from the Hebrew or Greek, calling attention to the MSS. which supported variants in the text. His children wrote:

74 Of course, his Bible readings were not mere occasions for textual criticism; rather were they opportunities for bringing forth stores of rich spiritual truth from his well-filled granaries. The history of some great key-word of the gospel would be unfolded, or of some wondrous foreshadowing in ancient scripture... No merely verbal adoration of the letter of scripture could survive many such experiences, yet the profound reverence for the inner spiritual truth and the zest with which he feasted upon the experience portrayed, could not fail to impress the most careless with a new reverence for the wonderful book.

Caroline Fox (1819-1871) *was the daughter of Robert Were Fox, a Victorian savant of Penjerrick, near Falmouth in Cornwall, and his wife Maria (described by a friend as 'imbued and steeped in the living waters of Divine Truth'). Her charm and intelligence won her the friendship of many leading figures of her time, notably the Coleridges, Carlyles, Sterlings and Mills; and her Journal is an important source of information about them.*

75 *The following passage was written when she was 21, to describe 'the struggle through which a spark of true faith was lighted in my soul' :*

I felt I had hitherto been taking things of the highest importance too much for granted, without feeling their reality; and this I knew to be a very unhealthy state of things... Carlyle admirably expresses my state of mind when he speaks of 'the spasmodic efforts of some *to believe that they believe*'. But it would not do; I felt that I was playing a dishonest part with myself, and with my God... A remark that Hender Molesworth one day incidentally made to me was often a gleam of comfort to me during this time of distress and warfare. He said that he thought 'a want of faith was sometimes permitted to those who would otherwise have no trials; for you know,' he added, 'a want of faith is a very great trial.' I did not tell him how truly he had spoken.

The first gleam of light, 'the first cold light of morning' which gave promise of day with its noontide glories, dawned on me one day at Meeting, when I had been meditating on my state in great depression. I seemed to hear the words articulated in my spirit 'Live up to the light thou hast, and more will be granted thee.' Then I believed that God speaks to man by His Spirit. I strove to lead a more Christian life, in unison with what I knew to be right, and looked for brighter days; not forgetting the blessings that are granted to prayer...

I by no means regret the perplexities and doubts and troubles through which I have passed. They have increased my toleration for others, and given me a much higher value and deeper affection for those glorious truths which make up the Christian's hope, than I could have had if they had only been passively imbibed. The hard struggle I have had to make them my own must rise to check future faithfulness; and the certain conviction that the degree of faith which has been granted was purely a gift from above, leads me with earnestness and faith to petition for myself and others, 'Lord, increase our faith'.   *1841*

76 I have assumed a name today for my religious principles—Quaker-Catholicism—having direct spiritual teaching for its distinctive

dogma, yet recognising the high worth of all other forms of Faith; a system, in the sense of inclusion, not exclusion; an appreciation of the universal and various teachings of the Spirit, through the faculties given us, or independent of them.   *1846*

Hannah Whitall Smith (1832-1911). *Hannah Tatum Whitall was born in Philadelphia of Quaker parents; at 19 she married Robert Pearsall Smith, and embarked with him on a career of religious evangelism in both America and Europe. She took part in the founding of the Women's Christian Temperance Movement in the U.S.A., and the Women's Suffrage movement. Her writings, especially 'The Christian's secret of a happy life', were translated into many languages and sold very widely. The passages below are taken from her spiritual autobiography, 'The unselfishness of God' (1903):*

77   By the discovery of God...I do not mean anything mysterious, or mystical, or unattainable. I simply mean becoming acquainted with Him as one becomes acquainted with a human friend; that is, finding out what is His nature, and His character, and coming to understand His Ways...My own experience has been something like this. My knowledge of God, beginning on a very low plane, and in the midst of the greatest darkness and ignorance, advanced slowly through many stages, and with a vast amount of useless conflict and wrestling, to the place where I learned at last that Christ was the 'express image' of God, and where I became, therefore, in a measure acquainted with Him, and discovered to my amazement and delight His utter unselfishness, and saw that it was safe to trust Him. And from this time all my doubts and questionings have been slowly but surely disappearing in the blaze of this magnificent knowledge.

78   In the very nature of things emotions are more or less variable, while convictions, where they are really convictions, and are not purely notions or ideas, are permanent...I learned in time therefore not to seek emotions, but to seek only for convictions, and I found to my surprise and delight that my convictions brought me a far more stable and permanent joy than many of my more emotional friends seemed to experience. In the time of stress, with many of them, their emotions flagged, and even often vanished, and they had hard

fights to prevent utter failure and despair, and some of them have been thankful at last to struggle back to the stable ground of conviction, which in their emotional days had seemed so barren and comfortless.

79 *She wrote to a friend three days before she died:*
Once my Divine Master sent me on His errands, and I knew His will was good, and was happy in trying to do it. And now He has shut me up to an invalid life, and tells me to sit in my wheeled chair, and to be content to let others do His errands and carry on His work, and I know His will is good just the same, and am happy in trying to accept it.

Caroline E. Stephen (1834-1909) *of Cambridge, daughter of Sir James Stephen and sister of Sir Leslie Stephen, had been passing through a long period of inward questioning as to the fundamental truths of religion, her difficulties made greater by the dogmatic statements and assumptions which she found in the Church of England service. She came to know the power that sprang from 'a deep quietness of heart and mind, a laying aside of all preoccupation with passing things ... a resolute fixing of the heart upon that which is unchangeable and eternal.' She embodied her findings in 'Quaker strongholds' (1890) from which the following extract is taken.*

80 I first found myself within reach of a Friends' meeting ⟨1872⟩, and, somewhat to my surprise, cordially made welcome to attend it. The invitation came at a moment of need, for I was beginning to feel with dismay that I might not much longer be able conscientiously to continue to join in the Church of England service; not for want of appreciation of its unrivalled richness and beauty, but from doubts of the truth of its doctrines, combined with a growing recognition that to me it was as the armour of Saul in its elaboration, and in the sustained pitch of religious fervour for which it was meant to provide an utterance...On one never-to-be-forgotten Sunday morning, I found myself one of a small company of silent worshippers who were content to sit down together without words, that each one might feel after and draw near to the Divine Presence, unhindered at least, if not helped, by any human utterance. Utterance I knew was free, should the words be given; and, before the meeting was over, a sentence or two were uttered in great simplicity by an old and apparently untaught man, rising in his place amongst the rest of us.

I did not pay much attention to the words he spoke, and I have no recollection of their purport. My whole soul was filled with the unutterable peace of the undisturbed opportunity for communion with God, with the sense that at last I had found a place where I might, without the faintest suspicion of insincerity, join with others in simply seeking His presence. To sit down in silence could at the least pledge me to nothing; it might open to me (as it did that morning) the very gate of heaven. And, since that day, now more than seventeen years ago, Friends' meetings have indeed been to me the greatest of outward helps to a fuller and fuller entrance into the spirit from which they have sprung; the place of the most soul-subduing, faith-restoring, strengthening, and peaceful communion, in feeding upon the bread of life, that I have ever known.

William Littleboy (1853-1936) *retired early from business in Birmingham and devoted himself to work for the Society and the Adult School Movement; he was a minister of exceptional depth and sensitiveness. He and his wife Margaret were wardens of Woodbrooke from 1904-1907.*

81 Men are always pre-disposed to make their own experience the standard for their judgment of others. One of life's hardest lessons is that there is no justification for expecting that our neighbour is to traverse precisely the same path as that which we ourselves have followed...The difficulty a man has in grasping this truth is increased in proportion as his own experience has been vivid and clearly defined. One who has been lifted out of the horrible pit, has had his feet set upon a rock, and a new song put into his mouth, finds it hard to believe that another who has arrived quietly and without crisis, with no strong consciousness of guilt and no corresponding ecstasy of deliverance, can really be a disciple at all. And he whose life is illumined with the brightness and joy of a heavenly companionship can with difficulty believe that his brother who walks in the shadows may yet be a humble and single-hearted follower of Jesus Christ...The fact is that...we habitually over-emphasize the place of the emotions in the spiritual life. We speak as if love (in the sense of conscious affection), rapture, overflowing peace were in themselves the essential characteristics of the life in Christ rather than the attitude of the soul toward God indicated by the qualities of faith and obedience...To be a Christian consists not in feeling, but in following; not in ecstasy, but in obedience.   (*1916*)

82   God is above all the God of the normal. In the common facts and circumstances of life He draws near to us, quietly He teaches us in the routine of life's trifles, gently and unnoticed His guidance comes to us through the channels of 'reason, judgment and determining circumstance'. We never felt God, we were never conscious of His control, nevertheless the fact remains that we have a store of experience which can only have come from Him; we have been taught by Him when we least suspected it; we have been guided— we know it—though the guiding hand rested upon us so lightly that we were unaware of its touch.   (*1916*)

83   Here is the unfailing attraction of the life in Christ. It is a life which even to old age, is always on the upgrade; there is always something calling for a joyful looking forward; it is a life where, across each revelation of God's grace as it comes to us is written, in letters of gold, Thou shalt see greater things than these. It gives full scope to our latent chivalry, to our desire for high adventure. No conceivable life can be so interesting, so stimulating, as that which we live in Christ.   (*1917*)

Edward Grubb (1854-1939) *teacher, author, and editor of 'The British Friend' (1901-1913), was 'one of the most influential figures in the Religious Society of Friends during the forty years which lay between 1890 and 1930,...a period when religious thought everywhere was disturbed and confused by the impact of the flood of new knowledge assailing it on every side.'*

84   *These quotations are from 'Flowers of the inner life' (1933) which he described as 'the outcome of a life's experience spread over many years'.*
       One of the chief troubles that beset many earnest seekers after God is the absence of direct experience of help from Him. We are told that we have only to ask and we shall receive; but we have prayed and prayed and nothing happens. We ask for help to overcome temptation, and then go and do, or say, the very thing we wished to avoid. We wonder what our Lord's promises mean, if they so constantly fail us. Is the grace of God a dream and not a reality?

Then it is that, if we only knew it, God is nearest to us, seeking us with an intensity of which our own longing for Him is but a pale reflection. If we cannot at once open our souls to His love and grace, let us in patience wait for Him; and we shall discover at last that it is He who has been infinitely patient with us. Trouble of soul can teach us things that raptures never could—not only patience and perseverance, but humility and sympathy with others. 'Blessed are they that mourn, for they shall be comforted.'

John William Graham (1859-1932) *came of a Quaker family. After teaching at Bootham and other schools he studied at Cambridge, where he helped to refound the meeting. As tutor and then as principal he spent 38 years at Dalton Hall, Manchester. In a period of crisis in religious thought he early became known in the Society for his bold advocacy of intellectual freedom. His clear mind, staunch spirit, and deep religious conviction enabled him to render a great service among students, who also valued, as many others did, his ministry in meeting. He was an acceptable 'chaplain' to many imprisoned conscientious objectors during the first world war, and peace took the first place among the good causes he worked for. No small part of his service was in writing: his most notable work was 'The faith of a Quaker'.*

85 When I sit down in meeting I recall whatever may have struck me freshly during the past week. This is in part, initially at least, a voluntary and outward act. It simply means that the outward man is ready to run if he is sent. It means that the will is given up to service; and it is quite possible to stop everything by taking an opposite attitude. So thoughts suggest themselves—a text that has smitten one during the week—new light on a phrase—a verse of poetry— some incident, private or public. These pass before the door whence shines the heavenly light. Are they transfigured? Sometimes, yes; sometimes, no. If nothing flames, silence is my portion. I turn from ideas of ministry to my own private needs. From these sometimes the live coal from off the altar is brought, suddenly and unexpectedly, and speech follows. Sometimes it does not. Again there are times when the initial thought strikes in of itself from the Inner Man beyond the will. These are times to be thankful for. Often two or three of the thoughts that have struck home during the week are woven together in unexpected ways. When the fire is kindled the blaze is not long. In five minutes from its inception, the sermon

is there, the heart beats strongly, and up the man must get. How trying is any outward interruption during these few rapt and fruitful minutes, when the whole scheme is unfolding itself, and flashing itself upon the brain. There are the five or six main points, the leading sequences of thoughts are there, the introductory expository teaching, the generalization, the illustrations, the final lesson and appeal, they fall into place. The sermon is made, but I, the slow compiler, did not make it.   (*1920*)

Mary Hughes (**1860-1941**) *was a daughter of Judge Thomas Hughes (author of 'Tom Brown's Schooldays') who was associated with Charles Kingsley, Frederick Denison Maurice and the Christian Socialists. She was born and reared in a house representing the best influences of Victorian England, but, as her Monthly Meeting wrote of her, 'became deeply convinced that the class to which she belonged was unjustly privileged, and as a member of that class felt convicted of sins against society, and strove to expiate them by a life of service and poverty'. In her late thirties she started to live in the East End of London and 'her home for many years was the Dewdrop Inn, formerly the "Earl Grey's Castle", a public house which she took over to redeem from its former purpose'. As Howard Spring shows in the following extract she identified herself completely with those around her, sharing their poverty, their privations and their lack of opportunities for cleanliness. She joined the Society of Friends in 1918 and Friends will not forget the stirring of conscience that was felt in Yearly Meeting when her white-haired, red-cloaked figure was present.*

86 The longest journey Mary Hughes made was in spiritual conception. In her youth she...took part in work on behalf of the poor and unfortunate. You drove to that work in a carriage and when the work was done you drove back to a beautiful house...Mary Hughes was never a one for condemning the way in which other people lived their lives; she was too busy with the way in which she chose to lead her own. If she had ever consciously wondered why this way, which she saw in her youth, was not satisfactory to her, she could have found the answer...in those words *when the work was done*. It became clear to her that what she had to do could never be *done*, not even for an hour. Her life itself must be her work, but it could be her work only if it were lived in the appropriate circumstances. She didn't want to *visit* the poor. She wanted to be *with* the poor and to be poor herself...

She had no set schemes. She founded no institution. Neither did Jesus...'He went about doing good.' So did Mary Hughes...It was a question of being rather than of doing. You trusted to the contagion of goodness rather than to homily or sermon. Necessarily, such a personality, linked as it was to endless sources of spiritual strength, became a magnet, and there again one hears the echo of an old phrase: 'I will *draw* all men unto Me.' As this magnet drew the poor and dispossessed, there was plenty to do; and Mary Hughes went about the doing of it in her own idiosyncratic way...She never turned down man or woman who had duped or bamboozled her. It was in the nature of things that the world contained sinners, and she wished above all to live close to the nature of things. This she could confidently do because of her belief that the over-riding reality is spiritual. She would have thought herself most faithless if a few sinners had shaken her...Burning with shame, radiant with love, she set her course and followed it...The whole point of her life will be missed unless we can share her faith that 'the things that are seen are temporal, the things that are unseen are eternal'. Looked at from that point of view, this shabby and sometimes verminous woman becomes one of the few, 'of whom the world is not worthy'.

A. Neave Brayshaw (1861-1940) *came of a Manchester Quaker family. After studying law he became a teacher at Bootham and was for some years a lecturer at Woodbrooke. He spent the last thirty years of his life in service for the Society of Friends, travelling in the ministry in England and the U.S.A. He was much loved by young people, on whom he had a great influence. His most important writings are 'The Quakers, their story and message', and 'The personality of George Fox'.*

87   I can remember my own disappointment when it opened out upon me that I was not going to find what I called a proof of God. I wanted something that was irrefutable; some chain of 'because' and 'therefore' leading up to a triumphant conclusion from which there could be no intellectual escape; and if I could not get that, nothing else seemed worth having; all was so shifting and unstable, so shadowy and unreal. I heard with impatience, amounting to anger, the saying of Pascal that 'the heart has reasons which reason

does not understand'; it seemed simply an evasion to be told that God was most truly to be found in the deepest experiences of life. I have come to see, first, that I shall get no better evidence, and second, that that which I have is good. Intellectual considerations are in no degree whatever to be undervalued and in their place they are invaluable—but, at best, they only point the way, and in themselves they never take us to the end. In thus trusting ourselves to that which is best in us we shall not, as I have said before, find a solution of many of the problems which we so much want to solve, but as we set our faces in the way of following Christ, who has shown to men the mind and love of God as they had never known them before, life takes on a new quality. This we cannot describe to one who insists on professing that he knows nothing of it, any more than we could describe colours to one who has never seen them; but as we follow His voice in the dark, if for the time we cannot see Him in the light, His words come true, not as a piece of poetic rhetoric, but as an experience of our own, 'He that followeth Me shall not walk in darkness, but shall have the light of life.'
(*1911*)

William Charles Braithwaite (1862-1922) *was the eighth child of Joseph Bevan and Martha Braithwaite. From young manhood he was very active in the Adult School Movement; after some years of legal practice in London he turned to banking, and Banbury became his home for the rest of his life. His great gifts of mind were notably employed in his histories, 'The beginnings of Quakerism' and 'The second period of Quakerism', which helped to reinterpret our seventeenth-century heritage. This same sense of historical perspective and his statesmanship were active in the transformation of the 'Book of doctrine' into the 1921 'Christian life, faith and thought'.*

88 I have no full definition to give of the word 'Spiritual'—which ranks high among the elusive words of the language...I hope myself that it will always escape capture and definition; we want some human-divine words, which belong both to earth and heaven; with meanings rooted in experience, but springing up into the regions where we walk by faith rather than by sight. At first 'spirit' was the breath of wind, and then the breath of physical life: but now we use the word for the breath of something higher—the life that is life indeed. It stands for something more than our physical vitality— and yet for something which we find incorporated to a considerable

extent in humanity as we know it at present, marking us off from the animal creation, and setting our wayward feet on the long road of a divine destiny. It has continually been touching life to finer issues, giving man a world of consciousness within him, thronged with the memory of the past, throbbing with the purpose of the present, thrilled with the hopes of the future, creating in him a personality which realizes itself most fully when it comes into closest fellowship with the personality of others and into that highest experience that we call union with God. And so for us the word 'spiritual' means all that belongs to the breath, the motion, of this larger life.

Most, perhaps all, of us know enough of this life to affirm that the hours when it controls our personalities are unforgettable, supreme. We think of great days when the spirit of nature embraced us lovingly and made us brothers and sisters of bird and flower and mountain. We recall times of fellowship, when one common life, one common service, thrilled us all. We remember hours of worship, in which we found ourselves, as Wordsworth says:

> Rapt into still communion that transcends
> The imperfect offices of prayer and praise.

We dwell again, very near to God, on some wide-viewed hill, the clamour of the world hushed, the peace of the blue sky around us and the grateful green of dewy mountain lawns. Or we revive some dark hour when He walked with us through the valley of the shadow and spread His table for us in the midst of our foes.   (*1914*)

Inazo Nitobe (1862-1933) *was by birth a member of the samurai, the ancient military caste of Japan. He was converted to Christianity in his student days, and then also arose in him the desire to be a link between the East and West. One of the first two Japanese students to study in America and Europe, he joined our Society in Baltimore about 1885, and married a Friend, Mary Elkinton of Philadelphia, in 1891. Having studied agriculture and taken his Ph.D. at Halle, he returned to Japan and effected great agricultural reforms. He was eminent also in education, and at their home in Tokyo he and his wife influenced countless students through the long years of his services to his country. After the first world war he became Under-Secretary-General of the League of Nations at its foundation, and spent some years in Geneva. On his return to Japan he was made a life-member of the House of Peers.*

89   When I began, in my boyhood, to hear Christian sermons and read Christian books, including the Bible, I confess that they were not at all convincing to me. Only in Quakerism could I reconcile Christianity with Oriental thought. Let it be far from me to turn Quakerism into Oriental mysticism. Quakerism stays within the family of Christianity. It professes to rest its structure on the person of Jesus Christ, whom it identifies with the Inner Light. It does not deny His incarnation and historicity, but it accepts His continued work of grace in each succeeding generation. Not only that, it believes His grace was retro-active, so that it was He who enlightened all the seers of old. He still dwells within us—in the least as in the greatest, even in the savage and the unlettered...Curiously enough, the Cosmic sense, as described by those who attain it, is very much the same everywhere—whether it be by a Buddhist priest, a Shinto votary, a Mohammedan saint, a French mathematician, an American farmer, or a Jewish philosopher. Nothing confirms the identity of the human race better than this spiritual expansion. But I can speak only as a close observer of those who attain this high and lofty sense, and not as one who has himself attained it...I believe Christianity has this advantage—not to call it a point of superiority—that it provides weak, ordinary mortals with a definite and concrete object upon which to focus their mind, thus facilitating their discovery of the Perfect Man. Acquaintance with Him makes us one with Him—at-one-ment. To follow Him is to be redeemed from a lower plane of life. To contemplate Him is to see God Himself and be saved.

'A Japanese view of Quakerism' (*1927*)

90   *A Supplication*

I ask for daily bread, but not for wealth, lest I forget the poor.

I ask for strength, but not for power, lest I despise the meek.

I ask for wisdom, but not for learning, lest I scorn the simple.

I ask for a clean name, but not for fame, lest I contemn the lowly.

I ask for peace of mind, but not for idle hours, lest I fail to hearken to the call of duty.

'Thoughts & essays' (*1909*)

Rufus M. Jones (1863-1948), *for many years Professor of Philosophy at Haverford College, Pennsylvania, was also an eminent historian and an authority on mystical religion. His wide influence as an author and speaker was enhanced by a gift for apt and humorous illustration. He made a great contribution towards ending the divisions among American Friends and towards creating the world community of Friends. He gave many years of service as chairman of the American Friends Service Committee, and on other bodies. He was brought up in a rural Quaker community in the state of Maine, lovingly described in his autobiographical volumes, from one of which this passage describing religion in the Quaker home is taken:*

91 While I was too young to have any religion of my own, I had come to a home where religion kept its fires always burning. We had very few 'things', but we were rich in invisible wealth. I was not 'christened' in a church, but I was sprinkled from morning to night with the dew of religion. We never ate a meal which did not begin with a hush of thanksgiving; we never began a day without 'a family gathering' at which mother read a chapter of the Bible, after which there would follow a weighty silence. These silences, during which all the children of our family were hushed with a kind of awe, were very important features of my spiritual development. There was work inside and outside the house waiting to be done, and yet we sat there hushed and quiet, doing nothing. I very quickly discovered that something real was taking place. We were feeling our way down to that place from which living words come, and very often they did come. Some one would bow and talk with God so simply and quietly that He never seemed far away. The words helped to explain the silence. We were now finding what we had been searching for. When I first began to think of God I did not think of Him as very far off. At a meeting some of the Friends who prayed shouted loud and strong when they called upon Him, but at home He always heard easily and He seemed to be there with us in the living silence. My first steps in religion were thus *acted*. It was a religion which we *did* together. Almost nothing was *said* in the way of instructing me. We all joined together to listen for God, and then one of us talked to Him for the others. In these simple ways my religious disposition was being unconsciously formed and the roots of my faith in unseen realities were reaching down far below my crude and childish surface thinking.

'*Finding the trail of life*' (*1926*)

92   *The following experience relates to the death of his son Lowell at the age of 11, while Rufus Jones was on a voyage to England in 1903:*

The night before landing in Liverpool I awoke in my berth with a strange sense of trouble and sadness. As I lay wondering what it meant, I felt myself invaded by a Presence and held by Everlasting Arms. It was the most extraordinary experience I had ever had. But I had no intimation that anything was happening to Lowell. When we landed in Liverpool a cable informed me that he was desperately ill, and a second cable, in answer to one from me, brought the dreadful news that he was gone. When the news reached my friend John Wilhelm Rowntree, he experienced a profound sense of Divine Presence enfolding him and me, and his comfort and love were an immense help to me in my trial...I know now, as I look back across the years, that nothing has carried me up into the life of God, or done more to open out the infinite meaning of love, than the fact that love can span this break of separation, can pass beyond the visible and hold right on across the chasm. The mystic union has not broken and knows no end.

'The luminous trail' (1947)

93   It is my great wish exceeding all others that I may feel in the last hours of my life that I have done my work and that the Great Father is satisfied with my life, so that death may be to me like falling asleep, as it is for all who faithfully walk the right road.

Letter to Sallie Coutant, July 1887

John Wilhelm Rowntree (1868-1905) *was the son of Joseph Rowntree of York, and at the age of 17 he started to work in his father's factory, two years later undertaking the reorganization of the cocoa and chocolate departments. He broke away from the narrowness characteristic of much of the Quakerism of his time, showed some talent for painting and became passionately interested in the theatre. As a young man he was highly critical of the Society, describing some of its practices as 'Quaker caution and love of detail run to seed', and at one time he considered resigning his membership. He was troubled by deafness from infancy, and, as hinted in this extract and recounted in §472, he learned in his mid-twenties of his mortal illness, involving ultimate blindness and loss of memory. It was at this time that he gained spiritual light.*

94 It is a great mistake to think that faith is exclusively or even mainly an affair of the heart, a question of the spiritual temper or attitude of the soul. As William Law expresses it, in one of his essays, faith 'is a living, working power of the mind, that wills, desires, and hopes and trusts and believes and obeys'. Aye, *obeys*. That is where our faith is weak. That is where we need the potency of the Gospel. We know better than we do. Perceiving the good we continually choose the evil...I am, shall we say, the average man...If anyone were to charge me with unorthodoxy, I should be painfully shocked. I read the Bible, perhaps sometimes wondering what I have read five minutes afterwards. I go certainly once, perhaps under favourable circumstances, twice, to church, chapel or meeting. I don't understand what is meant by the Trinity or the Atonement; I leave all that to the clergyman or the minister, but in a more or less definite way I believe that my earthly life is so irreproachable that my eternal future is sure to be pleasant. Christ, I say, is my Saviour, by which I mean (if I were ever so brutally frank with myself, which I am not) that He will leave me alone in this world, and save me in the next. So I go on. Now and then someone upon whose companionship I depend is called beyond the grave. On such occasions I am deeply touched...And then the tide of life, business and pleasure flows in again. The gap is filled. I forget and once more am satisfied to live on the surface. I flutter through the hours like a butterfly in a meadow—dipping aimlessly now here, now there. But let us suppose that the strong blow of some great catastrophe were to smite me. Something that destroyed the routine of self-pleasing and compelled me to face the realities which I have so steadfastly shirked. Let it be some permanent physical restriction like blindness, or some financial disaster involving penury—no matter what. Where do I stand now?..Everything is bitter, life and the interminable future are desolate. Suddenly I realise that my Christ was a lay figure. I made Him and draped Him myself. I realise that at the heart of what I called my religion was but selfishness...and that my insincerity has brought upon me the doom of spiritual emptiness...

But how are we to be saved? How are we to realise the Christ of our Gospel?..Beyond all question a first consideration is sincerity, the sincerity born for example of conviction for sin and the desire for pardon. We must honestly seek the true life, we must honestly wish to escape the toils of self-love. Assume this sincerity. Assume for example that I have grown dissatisfied with a drifting life, that I have felt a touch of that satiety which is the scourge of the worldling. How, then, am I to set about the business of salvation? I turn to Christ, the Christ of the Gospels. What is salvation by Christ? It is nothing mysterious, it is to be made like unto Him. Again I quote from William Law: 'From morning to night to keep Jesus in thy Heart, long for Nothing, desire Nothing, hope for Nothing, but to have all that is within thee changed into the Spirit and Temper of the Holy Jesus. Let this be thy Christianity, thy Church, and thy religion...'

But we must know the *steps* of this pilgrim's progress. Let me state the case again in terms of personal experience. I determine to seek the peace of God till I find it. My sincerity is not to be doubted. I am earnest in my quest. So far so good. I have the first condition requisite. I am willing to pull down the prickly cactus-hedge of my sins. I realise that self is the devil's workshop. I want to get away from the prison of my selfishness. I want to realise love. But I am not going to do it by mere mortification and penances... I am wrong in thinking that the Christian life consists merely in not doing things that other people do... Moreover, mortification of this sort breeds a judging temper and a spirit of pride. Self-sacrifice is self-realisation. I must approach my holy experiment from another side. I must seek not merely to lop off but to grow. I must acquire something I have not got. And here is a difficulty. In practical experience how am I to know what is meant by listening to the voice of Christ, obeying Him and following Him?.. Conscience is a guide I can follow. For example, be thoughtful of others, even in little things. Make a practice of forgetting yourself. In the past it was always *I*, what do they say and think of *me*, am *I* getting the recognition that is my due? Now let it be otherwise. Am I helping him, what can I do for him, what am I thinking of him? Am I giving him his due?..Someone angers me, insults me. I want to hit back, sting with a sharp repartee, crush with a jibe. I practise restraint. I return soft answers. And so I might illustrate at large.

But I cannot rest satisfied here. I seek not only discipline, but victory. I want to know not only conscience but Christ. Yes, but to the sincere experimentalist, using his conscience as a guide, and seeking always to focus his life on that of Jesus Christ, as he knows Him in the Gospels, and recognizes Him in His faithful disciples, there comes a time when the line between conscience and Christ grows very thin. There comes a time when the higher life of which I am always aware, and which I have tried to follow, becomes so merged in my thought of Christ and my devotion to Him, that I can hardly distinguish the two in my mind. There comes a time when suddenly I am on my knees, my whole soul flooded with light and love, tears in my heart and eyes, an unspeakable peace enfolding me. The pierced hands have reached through to me at last, and draw me gently forth to Him. 'Come unto Me and rest', and I answer, 'Yea, for I am hid with Christ in God'.

I have sketched, you say, a hypothetical career. No, it is a story from real life. You say I have spoken in mystical language. I answer, Yes, the supreme moment cannot be defined in the dry language of theology, nor can words express it. You say the experience is the result of mental suggestion practised over a term of years. I answer, No one believes that who has once been there and taken off his shoes on holy ground—the reality is too overpowering, the effect too profound...

But perhaps I have made haste too fast. If I go back to my pilgrim, I find in his experience something upon which I have not touched. It is not a smooth progress that he makes. His sincerity wavers before the fierce resistance of hereditary evil, ingrained selfishness, natural sloth. There are times when he cannot keep his eyes upon the cross, when the goal upon which he set his heart grows dim, when the baser self yearns for the flesh-pots of Egypt. How can he win through? There is only one way, the way of prayer. I do not mean formal praying, the rapid gabbling of the Lord's Prayer, or the set petition for outward benefits. I mean the prayer of the sinful man crying from the depths of his great need: 'Create in me a clean heart, O God, and renew a right spirit within me', the prayer of the longing soul seeking to escape from the clog of fleshly imperfection and to breathe the free, pure air of the spiritual life...

Amid the feverish activities of these modern days, when the loud-voiced interests of the world stun the ear, may we seek by devotional exercise in the private sanctuary of the home, no less than in public worship, to realise the saving love of God. And, as we turn our thoughts inward to face the solemn realities of eternal life, may the light of God's holiness reveal our sin as He sees it, that, knowing our weakness, we may seek His strength, and pray the Father whom Jesus has shown us to take us as children by the hand, and lead us into His everlasting truth, by the way of service and a life of love freely given.   *1905*

Following this experience John Wilhelm Rowntree became the prophet of a new era for the Society of Friends on both sides of the Atlantic, and the inspiration of his life and writings during the ten years that remained to him is still fruitful. At the age of 27 he took an outstanding part in the Manchester Conference of 1895 and in an address on 'Has Quakerism a message in the world today?' he asked:

95 Is there perplexity and change in religious thought? Then God grant to our church the spirit of understanding which shall give her the eye of a seer, the voice of a prophet, the place and power of a leader. Is there indifference to the higher life? Then, O Christ, convince us by Thy Spirit, thrill us with Thy divine passion, drown our selfishness in Thy invading love, lay on us the burden of the world's suffering, drive us forth with the apostolic fervour of the early church! So only can our message be delivered—'Speak to the Children of Israel that they go forward.'

Mary Ann Stokeley (1869-1941)

96 Mary Ann Stokeley was associated with Ratcliff Meeting from her earliest years. Born and bred in Stepney, within a stone's throw from the old Ratcliff Meeting House in Brook Street (now Cable Street), she first attended the Sunday School at the age of four, and thereafter made her spiritual home with Friends. Very short in stature and of comparatively frail physique, she knew poverty at first hand, and was never able to earn an adequate wage. Yet despite her physical and educational disadvantages, for many years she was responsible for a Sunday School class of rowdy Stepney girls, to whom she gave of her best.

Mary Stokeley did not apply for membership of our Society until she reached middle life, after many years as an attender. Her attendance at meeting for worship was regular and punctual and she took an interest in all the concerns of her Preparative and Monthly Meetings. Very conscious of her own limitations, her part was a silent one, but she was amazingly faithful to the tiny meeting to which she belonged. Our Friend was not a 'Oncer'—for many years she was in the meeting house morning, afternoon and evening every first-day. It was indeed the centre of her life.

During the air raids in the last war she was repeatedly pressed to leave the district, but she preferred to share the danger with her own kith and kin, and there can be no doubt that the anxiety of the time shortened her life. Ratcliff Meeting was reduced to one or two, yet up to her last illness she was in her place every first-day morning with unfailing regularity. Faithfulness was indeed the keynote of her life, and an example to us all.

That our Friend should, out of her poverty, have left us a substantial legacy is truly humbling. She lived in one room, enjoyed none of the refinements which most of us consider essential for a reasonable life, and might well have spent the money on comforts in her last years. But she preferred to leave her money to the religious fellowship of which she was so humble and unobtrusive a member.

Testimony of Ratcliff and Barking Monthly Meeting

Elizabeth Fox Howard (1873-1957) *came of a long line of Quaker ancestors, but did not herself join Friends until she was nearly thirty, when she soon found herself 'drawn into the full tide of useful service' with an outstanding generation of young Friends. She was one of the first students at Woodbrooke, travelled widely and edited 'Friends Fellowship Papers', as well as writing books of several kinds in prose and verse. She gave long service and profound love to Germany and its people, particularly through the Rest Home at Bad Pyrmont.*

97 When I was about seven years old, I announced that my favourite text was 'Hitherto hath the Lord helped me'. The elders were amused, but I am not so sure that it was funny after all. The distance from one birthday to the next seems infinite to a small child, and 'the thoughts of youth are long long thoughts'. Looking back over many years, I fancy my choice now would be much the same. I am not prepared, here and now, to analyse and define the reasons, but I can only say that this quiet certainty has run all through my life, linking up babyhood and youth and middle age with the latest stretch of the road . . . and 'hitherto', though sometimes almost slipping through one's fingers, that golden thread has never wholly escaped my grasp.   *'Midstream: a record of many years'* (*1943*)

J. Rowntree Gillett (1874-1940) *was a banker who gave up his business during the first world war, because all financial business had been diverted to its support. He devoted the rest of his life to the service of the Society of Friends, the Adult School Movement, relief work, help to the unemployed and many social causes. He acted as a Quaker chaplain to conscientious objectors in prison during the first world war. The crisis of his religious experience came during the Yearly Meeting of 1905 in Leeds, when the death of John Wilhelm Rowntree after a few short years of vital activity and ministry produced among Friends a mood of deep heart-searching. Rowntree Gillett's description of this occasion, and the following passage, are taken from an article published in 1937, 'What Quakerism means to me', in which he reflected on the events of 1905.*

98   I came to know God experimentally through the Quaker Fellowship. In November ⟨1905⟩ I wrote, 'I have been conscious this last few months of coming into a closer union with the Divine life and to some small extent have known something of the joy of obedience'... From the start of that experimental life in God I found my life challenged by the Divine Spirit. There were things in my life that had to go. I remember coming out of the Yearly Meeting weeping like a child. I lit up a cigarette and leaned on the wall of a bridge that stretched over a dirty canal in order to think out what difference this great new fact of experience—the reality of God—was going to mean in my life, and almost immediately the challenge came that I must drop smoking! I had tried to control this habit often but had always failed, so that the demand seemed quite unpractical, and it was not till three weeks later when the issue became so clear that it must be either obedience to the Divine challenge or failure to grow in the spiritual life, that all desire for smoking suddenly left me, and from that day to this I have never even wanted to take it up

again; some greater desire had mastered the old habit, it was the desire to know God. This is not an attempt to condemn smoking in general, but rather the record of the demands in an individual life of the Divine incoming.

I began to attend the Meeting that gathered in the Y.M.C.A. at Hampstead, and here after a short time the second challenge came— to get up and witness to the inward life in God that now was mine. I hesitated and shrank back: my wife had taken a friend to Meeting that morning, and that individual of all people was just the one I could not witness before; but once again the issue was plain and obedience was the only path to further growth, so I rose and falteringly spoke of the thing that had bound me to my seat, the subject of fear! The reward in both cases was instant and overwhelming, the joy of obedience, and also the realisation that a new power had come into my life and was working through me.

99 *Towards the end of the first world war he wrote:*
Brought up in a house where Jesus Christ was loved and honoured, I can never remember a time when His claims on me were not more or less a living issue, and although on attaining manhood I wandered for many years in a maze of doubt and unrest, nevertheless that issue remained. Just thirteen years ago I became convinced that God was a living reality and had revealed Himself to humanity in the character and personality of Jesus Christ. From that time I dedicated myself to Him, and have tried to lead men and women into a realisation of God's love and care for them.

T. Edmund Harvey (1875-1955) *was the eldest son of William and Anna Maria Harvey of Leeds. His early experience of social questions was gained in London on various public bodies. He sat in Parliament altogether about 18 years, which covered both the great wars. There his constant advocacy of magnanimity, justice and peace won him the high regard of men of all opinions. He worked in defence of conscientious objectors to military service, and in relief work for the civilian victims of war, especially in France. Less known was his personal help given over many years to prisoners and orphans. In our meetings his ministry was deeply valued, being simple and personal as well as profound, and it was enriched by the breadth and depth of his scholarship.*

100 I am far from having arrived at the mount of vision where so many more faithful disciples have stood, above all mists of doubt: yet to think of Christ has meant again and again a parting in the clouds through which a beam of light comes gleaming. Sometimes that light has shone into my vision reflected from word or deed of some man or woman who themselves have been illumined by the same Lord; sometimes the echo of His words in the New Testament; the impress of what He did, above all of what He was, and is and will be, has brought the help I needed.

I do not understand more than a very little of that life; there are passages in the gospels which puzzle me; I know there may be in the narrative things imperfectly reported or misunderstood by those who heard Him. But there He remains, and life goes forth from Him still into our lives, bringing hope and forgiveness and healing, a new vision and a new spirit.

A host of scholars have been at work for centuries to discover and understand the Jesus of history, and with strangely divergent results. The great quest still goes on and I seek to learn from it. But I cannot separate the Lord and Master of the first disciples from His risen spirit and personality which has gone on unfolding itself to those who seek Him, healing, renewing, inspiring, redeeming and guiding.

Thus I try to keep in touch with His life and message given first in Palestine, with the impact of His life and personality on the early disciples, as day by day I read a portion of the New Testament; I try, too, to learn something of what His Spirit has enabled others to be down all the ages since, from the study of the lives of the saints, both canonised and uncanonised, and by reading some of their writings. In the life of many who would not be called saints, and some even who might not be thought of as good men or women, I find flashes of light which to me are sparks or gleams from the light of Christ. I know that my own thoughts of God, my experience, my clumsy and imperfect prayer, are all penetrated by what Jesus Christ has meant to me. In doubts and difficulty His faith in God's love, His willingness to face even the awful burden of the cross and all that it involved, are a constant stay, bringing renewal of faith and of hope.   'Workaday saints' (1949)

101 Let us make Christ our teacher as his earliest disciples did, who knew nothing about His birth, and only followed Him at first just because they felt He was far better than they, and they had need of Him and loved Him. As we do this and simply endeavour to keep near to His thoughts, to think over the meaning of His words and to act as men who are seeking to follow Him, we shall begin to realise that there is in Christ himself a greater miracle than anything recorded of Him in the Gospels, and that whatever the correct theory of the Resurrection may be, He is still a living influence working upon our hearts and inspiring us onward to good. *'A wayfarer's faith' (1913)*

Henry T. Hodgkin (1877-1933) *came of a Darlington Quaker family, both his parents being prominent ministers. He was nurtured in the evangelical missionary tradition which inspired the work of the Friends Foreign Mission Association, of which he was for some years secretary. He was a born leader and he early developed gifts, both in the ministry and in administration. He was for many years an influential statesman in world missionary service, in which he served in various capacities in three continents. He was associated also with the Student Christian Movement and was one of the founders of the Fellowship of Reconciliation. He was truly an ecumenical Friend. From 1914 he was active in promoting the holding of a World Conference on Faith and Order, and in reminding Friends that they had their contribution of thought and experience to give. With Edward Grubb he was largely responsible for the statement on 'The true basis of Christian unity', extracts from which appear elsewhere in this book (§ 205, 217). The passage quoted here is taken from a letter written by Henry T. Hodgkin to his brother shortly before his death.*

102 When I was at school and college I had some very profound religious experiences which meant much in shaping my life and to which I now look back with the deepest thankfulness. While I can truly thank God that He continually comes to me in fresh experiences of His love and power, there was a certain quality of intensity and passion in those early experiences which made them, in one sense, unique.

I suppose it is almost inevitable that during such a period one should be so sure of the genuineness and value of one's own experience as to undervalue other types of experience. It is this which makes people eager missionaries or propagandists and it was as such that I went to China, still very sure of the 'greatness of the revelation' and but dimly aware that God, in His many-sided nature and activity, was not one whit less manifest in ways and persons with which or with whom I could have little sympathy. Of course in theory I believed that God used many methods and that all truth was not with me. Down deep I wanted all to be 'such as I', because I could not help feeling that, broadly speaking, what meant so much to me must be equally good for others.

By processes too numerous and diverse even to summarise, I have reached a position which may be stated in a general way somewhat like this: 'I believe that *God's best* for another may be so different from my experience and way of living as to be actually impossible to me. I recognise ⟨a change⟩ to have taken place in myself, from a certain assumption that mine was really the better way, to a very complete recognition that there is no one better way, and that God needs all kinds of people and ways of living through which to manifest Himself in the World.'

This has seemed to carry with it two conclusions which greatly affect conduct. One is that I really find myself wanting to learn from people whom I previously would have regarded as fit objects for my 'missionary zeal'. To discover another way in which God is operating —along lines it may be distasteful or dangerous to me—is a large part of the 'fun of living'. The second direction in which conduct is influenced is the deliberate attempt to *share* the life and interests of others who are not in my circle . . . ⟨for⟩ in such sharing I can most deeply understand the other's life and through that reach, maybe, fresh truths about God.

Pierre Ceresole (1879-1945), *the son of a former Swiss president, was a teacher of engineering by profession. From about 1920 he gave himself to work for peace, and became the founder of the International Voluntary Service ('Service Civil International'). Refusals of military service and public protests against war-like measures brought him many times into prison, twice for crossing the frontier into Germany in war time, without papers, with the message of peace. His conscience* *dominated his mind, and without narrowness or pride he dedicated his life to a master-purpose, the service of 'l'éternel', a word which he endowed with a meaning like that of the Seed for the early Friends.*

103 *From his letters of application for membership of London Yearly Meeting, 1936:*

I am of a scientific turn of mind upon the whole, and although I have always realised the essential importance of the Life of the Spirit—irreducible to the formulas of physics and mathematics—I have suffered within the restraints of a Christian orthodoxy which, in general, no longer really believes in its own dogmas...Because there is much that is forced and unnatural in the worship of the churches in which we were born, some of us have developed a 'complex' against all that recalls to us the attitude or special atmosphere of religious services. Thus I must confess even yet that it is not the meeting for prayer and mutual edification nor even the Quaker silence which creates for me the atmosphere where I can most really meet with God. God is seen, it seems to me, above all, there where one makes a true and sincere effort to do his will. I feel uncomfortable and disturbed by every kind of special arrangement, attitude, discourse or silence by which one is supposed to approach God. It is, in fact, life itself, ordinary life as it is called (and the more ordinary the more harmonious it is) which is our essential and constant communion with God...

It is, I think the idea of a special attitude or of a special moment peculiarly right for meeting with God which is especially difficult to me—the idea that one ought to, or even can, as it were, enter or leave the living and real presence of God at the moment when worship begins or ends.

I feel very strongly, on the other hand, that the spiritual life absolutely requires that we should not remain isolated. It is this deep need of getting out of a prolonged and dangerous relative isolation which urges me to ask now to be admitted among the Quakers. It is more and more clear to me that it is only in the bosom of a religious family, freely but very strongly constituted, that the individual can render to the world the services it sorely needs and which no politics, not based on a deep inspiration, can hope to organise.

104 *A prayer, written in his last note-book while in prison, 1945, for refusing payment of war-taxes.*

Eternal God, let thy spirit inspire and guide us. Thy will be done.

Give us the strength to fulfil our task without selfishness, slothfulness, or cowardice.

Give us the strength to withstand temptations, and to forgive others as we would wish them freely to forgive us.

Enable us to repay those who offend us only by redoubling our endeavours never to offend others.

Eternal God, we will listen to thy call and obey it in order that we may hear it ever more clearly.

Give us the honesty to examine our own acts and thoughts as scrupulously and severely as those of other people.

Deliver us from the fanaticism and pride which prevent us from welcoming truth even when it comes through the teaching and experience of others.

Give us the calm assurance that thou thyself wilt know how to reveal thy truth and thy righteousness to others even as we believe that thou hast in measure revealed them to us.

Teach us compassion and enable us to make a real effort to relieve the sufferings of others.

Give us the quiet courage needed in all circumstances, and natural to whoever has consecrated his life to thee.

At the highest level of existence where man and woman meet one another, let there be above all a passionate regard for the true values of life, for thy truth and thy love above all.

Do not let any defeat, any fall or backsliding ever separate us from thee; in the midst of all our weakness let thy love take hold of us and little by little lift us up to thee.

George Lloyd Hodgkin (1880-1918) *was a son of Thomas and Lucy Hodgkin of Newcastle. After a university education he travelled in the Near East, Australia, New Zealand and the United States, much of it 'in the service of Truth', in which he was ever welcome for his radiant and dedicated spirit. In 1918, leaving a young family in England, he set out on his second war-time journey to Armenia on behalf of the Lord Mayor of London's Armenian Relief Fund. He was taken ill at Baghdad and died there in June, 1918. 'His ruling desire it was to achieve such a life in God as shall result in the spontaneous shining forth of His spirit, joining others to him in the endeavour to increase the sweetness and light and reconciling influences in the world. He and his friends looked to the Father for the power for service. One of his prayers ended, "Wilt thou give us more humility in our hearts, more simplicity in our worship, and more reality in our lives."'*

105 The thing is just to live the highest life we know and leave everything else.   *1912*

106 So much of life is just going on and going on, long after the excitement and stimulus has faded...there is so much to ask for that I get very lost. And then I just come back to the simple longings, the simplest prayers of all; that Christ may be in those we love, that our love may be more Christ-like, more unmoveable, that we may be kept sinless by some immense miracle, and by God's side whatever happens. We must give up trying to hold His hand, and just stretch out our hands—even if they are just fists—for God to hold. There is all the difference...between holding and being held.   *1912*

Francis H. Knight (1881-1945) *was valued in our Society for his services in education as student, teacher, headmaster, general secretary of the Friends Education Council, and Fellow of Woodbrooke; and loved by his friends for his fresh unconventional manner, charm, sense of humour and honesty.*

107 I am by temperament a sceptic. But, at my feeblest, I am conscious of a power of choice, of a better and a worse. This 'ought' is my insignia of personality. Directly I admit that my life might be better than it is I have a sense of failure and feel a need of help from something or someone outside myself. This sense and this need are to me the meanings of the terms 'sense of sin' and 'need of salvation'. I recognise absolute moral or, rather, spiritual values, quite beyond reason or argument; very often indeed contradicting reason and flouting even scientific law. Suppose, for example, that I see a man throw away his life to rescue a dog, or one man of great intellectual power and moral leadership sacrifice himself in an attempt to save some apparently worthless drunken tramp. Natural science says 'What a waste!' but something else in me exclaims 'How grand!' My soul leaps to meet this nobility in another soul. Or again, something within me leaps to recognise the inspiration of an Amos, or Hosea, or George Fox, or Browning, or Shakespeare. Something of what inspired them inspires me. I am in touch with something or someone beyond myself...

I am not going to wait until I have fathomed all mysteries and secret lore before I begin to live. It has been my good fortune often to be in company with great souls, who have not only helped me in my intellectual quest for truth *about* religion, but have always encouraged me to strive towards experience, towards belief *in* religion. Fitfully and falteringly and with repeated failures I have tried to 'mind that which is pure' in me to guide me to God.

The faith of a sceptic, in 'The Wayfarer', 1945

Hilda Clark (1881-1955) *of Street, Somerset, trained as a doctor in Birmingham and worked devotedly against the then prevalent tuberculosis. When war broke out in 1914 she helped to found the Friends War Victims Relief Committee, and went to France as its medical organiser. She instituted the Châlons Maternity Hospital with the help of her friend Edith Pye. From 1919-1922 she was head of the Friends Relief Mission in Austria, which helped to rescue a whole generation of children there from starvation. Here, and later in work for Greek refugees, and in 1938 again in Vienna, she had the gift that 'lit up sparks in others, and released in them powers they did not know they possessed'. Her own crucial religious experience came just after she had qualified as a doctor, when her sister-in-law died in childbirth in 1908, as related in letters which she wrote at the time:*

108 I am thinking of those lovely fine days when Cara sat with me for hours sewing her little things. I feel as if my whole life might be better and more use to others from those two days, but what an awful price it is to pay. Do you know I actually felt that it was 'better' somehow than those awful hours with those two poor

creatures in the maternity hospital, when one's heart felt like ice within one, because one realised the tragedy with one's brain, and not with one's heart. And if I ever have to hold such a cold hand and feel such a death-stricken pulse, I think a little of the love I have for Cara will go out to the victim, whoever it may be...No, Justice is of the Spirit, not of the outside world—but our understanding is so wrapped up in outward things that we can only grow spiritually by applying spiritual things to material ones—therefore *we* must be just though Nature is not.

One thing I understand now is that one's intellect alone won't pull one through, and that the greatest service it can perform is to open a window for that thing we call the divine spirit. If one trusts to it alone it's like trusting to an artificial system of ventilation—correct in theory but musty in practice. How I wish it were as easy to throw everything open to the spirit of God as it is to fresh air.

Corder Catchpool (1883-1952) *as a young man practised mechanical engineering. During the first World War he served in the Friends Ambulance Unit, but returned to England and went to prison on the introduction of conscription, refusing to accept conditional exemption from military service. From then on he devoted himself to work for peace and reconciliation between peoples, particularly in Germany, where he and his wife Gwen lived for a time as well as paying extended visits. Always a lover of mountains, he died from physical exhaustion in his seventieth year, whilst climbing Monte Rosa in the Alps. Throughout his life of continuous activity he expressed his faith in God, in Christ his Master, and in his fellow-men, though he was at times assailed by intellectual and religious doubt.*

At the age of 28, following a period of frustration and misery, he was led to 'alter his whole conception of the way in which divine guidance may be sought and found. He came to see that God did not make our decisions for us, or give us special infallible directions for great occasions, if we prayed hard enough for them; that a feeling of certainty and joy in making a critical decision was no guarantee that it was going to work out well; that God could teach and lead us through frustration as well as through success; and, in sum, that no one could rightly understand or talk of Divine Guidance except one who had sought it daily in the smallest concerns of life; and so grown gradually to live more and more in the "mind of Christ" until his decisions in greater matters also were such as flowed out of a settled loving character, and were for that very reason in accord with the Will of God.'

109 *In 1934, when his work at the Berlin International Centre involved him in difficult decisions, anxiety and misunderstanding, and after arrest by the Secret Police, he wrote:*
I often wish earnestly that I had a more unwavering and unshakeable conviction, more of Paul and less of Thomas. But I am with the man who said: 'I believe; help thou my unbelief'. Perhaps such a frail faith brings me nearer to others who suffer similarly, and even better able to help them, as I have always been clear that I could not take the negative attitudes. By this I mean, I am for Christ, not for doubt—only I wish there were not so much that I don't yet understand. The difficulty is a hesitation as to whether I really desire 'revelation' in the sense of striking experience such as has brought conviction to some...I am by nature on my guard against subjectivity and feel that in my own case it may be best to share the occasional gleam with the multitude, rather than stand in the blaze on the mountain-top with the elect.

110 *Of his thoughts during an Alpine ascent, he wrote:* What then really is Christianity, if much that takes its name so fails to satisfy? I must face that problem; I felt no confidence that I was equal to it. But I seemed to be at least 50 per cent rationalist in make-up; that part of me demanded an answer. I began, fumblingly, an attempt to reason it out. I was by now high up on the moraine. The lazy clouds, that had hung all day as a light veiling about the snow-powdered rock peaks were just breaking up in the clear splendour of sunset. The dazzling mantles of Combin and Courbassière caught the last rays. It was no moment for reasoning. Too often my spiritual life runs shamefully shallow, lamentably in need of more living water from the eternal springs. May I be pardoned—I was utterly unworthy— but at that moment there swept over me unbidden, the *experience* of Christ. No more tiresome ratiocination, interpretations or misinterpretations, dogmas and differences. Just the fact that, in Christ, God was and is sharing the tragedy and sorrow, and the joy of the world. And—most glorious assurance—in his death and resurrection he faced the worst the world can do, faced these same problems and perplexities with all their mental anguish, which so often beat us till we cry inwardly for quarter—Christ faced them and triumphed over them and through them, with and for man in his struggle after righteousness, for all time.

Howard E. Collier (1890-1953), *besides having experience as a general practitioner, became successively a Medical Officer of Health, Reader in the Department of Industrial Hygiene and Medicine at Birmingham University, and a factory Medical Officer. The testimony of his Monthly Meeting says that 'through the Seekers Association and other groups he sought to stimulate and guide an active intellectual research into the basis of religion, taking a stand on trust in the Inner Light'. His personal religious experiences are related in a pamphlet entitled 'Experiment with a life' (1953), from which the following quotations are taken.*

111 On a certain summer afternoon towards the end of the first quarter of this century, I came home after a long and tiring day and, sitting down in the shade of the garden, I fell into a brown study. Quite unexpectedly I began to talk to myself, and to my surprise, I heard myself saying to myself, 'If you don't take care, you will end up by losing your soul!' The humour of this remark struck me, since, as far as I was aware, I did not believe at that time that I had a soul to lose. Looking back now I realise that particular afternoon marked a turning point in my life. Anyone who begins to refer to his soul as something that can be lost and found has discovered a new field of experience and a new inner reservoir of facts to be studied and related to the outward facts of his ordinary life. This redirection of my search—from an outward search for truth in nature, to an inward search for truth in myself—was the next step necessary for the healing of my own divided mind.

112 Learning during worship to turn my attention away from myself and me and mine, I soon, by a strange paradox, began to see myself as I really was and, because I discovered that I was, in fact, a much less estimable person than I had previously supposed, I was uncomfortable and ill at ease...To see those qualities in ourselves that we have hitherto been projecting upon other people and to see ourselves as truth sees us—these are experiences that are likely to shake the self-esteem of the hardiest...It is common experience in the spiritual life to find after an initial period of inspiration and emancipation that a period of deflation, even of despair, follows. But those who persevere soon find their boat sailing out into calmer waters again. As I persevered with the practice of worship I began to experience a measure of divine healing. A semblance of order, the outline of a coherent pattern, began to appear in my conduct as well as in my intellectual life...Jesus of Nazareth came alive for me, and I began to see Him as He was, shorn of the sentimental trappings of Victorian piety that had had hid Him from my view...He had become for me the Christ of the modern world. I had not hitherto realised that He was actually within the compass of myself.

Thomas R. Kelly (**1893-1941**) *came of a Quaker family in south-western Ohio, U.S.A. Most of his life was spent as Professor of Philosophy first at Earlham College and then at Haverford. In 1924-5 he and his wife spent fifteen months at the Berlin Quaker Centre, and in 1938 he returned to Germany, travelling amongst Friends. This visit clarified for him a vivid experience of a few months earlier, and he described himself as 'literally melted down by the Love of God'. His writings and spoken messages began to be marked by a note of experimental authority. During the remaining three years of his life, he poured out his experience in a series of essays and lectures, published after his death as 'A testament of devotion', a Quaker classic, from which the following extracts are taken.*

113 To you who are seekers, to you, young and old who have toiled all night and caught nothing, but who want to launch out into the deeps and let down your nets for a draught, I want to speak as simply, as tenderly, as clearly as I can. For God *can* be found. There *is* a last rock for your souls, a resting-place of absolute peace and joy and power and radiance and security. There is a Divine Center into which your life can slip, a new and absolute orientation in God, a Center where you live with Him and out of which you see all of life through new and radiant vision, tinged with new sorrows and, pangs, new joys unspeakable and full of glory...The reality of Presence has been very great at times recently. One knows at first hand what the old inquiry meant, 'Has Truth been advancing among you?'

114 Such a discovery of an Eternal Life and Love breaking in, nay, always there...makes life glorious and new. And one sings inexpressibly sweet songs within oneself, and one *tries* to keep one's inner hilarity and exuberance within bounds lest, like the men of Pentecost, we be mistaken for men filled with new wine. Traditional Quaker decorum and this burning experience of a Living Presence are only with the greatest difficulty held together.

John S. Hoyland (1887-1957) *was the son of John William Hoyland, who was for many years warden of the missionary training centre at Kingsmead, Birmingham. Jack Hoyland worked for 12 years as a missionary in India, and had an abiding love of that country and its peoples. From the time of his own undergraduate days he had a lifelong concern for the service of youth, organized Quaker tramps and interchange visits between young Friends in Britain and America, lectured at Woodbrooke for twenty-four years and constantly visited meetings and schools. In all that he did, whether fighting a cholera epidemic, digging with unemployed miners in South Wales, or campaigning for the United Nations Children's Fund or World Government, he was vociferous and whole-hearted. Like the seventeenth-century Quaker pioneers, he 'followed the movings of life rather than the counsels of prudence'.*

115 God who in every land and every age
Hast with divine compassion and divine desire
Sought to reveal thyself unto man:
Thou who hast truly shown thyself to all
Who truly have sought for thee with humble
        self-renouncing consecration—
We beseech thee that unto us this day thou wilt reveal thyself

We stand here, O Father,
Heirs of all the ages of thy creative effort,
Fruit of all the conflict, the hard-won progress,
        the sacrifice, the agony of the past;
We stand erect—for one brief moment—on the crest of thy history.

Unto us, O Father, without whom the past has no meaning,
Unto us, without whom the future has no existence,
Unto us, the men of thy world today,
Reveal thyself.

'*A book of prayers written for an Indian college*' (*1921*)

Chapter 2: God and man

*'To be like Christ, then, is to be a Christian. And regeneration is the only way
to the kingdom of God, which we pray for.'*   *William Penn (1693)*

Christian experience and the formulation of belief

116 In the seventeenth century, when the Quakers were often bitterly
attacked for 'heresy', they put out numerous statements as from the
body of Friends collectively, showing that they were broadly in
agreement with the historical Church of Christ in holding to what
were regarded as essential doctrines—such as the Unity of the
Father, Son and Holy Spirit; the Divinity and Humanity of Christ;
the reality of Sin and the need for Salvation; the resurrection of
Christ and His redeeming work; and the Inspiration of the Scriptures. This position our Society, speaking broadly, has always
maintained, and ⟨it⟩ has, therefore, claimed and still claims to be
essentially orthodox and evangelical. We are in line with our fellow-
Christians in the value which we, with them, attach to the historical
facts on which our religion rests, and to the witness that has been
borne to them through creeds, however far from final, and even
through liturgy and symbol, though these to us are non-essential.
But to us creeds have no value save as they testify to the eternal
realities which men must apprehend by spiritual experience and
express by life and conduct. A vital creed is not static but dynamic;
it can never be finally expressed in any form of words; it depends
upon and is held in the most intimate connection with the developing
life of the Spirit in the souls of men. Thus, while truth is eternal, our
apprehension of it enlarges, and our expression of it changes.

Faith & Order Commission, 1920

117 *The following extract, one of many similar statements of early Friends, is
taken from a tract written by William Dewsbury in 1656 entitled 'Christ
exalted: a true testimony of him, as is manifest, in answer to a book intituled
The Quakers Apostacy from the perfect rule of Scriptures, given forth by
John Timson of Great Bowden in Leicestershire':*

In the presence of God we witness against thee, no other Christ we bear testimony of, to be the salvation of lost Man and Woman, but that Christ according to Scripture testimony, who was born of the Virgin, and made a good confession before Pilate, and suffered at Jerusalem, and rose again the third day, and ascended into Heaven, and sitteth at the right hand of God; and this Christ we witness the true Light, Who lighteth everyone that cometh into the World and saith, I stand at the door and knock, who opens I will come into him and Sup with him and he with me (Rev. 3. 20), and we witness him faithful; And as many as receives him, to them he gives power to become sons of God, and this is the condemnation of all, because they believe not in him (John 1. 12).

118 *A somewhat fuller statement is given in the following extract from 'A testimony to the truth of God, as held by the people called Quakers' (1698) by William Penn & Benjamin Coole:*

We do, and hope we ever shall (as we always did) confess to the glory of God the Father, and the honour of his dear and beloved Son, that he, to wit, Jesus Christ, took our nature upon him, was like us in all things, sin excepted; that he was born of the Virgin Mary, went about amongst men doing good, and working many miracles; that he was betrayed by Judas into the hands of the chief priests, etc., that he suffered death under Pontius Pilate, the Roman governor, being crucified between two thieves, and was buried in the sepulchre of Joseph of Arimathea: rose again the third day from the dead and ascended into Heaven, and sits at God's right hand, in the power and majesty of his Father; and that by him God the Father will one day judge the whole world, both of quick and dead, according to their works.

119 Doubt and perplexity will often be the lot of travellers on this life's journey. Beyond the questions arising in our daily thought and conduct are those greater difficulties which seem to stop our progress and to render existence an insoluble riddle. Doubt has many sources. It may be true that some could find the origin of their doubts in an unwillingness to face their moral condition and obey the demands of duty. But at the present day, doubt frequently arises from a sense that received dogmas do not correspond with the facts of life or with the moral values which our truest insight reveals. In other cases there may be not so much perplexity and doubt as an exhilarating spirit of inquiry and exploration driving a man forward on the quest for truth for himself and all men. We strongly deprecate the attitude of mind, still too often current, which brands as unbelief that criticism of accepted ideas without which progress is impossible. We may often attain to a fuller understanding of the truth that God intends for us through doubts of the orthodoxy of the past. For true faith is not a passive acceptance of authority, but is an inner assurance of truth, asking, seeking, knocking until the door is opened. The enjoyment of idle questionings may indeed become an excuse for living a poor and careless life, but the genuine seeker is obeying the very call of God within him.   *1911; 1925*

120   Complete knowledge is always beyond us, and a recognition of this fact carries with it a demand that we 'prove all things; hold fast that which is good'. It is by this method that Christian thinkers in the past have advanced towards a more perfect understanding of the ways of God. This suggests on the one hand that even those ideas which we now see to be incomplete or erroneous often contained for those who first held them a vital expression of truth, and were in their time only gained as the result of painful strivings of heart and mind, and, on the other hand, that the ideas of God and man which have been held in the past must be re-expressed in the light of our own experience and further knowledge.   *1925*

121   The real meaning and worth of the confession of the Divine Humanity of Christ is the conviction which it brings us that in him we have a *revelation* of God in terms that we can understand—not by intellect only but by the response of our whole personality to the revelation. May it not be said that anyone whose inward eyes are opened to perceive and accept this revelation—who is able to think of God in terms of Jesus Christ, and feels that without Christ his knowledge of God would be vague and uncertain—and whose will is captured for living out in his own life what he has seen in Jesus—is fundamentally an *orthodox* Christian, whatever may be his intellectual attitude towards the Creeds of the Church? However we may define the word 'revelation', it must mean something quite different from the presentation by God to man of an intellectual theory or doctrine,

to be passively accepted on authority. It must involve the opening of the man's inward eyes to perceive and appropriate that which is being revealed; it must require for its acceptance *faith* and not only *belief*. In other words acceptance of the Divine Humanity of Jesus must be a religious and not merely an intellectual act. 'No man can say, Jesus is Lord, but in the Holy Spirit' (1 Cor. 12. 3.).

Edward Grubb (1928)

122 The intellectual forms in which religion finds expression are always inadequate to the reality with which they deal; and processes of reasoning by means of intellectual concepts in this region of experience are always liable to imperfection and error. God Himself is conceived as a Person like ourselves but greater; His grace is thought of as a quasi-mechanical force predestining and compelling the wills of men; the consciousness of self-abasement and nothingness in the presence of the 'Holy' is intellectualised into a dogma of total human depravity, and so forth. All this does not mean that theology is useless. It is inevitable and necessary, just because men are compelled to think out and express their experience as best they can; and real progress can be and has been made in reaching conceptions more adequate to the subject-matter of religious experience, closer in coherence with one another, and therefore nearer to the truth.

Edward Grubb (1928)

123 It ought to be recognised that at the present time, at least in this country, the real danger is not from a too narrow, cramping and militantly dogmatic theology, but rather from an inveterate haziness of mind, a half-heartedness and general belittlement of the importance of true thinking in religion. And the final outcome of this is the assumption...that Christianity may indeed reasonably claim to be 'good', that is, to put forward an elevated ethical standard and an edifying moral idealism, but makes and can make no claim to be 'true'. I do not think it likely that terms like 'theology', 'dogma' and 'creed' will ever evoke enthusiasm among members of the Society of Friends. But it ought to be possible to allay what almost amounts to a phobia with regard to them. *John W. Harvey (1947)*

124 In its early days our Society owed much to a people who called themselves Seekers; they joined us in great numbers and were

prominent in the spread of Quakerism. It is a name which must appeal strongly to the scientific temperament. The name has died out, but I think that the spirit of seeking is still the prevailing one in our faith, which for that reason is not embodied in any creed or formula. It is perhaps difficult sufficiently to emphasise Seeking without disparaging its correlative Finding. But I must risk this, for Finding has a clamorous voice that proclaims its own importance; it is definite and assured, something that we can take hold of—that is what we all want, or think we want. Yet how transitory it proves. The finding of one generation will not serve for the next. It tarnishes rapidly except it be preserved with an ever-renewed spirit of seeking. It is the same too in science. How easy in a popular lecture to tell of the findings, the new discoveries which will be amended, contradicted, superseded, in the next fifty years! How difficult to convey the scientific spirit of seeking which fulfils itself in this tortuous course of progress towards truth! You will understand the true spirit neither of science nor of religion unless seeking is placed in the forefront.

Religious creeds are a great obstacle to any full sympathy between the outlook of the scientist and the outlook which religion is so often supposed to require. I recognise that the practice of a religious community cannot be regulated solely in the interests of its scientifically-minded members and therefore I would not go so far as to urge that no kind of defence of creeds is possible. But I think it may be said that Quakerism in dispensing with creeds holds out a hand to the scientist. The scientific objection is not merely to particular creeds which assert in outworn phraseology beliefs which are either no longer held or no longer convey inspiration to life. The spirit of seeking which animates us refuses to regard any kind of creed as its goal. It would be a shock to come across a university where it was the practice of the students to recite adherence to Newton's laws of motion, to Maxwell's equations and to the electro-magnetic theory of light. We should not deplore it the less if our own pet theory happened to be included, or if the list were brought up to date every few years. We should say that the students cannot possibly realise the intention of scientific training if they are taught to look on these results as things to be recited and subscribed to. Science may fall short of its ideal, and although the peril scarcely takes this extreme form, it is not always easy, particularly in popular science, to maintain our stand against creed and dogma. I would not be sorry to borrow for our scientific pronouncements the passage prefixed to the Advices of the Society of Friends in 1656 and repeated in the current General Advices:

> 'These things we do not lay upon you as a rule or form to walk by; but that all with a measure of the light, which is pure and holy, may be guided; and so in the light walking and abiding, these things may be fulfilled in the Spirit, not in the letter; for the letter killeth, but the Spirit giveth life.'

Rejection of creed is not inconsistent with being possessed by a living belief. We have no creed in science, but we are not lukewarm in our beliefs. The belief is not that all the knowledge of the universe that we hold so enthusiastically will survive in the letter; but a sureness that we are on the road. If our so-called facts are changing shadows, they are shadows cast by the light of constant truth. So too in religion we are repelled by that confident theological doctrine which has settled for all generations just how the spiritual world is worked; but we need not turn aside from the measure of light that comes into our experience showing us a Way through the unseen world. Religion for the conscientious seeker is not all a matter of doubt and self-questionings. There is a kind of sureness which is very different from cocksureness.   *Arthur S. Eddington (1929)*

125 I should like to change the name 'seekers' to 'explorers'. There is a considerable difference there: we do not 'seek' the Atlantic, we explore it. The whole field of religious experience has to be explored, and has to be described in a language understandable to modern men and women.   *Ole Olden, 1955*

126 'Faith', said Sir Henry Newbolt, 'is a camp, not of armed men but of explorers on the march.' In this life of the spirit we may all start as seekers, but happy are we if we become explorers. And the field of our exploration is clearly set before us by St Paul, when he prays that his friends in Ephesus 'may be strong to apprehend with all the saints, what is the breadth and length and height and depth, and to

know the love of Christ which passeth knowledge'...St Paul invites us to explore the vast ocean of the love of Christ in which we shall find all the fulness of God.   *H. G. Wood, 1955*

For further extracts on Creeds see §205-207

The nature of God

127 The true faith (the faith of the gospel, the faith of the elect, the faith which saves the sinner from sin, and makes him more than a conqueror over sin and the powers of darkness) is a belief in the nature of God; which belief giveth entrance into, fixeth in, and causeth an abiding in that nature.   *Isaac Penington (1659)*

128 Spirit...is the best word there is to express the essential nature of God. It signifies that He is not to be confused with matter nor to be found in a framework of space. He is like that highest, purest inner nature in ourselves which we call 'spirit'. He is intelligent, He is purposeful. He is devoted to the realization of the good. He *is* what we are trying to be. And wherever in the universe the good is being achieved, wherever truth is triumphing, wherever holiness is making its power known—there is spirit, there is God.

Rufus M. Jones (1923)

129 *This extract has been selected and arranged from 'Some questions and answers, showing mankind his duty', (1662), by Isaac Penington. The form of question and answer was freely used by early Friends as a convenient way of expressing succinctly their fundamental convictions. It carried no suggestion of an officially adopted set of formulae embodying the rulings of some synod or assembly. These questions, as clearly as the answers, were deeply rooted in the spiritual travail of Isaac Penington himself: and he seems to have found the form particularly congenial as a means of communicating to others what the Lord had given him, in the hope that they also 'might meet with and enjoy the same, without passing through that misery and bitter anguish and distress of spirit, through which the Lord led me thereto'.*

What is the proper work of Man here in this world?

To fear God, and keep his commandments. This is all that God requires of him, and this is enough to make him happy.

What is God?

The fountain of beings and natures, the inward substance of all that appears; who createth, upholdeth, consumeth, and bringeth to nothing as he pleaseth.

How may I know that there is a God?

By sinking down into the principle of his own life, wherein he revealeth himself to the creature. There the soul receiveth such tastes and knowledge of him, as cannot be questioned by him that abideth there.

What is it to fear this God?

The spirit and soul of the creature standing in awe of his nature, and waiting to be kept in due subjection thereto, this is to fear him, and this is the proper means of preserving the spirit of the creature right in its motion towards him, attendance on him, and expectations from him.

What are his commandments?

They are such as are either general to all mankind, common to some sorts of men, or proper to particular persons.

What are those which are general to all mankind?

There are very many; but may all be referred to these two heads; to wit, *to love God above all, and one's neighbour as one's self;* even so in every respect doing to him, as one would be done by him in the like case.

How may man perform these?

Only by receiving a principle of life from God, and keeping close thereto.

How may a man come by a principle of Life from God?

God is near to every man with the breath of his life, breathing upon him at times according to his pleasure; which man's spirit opening unto, and drinking in, it becometh a seed or principle of life in him, over-spreading and leavening him up to eternal life.

How may a man come to believe in this principle?

In feeling its nature, in waiting to feel somewhat begotten by it, in this its light springs, its life springs, its love springs, its hidden power appears, and its preserving wisdom and goodness is made manifest to the soul that clings to it in the living sense, which its presence and appearance begets in the soul.

How may a man come to obey this principle?
In the faith, in the eyeing of it, in the clinging to it, the strength issues from it into the creature, which maketh it able to perform all that it calleth for.

Are there other commands besides these, common to all men?
Yes; according to the dispensation of life and mercy unto which they are called, and into which they are admitted by the love and kindness of God, which overspreadeth all his works, and who forgetteth not his creatures in their estate of separation and alienation from him.

Are there then more dispensations of life and mercy than one?
Yes. For though the life and mercy in itself is but one; yet it hath several ways of seeking-out after, and gathering into itself, the lost sons of Adam.

But how may men know that these are true commands of the Lord and not imaginations or opinions of their own?
When the principle of life is known, and that which God hath begotten felt in the heart, the distinction between what God opens and requires there, and what springs up in man's wisdom, reason and imagination, is very manifest.

130 The love of God is love past knowledge, which bears all things, endures all things, hopes all things, envieth not, thinketh no evil. And the love of God is the ground of all true love in your hearts.

George Fox, 1653

131 *William Penn, in reply to what he calls 'the perversion' that 'the Quakers deny the Trinity' writes:* Nothing less: they believe in the Holy Three, or Trinity of Father, Word and Spirit, according to Scripture. And that these Three are truly and properly One: of one nature, as well as will. But they are very tender of quitting scripture terms and phrases for schoolmen's; such as 'distinct and separate persons', and 'subsistences' &c. are; and from whence people are apt to entertain gross ideas and notions of the Father, Son and Holy Ghost. And they judge that a curious enquiry into those high and divine relations, and other speculative subjects, though never so great truths in themselves, tend little to godliness and less to peace; which should be the chief aim of true Christians. And therefore they cannot gratify that curiosity in themselves or others; speculative truths being, in their judgment, to be sparingly and tenderly declared and never to be made the measure and condition of Christian communion.   *William Penn (1692)*

132   *Penington's experience of the Trinity:*
I have not been taught to deny any testimony the scriptures hold forth, concerning the Lord Jesus, or any of his appearances, but am taught by the Lord more certainly and fully to own and acknowledge them. The first is concerning the Godhead, which we own as the scriptures express it, and as we have the sensible, experimental knowledge of it. In which, 'There are three that bear record in heaven, the Father, the Word, and the Holy Spirit; and these Three are One' (1 John 5. 7). This I believe from my heart, and have infallible demonstrations of; for I know three and feel three in spirit, even an Eternal Father, Son and Holy Spirit, which are but one eternal God. And I feel them also one and have fellowship with them (through the tender mercy of the Lord) in their life, and in their redeeming power. And here I lie low before the Lord in the sensible life, not desiring to know and comprehend notionally, but to feel the thing inwardly, truly, sensibly and effectively; yea, indeed, this is to me far beyond what I formerly knew notionally concerning them, and I cannot but invite others hither.
                    'An epistle to all serious professors'

It is now generally recognised that verse 7 of 1 John, ch. 5, is not part of the original Greek text. Erasmus omitted it from the first edition of the Greek New Testament, as he had no Greek manuscript containing it. He inserted it in his second edition when someone produced a Greek manuscript of the sixteenth century with it in. The verse came in from a Latin source of the fifth century, and it stood in all the English versions from Wyclif to the Authorised Version of 1611. Friends accepted it as Scripture, as did all their contemporaries. Isaac Penington cites it, not so much out of deference to the authority of Scripture, though he and other Friends protested their unity with the truth of the Scriptures, but rather as an example of a Scripture which had illuminated and been illuminated by his experience.

133 'I am the Good Shepherd; and I know mine own, and mine own know me, even as the Father knoweth me, and I know the Father.' These words are Johannine, but I do not therefore doubt that they expressed our Lord's thought. On some such lines Trinitarian and Unitarian, Orthodox and Liberal, may find reconciliation and an understanding, ceasing in their ignorance to draw lines of boundary through unmapped territory, ceasing to try to say where God ends and man begins; but owning allegiance to a Spiritual Order, in which vows were taken for us before we were born.

John William Graham (1920)

God as creator and father

134 After this I returned into Nottinghamshire again, and went into the Vale of Beavor... And one morning, as I was sitting by the fire, a great cloud came over me, and a temptation beset me; but I sat still. And it was said, 'All things come by nature'; and the elements and stars came over me so that I was in a manner quite clouded with it. But in as much as I sat, still and silent, the people of the house perceived nothing. And as I sat still under it and let it alone, a living hope arose in me and a true voice, which said, 'there is a living God who made all things'. And immediately the cloud and temptation vanished away, and life rose over it all, and my heart was glad, and I praised the living God. And after some time, I met with some people who had such a notion that there was no God but that all things come by nature. And I had great dispute with them and overturned them and made some of them confess that there was a living God. Then I saw that it was good that I had gone through that exercise. *George Fox, 1648*

135 He is the living God that clothes the earth with grass and herbs and causes the trees to grow and bring forth food for you, and makes

the fishes of the sea to breathe and live, and makes the fowls of the air to breed, and causes the roe and the hind and the creatures and all the beasts of the earth to bring forth whereby they may be food for you. He is the living God and causes the stars to arise in the night, to give you light, and the moon to arise to be a light in the night. He is the living God, that causes the sun to give warmth unto you, to nourish you when you are cold. He is the living God, that causes the snow and frost to melt, and causes the rain to water the plants... The living God is He that gives you life and breath and strength, and all things that are good; and would have you to feel after Him, with that which checks you for sin and evil; and would have you to worship Him in spirit, and serve Him who is holy and righteous, and to live in peace.   *George Fox, 1672*

136 Perhaps more wonderful still is the way in which beauty breaks through. It breaks through not only at a few highly organised points, it breaks through almost everywhere. Even the minutest things reveal it as well as do the sublimest things, like the stars. Whatever one sees through the microscope, a bit of mould for example, is charged with beauty. Everything from a dewdrop to Mount Shasta is the bearer of beauty. And yet beauty has no function, no utility. Its value is intrinsic, not extrinsic. It is its own excuse for being. It greases no wheels, it bakes no puddings. It is a gift of sheer grace, a gratuitous largesse. It must imply behind things a Spirit that enjoys beauty for its own sake and that floods the world everywhere with it. Wherever it can break through, it does break through, and our joy in it shows that we are in some sense kindred to the giver and revealer of it.   *Rufus M. Jones, 1920*

137 The spirit of the age is moving towards a belief in God as a pervading influence. We need to recapture the vivid sense of Him as a free agent in His own world, ever at liberty to help men. Jesus Christ had that sense, and, as He dwells within us, He can bring it to us. That is just what He has done for all the great pioneers in the spiritual history of mankind, and for multitudes of ordinary men and women.
                                             Yearly Meeting, 1912

Science and religion

Science as a spiritual activity

138 Science would not exist if man were not in some degree master of his thoughts and actions. Scientific inquiry is a spiritual activity, not possible for things or animals, only possible for rational persons. Science is itself the standing disproof of materialism, the clear evidence of the truth of Sir Thomas Browne's description of man as the great amphibium, a creature designed to live in two worlds, the physical and the spiritual, the natural and the supernatural.

H. G. Wood (1955)

139 God has set us in a universe governed by natural and spiritual law from which we cannot get exemption; the same consequence will always be reproduced if the same conditions are present. But the framework of law does not restrict our freedom; on the contrary, if it did not exist there would be no free choice at all, for no action could ever be deliberately directed to any end. Within the framework there is freedom for us, even in the most important matter of all, acceptance or rejection of fellowship with God.

John Hoare (1946)

140 It is, I think, of the very essence of the unseen world that the conception of personality should dominate it. Force, energy, dimensions, belong to the world of symbols; it is out of such conceptions that we have built up the external world of physics. What other conceptions have we? After exhausting physical methods we returned to the inmost recesses of consciousness, to the voice that proclaims our personality, and from there we entered on a new outlook. We have to build the spiritual world out of symbols taken from our own personality, as we build the scientific world out of the symbols of the mathematician. I think therefore we are not wrong in embodying the significance of the spiritual world to ourselves in the feeling of a personal relationship, for our whole approach to it is bound up with those aspects of consciousness in which personality is centred. *Arthur S. Eddington (1929)*

141 The main function which psychology can perform for the individual is to enable him to know himself better, and to see more clearly the way in which his thinking and feeling are influenced by unconscious motives, and, so far as he sees this, to make allowance for it and correct it, and to recognise the limitation and partiality of his point of view even when thus corrected. The man who has applied this discipline to himself will thereby understand others better, for he will recognise in them the mental processes he has discovered to exist in himself. But in all this the function of psychology is a negative one; to use a surgical term it is essentially orthopaedic, corrective of deformity. It will enable a man to walk better, but it will not tell him where to walk. He must look elsewhere for a dynamic. *W. Russell Brain (1944)*

142 The value of psychology is to show men the inescapable necessity of being honest with themselves and so with one another. If the object in this is truth pursued unswervingly, and the effect is to increase man's self-respect, the result will be all gain. Another path will have been made to the religion which widens out into the whole life. *Horace B. Pointing, 1945*

143 Our minds are open to every kind of fantasy and illusion, fixation, projection and wishful thinking; it has therefore frequently been suggested that religion is a fantasy to satisfy subconscious cravings. Such a view assumes that religion is an unreal answer to a hunger for which the real satisfaction would be on the natural and material level. There is however no proof that this is true. Indeed the hunger may be capable of full satisfaction only on the spiritual level, material and natural answers being outward signs of a spiritual reality which surpasses them as the substance surpasses the shadow. It is as reasonable to suppose that sexual love, for instance, is an image or reflection of the love between God and the soul as to suppose that religious hunger and adoration are transferred manifestations of the sex instinct. As Harold Loukes has put it: 'In all this argument, there are still two orders of experience: the facts and their meaning. We cannot dismiss the facts, but equally we cannot shirk the responsibility of looking, ourselves, for the meaning. And

on the facts, we can go either way. We can say, it is all illusion, and
the symbols of faith are but the shapes of dreams. Or we can say,
we will search on, for the shapes of our dreams may be the symbols
of reality. "The way is now open to us no longer to conceive of
God as a substitute for the physical father, but rather the physical
father as the infant's first substitute for God, the genetically prior
bearer of the image of the All-Father. God is less a Big Father than
the physical father a little god. Clearly we are not far from St. Paul's
'Father, from whom all fatherhood in heaven and earth is named'." '
Belief in God is always an act of faith, but faith on the lines of the
above argument is not contrary to reason, only to materialism. *1959*

The limitations of scientific knowledge

144 Science has its legitimate field and its legitimate methods, although,
like the theologian at whom he so often girds, the scientist is not
without his prejudices and his narrow dogmatism. He is to be
respected when he speaks according to what he knows. His knowledge is at least something more learned by man about God.
Unless we are to fall into an ancient fallacy and exclude God from
His universe, we must regard every fact of science as a fresh revelation of His creative activity and power. Nevertheless, scientific
knowledge lies on a plane different from that on which the knowledge we seek is to be found...⟨It⟩ cannot help a man to resist a
present temptation or to face death with Christian confidence and
hope. Science by itself is, and must always remain, powerless to
give us a God who will draw out the tendrils of the human heart
towards Himself. *John Wilhelm Rowntree, 1905*

145 The modern method of enquiry by experiment and inference, by
inductive generalisation and subsequent verification, has been
amazingly fruitful in the better understanding of physical nature.
But the very precision of its intellectual processes, and the inevitable-
ness of the garnered results are sometimes urged against it, as
tending to cramp and warp the perception of other kinds of truth.
It is charged sometimes with leading men to reject or despise other
kinds of truth which have not been discovered by the same sort of
process, and which cannot be verified by experiment, weighed in

the balance, or analysed in the test-tube. Doubtless there is some ground for this reflection. In any department of human activity the too-exclusive exercise of any one faculty or set of faculties tends to bring about a one-sided development; and the neglect of any faculty tends to its atrophy.   *Silvanus P. Thompson (1915)*

The contribution of science to our knowledge of God

146   If God is creator, then knowledge of his creation ultimately enlarges our understanding of him. The scientist and the theologian each believes in and seeks to understand a coherent ordered universe, and each needs the specialist knowledge of the other to form a comprehensive picture. This mutual dependence is too often un-recognised; it becomes a source of strength, even though also of tension, as men acknowledge the potentialities of each field of thought.

No argument can, of itself, prove the existence of God; our grounds for believing that God is, and is loving, come from his revelation of himself in the lives of men and women, all over the world, especially in the life, death, and resurrection of Jesus Christ, and in the repeated revelations received by the Christian church. Once we have acknowledged this, natural science has an immense amount to tell us about the nature of our loving God's creative activity.

Without the work of the scientist throughout the centuries, we might have no concept of the creation of the universe other than those derived from a literal interpretation of the first and second chapters of Genesis. The immensities of ordered space and time, which the chemist, the physicist, the mathematician, and the astronomer set before us, enrich and ennoble our idea of God. And his loving compassion for us, his intimate understanding of our least thought and need, fill us with new wonder and gratitude when we see it given to the souls living on this small planet, in all the great gathering of his creation.

Contemplation of the living world, of its diversity and beauty, brings to many a unique feeling of nearness to God. Others look at another side, and are appalled by what seems to them the essential cruelty and wastefulness of the natural order; they see in it a real obstacle to a belief in a creator who is also a loving father. But we now see creation as a process, involving numberless converging and diverging lines of development, still active, but almost inconceivably slow. This points the way to a new understanding of the travail, incompleteness, and apparent evil of the world of nature. Imperfections and misfits, which would be inconceivable in a completely preformed and determined world, begin to be comprehensible when seen as incidental steps in a continuing creative process. God is acting around us even now, albeit in a manner whose direction and purpose we begin only dimly to apprehend.

New knowledge helps us to understand better the apparent cruelty of nature. We know that animals can suffer, and we recognise our responsibility concerning suffering inflicted by man on domestic or on wild animals. We need not, however, think of the life of an animal in the wild as a long nightmare of fear and torment. There is now much evidence to suggest that, while animals can of course feel pain while it is being inflicted, the apprehension and imaginative anticipation which so intensify our own pains are human rather than animal characteristics: we should not read into the movements and behaviour of continuous alertness a mood of continuous anxiety. Thus the wild animal is not burdened by the fear of capture and death by its natural enemies which in like circumstances would make human life a nightmare, but spends much of its life in carefree enjoyment of its varied natural activities. For the great majority of wild animals, George Macdonald's words are probably very near the truth: 'The bliss of the animals lies in this ... that they live in the holy carelessness of the eternal now.'

It seems probable that the pain and fear which can be suffered by living creatures is in proportion to the degree of their nervous development. Thus we may recognise with humility, and some thankfulness, that our own power to suffer in body and spirit is enhanced far beyond that of other animals, by our mental development and spiritual nature. Through these God confers on us the possibility of being special instruments of his purpose, peculiarly his servants and friends, uniquely able to know, love, and worship him. The essential revolution in thought which gave rise to the scientific era consisted in an acceptance of first-hand knowledge, checked by repeated experiment, instead of trust in any dogmatic authority, ecclesiastical or secular. This approach in scientific enquiry leads men to new vistas of understanding, provided they be patient, humble, honest, and always ready to take into account the conclusions of other seeking minds. Such humility and integrity of mind is the very antithesis of pride, dogmatism, superstition, and prejudice. The early Friends, also in their sphere mistrusting traditional notions accepted merely on authority, gave witness to the validity of individual insight gained through devout meditation, nourished, tempered, and tested in corporate worship. They were ready to receive 'new light, from whatever quarter it may arise'.

There is thus a profound affinity between the scientific approach to truth, and that of the Society of Friends. The Quaker concept of the continuing individual and corporate revelation is wholly consistent with the spirit behind scientific research in so far as in both the bold personal adventure is tempered by humility in the face of individual fallibility and by the necessity for sharing experience with others.   *1959*

For other extracts on our responsibility towards animals see §478-480

147 Today Science is re-discovering the creative mystery of the universe. The old self-assurance is largely gone. Within the first quarter of the twentieth century a revolution has taken place. The laws of mechanics no longer explain all things. The intellect of man has become aware of something strange and unpredictable at the very heart of existence. Matter and radiation have assumed a complexity which was hardly guessed at in the eighteen hundreds. The exploration of the minute structure of matter seems to take us as far into the unknown as does the exploration of the farthest reaches of space.

Howard H. Brinton (1931)

All creation to be used to the glory of the Creator

148 We have met this year in the midst of the tragedy of war ... In the darkness of universal sorrow and desolation we cry for light. It seems to many that a God of love could not permit such terrible happenings. 'They continually say unto me: Where is thy God?' (Ps. 42. 3). We cannot give an answer of strength and consolation to such a cry in terms of any traditional faith. It is only as our faith is rediscovered and resettled on a rock foundation that we can help a bewildered world. We thank God that a new and living experience of His power and purpose has come to us. Our hope is in this word: God is Love—the power of God is the power of undying and persistent love. It is through the hearts and minds and wills of men and women that He works, and He waits for them to open their hearts to love and to follow with unwavering courage. In so far as men do this, they are helping to establish the Kingdom of God and of His Christ—the rule of love in the world... They too must act as their Master acted in unquestioning faith in the power of God's love and in the light which lighteth every man in every nation, and to which we can always make appeal... The world can only be won for Christ as men are possessed by the infinite power which we call the love of God—the love that will not let men go—the love that 'beareth all things, believeth all things, hopeth all things, endureth all things' (1 Cor. 13. 7) and that never faileth—the love that is Divine Omnipotence.   *Yearly Meeting, 1915*

149 To that which is pure take heed, that with that all your minds may be kept up to God, who is pure: that as the lily ye all may grow, and receive wisdom from God, how to use the creatures in their places, to the glory of Him that created them.   *George Fox, 1656*

The person and work of Christ

150 Wherefore, beloved brethren,.. let it be the frequent engagement of your souls, in deep reverence and humility, to 'consider the Apostle and High Priest of our profession, Christ Jesus'. The promised Messiah, He to whom all preceding dispensations had pointed, and in whom they were ended and fulfilled, He who was with God, and was God, the word who hath declared to man Him that is invisible, even He was made flesh, and dwelt amongst men. Though He was rich, yet for our sakes He became poor; veiling, in the form of a servant, the brightness of His glory, that, through Him, the kindness and love of God toward men might appear, in a manner every way suited to our wants and finite capacities. His righteous precepts were illustrated and confirmed by His own holy example. He went about doing good; for us He endured sorrow, hunger, thirst, weariness, pain; unutterable anguish of body and of soul even unto death; and was 'in all points tempted like as we are, yet without sin'. Thus humbling Himself that we might be exalted, He emphatically recognised the duties and sufferings of humanity as among the means whereby, through the obedience of faith, we are to be disciplined for heaven; sanctifying them to us, by Himself performing and enduring them; and, as 'the Forerunner', at once plainly marking and consecrating for His followers the path in which they must tread. But not only in these blessed relations must the Lord Jesus be ever precious to His people. Exalted to be a Prince and a Saviour, in Him has been revealed a Redeemer at once able to suffer and almighty to save; an High Priest, 'touched with the feeling of our infirmities', who, having made reconciliation for our sins by the offering up of Himself once for all, 'is gone into heaven', there to appear, our Mediator and Advocate, in the presence of God. *Yearly Meeting, 1852*

151 It is not possible for the Father to *beget*, or put forth a being that can work good independently of himself; for then there would be two good, or, which is the same thing, *two Gods*. Hence, when one called Christ, 'Good Master', he refused to accept the title, as applied to himself independently of the one only real goodness, the goodness of God, and makes this return, 'Why callest thou *me* good? There is none good but *one*, that is, *God.*' This must hold good forever; for the moment any other independent source of real goodness is admitted, another God is that moment admitted; or good is admitted, which the *one God* is not the source and author of. *Job Scott, 1792*

152 God is like Jesus Christ, and we can rule out of our thoughts of Him everything that conflicts with the character of Christ. 'He that hath seen Me hath seen the Father' (John 14. 9). Jesus was the man of the people, who knew their joys and sorrows because He lived as one of them. He learnt life at the carpenter's bench in Nazareth. He knew the trouble His mother had in patching the old garment, the value of the woman's lost coin, the cost to the widow of her two mites, the difficulty of the poor woman in getting justice from the unjust judge. He took our common life and daily toil and made them into divine things. The crowded cities of Galilee were His home. His heart went out to the helpless and the diseased, to the oppressed poor, to the rich, starved of true fellowship, and to the self-righteous, separated by their hardness of heart from their fellows and from God. He gave Himself to men without reserve, in loving fellowship; their life and lot came into His life; those who opened their hearts to Him knew His life; and overcoming love came into their lives. When His people refused Him, and crucified Him, His love still sought them undespairing.

This is how Jesus lived and died, and still lives on among men.
This is how God lives among men.
This is how we are to live among men.

In our hearts we must know this life of unity with God and our fellows, and we must then, from our hearts, live it out as God's way of life for the world. It will open our eyes to the oppression caused by many of the economic and other privileges which we have often taken for granted, and in opening our eyes will abase our hearts. It will send us forth to break down the social and educational barriers and to abolish the servitudes, which mar the fellowship of the human family. It will take us with Jesus not only into lowly service but also into clear-sighted truth. We shall find our lives brought alongside the lives of others in practical fellowship. We may have to give up what the world counts most dear, but we shall be lifted into the joy of love. *Yearly Meeting, 1920*

153 'I and the Father are One.' That means to me that I think of God in terms of Jesus Christ, that I pray to Jesus as representing the Father to my consciousness, or to the Father as I see Him in Jesus. Carry that thought to Calvary itself. See in the Crucifixion not merely a martyr's death, not merely a passing gleam of God's love, certainly not a sacrifice to God carrying a legal significance, but in truth the flashing into light of an eternal fact, the nature of God's relation to sin, of the pain we inflict on His heart by our own wrongdoing. Here is the wonderful dynamic of the Cross. God calls you to Him. He shows you His suffering, He shows you the hatefulness of the sin that caused it, and, in showing you His love, shows you the punishment of alienation from Him, the hell of the unrepentant, in which we must remain until repentance opens the gate for the prodigal and gives entrance to the free forgiveness and love of the Father's house. In Jesus, in His life and His death upon the cross, we are shown the nature of God, and the possibilities that are within our reach. We are shown the world as the Father sees it, are called to live in harmony with His will and purpose, to hate the sins that made Him mourn, to scale the barrier of sin and discover that the way of penitence lies open and direct to the Fatherly heart. No legal bargain, but a spiritual conflict, an inward change, the rejection of the living death of sin, the choice of the new birth, of the purified self, the conversion from a low and earthly to a high and spiritual standard of life and conduct—here you have the practical conditions of salvation, and in the active, free and holy love of God, ever seeking entrance, ever powerful if we but yield the gateway of our heart, is the substance of the Gospel. The revelation of God's Fatherhood and the possibility of unity with Him through Christ, meet the deep need of the soul for a centre of repose apart from the transitory interests and the things of time. Hear then the gentle appeal 'Come unto Me and rest'.

John Wilhelm Rowntree, 1905

154 What was ⟨Christ's⟩ cup He drank, and baptism He suffered? I answer: They were the denial and offering up of Himself by the eternal Spirit to the will of God, undergoing the tribulations of His life and agonies of His death upon the Cross, for man's salvation. What is our cup and cross that we should drink and suffer? They are the denial and offering up of ourselves, by the same Spirit, to do or suffer the will of God for His service and glory, which is the true life and obedience of the cross of Jesus, narrow still, but before an unbeaten way. For, when there was none to help, not one to open the seals, to give knowledge, to direct the course of poor man's recovery, He came in the greatness of His love and strength; and, though clothed with the infirmities of a mortal man, being within fortified by the almightiness of an immortal God, He travelled through all the straits and difficulties of humanity, and, first of all others, trod the untrodden path to blessedness.

O come, let us follow Him, the most unwearied, the most victorious Captain of our Salvation! To whom all the great Alexanders and mighty Caesars of the world are less than the poorest soldier of their camps could be to them. True, they were all great princes of their kind, and conquerors too, but on very differing principles. For Christ made Himself of no reputation to save mankind, but these plentifully ruined people to augment theirs. They vanquished others, not themselves; Christ conquered self, that ever vanquished them, of merit therefore the most excellent prince and conqueror. Besides, they advanced their empire by rapine and blood, but He by suffering and persuasion. He never by compulsion, they always by force, prevailed. Misery and slavery followed all their victories; His brought greater freedom and felicity to those He overcame. In all they did they sought to please themselves; in all He did He aimed to please His Father, who is God of Gods, King of Kings, and Lord of Lords. *William Penn (1682)*

155 *As a son,* Christ was and is as absolutely and entirely dependent upon the Father as any of us. Indeed, were he not so, he could not be *like us in all things,* sin excepted. As we can do no good thing merely of ourselves, so he, if like us in all things but sin, can do no good thing of himself, merely, and independently. Hence, he could not do many mighty works in some places, because of the people's unbelief; the Father, by his eternal power, not making way there for the visible display of the glory and power of the sonship. Nor was this total dependency confined wholly to power; it was as real in regard to wisdom and knowledge; and so certainly as *we* have no real wisdom and knowledge, but what we have received, so certainly was the case the same with the blessed Jesus. Hence, he himself speaks of a day or hour, which no man, nor angel, nay, nor even the *son* himself, but the Father *only,* knoweth. Some may think this is very strange, but it must be so, if he is, except sin, like us in all things; and if he were not in all things else like us, his triumph and

victory over all the powers of death and darkness, could not assure us of the possibility and certainty, upon our standing faithful, of our victoriously triumphing in like manner. *Job Scott, 1792*

156 Christ has not conquered to excuse us, but that we should follow in his steps. *Job Scott, 1792*

157 The New Testament clearly sets out Christ as fully human and as fully divine. The writers are conscious of no difficulty or contradiction involved in this position. It seemed to them the most natural thing in the world. Probably the sense of contradiction only arises in our minds through ignorance of what is meant by personality. We have set divinity over against humanity, on the assumption that so much added to the one must be so much subtracted from the other. Some have so emphasised Christ's divinity as to leave no room for His humanity, while others have done just the reverse. It seems so easy to solve the problem by cutting the knot; either say that Christ was absolute God, or that He was ordinary man. But this does not solve the problem, for either solution fails to take account of many of the facts. The difficulty is to get a conception of Jesus that is true to all the facts—of one who was the Incarnate Son of God and yet (perhaps we should say 'and *therefore*') was truly man. It is a pity that we insist on using the terms 'humanity' and 'divinity' as though they imply opposition. May we not rather say that Jesus 'shows us the divine life humanly lived and the human life divinely lived'? But of one thing we can be certain—there are depths beneath depths, and heights above heights in the personality of Jesus, which make rash generalisations or superficial solutions absurd. We are standing before the greatest character in history and we may well hesitate before trying to express Him in a formula. *Yorkshire Q.M., 1919*

158 The Society of Friends as such has never departed from its claim to be within the Christian tradition, nor from its assent to the Lordship of Christ. But the Society, abjuring doctrinal notions and credal statements, has not felt it necessary to depart from this practice in regard to the person of Christ. We thus have within our membership men and women with differing conceptions of this subject held together as heretofore, in a common loyalty to the ever living Christ, known to us in the Jesus of history.

Edgar G. Dunstan (*1956*)

159 The crux of Fox's discovery was that in the present spiritual reality he was aware of the same living Christ to whom the scriptures and the doctrines bore witness. It was a mystical apprehension of the fact that the person of Christ belongs not only to history at a given time and place, but also to an eternal world into which Fox and his friends knew that Christ had brought them. A statement made by London Yearly Meeting in 1906 reflects the close relation between spiritual experience and Christian practice. It deals also with the essential unity between spiritual experience of the living Christ, and the historic revelation of God in Jesus.

'Christ is not divided; the Christ who dwells within, the hope of glory, is the Christ of history. Only as we follow the guidance of the Holy Spirit and by faith embrace the Lord Jesus as the Redeemer of the world, and as our personal Saviour, can we hope to perform an adequate part in the social and other service that lies before us; for, after all, the world's misery is the result of the world's sin. War, intemperance, avarice, lust, the chief sources of suffering and poverty, are the outcome of selfishness; and all selfishness is sin. Civilisation makes but small progress against its ravages. We need a fresh vision of the cross of Christ. Coming as penitents to the foot of that cross, we find pardon, peace and power...Christ's life is the key to our life, and His service the key to our service. Underlying all difference of view, is the reality of the power of the living Christ, whose love goes deeper than all our experience. By grace may it be given to us humbly and gratefully to confess: "The life which I now live in the flesh I live by the faith of the Son of God, who loved me and gave Himself for me" (Gal. 2. 20).'

'*The nature of the church*' (*1945*)

In joy of inward peace, or sense
  Of sorrow over sin,
He is His own best evidence,
  His witness is within.

No fable old, nor mythic lore,
  Nor dream of bards and seers,
No dead fact stranded on the shore
  Of the oblivious years;

But warm, sweet, tender, even yet
  A present help is He;
And faith has still its Olivet,
  And love its Galilee.

The healing of His seamless dress
  Is by our beds of pain;
We touch Him in life's throng and press,
  And we are whole again.

Through Him the first fond prayers are said
  Our lips of childhood frame,
The last low whispers of our dead
  Are burdened with His name.

Our Lord and Master of us all!
  Whate'er our name or sign,
We own Thy sway, we hear Thy call,
  We test our lives by Thine.

We faintly hear, we dimly see,
  In differing phrase we pray;
But, dim or clear, we own in Thee
  The Light, the Truth, the Way.

John Greenleaf Whittier, 1866

161 We must not have Christ Jesus, the Lord of Life, put any more in the stable amongst the horses and asses, but he must now have the best chamber, the heart, and the rude, debauched spirit must be turned out. Therefore let him reign, whose right it is, who was conceived by the Holy Ghost, by which Holy Ghost you call him Lord, in which Holy Ghost you pray, and by which Holy Ghost you have comfort and fellowship with the Son and with the Father. Therefore know the triumph in the Seed, which is first and last, the beginning and ending, the top and cornerstone. *George Fox, 1657*

162 Everything in the Kingdom, every spiritual thing, refers to Christ and centres in him. His nature, his virtue, his presence, his power makes up all. Indeed he is all in all to a believer, only variously manifested and opened in the heart by the Spirit. He is the volume of the whole book, every leaf and line whereof speaks of him and writes out him in some or other of his sweet and beautiful lineaments. So that if I should yet speak further of other things...I should but speak further of his nature brought up, manifested and displaying itself in and through the creatures, by his turning the wheel of his life in their hearts. But my spirit hasteneth from words... ⟨that it⟩ may sink in spirit into the feeling of the life itself, and may learn what it is to enjoy it there and to be comprehended of it, and cease striving to know or comprehend concerning it.

Isaac Penington (1663)

The Spirit

The Spirit as the Light of God in all men

163 Now the Lord God hath opened to me by His invisible power how that every man was enlightened by the divine Light of Christ; and I saw it shine through all, and that they that believed in it came out of condemnation and came to the Light of Life, and became the children of it, but they that hated it, and did not believe in it, were condemned by it, though they made a profession of Christ. This I saw in the pure openings of the Light, without the help of any man, neither did I then know where to find it in the Scriptures, though

afterwards, searching the Scriptures, I found it. For I saw in that Light and Spirit which was before Scripture was given forth, and which led the holy men of God to give them forth, that all must come to that Spirit, if they would know God or Christ or the Scriptures aright, which they that gave them forth were led and taught by.   *George Fox, recalling his experiences in 1648*

164 The Spirit which illuminateth and the Spirit which sanctifieth, is one and the same Spirit, and the illumination of the Spirit is in order unto sanctification. The same Light which discovereth the darkness, also chaseth away the darkness, as it is received and subjected to, and purifieth the mind: for the light hath not only a property of enlightening, but also of cleansing and sanctifying.
                                               Isaac Penington (1674)

165 And this I declare to all the inhabitants in England and all that dwell upon the earth, that God alone is the Teacher of His people and hath given to everyone a measure of grace, which is the light that comes from Christ, that checks and reproves for sin, in the secrets of the heart and conscience; and all that wait in that light which comes from Christ—which is the free grace of God—for the power of Jesus Christ to destroy sin and to guide them in obedience to the Light, so shall they come to know the only true God and Father of Light, in Christ Jesus who is the Way to Him. And this I witness to all the sons of men, that the knowledge of eternal life I came not to by the letter of the Scripture nor hearing men speak of the Name of God. I came to the true knowledge of the Scripture and the eternal rest... by the inspiration of the Spirit of Jesus Christ.
                                            William Dewsbury (1655)

166 In the afternoon the people gathered about me, with several separate teachers, where it was judged there were above a thousand people;... amongst whom I declared freely and largely God's everlasting truth and word of life about three hours, directing all to the Spirit of God in themselves; that they might be turned from the darkness to the light, and believe in it, that they might become the

children of it; and might be turned from the power of Satan, which they had been under, unto God; and by the Spirit of Truth might be led into all truth, and so sensibly understand the words of the prophets and of Christ and of the apostles; and might all come to know Christ to be their Teacher to instruct them, their Counsellor to direct them, their Shepherd to feed them, their Bishop to oversee them, and their Prophet to open divine mysteries to them; and might know their bodies to be prepared, sanctified and made fit temples for God and Christ to dwell in. And, in the openings of the heavenly life, I opened unto them the prophets and the figures and shadows and directed them to Christ the Substance. *George Fox's Sermon on Firbank Fell, near Sedbergh, Whitsuntide, 1652*

167 *This account of George Fox's visit to North Carolina is printed in the slightly modernized version of the Journal, given by Rufus Jones in 'George Fox, an autobiography'.*
The Governor, with his wife, received us lovingly; but a doctor there would needs dispute with us. And truly his opposing us was of good service, giving occasion for the opening of many things to the people concerning the Light and Spirit of God, which he denied to be in everyone; and affirmed that it was not in the Indians. Whereupon I called an Indian to us, and asked him whether when he lied, or did wrong to any one, there was not something in him which reproved him for it. He said there was such a thing in him, that did so reprove him; and he was ashamed when he had done wrong or spoken wrong. So we shamed the doctor before the Governor and the people; insomuch that the poor man ran out so far that at length he would not own the Scriptures.   *1672*

168 Paul asked the Jews to find the nature of Abraham in the face of Jesus Christ and in Gentile converts. We ought to recognise the faith of Jesus Christ wherever we find it, outside our own or any Church, and in unexpected forms. The fellowship of Christ must be inclusive; there must be no 'fencing of the Table'. What really differentiates people is only that they grasp less or more of the vital store of the Universe. Jesus is not beyond our sufficient if incomplete comprehension, however much He is beyond our achievement.
John William Graham (1920)

169 As the spirit of Christ works in the Eastern nations, we look for ever fresh expressions of Christian thought and method; and, since we are all seekers, we hope to receive from them, as they also do from us, new light and leading in the way of the Kingdom.

Friends Foreign Mission Association, 1919

170 The Lord Jesus died not for a favoured few only, but for all. 'He is the propitiation* for our sins, and not for ours only, but also for the sins of the whole world.' His Church must ever testify to the unsearchable riches of His Grace. The invitation is all-embracing. 'Whosoever will, let him take the water of life freely'. Firmly as we believe this truth, we think it right once more plainly to declare that we have never acknowledged any principle of spiritual light, life or holiness, inherent by nature in the mind or heart of man... The light that shines into man's heart is not of man, and must ever be distinguished both from the conscience which it enlightens, and from the natural faculty of reason which, when unsubjected to its holy influences is, in the things of God, very foolishness. As the eye is to the body, so is conscience to our inner nature, the organ by which we see; and as both light and life are essential to sight in the natural eye, so conscience, as the inward eye, cannot see aright without the quickening and illumination of the Spirit of God. It is the capacity to receive this blessed influence which, in an especial manner, gives man pre-eminence above the beasts that perish; which distinguishes him, in every nation and in every clime, as an object of the redeeming love of God, as a being not only intelligent, but responsible; for whom the message of salvation through our crucified Redeemer is, under all possible circumstances, designed to be a 'joyful sound'.

Yearly Meeting, 1879

171 We misunderstand the truth of the Inward Light if we imagine that it means a present inspiration independent of the past. Fox claimed that he had a word from the Lord as sure as any of the Apostles ever had. We join him in affirming our faith in the contemporary inspiration of the Holy Spirit. But Fox could never have made his claim if he had not recognised the word of the Lord which came to the Apostles.

H. G. Wood (1951)

* The word 'propitiation' is, in the Revised Standard Version, translated 'expiation'.

The work of the Spirit in the Old Testament in preparation for Jesus

172 While we are not to confine the thought of Revelation to that which Jesus brought to men—while with the Apostle we recognise that God has 'not left Himself without witness' in all human history—it seems that in a very special way He revealed Himself in Christ. And, in the long history of the Hebrew race, we see the long process of preparation for this climax. Without such a spiritual preparation —of a seed-bed, as it were, in the hearts of a few for the sowing of the seed of the Gospel that it might later spread to all—it is impossible to see how that Divine seed could ever have taken root. At Athens, or Rome, or even Alexandria, it is more than doubtful whether Jesus could have made himself understood at all; as it was (humanly speaking) he only just succeeded. And it is as the record of this gradual process of revelation that the Bible is unique in human literature and indispensable for the understanding of Christianity.

Edward Grubb (1928)

173 It was the same Spirit that came upon Moses, which came upon John the Baptist; and it was also the same Spirit that came upon Gideon and Samson, that fell upon Peter and Paul; but it was not the same dispensation of that Spirit. *William Penn (1696)*

Christian experience of the Spirit

174 Now therefore, everyone that thirsts, come unto Christ Jesus, who is near you, and wait to know his word in you, which is in the heart, which faith comes by the preaching of it in you, as you diligently wait and keep your minds unto it. And this which shows you sin and evil, is in you, and makes manifest all that you have acted contrary unto it, yea, all that you have ever done, and will search your hearts, and is the eye that sees the deceit in all its transforming in you; and it will let you see, it hath often checked and called, but you have not answered its call, and so have chosen your own way, and so have gone from the way which is the Light of Christ in you, and so you have run into the broad way; and that which desired God hath not been nourished and fed but hath been famished, and another hath been fed, which is now for the slaughter. But now as ye return home to within, to the true Light of Jesus which is that one thing which leads all men that own it, to be guided by it, you shall have true rest and peace. *Francis Howgill (1656)*

175 By far the greater part of any 'Inner Light' that we know is, ultimately, whether we recognise the fact or not, due to Jesus of Nazareth and to the Scripture; and our spiritual life is hurt by a confused thinking that leads to any neglect of these, setting the Light over against them as if it were their rival and superior.

A. Neave Brayshaw, 1915

176 If you build upon anything or have confidence in anything which stands in time and is on this side eternity and ⟨the⟩ Being of beings, your foundation will be swept away, and night will come upon you, and all your gathered-in things and taken-on and imitated will all fail you...Why gad you abroad? Why trim you yourselves with the saints' words, when you are ignorant of the life? Return, return to Him that is the first Love, and the first-born of every creature, who is the Light of the World...Return home to within, sweep your houses all, the groat is there, the little leaven is there, the grain of mustard-seed you will see, which the Kingdom of God is like; ...and here you will see your Teacher not removed into a corner, but present when you are upon your beds and about your labour, convincing, instructing, leading, correcting, judging and giving peace to all that love and follow Him. *Francis Howgill (1656)*

177 The divine mystery of this infinite God is revealed and discovered in the hearts of the sons of men whom He hath chosen; and He hath given us to enjoy and possess in us a measure of that fulness that is in Himself, even a measure of the same love and life, of the same mercy and power, and of the same divine nature...These things ye know, if ye be born from above, and if the immortal birth live in you and you be constant in the faith, then are you heirs through it of the everlasting inheritance of eternal life...and all are yours because you are Christ's, and he is God's; and you have the Father and the Son. *Edward Burrough (1660)*

178 Glory to God for ever! who hath chosen us as a first-fruits to himself in this day wherein he is arisen to plead with the nations, and therefore hath sent us forth to preach this everlasting gospel unto all, Christ nigh to all, the light in all, the seed sown in the hearts of all, that men may come and apply their minds to it. And we rejoice that we have been made to lay down our wisdom and learning... and our carnal reasoning, to learn of Jesus and sit down at the feet of Jesus, in our hearts, and hear him, who there makes all things manifest and reproves all things by his light (Eph. 5. 13).

Robert Barclay (1678)

179 It is a distinguishing feature of the work of the Holy Spirit, that it bears an effectual witness to Christ, and brings to the enjoyment of His grace in those various relations in which He has been pleased to reveal Himself. Under the power of heart-searching conviction, it draws the believing soul, in contrition and humiliation, to the Saviour's feet. Here, through the acceptance of Him, in living faith, as the propitiation for sin, the reconciling love of God is shed abroad in the heart, and we are enabled to realise the inestimable privilege of access unto God; not in our own right, or for any works of righteousness that we have done, but for the sake of Christ alone. In thus witnessing of Him, and establishing the soul upon Him, the Holy Spirit becomes a Comforter indeed. Through His sanctifying power, the righteousness of God through faith is more and more manifested in the life and conversation, whilst all boasting is excluded. The promise of the New Covenant, in its most precious import, is fulfilled. The law of God becomes more and more plainly written upon the heart, whilst a yet clearer and clearer view is granted of the depth of that love which, in Christ Jesus, pardoneth iniquity, transgression and sin. Fervently do we desire that our dear Friends, everywhere, may press after an individual acquaintance with this heart-searching and heart-sanctifying knowledge of the Son of God. May none, under the heavy weight of conviction, stop short in the first stage of Christian experience; but, yielding without reserve to the further manifestation of light and truth, may they be brought, from step to step, in faith and faithfulness, to the full enjoyment in their own souls of the covenant of life and peace.

Yearly Meeting, 1857

180 The revelation of the Son of God is by the Spirit... I shall prove this by diverse arguments, and first from the promise of Christ in these words: 'I will pray the Father and He will give you another Comforter, that He may abide with you for ever... The Comforter, which is the Holy Ghost,.. He shall teach you all things, and bring all things to your remembrance' (John 14. 16, 26).

Hereunto have all Christians in all ages attributed their strength and life. It is by this Spirit that they avouch themselves to have been converted to God, to have been redeemed from the world, to have been strengthened in their weakness, comforted in their afflictions, confirmed in their temptations, emboldened in their sufferings, and triumphed in the midst of all their persecutions. It is this Spirit that bearest witness with our spirit that we are the children of God (Rom. 8. 16)... It is by this Spirit that the glorious things which God hath laid up for us, which neither outward ear hath heard, nor outward eye hath seen, nor the heart of man conceived by all his reasonings, are revealed unto us. It is by this Spirit that both wisdom and knowledge, and faith and miracles, and tongues, and prophecies are obtained. But they cry out, that it is not without great temerity that we dare so boast of the Spirit of Christ... Why should any be so foolish as to deny... this Spirit which Christ hath promised shall dwell in his children? They that do suppose the indwelling and leading of his Spirit to be ceased, must also suppose Christianity to be ceased, which cannot subsist without it.

What the work of this Spirit is,.. Christ compriseth in two or three things, 'He will guide you into all truth; He will teach you all things, and bring all things to your remembrance'. Since Christ hath provided for us so good an instructor, why need we then lean so much to those traditions and commandments of men wherewith so many Christians have burdened themselves?.. But to conclude, He in whom the Spirit of God dwelleth, it is not in him a lazy dumb useless thing; but it moveth, actuateth, governeth, instructeth and teacheth him all things whatsoever are needful for him to know: yea, bringeth all things to his remembrance.

Robert Barclay (1678)

181   The central Quaker testimony to the Divine Light, which enlightens
every human soul, identified that Light from the first with the
Light and life of Jesus Christ. Today as in the past, we need to have
faith in the Divine Immanence and to find its completion and its
explanation for our own lives in the personality of Jesus Christ.
We think of him not as someone far off in bygone history, but as one
who has been a present reality to his disciples all down the ages and
is the guiding head both of the disciple and of the whole fellowship
of disciples that we call the Catholic Church of Christ. Christ
himself, manifested not only in the pages of the Gospels, but through
the lives of his saints, and apprehended through communion in
worship with our fellow-believers, and in individual communion in
our own hearts, is the authority to whom as Christians we turn to
check our hopes, control our acts and guide our lives. We need all
these windows to receive his light. If we neglect the study of the
Gospels our loss is immeasurably great: we lose something very
precious if we do not seek the light reflected in the lives of our fellow
Christians, and if we do not seek for guidance along with others, as
well as by ourselves. But in the last resort a man must seek to obey
the leading of God as he sees it in his own conscience, after seeking
the light in all these different ways.   *T. Edmund Harvey (1935)*

182   The Inner Light does not lead men to do that which is right in their
own eyes, but that which is right in God's eyes. As the Light is One,
so its teaching is ultimately (though not superficially) harmonious.
In actual experience, it is not found that souls truly looking to the
Inner Light as their authority will break away from each other in
anarchy.   *Ellen S. Bosanquet (1927)*

Life in Christ

Growth in the Life

183   If you would know God, and worship and serve God as you should
do, you must come to the means He has ordained and given for that
purpose. Some seek it in books, some in learned men, but what they

look for is *in themselves*, yet they overlook it. The voice is too still, the Seed too small, and the Light shineth in darkness. They are abroad and so cannot divide the spoil; but the woman that lost her silver found it at home after she had lighted her candle and swept her house. Do you so too, and you shall find what Pilate wanted to know, *viz.*, *Truth*. The Light of Christ within, who is the Light of the world, and so a light to you that tells you the truth of your condition, leads all that take heed unto it out of darkness into God's marvellous light; for light grows upon the obedient. It is sown for the righteous and their way is a shining light that shines forth more and more to the perfect day.

Wherefore, O Friends, turn in, turn in, I beseech you! Where is the poison, there is the antidote; there you want Christ and there you must find Him: and, blessed be God, there you may find Him. 'Seek and you shall find', I testify for God. But then you must seek aright, with your whole heart, as men that seek for their lives, yea, for their eternal lives, diligently, humbly, patiently, as those that can taste no pleasure, comfort or satisfaction in anything else, unless you find Him whom your souls want and desire to know and love above all. O, it is a travail, a spiritual travail, let the carnal, profane world think and say as it will. And through this path you must walk to the City of God, that has eternal foundations, if ever you will come there... Here you will come to love God above all and your neighbours as yourselves. Nothing hurts, nothing harms, nothing makes afraid on this holy mountain; now you come to be Christ's indeed, for you are His in nature and spirit, and not your own.   *William Penn (1694)*

The place of the Church

184 *The corporate experience of the Early Friends*
⟨We⟩ were reckoned, in the north part of England, even as the outcasts of Israel, and as men destitute of the great knowledge, which some seemed to enjoy; yet there was more sincerity and true love amongst us and desires after the living powerful presence of God than was among many in that day who ran into heaps and forms but left the cross behind them. God out of his everlasting

love did appear unto us, according to the desire of our hearts, who longed after him; when we had turned aside from hireling-shepherds' tents, we found him whom our souls loved; and God, out of his great love and great mercy, sent one unto us, a man of God, one of ten thousand, to instruct us in the way of God more perfectly;* which testimony reached unto all our consciences and entered into the inmost part of our hearts, which drove us to a narrow search, and to a diligent inquisition concerning our state, through the Light of Christ Jesus. The Lord of Heaven and earth we found to be near at hand, and, as we waited upon him in pure silence, our minds out of all things, his heavenly presence appeared in our assemblies, when there was no language, tongue nor speech from any creature. The Kingdom of Heaven did gather us and catch us all, as in a net, and his heavenly power at one time drew many hundreds to land. We came to know a place to stand in and what to wait in; and the Lord appeared daily to us, to our astonishment, amazement and great admiration, insomuch that we often said one unto another with great joy of heart: 'What, is the Kingdom of God come to be with men? And will he take up his tabernacle among the sons of men, as he did of old? Shall we, that were reckoned as the outcasts of Israel, have this honour of glory communicated amongst us, which were but men of small parts and of little abilities, in respect of many others, as amongst men?' And from that day forward, our hearts were knit unto the Lord and one unto another in true and fervent love, in the covenant of Life with God; and that was a strong obligation or bond upon all our spirits, which united us one unto another. We met together in the unity of the Spirit, and of the bond of peace, treading down under our feet all reasoning about religion. And holy resolutions were kindled in our hearts as a fire which the Life kindled in us to serve the Lord while we had a being, and mightily did the Word of God grow amongst us, and the desires of many were after the Name of the Lord. O happy day! O blessed day! the memorial of which can never pass out of my mind. And thus the Lord, in short, did form us to be a people for his praise in our generation.

Francis Howgill (1672)

* *For another account of this visit of George Fox among the Westmorland Seekers,* see §15

185 *Their generalizing conception of its nature*

The Church is to be considered as it signifies a certain number of persons gathered by God's Spirit...unto the belief of the true principles and doctrines of the Christian Faith, who, through their hearts being united by the same love and their understandings informed in the same truths, gather, meet and assemble together to wait upon God, to worship Him and to bear a joint testimony for the truth against error, suffering for the same. And so becoming, through this fellowship, as one family and household in certain respects ⟨they⟩ do each of them watch over, teach, instruct and care for one another, according to their several measures and attainments.   *Robert Barclay (1678)*

186 *A more recent statement on the place of the Church*

The earthly pilgrimage of the Christian is not to be a solitary one; he has become a member of a body, a citizen of a heavenly Kingdom, a constituent part of the household of faith. The followers of Christ are, in the words of the Apostle Peter, to be 'built up a spiritual house, a holy priesthood, to offer up spiritual sacrifices, acceptable to God through Jesus Christ'. It was to the whole company of Christians in Asia Minor, not to any special order, that these words were addressed; it was the whole company of Christians at Rome whom the Apostle besought 'by the mercies of God' to render a holy, acceptable and reasonable service, through the dedication of their bodies 'a living sacrifice' unto God. For the redeemed man, the incarnation of Christ has consecrated all life; to him the distinction between things secular and things religious fades away; whether he eats or drinks or whatsoever he does he recognises the glory of God to be his constant aim and object. Membership in the royal priesthood is not conditioned by the distinctions of age or sex. Especially, though by no means exclusively, in the ministries of home life are Christian women called to fulfil their spiritual priesthood, and we desire earnestly to urge them not to be neglectful of this holy calling. And how great is the privilege to themselves and to the Church when, through obedience to the teachings of the Spirit of Truth, children are early introduced into the same honourable vocation.   *Yearly Meeting, 1899*

187 *The personal application*

Membership in the Christian Church is a high privilege which entails a corresponding responsibility. Ideally it is an outward sign of an inner union with Christ the living head and with other members of a living body. This true and inner union cannot be infallibly discerned by men, and outward membership can never perfectly mark it. *Yearly Meeting, 1940*

For further extracts on the Basis of Membership see §365-371

Life beyond death

188 The Apostle Paul saith, 'For we know that if our earthly house of this tabernacle be dissolved, we have a building of God, an house not made with hands, eternal in the heavens, for in this' (namely, earthly house) 'we groan earnestly desiring to be cloathed upon with our house that is from heaven'...Here you may see what the spiritual groaning was for, for an house and cloathing from Heaven and that mortality might be swallowed up of life, and so to be ever with the Lord. And here you may see how Christ is the Resurrection and the Life; and in the resurrection the vile body is changed like unto his glorious body; and in the resurrection they are spiritual and Mortal puts on Immortality, and Corruptible puts on Incorruption. And so as we have borne the image of the earthly, we shall also bear the image of the heavenly. *George Fox (1685)*

189 We deny not, but believe, the resurrection, according to the scriptures; not only from sin, but also from death and the grave; but we are conscientiously cautious in expressing the manner of the resurrection because it is left a secret by the Holy Ghost in the Scripture. Should people be angry with ⟨us⟩ for not expressing or asserting what is hidden, and which is more curious than necessary to be known, and in which the objectors themselves cannot be positive? 'Thou fool', is to the curious enquirer, as says the apostle (1 Cor. 15. 36-54); which makes the Quakers contented with that body, which God shall please to give them hereafter; being assured 'That their corruptible shall put on incorruption, and their mortal shall put on immortality', but in such a manner as pleaseth God. And in the meantime they esteem it their duty, as well as wisdom, to acquiesce in his holy will. It is enough they believe a resurrection, and that with a glorious and incorruptible body, without further niceties; for to that was the ancient hope.   *William Penn (1692)*

190   The truest end of life, is to know the Life that never ends.
          He that makes this his Care, will find it his Crown at last.
          And he that lives to live ever, never fears dying:
          nor can the means be terrible to him
          that heartily believes the end.

      For though Death be a Dark passage, it leads to Immortality,
          And that's Recompence enough for Suffering of it.
          And yet Faith lights us even through the Grave,
          being Evidence of Things not seen.

      And this is the Comfort of the Good,
          that the Grave cannot hold them,
          and that they live as soon as they die.
          For Death is no more
          than a turning of us over from time to eternity.
          Death, then, being the way and condition of Life,
          we cannot love to live,
          if we cannot bear to die.

      They that love beyond the World, cannot be separated by it
          Death cannot kill what never dies.
          Nor can Spirits ever be divided
          that love and live in the same Divine Principle,
          the Root and Record of their Friendship.
          If Absence be not Death, neither is theirs.

      Death is but Crossing the World, as Friends do the Seas;
          they live in one another still.
          For they must needs be present,
          that love and live in that which is Omnipresent.
          In this Divine Glass, they see Face to Face;
          and their Converse is Free, as well as Pure.
                                               William Penn (1693)

191 *The last two verses of a poem written in 1868 by Thomas Hodgkin (1831-1913) 'show the peace he had won and the glad certainty of his faith':*

> Oh, Son of Man, if Thee and not another
> I here have known,
> If I may see Thee then, our First-born Brother,
> Upon Thy Throne;
>
> How stern soe'er, how terrible in brightness
> That dawn shall break,
> I shall be satisfied with Thy dear likeness
> When I awake.

192 I must confess to a passionate devotion to God, as the spiritual reality *par excellence*. If He be real, and if He be concerned for me, I ask no more. I believe He cares, and that He continues our lives after death, in a fellowship of which we have a foretaste here. And I believe that the Eternal Christ, who is this same God, viewed as active and creative, is ever in the world, seeking, knocking, persuading, counselling men to return to their rightful Home.

Thomas R. Kelly, 1940

193 *Rufus Jones here describes an experience (mentioned also in §92) following the death at the age of 11 of his son Lowell:*

When my sorrow was at its most acute stage I was walking along a great city highway, when suddenly I saw a little child come out of a great gate, which swung to and fastened behind her. She wanted to go to her home behind the gate, but it would not open. She pounded in vain with her little fist. She rattled the gate. Then she wailed as though her heart would break. The cry brought the mother. She caught the child in her arms and kissed away the tears. 'Didn't you know I would come? It is all right now.' All of a sudden I saw with my spirit that there was love behind my shut gate. Yes, 'where there is so much love, *there must be more*'.

194 *Carl Heath writes in the summer of 1940 to some friends on the east coast in the early days of air raids during the second world war:*

I was very glad to hear from you, for in these days one is anxious in one sense though in another *not at all* ... What I mean is that ultimately whether you are in Suffolk or South Heaven, Norfolk or North Heaven, you exist and live, and it's the joy I have in the quality of your living that is important, not where you are at a given moment. Which has its bearing on this constant raiding.

195 Our beloveds are become now a part of the life of the place. There is One who is peculiarly the Life itself: '*I will come again and receive you unto myself.*' *J. Rendel Harris (1905)*

For further extracts on death and the life to come see §525-530

Chapter 3: Friends and the Christian Church

The historic witness

196 As members of the Church Universal, we share its world-wide life: we must learn from its history; the triumphs and failures, the shortcomings and the growth in Truth of our fellow Christians in all ages are bound up with our own lives today. Through all and over all there shines the grace of God. Neither difference of dogma, nor of ritual, nor of church government can wholly separate and keep apart the great family to which we belong.

T. Edmund Harvey, 1937

197 Historically our Society stands in the Christian tradition;...we unite in the desire that Friends everywhere should share in the life and fellowship of the wider Christian community and co-operate as fully as possible in its work...Many of us value opportunities for worship and service with our fellow Christians. No one can measure the debt we owe to the influence and inspiration and leadership of many of our fellow Christians, to the stimulus and fellowship some of us have known in inter-church groups and inter-denominational movements. And there is, too, the valuable service rendered by Christian scholars and thinkers for which we are profoundly thankful.

On the other hand, we have realised how far short we ourselves fall of what we ought to be and yet we believe our Society has something of value to contribute to the life and thought of the ⟨ecumenical⟩ movement. Our witness to the non-necessity of the outward forms, to the essentially inward nature of communion and to our peace testimony are examples.

Our Quaker experience embodies elements that are both protestant and catholic; we claim to be a movement rather than a sect. This lays on us an added responsibility. To achieve the ideal of unity in diversity we must have confidence in the integrity of one another.

Dependence on the Holy Spirit will lead us into unity at the deepest level of fellowship. At that point differences are accepted, yet transcended, in a common loyalty to Jesus Christ.

Friends World Conference, 1952

198 The whole Christian community still needs the witness of a corporate body like the Society of Friends to the Quaker type of sainthood, to the value of silence, to the true nature of Christian democracy, and to the paramount claims of positive goodwill on Christian thought and effort. *H. G. Wood (1920)*

The Scriptures

199 And as concerning the Holy Scriptures, we do believe that they were given forth by the Holy Spirit of God, through the holy men of God, who, as the Scripture itself declares (2 Pet. 1. 21) 'spake as they were moved by the Holy Ghost'. We believe they are to be read, believed and fulfilled—He that fulfils them is Christ—and they are 'profitable for doctrine, for reproof, for correction and for instruction in righteousness, that the man of God may be perfect, throughly furnished unto all good works' (2 Tim. 3. 16, 17), and are able to make wise 'unto salvation through faith in Christ Jesus'...We call the Holy Scriptures, as Christ and the Apostles called them, and holy men of God called them, viz.: the 'words of God'...We do declare that we do esteem it a duty incumbent on us to pray with and for, to teach, instruct and admonish those in and belonging to our families. *George Fox, 1671*

200 From these revelations of the Spirit of God to the saints have proceeded the Scriptures of Truth, which contain:

(1) A faithful historical account of the actions of God's people in divers ages, with many singular and remarkable providences attending them.

(2) A prophetical account of several things, whereof some are already past, and some are yet to come.

(3) A full and ample account of all the chief principles of the doctrine of Christ, held forth in divers precious declarations, exhortations and sentences, which, by the moving of God's Spirit, were at several times and upon sundry occasions spoken and written unto some Churches and their pastors.

Nevertheless, because they are only a declaration of the fountain and not the fountain itself, therefore they are not to be esteemed the principal ground of all truth and knowledge, nor yet the adequate, primary rule of faith and manners. Yet, because they give a true and faithful testimony of the first foundation, they are and may be esteemed a secondary rule, subordinate to the Spirit, from which they have all their excellency and certainty: for, as by the inward testimony of the Spirit we do alone truly know them, so they testify that the Spirit is that Guide by which the saints are led into all truth: therefore, according to the Scriptures the Spirit is the first and principal Leader.   *Robert Barclay (1678)*

201 The Bible is the record of what God did with and for Israel, and of what He has done for mankind through the discipline of Israel and the coming of Jesus Christ. The Old Testament relates the call of a nation to become a moral and spiritual example to all nations, the training of a people to be the bearers of God's truth and mercy to all peoples. It was the mission of Jesus 'to make the treasures of Israel available for mankind'. Throughout the story, from the call of Abraham to the coming of Jesus Christ and the gift of the Holy Spirit, the divine initiative is manifest with a unique intensity in a continuous and progressive revelation. As the record of this revelation the Scriptures become the primary and indispensable witness to the history and nature of salvation.

Meeting for Sufferings, 1956

202 The canon of Scripture may be closed, but the inspiration of the Holy Spirit has not ceased. We believe that there is no literature in the world where the revelation of God is given so fully as in our New Testament Scriptures; we go back to them for light and life

and truth. But we feel that the life çomes to us, not from the record itself, but from communion with him of whom the record tells. Through his own Spirit we commune with Him himself. In the words of Coleridge, 'I meet that in Scripture which finds me'.

Yorkshire Q.M., *1919*

203 '*Something that lately passed in discourse between the King and R.H.*' in *1660*:

Charles II: How did you come to believe that the Scriptures were true?

Richard Hubberthorne: I have believed the Scriptures from a child to be a declaration of truth, when I had but a literal knowledge, natural education and tradition; but now I know the Scriptures to be true by the manifestations and operation of God fulfilling them in me.

204 And the end of words is to bring men to the knowledge of things beyond what words can utter. So, learn of the Lord to make a right use of the Scriptures: which is by esteeming them in their right place, and prizing *that* above them which is above them.

Isaac Penington

Creeds

205 We do not in the least deprecate the attempt, which must be made, since man is a rational being, to formulate intellectually the ideas which are implicit in religious experience...But it should always be recognised that all such attempts are provisional, and can never be assumed to possess the finality of ultimate truth. There must always be room for development and progress, and Christian thought and inquiry should never be fettered by theory. Among the dangers of formulated statements of belief are these:

> (1) They tend to crystallise thought on matters that will always be beyond any final embodiment in human language;
>
> (2) They fetter the search for truth and for its more adequate expression; and

(3) They set up a fence which tends to keep out of the Christian
fold many sincere and seeking souls who would gladly
enter it.

Particularly in these days we need to be on our guard against
these dangers. Multitudes of people are being shaken out of their
comfortable beliefs by the terrific experiences through which the
world is passing, and are seeking a secure basis for their faith. And
some are finding a Reality which is much too great to be confined
within the narrow limits of a creed.

'True basis of Christian unity' (*1917*)

206 The original message of George Fox which gathered the Society of
Friends was never systematically formulated by him. It was essentially the faith, based on personal experience, that God and man
have direct relationship and mutual correspondence. This was not,
in the first instance, a doctrine, but a live and throbbing experience.
George Fox kept his faith as concrete as possible and avoided, as far
as one can, abstract phrases which tend to become mere words.
The principle which he named 'that of God in man' was first of all
for him a personal discovery that something not himself, something
beyond himself, was operating in him as an invading spiritual power.
He seemed to have found a central stream of life, flowing over the
ocean of darkness and death, and revealing to him the infinite
love of God present here in the world where we live.

Rufus M. Jones, 1937

207 Quakerism, indeed, has always found the bond of union for itself,
and for the wider fellowship of the Church Catholic, in inward
experience—the experience of the one Divine Life that is reproduc-
ing in men the character of Jesus Christ. It has refused to lay the
emphasis on creed or ritual or, in its days of vigour, on institutions.
Where Christ is, there is His Church, made up of all who seek to
live in His spirit, whatever the words by which they try to find
expression for their faith, or the practices which have become means
of grace to their souls...

A rich variety of expression and of practice is to be expected as the Life streams through disciples of every race and clime and condition. ...It does not press men into a rigid mould of thought or action; rather would it pour its own joy into every mould of humanity. We have sought unity through agreement in doctrines and institutions; and the track of Church history, like some new road through the desert, is strewn with the parched skeletons of our failures.

William Charles Braithwaite (1918)

Sacraments

208 Neither silence, nor words, nor music, nor baptism with water are in themselves religious ends. We are called upon to partake of the sacrament of communion at every meal; when alone; and when in Friends' Meetings, where our form of worship gives a unique opportunity for corporate union in the Spirit of God.

Friends World Conference, 1937

209 To Fox and the early Friends the whole of life seemed sacramental, and they refused to mark off any one particular practice or observance as more sacred than others. They took the same stand with regard to Sunday, or First Day; it was not in itself more holy than Saturday or Monday; every week-day should be a Lord's Day. Their whole attitude was gloriously positive, not negative. They were 'alive unto God' and sensed him everywhere.

We do not say that to observe the sacraments is wrong, but that such observance is not essential to wholehearted Christian discipleship and the full Christian experience. We do not judge our fellow Christians to whom the outward sacraments mean so much. Rather do we wish, by prayerful fellowship with them, to be led unitedly with them to a deeper understanding of what underlies those sacraments, and so to share a richer experience of the mind of Christ.

Gerald K. Hibbert (1941)

210 Our experience leads us to emphasise the fact that entrance into the community of Christ's people requires no outward rite, but is to be known only through trust, obedience, love, and commitment. As these are brought forth in us, we find ourselves drawn together into a unity with one another in which the presence of the Spirit of God is realised. Similarly we believe that our corporate experience at its best justifies us in claiming, in humility, that Christ's real presence is indeed known by us when even two or three are gathered together, in quiet expectancy, in his name. And some Friends would even say that they have come to know, in Quaker worship and fellowship, a communion with Christ and a baptism of the Spirit which go beyond anything they had previously experienced in the sacramental practice of other Christian groups...

We desire to bear a corporate testimony to the fact that, while to be made a member of Christ's Body does not necessarily involve any outward rite, it does inescapably require an inner transformation of the whole self by the indwelling Spirit of God. And we would bear witness to the certain fact that, in a gathered company of worshippers, and apart from the use of the outward elements of bread and wine, the real presence of Christ is to be truly and effectually known, bringing us into unity with one another and with himself.

Maurice A. Creasey (1956)

211 If we go back to their origin we shall see that the two chief sacraments of the church were most simple acts expressing in visible language the life of the spirit, acts perfectly natural and full of significance to those who first took part in them, but which in later days have too often lost their meaning because the mere form was held to have some magical efficacy in itself. To understand these sacraments aright do we not need to enter into the spirit of the Teacher in whose name they are celebrated, and who is believed to have instituted them? As we read the evangelists' record of the life and words of Jesus, we must surely feel that to him all life was a sacrament, a continual unfolding of the Divine through the visible world and through human life... Because he is in unbroken communion with the Father unseen, he constantly brings all the little things of daily life into communion with him.

T. Edmund Harvey (1913)

212   We know the grace of God ministered to us in countless ways —in the sacraments of nature, of the family, of friendship, of books, of music, of art. These and other such ministries become the symbols of God's ever-loving presence and of his care for even the least of his wayward children. Through such manifestations he has revealed himself to us: they are sacraments, and as we remember them we 'feed on him in our hearts with thanksgiving'.

Edgar G. Dunstan (1956)

213   It is not true, as we sometimes hear people say, that Friends do not believe in baptism and the Lord's supper. We do believe both in spiritual baptism and spiritual communion...Baptism to us means the Holy Spirit's power so known and yielded to in our hearts that we live in continual dependence upon His help and guidance. He brings us into such conscious fellowship with God and Christ that we can truly say, 'The life which I now live in the flesh I live by the faith of the Son of God, who loved me and gave Himself for me'. 'I live, yet not I, but Christ liveth in me' (Gal. 2. 20). Communion is opening the door of our hearts to the Lord Jesus and finding His promise fulfilled, 'I will come in to him, and will sup with him, and he with Me' (Rev. 3. 20)... We who set aside the outward ought to make sure that we do know these inward realities.

Elizabeth B. Emmott (1908)

214   Jesus, when He took up the little children and said, 'Of such is the Kingdom of Heaven', was speaking of Jewish children, who, according to the Jewish custom, would not have been baptised, and the Quaker position is really summed up in the words 'John indeed baptised with water, but ye shall be baptised with the Holy Spirit'. It is the inward change, the inward purification, the spiritual fact and not the outward symbol, that belongs in truth to the Kingdom of God. Neither in the refusal to baptise nor to take the supper do Friends set forth a negation. They assert, on the contrary, the positive truth that the religious life is the inward life of the spirit. But no place or time can limit its action, nor any symbol adequately express it, and that therefore of necessity no priest can claim to intervene between that inward life and its source of strength and power.

To the soul that feeds upon the bread of life the outward conventions of religion are no longer needful. Hid with Christ in God, there is for him small place for outward rites, for all experience is a holy baptism, a perpetual supper with the Lord, and all life a sacrifice, holy and acceptable unto God. This hidden life, this inward vision, this immediate and intimate union between the soul and God, this, as revealed in Jesus Christ, is the basis of the Quaker faith.

John Wilhelm Rowntree, 1902

215 We need to guard against under-valuing the material expressions of spiritual things. It is easy to make a form of our very rejection of forms. And in particular we need to ask ourselves whether we are endeavouring to make all the daily happenings and doings of life which we call 'secular' minister to the spiritual. It is a bold and colossal claim that we put forward—that the whole of life is sacramental, that there are innumerable 'means of grace' by which God is revealed and communicated—through nature and through human fellowship and through a thousand things that may become the 'outward and visible sign' of an 'inward and spiritual grace'.

A. Barratt Brown (1932)

Daniel Wheeler's sense of communion in the meeting for worship is described in §56; Stephen Grellet's experience of the common meal as a sacrament is expressed in §61.

Christian unity

216 True unity may be found under great apparent differences. This unity is spiritual, it expresses itself in many ways, and we need divine insight that we may recognise its working. We need forbearance, sympathy, and love, in order that, while remaining loyal to the truth as it has come to us, we may move forward with others to a larger and richer experience and expression of the will of God.

Yearly Meeting, 1916

217 *In 1917 Yearly Meeting received from its Faith & Order Commission a statement entitled 'The true basis of Christian unity'. As revised in 1937 the statement opens:*

The unity of Christians is not something that needs to be created; it is already here, and needs only to be recognised and acted upon. All those who love our Lord Jesus Christ, and in whose lives his character is being manifested, know this inner unity, whatever diversities there may be in the formulas by which they express themselves, or in the practices by which they seek to cherish his life in their souls.

218 In face of the wide and deep spiritual need of the modern world . . . we believe that the call to united witness and action on the part of Christians is becoming more insistent, and that Friends will be bound to consider their work in relation to that of the other Churches. Friends will be concerned to share whatever burdens of suffering and responsibility may fall on our fellow Christians, wherever they may be, and to bring into the life of the Church whatever wisdom and strength may have been given to Friends through worship and communion, not only as a contribution to unity but as a witness to the world and as a challenge to its current trend of thought. *Faith & Order Commission, 1935*

219 Friends have sought ⟨in all discussions with their fellow Christians⟩ to maintain their conviction concerning the freeness and spirituality of the Gospel. Thus in 1917 the statement on 'The True Basis of Christian Unity' declared that unity can only arise from a personal and corporate life in which the power of Christ to reproduce in us his own character is being in some real measure experienced. Negatively, Friends have always adhered to the view that unity cannot permanently be found in creed or sacrament. It was this conviction that caused Yearly Meeting in 1940 to decline the invitation to join the World Council of Churches because the Council's basis seemed to London Yearly Meeting to require acceptance of a credal formulation. In the case of a similar invitation from the British Council of Churches, however, the same stand was taken by Friends, but in this case it was met by the Council's decision to extend its basis so as to include in its membership those bodies which had previously been associated with the ecumenical movement, thus including the Society of Friends.

Christian Relationships Committee, 1957

The second Article of Amalgamation (1942) of the British Council of Churches reads: 'The basis of the British Council of Churches shall be that of the World Council of Churches, namely a "fellowship of churches which accept our Lord Jesus Christ as God and Saviour", with the understanding that any body which has hitherto been represented on the Commission shall continue in membership of the Council, if so willing, even though it does not itself accept the basis.'

220 Fellowship with those who are concerned in 'strengthening the Christian witness throughout the world' has helped Friends in appreciating the importance of standing together for a belief in the purposes of God in a world where indifference and materialism prevail. Friends have come to see the importance of a common witness with others arising from a common Christian faith rather than because they happen to agree in some one application of such faith. Responsibility for maintaining our special testimonies remains; but these should be seen not in isolation, but as expressions of our Christian faith. *Christian Relationships Committee, 1954*

221 The unity of Christians never did nor ever will or can stand in uniformity of thought and opinion, but in Christian love only.

Thomas Story (1737)

222 Even in the Apostles' days, Christians were too apt to strive after a wrong unity and uniformity in outward practices and observations, and to judge one another unrighteously in those things; and mark, it is not the different practice from one another that breaks the peace and unity, but the judging of one another because of different practices. He that keeps not a day may unite in the same Spirit, in the same life, in the same love, with him that keeps a day; and he who keeps a day may unite in heart and soul with the same Spirit

and life in him who keeps not a day; but he that judgeth the other because of either of these errs from the Spirit, from the love, from the life, and so breaks the bond of unity... And here is the true unity, in the Spirit, in the inward life, and not in an outward uniformity... Men keeping close to God, the Lord will lead them on fast enough... for He taketh care of such, and knoweth what light and what practices are most proper for them...

And oh, how sweet and pleasant it is to the truly spiritual eye to see several sorts of believers, several forms of Christians in the school of Christ, every one learning their own lesson, performing their own peculiar service, and knowing, owning, and loving one another in their several places and different performances to their Master, to whom they are to give an account, and not to quarrel with one another about their different practices (Rom. 14. 4). For this is the true ground of love and unity, not that such a man walks and does just as I do, but because I feel the same Spirit and life in him, and that he walks in his rank, in his own order, in his proper way and place of subjection to that; and this is far more pleasing to me than if he walked just in that track wherein I walk. Nay, so far as I am spiritual, I cannot so much as desire that he should do so, until he be particularly led thereto, by the same Spirit which led me; and he that knows what it is to receive any truths from the Spirit, and to be led into practices by the Spirit, and how prone the fleshly part is to make haste, and how dangerous that haste is, will not be forward to press his knowledge or practices upon others, but rather wait patiently till the Lord fit them for the receiving thereof...

The great error of the ages of the apostacy hath been to set up an outward order and uniformity, and to make men's consciences bend thereto, either by arguments of wisdom, or by force; but the property of the true church government is, to leave the conscience to its full liberty in the Lord, to preserve it single and entire for the Lord to exercise, and to seek unity in the light and in the Spirit, walking sweetly and harmoniously together in the midst of different practices. Yea, and he that hath faith, and can see beyond another yet can have it to himself, and not disturb his brother with it, but can descend and walk with him according to his measure; and if his brother have any heavy burthen upon him, he can lend him his shoulder, and bear part of his burthen with him.

Oh, how sweet and lovely it is to see brethren dwell together in unity, to see the true image of God raised in persons, and they knowing and loving one another in that image, and bearing with one another through love, and helping one another under their temptations and distresses of spirit, which every one must expect to meet with...The way is one; Christ the truth of God; and he that is in the faith, and in the obedience to that light which shines from his Spirit into the heart of every believer, hath a taste of the one heart and of the one way, and knoweth that no variety of practices, which is of God, can make a breach in the true unity.

Isaac Penington (1659)

Friends and other faiths

223 The Quaker faith is Christian. This involves a belief that all people everywhere are within the family of God who is our Father. God has been apprehended in other religions and we feel in fellowship with all who truly seek him...We are all children of God in that his care for man includes all. Only potentially are we sons of God. The sons of God are those who are led by the Spirit, who do the will of God. All those who do the will of the Father are brethren of Jesus in the Spirit. *Friends World Conference, 1952*

224 The church ⟨is⟩ no other thing but the society, gathering or company of such as God hath called out of the world, and worldly spirit, to walk in his light and life. The church, then, so defined, is to be considered, as it comprehends all that are thus called and gathered truly by God, both such as are yet in this inferior world, and such as having already laid down their earthly tabernacle, are passed into their heavenly mansions, which together do make up the one Catholic church... Out of which church we freely acknowledge there can be no salvation: because under this church...are comprehended all, and as many, of whatsoever nation, kindred, tongue, or people they be, though outwardly strangers, and remote

from those who profess Christ and Christianity in words, and have the benefit of the Scriptures, as become obedient to the holy light, and testimony of God, in their hearts... There may be members therefore of this Catholic church both among heathens, Turks, Jews, and all the several sorts of Christians, men and women of integrity and simplicity of heart, who... are by the secret touches of this holy light in their souls enlivened and quickened, thereby secretly united to God, and there-through become true members of this Catholic church.   *Robert Barclay (1678)*

225 We are conscious of Christianity as one among a number of religions competing for the allegiance of intelligent and spiritually-minded men, and the relationship between them exercises men's minds and hearts. The world is much smaller, much more interdependent than it used to be, and Christendom is no longer a self-contained unit. Few may have the privilege of intimate friendship with the saints of other faiths like Gandhi or Vinoba Bhave, but... an increasing number of people have had personal contacts with humble men and holy of heart in all walks of life of whom they dare not deny that they have been taught of God.   *Margaret B. Hobling (1958)*

The experience of a Japanese Friend, Inazo Nitobe, is described in §89.

226 'What think ye of Christ?' is central both in our relationships with other religions and in our relationship with one another within the Society of Friends... We are truly loyal to Jesus Christ when we judge the religious systems of the world by the standard which he himself used: 'Not everyone that saith unto me, Lord, Lord... but he that doeth the will of my Father'. Every tree is to be known by its fruits: not by its dead wood, or thorns, or parasites, but by the fruit of its own inner life and nature. We all know the fruits of the Spirit, and recognise the beauty of holiness, in our own ancestral tree... The flowers of unselfish living may be found growing in other men's gardens and... rich fruits of the Spirit may be tasted from other men's trees. They spring from the same Holy Spirit of Truth, the same Seed of God, whose power moves us through Christ.   *Marjorie Sykes, 1957*

227 The humble, meek, merciful, just, pious, and devout souls are everywhere of one religion; and when death has taken off the mask they will know one another, though the divers liveries they wear here makes them strangers. This world is a form; our bodies are forms; and no visible acts of devotion can be without forms. But yet the less form in religion the better, since God is a Spirit; for the more mental our worship, the more adequate to the nature of God; the more silent, the more suitable to the language of a Spirit.

William Penn (1693)

Chapter 4: The meeting for worship

In this chapter extracts are included expressing Friends' beliefs on the nature of worship which 'is not so much an attitude of mind which we cultivate as a response drawn from us by a consciousness of God's presence'. It is in our corporate worship that our common life is grounded. To this worship each has the responsibility of offering his gift, whether it be 'the broken and the contrite heart, the confession of the soul prostrate before God, the prayer of the afflicted when he is overwhelmed, the earnest wrestling of the spirit, the outpouring of humble thanksgiving, the spiritual song and melody of the heart, the simple exercise of faith, the self-denying service of love'.

Our response to God

228 All true worship is inspired by God. The place of worship is the place of dependence, the place of wonder and of power, the place of fellowship and of communion... Worship links us to God and implies faith in a God who is in some sense personal. Personality is the highest category we know and we cannot worship a Being who is less than the highest of which we can conceive... Thus the act of worship presupposes on our part a sense of dependence on God and the acknowledgment of our need of him, and this means that the element of adoration and thanksgiving should always be present in worship. Worship in Christian experience is our response to the God of Love. *Robert Davis, 1933*

229 In this humanistic age we suppose man is the initiator and God is the responder. But the living Christ within us is the initiator and we are the responders. God the Lover, the accuser, the revealer of light and darkness presses within us. 'Behold, I stand at the door and knock.' And all our apparent initiative is already a response, a testimonial to His secret presence and working within us. The basic response of the soul to the Light is internal adoration and joy, thanksgiving and worship, self-surrender and listening.

Thomas R. Kelly

230 Worship is essentially an act of adoration, adoration of the one true
God in whom we live and move and have our being. Forgetting our
little selves, our petty ambitions, our puny triumphs, our foolish
cares and fretful anxieties, we reach out towards the beauty and
majesty of God. The religious life is not a dull, grim drive towards
moral virtue, but a response to a vision of greatness...The pattern
prayer given by our Lord offers us the clue to right worship. It
begins and ends with words of adoration.   *Thomas F. Green (1952)*

231 Adoration leads naturally to the other responses which must always
be present in worship—confession, dedication, thanksgiving and
intercession...A clear awareness of failure and unworthiness must
always follow a vision of the highest, and it is a sure sign that our
worship has been a failure if we have not known afresh a deep need
of God's forgiveness... To reaffirm our loyalty, renew our vows,
and rededicate ourselves as instruments of his will is surely pleasing
to God.   *Thomas F. Green (1952)*

232 If worship is to be, as it must be, the core of our religion then it must
be concerned primarily with the divine Being whom we worship
and very much less with ourselves and our states of mind...This
should mean a more determined endeavour to render the character
of the divine Being clear and meaningful, to mind as well as heart,
and especially to consider more seriously, and as a challenging
problem for our religious experience to grapple with, the significance
of the life and death of Jesus Christ. And...we shall not be too
easily frightened back into a contented haziness of mind or negative-
ness of attitude by our traditional mistrust of formulating religious
beliefs.   *John W. Harvey (1947)*

233 In our life as a religious society we have found it true that the
spirit of man can come into direct contact with the Spirit of God,
and can thereby learn of God. A man who has experienced the
sense of contact with the Spirit will not only wish to listen for himself
to what God may say, and in the secret of his own soul speak with
God, but he will become conscious that fellowship with other

human beings, especially if they be seekers like himself, will strengthen and deepen the sense of communion. The way of worship through silent communion, in which there is freedom for spoken prayer or ministry, springs from the fundamental experience of the Society of Friends, and is a constant expression and working out of its central principle. *Berks & Oxon Q.M., 1919*

Corporate worship

234 In common with our fellow Christians we realise the need for a deep individual devotion finding expression in life and action. We believe that the power for its exercise is most fully given through the faithful practice of a corporate devotional life under the immediate guidance of the Spirit. In a meeting for worship Friends gather in silence as a congregation of seeking souls, and as they unite together in worship there comes a spiritual harmony, 'the still life, in which the fellowship is attained to in the spirit of God, when there are no words spoken'. But often, out of that silence, is born the message of that meeting, expressed it may be by several speakers and yet with a central thought common to each which frequently meets many individual needs. True worship may be experienced at any time; in any place—alone on the hills or in the busy daily life—we may turn to God, and find him, for in him we live and move and have our being. But this individual experience is not sufficient, and in a meeting held under the influence of the Spirit there is a giving and receiving between its members, one helping another with or without words. So there may come a wider vision and a deeper experience. *1925*

235 The gathered group depends utterly upon the Spirit of God for direction and leadership, and meets in the faith that that Spirit is available and can be known to all. He may be known in that 'sound of gentle stillness' in which the ancient Hebrew prophet found him; in private and personal pressures and restraints which are significant for the individual worshipper and known to him alone; in vocal ministry which is initiated by the Spirit of God in the midst; in the

spoken prayer, sometimes haltingly uttered and perhaps offered in deep misgiving, yet in the belief that he to whom the prayer is addressed has prompted it. In all the rhythm of our worship we seek to be guided by and sensitive to the movement of God's Spirit in our own hearts within the gathered community...It would, however, be a great mistake were it to be assumed that only in the spoken word is God's message given to the worshipper. In the silence the faithful listener may catch the accents of a Voice within and become vividly aware of a demand which has absolute authority, a demand to which he must be obedient or betray something deep within him—which has, for him, become the voice of God himself.

Edgar G. Dunstan (1956)

236 With diligence meet together, and with diligence wait to feel the Lord God to arise, to scatter and expel all that which is the cause of leanness and barrenness upon any soul; for it is the Lord must do it, and he will be waited upon in sincerity and fervency of spirit; ...and let none be hasty to utter words, though manifest in the light in which ye wait upon the Lord; but still wait in silence, to know the power working in you to bring forth the words, in the ministration of the eternal word of life to answer the life in all.

Stephen Crisp, 1663

237 The living power of a meeting for worship depends not only on the sincere dedication of heart and thought on the part of each individual member, but also on united communion in the presence of God wherein each one overpasses the bounds of his individual self and knows a union of spirit with spirit, bringing him into a larger life than that which is known in spiritual separateness...We cannot come to a true understanding of life's purpose apart from knowledge of one another in the deepest place of our being. This was the thought of George Fox as he gave counsel: 'Friends, meet together and know one another in that which is eternal, which was before the world was'. Out of such fellowship there will arise a sense of a common purpose in life, and the united worship will be deepened and enriched by the consciousness that in varied fashion all are ministering in the service of God.

1925

238 It might be assumed that the ideal meeting for worship would consist entirely of Christian disciples who were all 'of one accord' in the deep desire to present themselves to God and to help one another in the spiritual life. And yet it is clear that normally it cannot be so—and, indeed, *ought* not to be so—as long as sin and earthliness remain in the world. The true meeting for worship will be gathering in, Sunday by Sunday, many sorts of human souls, not all of whom are yet in the experience of deep communion with God. *Edward Grubb (1917)*

239 The mind wanders and the will falters again and again. Even the great masters of the religious life have confessed they were always liable to be invaded by the most frivolous thoughts during their meditations. But it is foolish to allow failures in concentration to plunge us into profitless self-condemnation. A mother does not condemn her child who is struggling with many a failure to learn how to walk, but rather is she pleased by each successful effort. Man is at the corresponding stage in his spiritual development, and I like to believe that God is similarly pleased with our efforts and understanding of our many failures. What matters is whether or not the will, like a compass needle when deflected, is so pivoted that it can swing back to the true direction. St Francis de Sales is reassuring:

> 'When your heart is wandering and distracted, bring it back quickly to its point, restore it tenderly to its Master's side, and if you did nothing else the whole of your hour but bring back your heart patiently and put it near our Lord again, and every time you put it back it turned away again, your hour would be well employed.' *Thomas F. Green (1952)*

240 In our meetings for worship our attitude of mind will not always be the same. There will be times of seeking to know the Light of Christ guiding our course amid tangled ways of action or thought, times of sorrow for failure and of search for strength to overcome temptation known to be before us, or to come into a right mind toward those who have hurt us; times also when the active part is less forward and in the silence we lie open to what God, the Lord, shall speak, the eternal word, the heavenly vision setting before us 'things invisible to mortal sight'. And all this will be coloured or transfused by the sense, subconscious or explicit, of others met with us seeking, failing, finding, even as we, and sometimes a great love glows within us, a mightiness of longing for a coming near to one another for the help of us all. There will be with us some who are bewildered seekers, some who are finders and ever finding more of the things of God, some for whom the outward life is going well, but most of the company battered by the week's labour, people in anxiety, finding it hard to prevent the cares of the world choking the good seed, women with the care of home and family, young ones with examinations upon them, business men closely pressed; there will be lonely people longing for friendship and those on whom the storm of temptation is beating sore, some giving way and some coming over it, people who feel themselves to have been badly treated and finding it hard to forgive, some who are knowing success in their work as builders of the holy city and some disheartened at the steepness of the way—everyone, however placed, in need of renewed strength. The realisation of this will bring the worshippers into community of spirit as children in the house of their Father, drawing strength from him and sharing with one another, knowing bitterness of soul to give way to his peace.

A. Neave Brayshaw (1926)

Silent waiting

241 In silence, without rite or symbol, we have known the Spirit of Christ so convincingly present in our quiet meetings that his grace dispels our faithlessness, our unwillingness, our fears, and sets our hearts aflame with the joy of adoration. We have thus felt the power of the Spirit renewing and recreating our love and friendship for all our fellows. This is our Eucharist and our Communion.

Yearly Meeting, 1928

242 We highly prize silent waiting upon the Lord in humble dependence upon him. We esteem it to be a precious part of spiritual

worship, and trust that no vocal offering will ever exclude it from its true place in our religious meetings. Let not the silence... be spent in indolent or vacant musing but in patient waiting in humble prayerful expectancy before the Lord.

Yearly Meeting, 1884, 1886

243 The *silence* of a religious and spiritual worship is not a drowsy unthinking state of the mind, but a sequestring or with-drawing of it from all visible objects and vain imaginations, unto a fervent praying to, or praising the Invisible Omnipresent God, in his Light and Love; his Light gives wisdom and knowledge, and his Love gives power and strength, to run the ways of his commandments with delight. But except all excesses of the body and passions of the mind are avoided (through watchfulness) the *Soul* doth not attain *True Silence*.

He that lets his mind be ungoverned out of meeting, cannot set it so right as it should be, when he comes into one; and such as get not forward in their spiritual journey when in meeting, it's certain they will go backwards, when out of them. *John Bellers (1718, 1703)*

244 ⟨The early Friends⟩ made the discovery that silence is one of the best preparations for communion ⟨with God⟩ and for the reception of inspiration and guidance. Silence itself, of course, has no magic. It may be just sheer emptiness, absence of words or noise or music. It may be an occasion for slumber, or it may be a dead form. But it may be an intensified pause, a vitalised hush, a creative quiet, an actual moment of mutual and reciprocal correspondence with God. The actual meeting of man with God and God with man is the very crown and culmination of what we can do with our human life here on earth. *Rufus M. Jones, 1937*

245 Really powerful hours of unbroken silence frequently carry a genuine progression of spiritual change and experience. They are *filled* moments, and the quality of the second fifteen minutes is definitely different from the quality of the first fifteen minutes.

Outwardly all silences seem alike, as all minutes are alike by the clock. But inwardly the Divine Leader of worship directs us through progressive unfoldings of ministration, and may in the silence bring an inward climax which is as definite as the climax of the Mass when the host is elevated in adoration... ⟨Words⟩ should not break the silence, but continue it. For the Divine Life who was ministering through the medium of silence is the same Life as is now ministering through words. And when such words are truly spoken 'in the Life', then when such words cease the *uninterrupted* silence and worship continue, for silence and words have been of one texture, one piece.

Thomas R. Kelly, 1940

The gathered meeting

246 A Friends' meeting, however silent, is at the very lowest a witness that worship is something other and deeper than words, and that it is to the unseen and eternal things that we desire to give the first place in our lives. And when the meeting, whether silent or not, is awake, and looking upwards, there is much more in it than this. In the united stillness of a truly 'gathered' meeting there is a power known only by experience, and mysterious even when most familiar. There are perhaps few things which more readily flow 'from vessel to vessel' than quietness. The presence of fellow-worshippers in some gently penetrating manner reveals to the spirit something of the nearness of the Divine Presence. 'Where two or three are gathered together in His name' have we not again and again felt that the promise was fulfilled and that the Master Himself was indeed 'in the midst of us'? And it is out of the depths of this stillness that there do arise at times spoken words which, springing from the very source of prayer, have something of the power of prayer—something of its quickening and melting and purifying effect. Such words as these have at least as much power as silence to gather into stillness.

Caroline E. Stephen (1908)

247 True worship is intensely active. It consists in offering ourselves to God—body, mind, and soul—for the doing of his will. We have

a gift to bring to him and not only a grace to receive... May we come into the presence of Christ as disciples—in earnest devotedness and lowly teachableness—and into the presence of one another as brethren—in a living fellowship of love and sympathy. 'One is your Teacher and all ye are brethren.'   *'Worship & ministry', 1899*

248 In our experience there is unique value in the meeting for worship held in life and power. The basis of such a meeting is the presence in our midst of him whom we recognise as love and truth, discovered in the silent waiting, drawing us to himself and to one another, opening mind and heart to fresh visions both of the world and of himself, giving us guidance and power for everyday life. This is a very wonderful thing. In many of our meetings such experiences are not uncommon. In others they may be rare. Perhaps we do not wait long enough in living silence that the life of God may stir our hearts as the sap presses up to open the buds in spring. Perhaps, preoccupied with our own concerns, we think too little of other worshippers, lacking that spiritual sensitiveness which is itself so rich a gift of the Spirit.   *Yearly Meeting, 1929*

249 In the gathered meeting the sense is present that a new Life and Power has entered our midst... We are in communication with one another because we are being communicated to, and through, by the Divine Presence... We may not issue from a gathered meeting with a single crisp sentence or judgment of capsuled knowledge, yet we are infinitely more certain of the dynamic, living, working Life, for we have experienced a touch of that persuading Power that disquiets us until we find our home in Him... When one rises to speak in such a meeting one has a sense of *being used*, of being played upon, of being spoken through. It is as amazing an experience as that of being *prayed through*, when we the praying ones are no longer the initiators of the supplication, but seem to be transmitters, who second an impulse welling up from the depths of the soul. In such an experience the brittle bounds of our selfhood seem softened, and instead of saying 'I pray' or 'He prays' it becomes better to say 'Prayer is taking place'.   *Thomas R. Kelly, 1940*

250 One of the paradoxes of the spiritual life is that those who have suffered most are among those who are most certain of 'an infinite ocean of light and love flowing over the ocean of darkness and death'... It is one of our Christian mysteries that we can share the sorrows of the world and at the same time be certain of the love of God. A grateful heart is one of the fruits of the spirit, and thanksgiving will always be a dominant theme in Christian worship.

Thomas F. Green (1952)

251 Sometimes...the prayer following meditation leads to an inner silence, a stillness in the depths, which is the peace of God, passing all understanding. It cannot be commanded at will for it is the gift of God, a blessing which he gives only to those who can cease from anxious striving and desiring. Some of us, alas, have known it only on a few occasions, but these are our richest memories, the real grounds for our faith in the reality of the realm of spirit... We should always go to meeting expecting this tremendous thing to happen, but never be discouraged if it does not. *Thomas F. Green (1952)*

252 Our meetings for worship...are at the very centre of our life. We need to banish from them the spirit of criticism, the lazy indifference, and the self-centred thinking, which too often mar their harmony and power. Do we come to our meetings as prepared men and women? Do we give of our best, of that which costs us something? Whether in speech or in silence, are we helpers one of another? It is here that we should find strength for the discharge of our individual and our corporate duty to the world. The stillness in which every soul is turned to God may bring us together into new regions of experience such as we could not hope to explore as isolated units.

Yearly Meeting, 1912

Personal experiences of meetings for worship are narrated by Thomas Ellwood (§35), Robert Barclay (§41), Thomas Story (§44), Samuel Bownas (§45), Daniel Wheeler (§56), Stephen Grellet (§58), John G. Whittier (§71), Caroline E. Stephen (§80).

253 Friends ought to put the meeting for worship and its service in the forefront of their lives, for it stands as a public testimony to the two great essentials of their experience—the assurance that all men who seek God in their hearts can find Him, and the knowledge that both as individuals and as groups those who ask and accept His guidance are led of Him. The meeting for worship is the centre of the corporate life of the Society, and its health is a condition of our usefulness. It is also a possible channel of much blessing to many outside our membership. *1925*

Further reference to the place of the meeting for worship in publishing truth will be found in §387.

254 *In 1675, during a time of great persecution, a 'solemn general meeting of many faithful friends and brethren', issued the following advice:*
It hath been our care and practice from the beginning that an open testimony for the Lord should be borne and a publick standard for truth and righteousness upheld in the power and Spirit of God by our open and knowne meetings, ... so it is our advice and judgment that all Friends gathered in the name of Jesus keep up these publick testimonies in their respective places, and not decline forsake or remove their publick assemblies, because of times of sufferings as worldly, fearful and politique professors have done because of informers and the like persecutors; for such practices are not consistent with the nobility of the truth and therefore not to be owned in the Church of Christ.

255 'Where two or three', saith our Lord, 'are gathered together in my name, there am I in the midst of them' (Matt. 18. 20). In these words he...invites us not only to meet one with another but, in so doing, with himself also...Shall the poor perishing gratifications of sense and self-love, or any inconveniences of a trivial nature, be suffered to prevent our dutiful attendance upon him, in whom alone stands our everlasting interest? Shall a cloudy sky, a little wet,

a little cold, a little ease to the flesh, a view to a little earthly gain, or any common incident, furnish an excuse for declining this duty, and thereby depriving ourselves of the blessed advantage, often vouchsafed to the faithful, of enjoying heavenly communion together in spirit with the Lord of life and glory?

Yearly Meeting, 1765

256 There are times of dryness in our individual lives, when meeting may seem difficult or even worthless. At such times one may be tempted not to go to meeting, but it may be better to go, prepared to offer as our contribution to the worship simply a sense of need. In such a meeting one may not at the time realise what one has gained, but one will nevertheless come away helped.

Berks & Oxon Q.M. Ministry & Extension Committee, 1948

257 None of us can afford to miss opportunities of gaining power and inspiration for daily life, that we may 'take the common things of life and walk truly among them'. Earnest labour for the good of others, however necessary and beneficent, is no substitute for the times of refreshing when we may gain the vision, the faith, the insight and the love, without which our efforts to raise and help the lives of men will be largely vain. If the more active and thoughtful members of a meeting allow themselves to be drawn away from its service, they leave the main responsibility for vocal ministry to be borne by others who may be less in touch with the needs of the time, and the meetings in consequence will almost certainly fail in power and grip.   *1911*

258 It is the individual faithfulness of each Friend which is needed if our meetings for worship are to be held to the glory of God. Each one of us must come expecting not only to receive but to be used. This involves a preparation of spirit, but many interpret the phrase 'Come with heart and mind prepared' too narrowly. The preparation needed is the living of our daily lives in constant awareness of the presence of God. In the rush of living we may miss the true Life. We must face realities, however, and try to overcome the practical

difficulties which we do encounter. Our lives are sometimes inevitably rushed. This means that we may come to meetings for worship in turmoil or trouble. We may be tired, irritable or sleepy. We should not in such cases turn away from the meeting for worship, but should realise the value of such occasions as training times.

Important though our part of preparation, dedication and faithfulness is, we have always to remember that *our* part is dependent upon that Power which comes to us, unlooked-for and undeserved, the power of the grace of God.

Berks & Oxon Q.M. Ministry & Extension Committee, 1948

259 Regular attendance at your own meeting, leading to a deeper knowledge of the members and their needs, will contribute to the quality of its corporate life. We both recognize and encourage concerned visitation of other meetings and opportunities of worship with those of other communions, but continued casual or undisciplined attendance sometimes at one place of worship and sometimes at another is a source of weakness alike to the individual and to his meeting. *1959*

260 A punctual attendance at the hour appointed is...a matter of no small importance. If we hurry away from our outward occupations to the meeting house, thinking that, by the delay of a few minutes, we shall not be long behind our brethren, we are in great danger of having our thoughts employed on that in which we have been engaged, and of interrupting that holy silence which... would often prevail, if all the members of a meeting were assembled not only in one place, but at one time, with one and the same great object in view. *Yearly Meeting, 1821*

Promoting the spirit of worship

261 We earnestly advise all who attend our meetings to lift their hearts to God immediately on taking their seats. The avoidance of dis-

tracting conversation beforehand is a great help to this end, and the walk to meeting may often prove a true preparation for divine worship. *1911*

262 *Alexander Parker wrote to Friends in 1660:* The first that enters into the place of your meeting...turn in thy mind to the light, and wait upon God singly, as if none were present but the Lord; and here thou art strong. Then the next that comes in, let them in simplicity of heart sit down and turn in to the same light, and wait in the spirit; and so all the rest coming in, in the fear of the Lord, sit down in pure stillness and silence of all flesh, and wait in the light... Those who are brought to a pure still waiting upon God in the spirit, are come nearer to the Lord than words are; for God is a spirit, and in the spirit is he worshipped...In such a meeting there will be an unwillingness to part asunder, being ready to say in yourselves, it is good to be here: and this is the end of all words and writings—to bring people to the eternal living Word.

263 In the Quaker discovery of an inward order, an inward discipline that would bear a worshipper into the heart of the silent corporate waiting, much can be learned from a study of the nature of attention. For it is the focussing and refocussing of attention upon the Divine Listener that is the small part which the frail worshipper can perform and which he must perform if this form of service is to be fruitful for him. The presence of a group of earnest worshippers is of itself a great encouragement to him. But it is not enough. He must do more than bring his body to the place where others have also gathered. He must learn the art of voluntary attention, either as a child brought up in it until it becomes a natural thing to enter into the silence, or, if this training has not been adequate or is totally wanting, then he must learn it in adult life.

Douglas V. Steere (1955)

264 The meeting for worship raises to the highest plane the relationship of the individual to the group. Since in meeting together for worship we seek as a group to worship God—for this is the essential difference between corporate worship and private devotion—this fact must be consciously or unconsciously present to all taking part, and it would seem a good plan that in the early part of a meeting it should be consciously present and that each should lift up the group to God in prayer.   *W. Russell Brain (1944)*

265   *The following story is attributed to Rebecca Jones, speaking in the Yearly Meeting of Philadelphia in 1792:* A Friend of Philadelphia, who was by profession a tanner, once dreamed that he was sitting in a religious meeting, wherein he was surprised to observe the congregation with tables before them, at which they were pursuing their usual avocations. The merchant had his books there, the retailer his goods, the mechanic his tools. Indignant at such employment, among those professedly assembled for the awful and soul-important purpose of divine worship, he was about rising to reprove them sharply when, incidentally placing his hands behind him, he found a bundle of calfskin suspended from his own shoulders! How much easier is it to discover the errors of others than our own, and how often we richly deserve the very condemnation we mete out to our neighbours.

266   All of you have godly care of judging or contradicting one another in public meetings, or showing any marks or signs of division therein, among ministers or others; that being of very pernicious consequence, to bring blame or contempt upon the ministry, and a great hurt to our youth and others.   *Yearly Meeting, 1716*

Visits to neighbouring meetings;   Small meetings

267   We should take an interest not merely in our own particular meetings, but also in other adjacent meetings, especially if they are few in numbers or otherwise in need. The visitation of another meeting in the spirit of Christian fellowship is an act of service, even if unaccompanied by any words of spoken ministry. When carried out under right concern it may bring encouragement and refreshment both to those who visit and those who are visited.   *1925*

268 We desire, dear friends, that such of you as often meet in small companies for the solemn purpose of worship, may not relax in your diligence. Your situation will at times appear discouraging; but although you may be seldom assisted by the company and travail of your brethren, never forget that you are under the continued notice of the Lord; and that his tender regard extends to all those who wait upon Him in reverence and humility...If with faithfulness and integrity you perform your Christian duties, your example will prevail with others who have been too negligent of the concerns of a future life; and by your consistent conduct, the truth which we profess will be exalted—the name of the Lord glorified.

Yearly Meeting, 1813

269 We urge Friends, when staying from home during holiday or on business, to attend a meeting for worship if there is one within reach. Such attendance may well have the effect of strengthening the meeting, and of bringing Friends who were hitherto strangers into fellowship with one another.   *1925*

Place of residence and attendance at meeting

270 The importance, both for ourselves and for our children, of active association with our fellow members in work and worship has led our Society in the past strongly to encourage Friends to live near meetings. We ⟨urge⟩ Friends in fixing their places of residence to bear this in mind. But we are aware that there are many whose duties oblige them to reside where there is no meeting. We do not desire in any way to discourage these from associating in worship with members of other religious denominations. It is our concern that Friends thus situated should ⟨consider holding⟩ meetings of a simple spiritual character with their neighbours, either on first-day or during the week. The world needs this message, and it is one for which many souls are hungering. Where a meeting on first-day may not seem a wise arrangement a quiet hour of worship with neighbours of other religious denominations on a weekday may be found mutually helpful, and may serve to draw away from too great a dependence on the outward in religion.

Sometimes opportunities may be found in simple informal gatherings in private houses for brief times of quiet worship and communion, springing up after the consideration of some subject of vital interest, and in such reunions neighbours and friends may take part who would be unlikely to go with us to one of our regular places of worship. There should be no cause for discouragement if such meetings be very small. Let us seek and find opportunities of true fellowship in worship with others, which may be of help to those who are standing for a free spiritual worship, or those who are out of touch with any form of organised Christianity.

Yearly Meeting, 1905

Meetings on special occasions

Mid-week meetings

271 The need for finding other opportunities for united devotion beyond those held on first-day should be kept before us. Experience shows that there is an individual and a corporate gain. Some who are burdened with work and pressing engagements can speak with thankfulness of the rest and refreshment they have found in the attendance of mid-week meetings. We should realise the importance of finding occasion for worship during the week, whether in our meeting houses, in other public halls or in private houses. *1925*

Weddings

272 In meetings held for the solemnisation of marriage a true spirit of worship is required, so that the sacramental character of the marriage tie may be realised when thus entered upon in the fear of the Lord. Assembled as a waiting company of worshippers, those who gather on such an occasion are witnesses of a solemn covenant made in the presence of the Lord. A meeting held in life and power may be rich in blessing for those for whose union it is called. The commencement of their united life in the company of loving and prayerful friends, who thus join with them in this solemn act of

worship, may be the prelude to a united life of continued dependence upon Him before whom their marriage vow has been taken.

1911, 1925

Funerals

273 Friends should not adopt any rigid pattern for the conduct of funerals. In some cases it is best to hold, separately from the committal or cremation, a 'meeting for worship on the occasion of the death of our Friend', at a week-end, when Friends are free to attend and there is time for the spirit of quiet trust and dependence on God to overcome natural grief. In other cases the brief meeting for worship at the crematorium is all that is either possible or desired... If Friends really believe that all meetings of every kind are meetings for worship in which the presence of Christ is with them and that they are in unity with the living and the dead, they will not experience difficulties or find the occasion of a funeral imposing a pattern of unbalanced eulogy of the deceased. Arising from a gathered meeting, messages of a general character, even from those who have not known the deceased, will enrich the worship of all who are there.

Berks & Oxon Q.M. Ministry & Extension Committee, 1951

274 A feeling of hesitation as to speaking at funerals is most natural, for great wisdom and tenderness are required. On the other hand, these gatherings give opportunities of a very special character, and we urge all on whom the gift of the vocal ministry has been bestowed to consider whether it may not be their duty and privilege to use it on these occasions, even if in some degree contrary to their convenience and inclination. There is also need for the presence of others, and ⟨their⟩ attendance in a loving and sympathetic spirit is a very real service.

Warwickshire North M.M. Ministry Committee, 1912

For further extracts on the solemnisation of marriage, see § *487-488; on the conduct of funerals, see* §*529.*

Chapter 5: Vocal ministry

A shared responsibility

275 Priesthood is the highest expression of man's social nature, by which he enters into communion with his fellows and with God. It is only because we narrow the use of the name of priest that we do not honour it aright, for in its essence priesthood is not a profession but a high duty to which all are called. If we were to try to define this true priesthood, might we not say that a priest is one who, reaching out after the higher and better than himself, helps others onward too, bringing to them something to which they could not of themselves have attained, who shares his good with his fellows and takes upon himself their ill, making communion possible for them, because he has entered into communion with them himself. But it is not easy thus to summarise in a sentence a work which is in truth as wide as human life; wherever a man interprets in the terms of his own day the unseen and enduring realities, and helps those about him to view things in their true relations, he is performing a priestly function; whenever he takes up their disadvantages as his own, in fellowship with suffering, and shares with others willingly the result of their own wrong-doing, then is he doing a part of the priest's divinest work.   *T. Edmund Harvey (1913)*

276 All true ministry of the Gospel is from the appointment of the Lord Jesus Christ; and it is He who, by His Spirit, prepares and qualifies for the work. The gift must be exercised in continued dependence upon Him; and blessed is that ministry in which man is humbled, and Christ and His grace exalted.   *Yearly Meeting, 1871*

277 *In 1949 the following Additional Advice on the Ministry was adopted by Yearly Meeting as it felt the need 'for a message of encouragement to those who are beginners or who have not yet taken part in the ministry':*
When we gather together in worship let us remember that there is committed to each of us, as disciples of Christ, a share in the priest-

hood. We should help one another, whether in silence or through spoken prayer or words of ministry. Let none of us assume that vocal ministry is never to be our part.

Our daily lives should be linked with the meeting for worship. Day by day we can dwell prayerfully on thoughts which may at some time lead to ministry. We should try to discern and to interpret the spiritual meaning of the movements of thought and action at work in the world around us, entering into understanding sympathy with our fellow worshippers.

If the call comes, there should be no quenching of the spirit; the sense of our own unworthiness must not exempt us from this service, nor the fear of being unable to find the right words.

Faithfulness in speaking, even very briefly, may open the way or fuller ministry from others. The tender and humble-minded utterance, given faithfully, can carry its message to the hearts of its hearers. Above all in vocal prayer even broken and imperfect words springing from a deep place in the heart may wonderfully draw those present into communion with God and with one another.

True ministry is rooted in prayer. If our prayer life is wide and deep it will lead each one to some form of ministry in the service of God which is also the service of man.

278 To admit freely that the precise words, the illustrations, the capacity to quote scripture, or the telling lines of some poem have been drawn from the worshipping minister's lifetime of preparation is in no sense to minimise the source of the insight which they are used to search and to communicate. George Fox was an assiduous student of the Bible and knew it almost by heart. The mighty works of God recorded in Scripture were always before him and this knowledge was always at the disposal of the inward insights that were given to him. Fox was also a man of prayer, a man who was 'energised in secret for life in the open world'. By being continually open to inward guidance, the exercise in the meeting for worship was a natural one for him and he came to it attentive and inwardly gathered. The practice of regular prayer and a continual intent to listen for the deeper meaning in everything that happens in life is an indispensable preparation for this type of ministry...

This in no sense suggests that formal education necessarily cultivates or prepares the spirit for ministry or that the humble spirit-tipped word of an utterly unlearned man or woman or child in a meeting may not minister to its deepest need, but it does propose that nothing is too good for God and that over the years there is no preparation of the mind and heart and will that God cannot use and use with power to further his ministry.

Douglas V. Steere (1955)

279 The whole fellowship of disciples without distinction of sex or of official position are called to be priests, and to each one may be given some work of ministry. Our common worship must give opportunities for this, and in our experience we have found that in waiting upon God in silence we have the freedom and opportunity for such ministry and also for a deep experience of communion.

T. Edmund Harvey, 1937

280 From its earliest days the Society of Friends has emphasised the importance to the Christian community of a living ministry, freely given in the service of God and man, a task calling for dedication of life and often for the sacrifice of other claims, because it involved not the pursuit of a profession, but obedience to a vocation. The call to the service of the ministry comes to very many. No one should put from him the thought that it may be his duty to take part in the ministry, even though it be but seldom. 'In the Light, everyone should have something to offer.'

To some the service of the ministry will come as a duty, to make way for which other valuable work must be set aside. It will involve the dedication of thought and leisure, the giving of the best that is in them, above all the preparation of meditation and of prayer, not only at the time of meetings for worship but throughout the week. If a Christian society is worthy of its name and is to achieve its task of proclaiming and serving the kingdom of God, it must be through a succession of lives touched and transformed by the spirit of Christ and dedicated to this service in His name. In the service of the kingdom the work of the ministry has an essential place.

1931

281 Let the hearers be watchful over their own spirits...for if they be not very careful and diligent in attending upon the Lord in meetings, they are liable to mistake in the judgment they may pass on the ministry. Now this being...a matter of great moment for the preservation of love and concord in the churches, and knowing the danger and ill consequences which attend a hasty and censorious judging of the ministry, we thought it very necessary to caution ...⟨Friends⟩ not to let their own spirits sway them, but let the Spirit of God rule and reign in the hearts of Friends, for that will preserve all in sweetness and tenderness one towards another.

Yearly Meeting, 1731

282 The meeting affects the ministry quite as truly as the ministry affects the meeting. If those who come together do so in expectant faith, and in genuine love and sympathy with one another, striving to put far from them thoughts of criticism and fault-finding, and praying earnestly that the right persons may be led to speak and the right messages be given, they will not go away unhelped. It is in such an atmosphere that the Holy Spirit can work effectively to bring forth the utterances that are needed, and to check those that are not required. On the other hand, the spirit of indifference or of cold and unfriendly criticism injures the whole life of the meeting, and we need not wonder if in such an atmosphere speakers mistake their guidance.

1911

283 When we are inclined to 'pass judgment on the ministry', or feel out of unity with what is said, let us ask ourselves whether the reason may not be that we are listening to a truth to which our own psychological make-up has made us blind and which therefore has a special value for us. By recognising this we may avoid the impulse

to criticise or correct others, our own vision will be enlarged and any contribution we may make will be of greater worth.

W. Russell Brain (1944)

284 How large the wisdom, how tender the sympathy, required to be exercised towards those who are called to bear a public testimony to their Lord, especially in the earlier stages of their ministry. On the other hand, ⟨they ought⟩...to be open to the counsel of their more experienced brethren and, whilst seeking to minister for their Lord and only in the ability which He giveth, to be ever subject to one another in love.

Yearly Meeting, 1868

285 All my dear friends in the noble seed of God, and who have known his power, life and presence amongst you, let it be your joy to hear or see the springs break forth in any, through which you have all unity in the same feeling, life and power.

George Fox, 1656

286 It should be the care of elders to foster the spiritual life of all members and to give caution and advice to Friends who share in the vocal ministry. They should look out for Friends who may be likely to help the ministry and lead them to make their right contribution to the life of their meeting, and to encourage our members to think deeply on the great issues and problems of life and the fundamentals of our faith.

This, however, is not the duty of elders alone; as any Friends may hinder the work of the ministry by a critical or unloving spirit, so their sympathy and prayers for those who may speak will help to create an atmosphere in which an inspired and inspiring ministry may grow. A friendly word of thankfulness from one who has been helped is often a great source of encouragement to the minister.

1925, 1959

The nature of eldership is considered in §341-345.

287 A Friends' meeting for worship finds no room for debate or for answering (still less for contradicting) one another; if this is desirable, it will be left for another occasion. And if anything should seem to be spoken amiss, the spiritually minded worshipper will have the wit to get at the heart of the message, overlooking crudity and lack of skill in its presentation, and so far from giving way to irritation at what seems unprofitable, he will be deeply concerned for his own share in creating the right spiritual atmosphere in which the harm fades out and the good grows. Many a meeting has known this power, transforming what might have been hurtful into a means of grace...The minister who, it is to be assumed, has wished to speak for the help of the congregation and not for the advertisement of himself, will be willing at least *to consider* the suggestions of those whose concern for the meeting's welfare is as deep as his own. The hard assertiveness which is determined to have its own word, resenting kindly counsel, even if such seems to be mistaken, is wholly out of place in a Friends' meeting, being alien to the spirit in which alone right ministry can be exercised. The true message, however plain spoken it be, will win its way, not by truculence and discourtesy but by persuasiveness and love.   *A. Neave Brayshaw (1921)*

Obedience to the call

288 When the call comes, there should be no 'quenching of the Spirit', no 'contempt for prophesyings', on the ground that the offering is small, but instead, a willing-hearted, humble-minded obedience. Faithful use of a gift brings increase; unfaithfulness leads to the withdrawal of the talent... entrusted to us not for neglect but for service...More important than the actual words used is the atmosphere the speaker brings with him, the evidence, which his hearers instinctively discern, that he is speaking of what he knows. The very fact that a member has seldom or never taken vocal part hitherto may give a special influence to his words...The Church wants the vigour and freshness of youth—its sympathy with those of like age, its lofty aspirations and its grasp of the needs and thoughts of the time—as well as the matured strength of manhood and womanhood and the ripe spiritual experience of old age.

'Worship & ministry', 1899

289 Older Friends in particular do well to realise that their continued silence ten years after ten years is making the service hard for the young. I am not, of course, suggesting that anyone should speak words merely in order to make it easy for someone else to do so and for no other reason. I am pointing out that the knowledge of the harm that we may be doing and of the help that we might be giving turns our faces in the direction of the work, giving us encouragement to it and power to come over the fear that would keep us back...

And to this end we shall know a spiritual alertness. We speak of the danger inherent in the resolve or arrangement to preach a sermon at a particular time in the future for a fixed length of time, and we may fail to understand that our freedom gives us no assurance of safety. There is no easy way in which we are spared the effort of watchfulness. The fact of our being under no engagement to speak, no one having the right to call us to account if we do not, may breed slackness. Easily may we say that we have had no call, and fail to consider whether we might not have heard one; the exploitation of Quaker principles in the way of repression has never been a difficult feat. We do well to remember that even if the preaching of certain 'paid' ministers is mechanical or superficial, there is many a one who, knowing that a sermon will be required of him, looks forward to it in the spirit of prayer and love for his congregation, of watchfulness over his lower self and of expectation of power, so that when the appointed time comes it is right for him to give his message. Our way of worship and conception of ministry give no excuse for our prayer and love, our watchfulness and expectation, being less than his.   *A. Neave Brayshaw (1926)*

290 Each Friend who feels called upon to rise and deliver a lengthy discourse might question himself—and herself—most searchingly, as to whether the message could not be more lastingly given in the fewest possible words, or even through his or her personality alone, in entire and trustful silence. 'Cream always must rise to the surface.' True. But other substances rise to the surface besides cream; substances that may have to be skimmed off and thrown away before bodies and souls can be duly nourished. 'Is my message cream or scum?' may be an unusual and is certainly a very homely query. Still it is one that every speaker, in a crowded gathering especially, should honestly face. Some of the dangers of silent worship can best be guarded against by its courtesies.

L. Violet Holdsworth (1919)

291 What it is that constitutes guidance in ministry, and the means by which it is to be sought and found, is a difficulty with many. Some are afraid to speak in a meeting for worship, because, though they know something of the love of Christ, they do not seem to have any experience of a call that is undeniably supernatural. Others may be too readily taking their own thoughts and feelings as a warrant for obtruding them on others. Our natures differ greatly, and it is not possible to lay down any precise rules that all can follow. To some it seems that God speaks, as it were, by the earthquake and the whirlwind; to others it is in a very still small voice. There are strong impulses which make the heart beat and body tremble; there are, on the other hand, faint whispers which we need to be on the alert to hear. Both may be equally the voice of the true Shepherd, calling us to follow His leading. What we can safely say is that His guiding hand and voice are not confined to meetings for worship, and that we need to recognise it along the common ways of life, and to find it through the right use of our natural faculties. If we are going our own way six days in the week it is presumptuous to expect that He will guide us miraculously on the seventh. 'My sheep hear my voice, and I know them, and they follow me.'

But while guidance must be sought and followed in all the affairs of life, not by the displacement or disuse of our natural faculties, but by their consecration to God's service, there is, we are convinced, a yet more intimate guidance to be known in our meetings for worship. True ministry is not simply the expression of views of truth or ideals of conduct. It arises out of personal communication with God in the atmosphere of fellowship with others, whether before or at the time of meeting with them. It should have in it a direct message adapted to their present spiritual needs. To find the right words for a gathered company, whether of vocal prayer or testimony, we need to wait for that sense of call that comes to us from God through the fellowship of hearts that are bound into harmony by the flowing through them of the tides of His living presence. Hence, whatever may have been on our minds beforehand—whatever thoughts we may have worked out under the sense of help from God—must be held loosely, with perfect willingness to refrain from uttering them if the right time has not come. In a large company, where there may be many speakers, it is of special importance that we should thus quietly wait for clear guidance.   *1911*

292   *The experience of John Fothergill, about 1697:*
I was often exceedingly distressed after meetings, under a thought that I had refused to answer the requiring of God...When the time came indeed, that I was to open my mouth in a few words for the Lord among his people it was so indisputably clear, that I had no scruple of its being certainly the holy requiring: and yet in fear I reason'd it away one meeting, to my deep sorrow. But the all-seeing One knew it was from an innocent fear...and therefore he graciously owned me again; And in another meeting shortly after, a fresh, strong motion, or concern, came upon me, and I broke forth in a few words, but scarcely durst I stand upon my feet: And after the meeting I got quietly away, with some ease and an holy peace of mind...It is only his fresh and renewed requiring, not only opening matter to speak, but engaging to speak it at this time, whereby the Church or particulars are edify'd, as our Father would have his children edify'd.

293   *The expereince of John Woolman, 1741:*
I went to meetings in an awful frame of mind, and endeavoured to be inwardly acquainted with the language of the true Shepherd, and one day, being under a strong exercise of spirit, I stood up, and said some words in a meeting, but not keeping close to the Divine opening, I said more than was required of me and being soon sensible of my error, I was afflicted in mind some weeks, without any light or comfort, even to that degree that I could take satisfaction in nothing. I remembered God and was troubled, and in the depth of my distress he had pity upon me, and sent the Comforter. I then felt forgiveness for my offence, and my mind

became calm and quiet, being truly thankful to my gracious Redeemer for his mercies. And after this, feeling the spring of divine love opened, and a concern to speak, I said a few words in meeting in which I found peace; this I believe was about six weeks from the first time, and as I was thus humbled and disciplined under the Cross, my understanding became more strengthened to distinguish the language of the pure spirit which inwardly moves upon the heart, and taught me to wait in silence sometimes many weeks together, until I felt that rise which prepares the creature to stand like a trumpet, through which the Lord speaks to his flock.

Further personal experiences are narrated by Sarah Lynes Grubb (§57), John William Graham (§85) and J. Rowntree Gillett (§98).

Content and purpose

294 The intent of all speaking is to bring into the life, and to walk in, and to possess the same, and to live in and enjoy it, and to feel God's presence. *George Fox (1657)*

295 There is no occasion at all, for those who regard ⟨Christ's⟩ power as the substance of their ministry, to be any wise solicitous about words; as the lowest and most simple are really beautiful, when fitly spoken under that holy influence. *John Griffith, 1734*

296 Endeavour to express yourselves audibly and distinctly, and guard against all tones and gestures inconsistent with Christian simplicity. Speak with reverence, as in the Master's presence. Beware of using unnecessary preambles and of making additions towards the conclusion of a meeting, when it was left well before.
Advices on ministry, 1928

297 There is a place for the ministry of interpretation and teaching which bears upon the intellectual as well as the moral and spiritual needs of the congregation, and there is the ministry of prayer—in some ways the most difficult and often the most helpful service of all. But however varied may be the individual needs in any company of worshippers there is common to all the need to hear the voice of the Lord, the prophetic word that comes with power from God to awaken the sense of sin, to heal the soul, to inspire with vision and hope, to challenge the complacent, to persuade the fearful, to convince the doubter—in a word, to win men and women for Jesus Christ.   *Robert Davis, 1933*

298 A living meeting is moulded not according to prescribed pattern, but by the Master's own hand. The right holding of our meetings is not to be judged by their adherence to routine, but by the exercise in them 'unto edifying', and under the control of the Holy Spirit, of spiritual gifts. Varied gifts thus exercised will be kept in their true harmony and proportion, and the variety will enrich without enfeebling the life of the congregation. There is especially a place today for the gift of religious teaching, which may greatly promote that comprehensive grasp of truth and that enlightened knowledge of the Holy Scriptures which the Church is responsible to God for giving to its members.   *'Worship & ministry', 1899*

Prayer and thanksgiving

299 Those who meet together for public worship should come in the spirit of prayer. As this is the case, we believe that the vocal utterance of thanksgiving and prayer will more often find a place early in our meetings. Let all yield to the gentle promptings of the Holy Spirit as He constrains them, it may be very simply, to acknowledge, in the midst of their brethren, the mercy and faithfulness of the Lord, and to seek His renewed blessing.   *Yearly Meeting, 1898*

300 Prayer offered in the right spirit...is a great power and has a wonderfully unifying and quickening effect. The times of silent waiting in our meetings for worship are not intended only for the refreshment of the individual worshipper. If the silence be a living one, in which the worshippers seek to enter into each other's needs and to bear in their hearts the sufferings of the world without and the call to dedication in the service of the kingdom of God, silent prayer may naturally lead also to vocal prayer. The expression of prayer will not be of the nature of an address to the congregation, neither exhortation nor exposition of doctrine. If it is offered simply and humbly in fellowship with others and as a heart-felt cry of man's spirit to his Heavenly Helper, it is of the utmost value in building up our common religious life. If we meet as members of one family in the presence of our Father, we should not shrink unduly from this offering of love. Sometimes broken words and thoughts may be made sacramental to ourselves and others and lead on to a deeper experience of worship, or open the way to some helpful and inspiring communication from a fellow-worshipper which might not otherwise have found utterance. It was to encourage such simple ministry that William Dewsbury from his prison in 'York Tower' in 1660 wrote the words, 'And thou, faithful babe, though thou stutter and stammer forth a few words in the dread of the Lord, they are accepted'. *1925*

301 Public prayer, thanksgiving and praise ought ever to spring from a living sense of the wants and condition of the congregation. In this solemn service may all be impressed with the importance of their words being few and full. *Yearly Meeting, 1868*

302 Even though the words of vocal prayer may sometimes barely be audible, the whole meeting may enter into its spirit, simply and humbly, in thanksgiving, adoration, intercession, petition or dedication. *1959*

William Penn's description of George Fox at prayer will be found in §13.

Chapter 6: Retirement and prayer

'Do you make a place in your daily life for inward retirement and waiting upon God, that you may learn the full meaning of prayer and the joy of communion with him? And do you live in daily dependence upon his help and guidance?' Query 8, 1928

303 Be still and cool in thy own mind and spirit from thy own thoughts, and then thou wilt feel the principle of God to turn thy mind to the Lord God, whereby thou wilt receive his strength and power from whence life comes, to allay all tempests, against blusterings and storms. That is it which moulds up into patience, into innocency, into soberness, into stillness, into stayedness, into quietness, up to God, with his power. *George Fox, 1658*

304 Prayer is an exercise of the spirit, as thought is of the mind. To pray about anything is to use the powers of our spirit on it, just as to think clearly is to use our mental powers. For the best solution of every problem, the best carrying out of every action, both thought and prayer are necessary...To pray about any day's work does not mean to ask for success in it. It means, first, to realise my own inability to do even a familiar job, as it truly should be done, unless I am in touch with eternity, unless I do it 'unto God', unless I have the Father with me. It means to see 'my' work as part of a whole, to see 'myself' as not mattering much, but my faith, the energy, will and striving, which I put into the work, as mattering a great deal. My faith is the point in me at which God comes into my work; through faith the work is given dignity and value. And if, through some weakness of mine, or fault of others, or just 'unavoidable circumstances', the work seems a failure, yet prayer is not wasted when it is unanswered, any more than love is wasted when it is unreturned. *Mary F. Smith, 1936*

305 How, then, shall we lay hold of that Life and Power, and live the life of prayer without ceasing? By quiet, persistent practice in turning of all our being, day and night, in prayer and inward

worship and surrender, toward Him who calls in the deeps of our souls. Mental habits of inward orientation must be established. An inner, secret turning to God can be made fairly steady, after weeks and months and years of practice and lapses and failures and returns. It is as simple an art as Brother Lawrence found it, but it may be long before we achieve any steadiness in the process. Begin now, as you read these words, as you sit in your chair, to offer your whole selves, utterly and in joyful abandon, in quiet, glad surrender to Him who is within. In secret ejaculations of praise, turn in humble wonder to the Light, faint though it may be. Keep contact with the outer world of sense and meanings. Here is no discipline in absent-mindedness. Walk and talk and work and laugh with your friends. But behind the scenes keep up the life of simple prayer and inward worship. Keep it up throughout the day. Let inward prayer be your last act before you fall asleep and the first act when you awake. And in time you will find, as did Brother Lawrence, that 'those who have the gale of the Holy Spirit go forward even in sleep.'   *Thomas R. Kelly*

306 The pearl of great price is for him who is prepared to sell all that he has that he may possess it. Furthermore our prayer to be effective must be in accordance with the mind of God; which means, I think, that our request should be rather that we may be perfectly con- formed in all things to His will and character than that we may receive the spiritual luxury of a vivid emotional experience... To the non-mystic, to whom prayer is the most difficult of life's duties because it elicits no sensible response from Him to whom he prays, we may say that the prayer which he thinks of as a spontaneous appeal on his own part to a God who for some unknown reason has covered himself with a cloud so that no prayer can pass through, is in fact always his own response to *God's* prompting...

God is always beforehand with us; and the impulse to pray, the necessity that is laid upon us to persist in apparently unavailing petition, is in itself a certain indication that God is not afar but is living and active in our life. In the well known words of Pascal, 'Thou wouldst not seek God if thou hadst not already found Him', or perhaps more accurately, if He had not already found thee.

William Littleboy (1916)

307 Consider now the prayer-life of Jesus. It comes out most clearly in the record of St Luke, who leaves us with the impression that prayer was the most vital element in our Lord's life. He rises a great while before day that he may have some hours alone with His Father. He continues all night in prayer to God. Incident after incident is introduced by the statement that Jesus was praying. Are we so much nearer God that we can afford to dispense with that which to Him was of such vital moment? But apart from this, it seems to me that this prayer-habit of Jesus throws light upon the *purpose* of prayer.

I think of those long hours alone with God. Quite obviously *petition* can have had a very small place in our Lord's thought. We cannot suppose that He whose chief desire was that God's will should be done in all things could have been incessantly asking, asking. There must have been a sacred interchange far deeper than this. Especially are we sure that He was not praying for material blessings to be enjoyed by Himself alone. On the only occasion recorded in which He asked (in perfect submission) something for Himself, at Gethsemane, His request was not granted.

My own belief is that outward circumstances are not often (I will not say *never*) directly altered as the result of prayer. That is to say, God is not always interfering with the working of the natural order. But indirectly by the working of mind upon mind great changes may be wrought. We live and move and have our being in God; we are bound up in the bundle of life in Him, and it is reasonable to believe that prayer may often find its answer, even in outward things, by the reaction of mind upon mind. Prayer is not given us to make life easy for us, or to coddle us, but to make us strong,... to make us masters of circumstance and not its slaves. We pray, not to change God's will, but to bring our wills into correspondence with His. *William Littleboy*

308 If the Master felt the need of prayer and made special opportunities for it before occasions of great strain or difficulty, must not the disciple try to follow His example? When we have before us a difficult decision to make or a hard task to do, we must prepare

ourselves by prayer. Some difficulties will come unforeseen, and sometimes we must suddenly make a decision of great importance. The practice of prayer will make all the difference to the way in which we meet the emergency, and will make easier that instantaneous act of prayer by which, without any word spoken by the lips or even in the mind, we seek the strengthening help of God in our moment of need. What matters to us at such moments is the realisation of the presence of God. At the heart of all prayer is the realisation of God's presence, and this is the crown of fellowship, the light which shines in the purest joy, and that may be felt, even though it be not seen, in the deep night of sorrow.

T. Edmund Harvey (1929)

309 Against the rush of modern life... we must make time for the silent grace of recollection before a meal, for the common daily worship of the family, and for regularity and depth in our private devotions. As A. Neave Brayshaw...used to remind us, we have as much time as there is, and we spend much of it letting ourselves down lightly. When we say we haven't time we merely mean that we choose to do other things instead. Above all we need to learn more about the practice of prayer, whether by way of petition, intercession or adoration, cheerfully accepting whatever psychological study has to tell us about its mechanism, but having no doubt about its end... If, as we believe, prayer is an opening of the whole of our life to the spirit of God, it is natural that we should bring before Him our needs, that before Him we should hold our friends in mind, and that at the end, we should say, Holy, Holy, Holy.

R. Duncan Fairn (1951)

310 The true warrant for prayer is the sense of need. The blessing is still for the poor, for the mourners, for them that hunger and thirst after righteousness. Let none allow the rush of engagements or the hurry of business to crowd their opportunities for private retirement and waiting upon God. The more our engagements multiply, the greater is the call to watch unto prayer. He who is a stranger to prayer enters upon them in his own strength, and finds, to his unspeakable loss, that a life without prayer is a life practically without God.

Yearly Meeting, 1888, 1877

311 There is no use trying to conceal how difficult it is to find time for private prayer in the congested schedules under which most modern people live. But at the bottom it is not a question of finding time ... ⟨but⟩ of the depth of the sense of need and of the desire. Busy lovers find time to write letters to one another, often... long letters; although what really matters is not the length of the letter any more than it is the length of the prayer. In this life we find the time for what we believe to be important. God never asks of men what is impossible. *Douglas V. Steere (1938)*

312 To many there are difficulties in prayer; how can we influence God? Ought we to try to do so? How can we pray aright? What are we to think when our prayers go apparently unanswered? No solution ot these problems can here be attempted. We would only say that the testimony of multitudes who have persisted in prayer is that it is the most real fact of experience and that whether or no it receives its answer in the sense of gaining the immediately desired object, it always ultimately attains the far fuller end of knowledge of God and increase of His power to life. To those therefore who feel these difficulties we would say, do not wait till you have solved them but pray.

No living creature can create energy; the physical energy which we derive from our food comes from the sun's light and heat. So also we cannot create spiritual power; we can only draw on the springs which flow from God. Prayer is the attitude of mind in which we may get into contact with God and renew our strength. In it our desires are brought before God with an open mind to try to understand His will. This attitude involves a complete surrender on our part.

We would encourage Friends, therefore, reverently yet daringly to make fuller experiment of the life of trust and consecration through prayer, that they may know relief from the burden of anxiety and perplexity and realise the joy of health and victory, whereby they may become centres of radiant energy for the help and healing of others. *1925*

6: Retirement and prayer

For further extracts on prayer in relation to health and sickness, see §338, 339, 470-477.

313 Do not let us be discouraged because we find the path of silent prayer difficult or because we do not experience that joy of conscious communion which is given to some. The sunlight shines through the cloud; even when the cloud is so thick that we cannot see the sun at all, its rays carry on their healing work, and it does us good to go out into the open, even on a grey day. The experience of many of the greatest saint spoints to the traversing of a dark night of the soul before the light of full communion dawns, and to times of dryness of spirit coming at intervals to test the faith and perseverance of the seeker. *T. Edmund Harvey (1929)*

314 In intercession we share with ⟨God⟩ our deepest desires for others... We need constantly to remind ourselves that we can have no right desire for others in which God has not forestalled us. It was His desire before it was ours...All intercession is a self-offering, a self-giving, a longing that what we ask for others may be done, if need be, through ourselves. *Edgar G. Dunstan, 1946*

315 The place of prayer is a precious habitation; I saw this habitation to be safe, to be inwardly quiet, when there was great stirrings and commotions in the world. *John Woolman, 1770*

316 Prayer, then, is *communion,* whether it take the form of petition, intercession, thanksgiving, or whether it be just the quiet unveiling of the heart to a trusted friend, the outpouring of the soul to the one who is nearest of all. *William Littleboy*

Chapter 7: The meeting as a fellowship

Unity of spirit

317 The life of a religious society consists in something more than the body of principles it professes and the outer garments of organisation which it wears. These things have their own importance: they embody the society to the world, and protect it from the chance and change of circumstance; but the springs of life lie deeper, and often escape recognition. They are to be found in the vital union of the members of the society with God and with one another, a union which allows the free flowing through the society of the spiritual life which is its strength. Such words as 'discipleship', 'fellowship', 'brotherhood', describe these central springs of religious life...

Fellowship in a common faith has often brought a religious society into being before it was in any way organised into an institution. It was so with the primitive Church and with the Society of Friends. Organisation is a good servant but a bad master; the living fellowship within the Church must remain free to mould organisation into the fresh forms demanded by its own growth and the changing needs of the time. Where there is not this freedom the Church has its life cramped by ill-assorted clothes, and its service for the world becomes dwarfed or paralysed.   *William Charles Braithwaite, 1905*

318 The Church is not simply, in the Quaker conception, a fellowship of disciples at work for the Kingdom of God; it is such a fellowship, *plus* Jesus Christ Himself, in whose spirit, the spirit which unites them one to another and to Him, they become together 'one flock, one Shepherd'.   *William Charles Braithwaite (1912)*

319 The way that Jesus lived among men shows us the way that God lives among men and the way in which we are to live with one another. It was a way of fellowship. And fellowship, as Jesus understood it, was not mastery, but a living comradeship which respected the freedom of others and safeguarded instead of crushing out the growth of their personalities. In His intercourse with His disciples, and with others, we always find·Him respecting personality: He never forced men's wills or violated their moral freedom.

William Charles Braithwaite, 1921

Self discipline

320 A loving spirit should be the mark of the Friend at all times. Outspoken comment within the family circle it would be unreasonable to check, but it must be remembered that bitter criticism is more hurtful to those who indulge in it than to those of whom it is uttered, though the latter may suffer indirectly through the creation of a hostile atmosphere; also that remarks uttered half in jest may have more effect than is imagined on the younger members of the circle. Seek ever to speak the truth in love. *1925*

321 Where any have received offence from any other, first to speak privately to the party concerned, and endeavour reconciliation between themselves; and not to whisper or aggravate matters against them behind their backs, to the making parties, and the breach wider. Even though efforts for agreement by private conference should fail, Friends should avoid engaging one another in legal disputes. *Yearly Meeting, 1692*

322 If we hope to be forgiven, we must also forgive one another. He who yields to a suspicious and unforgiving spirit is led on to imagine things against his brother that are exaggerated, or even false. How can they, whose only hope is in the Lord's mercy, indulge in hard and unforgiving thoughts towards a brother or a sister? It may be that thou hast just ground for offence. Is thy brother's trespass against thee any warrant for thy own disobedience? Consider how exceeding broad is the 'new commandment' of thy Lord: 'Love one another, as I have loved you'...Wait not until thy brother be reconciled unto thee, or until he shall make the first overture. Be thyself the first to seek reconciliation, and to prove that thou art

honestly desirous to submit thyself to the government of the Prince
of Peace. *Yearly Meeting, 1870, 1872*

323 Maintain that charity which suffereth long, and is kind; put the
best construction upon the conduct and opinions one of another
which circumstances will warrant. Take heed...that the enemy
produce no dissensions among you; that nothing like a party spirit
be ever suffered to prevail. Let each be tender of the reputation of
his brother; ⟨and⟩ be earnest to possess the ornament of a meek
and quiet spirit. Watch over one another for good, but not for evil;
and whilst not blind to the faults or false views of others, be especially
careful not to make them a topic of common conversation. And even
in cases in which occasion may require that the failings of others
should be disclosed, be well satisfied, before they are made the
subject of confidential communication, either verbally or by letter,
that your own motives are sufficiently pure. *Yearly Meeting, 1834*

324 *The example of John Woolman reminds us of the way in which admonition
should be received:*
Last night in my Sleep I thought I was in a room with thee, and
thou drawing thy chair nigh mine, did, in a friendly way, tell me
of Sundry particular failings thou had observed in me, and Express'd
some desire that I might do better. I felt inwardly thankful for thy
care over me, and made little other reply than to tell thee I took it
very kind. Almost as soon as I woke I remembered it, and though
I could see some things in which I had not done as well as I might,
yet the particulars thou pointed out were gone from me, nor can I
yet remember them. *Letter to John Smith, 1760*

For further extracts relating to this subject see §402-405.

Caring for one another

325 The spiritual welfare of a meeting is greatly helped if its social life
is vigorous, and its members take a warm personal interest in one

another's welfare. The pastoral work of the Society is specially committed to the overseers, but our members generally should not allow themselves to feel that they are relieved from responsibility. In the greater events of life, such as marriage, the birth of a child, illness or death, it is our duty and privilege to share in one another's joys and sorrows; and sympathy thus shown is a potent means of binding us in closer fellowship.

Those who hold public offices, or are engaged in various forms of social service, should be made to realise that they have the sympathetic support and prayers of their friends in their work. Opportunities might well be found for such Friends to tell of their activities, and receive encouragement and counsel; the other members of the Meeting would thus acquire a deeper sense that they are called to a real share in the service.   *1925*

326 Recognising that our end is one, even though the work of each has its own emphasis, we shall not want to be always out of one another's sight, casually hearing of what others are doing...Many of our members so far give their attention to what is called 'outside work', as to leave them with little interest in the Society itself. Of some of them the attendance at worship is fitful and listless and in the necessary work of their meeting they take no part. Conversely their meeting takes no interest in their doings and the separation grows wider...I would propose that each congregation should...come together in social gathering and hear from one and another not only of his work done for the church outside his own congregation, but also of his 'outside work'...and in the atmosphere of thankfulness for service and prayer for wisdom and strength the worker and his friends would be drawn into unity and the work would no longer be 'outside', but would be done in the strength that comes from the fellowship known by those who are labourers together with Christ...

There are times when this unity is known deeply. The serious illness or the death of one of the congregation does cause a coming together on the part of all, drawn near not only to the stricken family but to one another; we do weep with those who weep, we do not know enough of rejoicing with those who rejoice. I would reckon it the natural thing for the father and mother of the new born child, as soon as they are able to do so, to bring the child to meeting that the Friends there might rejoice with them and with one another in thankfulness for the new life. So might the parents be strengthened for the holy work, and the congregation understand that to them also is their Lord's commission: 'Take this child and nurse it for me.'

A. Neave Brayshaw (1926)

327 Christian education is not for the most of us a matter of solitary study—though it will play its part—but study in fellowship, in which we may share our insight by teaching each other, loving each other, and challenging each other in the living of the life. ..The emphasis we have laid in the Society on the necessity of an individual apprehension of God makes it all the more urgent that we should study the faith together in a living community. Oddity, whimsy, anarchy beset the path of the Christian who tries to push his insight too far alone; and from the earliest days the Society has rightly sought to maintain unity among Friends by providing for the sharing and pooling of individual judgments.

'The nurture of our spiritual resources' (1954)

For further extracts on religious education see §74, 455.

328 In our own Meetings, as members one of another, we must be alert to the changing situations that come to each of us from youth to old age. There will be some who need help in the experiences of marriage and parenthood, others in business or personal relationships, or because they are living in isolation.

Responsibility for this ministry of love and service cannot be left to others. It rests upon each one of us, by action and in prayer, to make human need our own wherever we may find it, being quick to see, and moved to respond, as God gives us the vision and the opportunity. As we worship together, opening our hearts and minds to the source of all grace and power, we shall experience that living

unity with God and with our fellow men from which true caring
springs. *Yearly Meeting, 1956*

329 *Testimony concerning Thomas Ellwood:*
He was greatly respected by his neighbours for his services amongst
them; his heart and doors were open to the poor, both sick and lame,
who wanted help, and had it freely, taking care to provide things
useful for such occasions...often saying, he mattered not what cost
he was at, to do good.

He was an early comer to meetings, seldom hindered by weather
(though he lived three miles distant) when bodily weakness did
not hinder. The Monthly Meeting was held at his house about
forty years, and he always looked very kind and courteous on
Friends, when they came there, and took care and notice of the
meanest, who came in sincerity...We, who knew him in his conversation, are engaged to set forth how kind and condescending he
was to the weakest capacity, and would help out when they wanted
a word. *Upperside Women's Monthly Meeting, 1713/4*

330 *Testimony concerning Herbert Grubb:*
What he said and what he did sprang from what he was. His
bearing was erect, yet not formal; his manner gracious, yet not
artificial. He was a man of wide interests, of discriminating taste
and of a wise and balanced judgment. He had a contagious sense
of humour which was almost boyish; he spoke with quiet exuberance,
and in a delightful Irish brogue. He was shocked only by insincerity
or by unkind or cheap gibes at others. He was a courteous, friendly
and loveable man.

His quiet but deep personal interest in people enabled him to enter
into their problems and, by sharing them, to lighten them. He was
eminently approachable, and did not postpone discussion of problems until the quiet of the fireside: he gave his help and advice when
it was needed, whether the discussion was at the kitchen sink or
over the telephone. Nor did he wait for those in need to come to
him: isolated or sick Friends, small and discouraged Meetings,

conscientious objectors in prison during two wars—all have memories of his visits and help to them in need or difficulty. No consideration of personal inconvenience or trouble, however great, kept him back from giving all that friendship could give.

Alton, Southampton & Poole M.M., 1952

331 To put out the hand to help another may often be the surest way to obtain help for ourselves in overcoming temptation. Let us not be too much afraid to take a friend into our confidence. Open confession is good for the soul, and the knowledge that some one else is watching to see the issue of our conflict, and bearing us up in prayer before the throne of grace, may be a real strength to us when we are tempted.   *1911*

332 If in our pastoral care we are cumbered with much serving, hardly knowing where to find time for all that weighs on us, let us sit at the Lord's feet. Those who live with Him always seem to have time to love and care for their fellow-men, which is denied to those of us who think we can accomplish it in our own strength.

Edward H. Milligan, 1951

Care for young people

333 Religious education in our Society cannot be left as the concern of individual Friends in a meeting, nor of the full-time officers of permanent committees. The drive behind it must come from the membership as a whole. While the problem of meeting the existing demands for such instruction is a pressing one, a much more urgent matter is that of awakening a sense of the need for this task to be undertaken. It is not too much to say that the two most important duties of our Society are to publish the truth as we understand it and to educate our children in our faith and life. Friends are too often indifferent about the latter, at any rate as far as the work of the local meetings is concerned. It is of the utmost importance therefore that Friends everywhere should take this matter much

more seriously, for without a renewal of interest in it, all schemes and syllabuses are of little use...We feel that elders in particular should give more attention to the spiritual needs of the adolescent boys and girls within our Society, and that overseers should concern themselves more actively with the organisation and supervision of all sides of religious education.   '*Up to eighteen*' (*1949*)

334 After asking what is the effect of children upon the group it is natural to enquire what is the effect of the group upon the children? Here I cannot feel that we have done all that we should do to meet our responsibilities as a religious society. We have special difficulties; at many meetings the number of children is small and their ages mixed. Some children may be able to share in meeting for worship at a fairly early age, but others require to be ministered to, and does it not often happen that the hungry look up and are not fed? Even our young people are apt to feel that we do not sufficiently give them a reason for the faith that is in us. It may not be appropriate to do this in meeting for worship. Do we not need more diversity of method and a more experimental spirit both to meet the spiritual needs of the young and to educate in our own ways of thought attenders and newly-joined members of the Society?

W. Russell Brain (*1944*)

335 In the Society of Friends we are members one of another in worship in a very particular way, and we rejoice that it is so, but often we take too lightly the responsibility that this lays upon us individually...We ought to see to it that we are...equipped to be of use to younger members ⟨and⟩...to make the maximum use of the variety of gifts represented in the membership of our meeting. Some Friend, for example, may feel rightly hesitant about teaching in the children's class or leading a discussion, but as a keen gardener, as a gifted pianist or as a skilled craftsman he may bring delight and interest to the younger members of his meeting and enrichment to the life of the meeting as a whole. There are many and varied ways in which we can become bound together as a family, helping one another and encouraging one another. We ought not to become stereotyped in our methods, or to be too timid to experiment; for boys and girls,

who love life and movement and adventure, should find these qualities in our meetings. *'Growing up in Quaker worship'* (*1952*)

336 There are many ways in which we can help ⟨the children's⟩ class to appreciate Quaker worship. The simplicity and beauty of the surroundings is important. Hymns are a natural means of expressing praise and thanksgiving. Children love singing and often gain in this way a sense of unity with the group and of release and joy. Praise and thanksgiving are also forms of prayer; silent prayer, following thoughts suggested by simple Bible or poetry reading, opens the way to Quaker worship with its quiet listening...The older boys and girls will spend many or all their Sunday mornings in the adult meeting, and they should have real help in preparation for worship there...The young people should be encouraged to attend regional gatherings—Junior Quarterly and Monthly Meetings; and, if possible, Junior Yearly Meeting. For those who are already having local instruction these larger gatherings will give supplementary assistance as well as valuable experience in sharing worship, fellowship and discussion with larger groups. Reports of such gatherings should be given by the young people in their own meetings, thus helping them to realise that they are not only contributing to the life of the local meeting, but that they are members of the whole Society. *'Up to eighteen'* (*1949*)

For further extracts on the religious education of children see §445-447.

337 We are anxious that, when young people enter upon business life, both their employers and other Friends in the meetings near to which they reside may watch over them for good, and be willing in various ways to show an affectionate interest in their comfort and welfare. *Yearly Meeting, 1828*

Care for the lonely, sick and elderly

338 Let us remember...the need of isolated Friends and invalids for

spiritual fellowship and encouragement. Caring for such need is a priestly service in which all of us should seek to share.

Meeting for Sufferings, 1949

339 The sick and those caring for them have need of our prayers. But let us not imagine...that a few sentimental good wishes from a distance are all that is needed. Whenever we intercede in prayer we must be prepared for an answer which places a practical obligation upon us. A prayer is always a commitment.   *Thomas F. Green (1952)*

For further extracts on health and sickness, see §470-477; on intercession, see §314.

340 Isolation of spirit...comes to most—perhaps all of us—at one time or another. There are times in our lives when the tides of faith seem far out, times of dryness, times when we do not feel the comfort and guidance of God's hand. At such times we may stay away from meeting feeling that it does not give us the spiritual help that we need; or it may be that we continue to go and are to outward appearance actively engaged on the meeting's life and business, while, within, we feel the agonies of isolation and the longing for light to lighten our darkness. I can think with thankfulness of Friends who have brought light to my darkness—perhaps a single sentence, a friendly letter, a walk on the downs: their help was perhaps given unconsciously, but it was because they were sensitive to God's leadings that they were able to do it. Do we seek to be the channels of God's love and caring? Caring matters most.

Edward H. Milligan, 1951

Eldership and oversight

341 The offices of elder and overseer amongst us are...when rightly filled of great value...We encourage ⟨those appointed⟩ to cherish an interest in the spiritual welfare of all their fellow members, to exercise a watchful care and affectionate oversight, and more especially to show sympathy with younger members, that they may be drawn to a living, experimental faith in Christ. If counsel or warning be given, let it be done privately in faithfulness and love.

Nor would we limit the performance of these duties to those who occupy these stations; we are all to watch over one another for good and to be mutually interested one for another, being united together as lively stones in the spiritual building of which the Lord Jesus Christ is the chief corner stone.   *Yearly Meeting, 1851*

342   The good of the body, not the personal interest or prestige of individuals, should always be kept in mind. Appointment is not to be regarded as a prerogative that can be rightly claimed by those who have served in the past, or as a testimonial to 'weight' in the affairs of the Society. The purpose is to secure the best available help for its most important duties.   *Edward Grubb, 1933*

343   And all such as behold their brother or sister in a transgression, go not in a rough, light or upbraiding spirit to reprove or admonish him or her, but in the power of the Lord, and spirit of the Lamb, and in the wisdom and love of the Truth, which suffers thereby, to admonish such an offender. So may the soul of such a brother or sister be seasonably and effectually reached unto and overcome, and they may have cause to bless the name of the Lord on their behalf, and so a blessing may be rewarded into the bosom of that faithful and tender brother or sister that so admonished them.
George Fox, 1669

344   The primary duties of elders are to seek for true discernment in respect to offerings in the ministry, and to be loving and faithful in the exercise of that discernment; to be diligent in spiritual travail and prayer for those on whom the ministry of the word devolves; to sympathize with them in seasons of conflict and discouragement. ..It is ⟨the elder's⟩ part also to consider how far the varied needs of the congregation are met by a corresponding variety in the vocal ministry, so that all may be alike edified by the due exercise of a

diversity of spiritual gifts. In this service he may at times be called upon to consider prayerfully, in consultation with his fellow elders, whether any Friends, in younger or older life, are failing to offer such service as they may be qualified to render, and, if this appear to be the case, lovingly to urge upon such a faithful obedience to the voice of the Divine Guide within the heart.   *1931*

345 Elders have a duty to the whole of our membership. Prayer and thought are needed on behalf of each one. Vocal prayer in our meetings should be a natural outcome of such concern, and may be peculiarly helpful when it comes from one who does not often take vocal part in a meeting for worship. If elders are to advise and help others aright, they must have deep inward sympathy with the exercise of spirit from which true ministry proceeds.   *1931*

346 ⟨Let not⟩ Friends in the station of overseer...take a limited view of their duties...To them is committed the oversight of the flock, in the love of Christ. ⟨Let them⟩ give themselves to this... duty in faith and prayer, seeking, in the wisdom of God, to encourage all in the right way of the Lord; to bind up that which is broken; to bring home the wanderers; to visit the sick and the afflicted; and to extend a loving care over the young and inexperienced. Desirable as it is that some should be specially entrusted with these duties, an earnest concern has prevailed that all may take their right share in the privilege of watching over one another for good.
Yearly Meeting, 1871

347 An overseer may be described as one who should tend, as a shepherd tends his flock, the individuals of his monthly meeting. The overseer needs to carry out all his duty in a brotherly spirit. He should, so far as practicable, make himself personally acquainted with the individual members of his meeting, by home visiting, and speaking to Friends as opportunity may arise. Each overseer should endeavour to pursue that particular branch of the work to which he is best adapted. It is only a part of the service of overseers to deal with those who go astray, and if their other duties are faithfully carried out, there will be less of this painful duty required.   *1931*

348 The group of overseers should between them strive to discharge the duties for which they are appointed so that not even the least one be overlooked. It is a service bringing its own rich reward, for it cannot rightly be undertaken in one's own strength. We need to recapture the sense that we are indeed working with God and to keep our hearts and minds open to his leadings—for he careth for us all and not one of us is in need but he knows. If we keep this attitude of receptive dependence we shall be ready to obey his promptings, we shall become aware of the needs of our fellow members and be prepared in his strength to play our part in helping all our members to find their right place in the life of our Meeting.

Stephen J. Thorne (1959)

Meetings for church affairs

'Are your meetings for church affairs held in loving dependence upon the spirit of God, and are they vigilant in the discharge of their duties?.. Do you individually take your right share in the attendance and service of these meetings so that the burden may not rest upon a few?' *Query 7, 1928*

349 If a real religious fellowship grows out of our meetings for worship, it will naturally be carried over into our business meetings and into our social life, so that the whole congregation will be interested in all its members, and be knit together as a body of workers for the cause of Christ. The right conduct of our business meetings even in matters of routine is important to the spiritual life of our Society, and in so far as Friends are concerned in promoting the kingdom of God, we may rightly feel that its business is a service for him.

1925

350 The custom of appointing representatives to our meetings for church affairs may lead some Friends to the mistaken conclusion that their responsibility for these gatherings is of less importance than that for the meeting for worship. But the privilege of membership implies that every Friend should feel concerned to attend these meetings, and Friends should not lightly refuse any service to which they are called by their fellow members even though the work at times may prove onerous and exacting.

'The least member hath an office and is serviceable', and those Friends who are habitual non-attenders, without good cause, are depriving their fellow members of the help and counsel which perhaps they are well fitted to give. They are also depriving themselves of the opportunity for growth which comes with service, whether in the Society's routine business or the more specialized work of its committees.   *1959*

351 ⟨It is⟩ our concern that Friends should work with one another in a humble and loving spirit, each giving to others credit for purity of motive, notwithstanding differences of opinion, and being ready to accept the decision of the meeting even when it may not accord with his own judgment. The mutual forbearance and understanding which are produced by a constant dwelling under the power and control of Christ do much to prevent jealousies, misunderstandings, or any breach of love.   *1931*

352 When we meet together to transact the business of the Society the fellowship realised in our times of worship should be the atmosphere also of our meetings for discipline. The practice of beginning and concluding meetings for church affairs and committees or conferences with a time of worship is of great value and significance, and we would plead for the maintenance and extension of these opportunities for communion and spiritual refreshment, in which the business and interests of daily life may be kept in conscious relationship with the eternal source of our strength, and in which too we may be brought into the quietness and collectedness of spirit so essential to the right discharge of business.   *1925*

353 As it is our hope that in our meetings for discipline the will of God shall prevail rather than the desires of men, we do not set great store by rhetoric or clever argument. The mere gaining of debating points is found to be unhelpful and alien to the spirit of worship which should govern the rightly ordered meeting. Instead of rising hastily to reply to another, it is better to give time for what has been said to make its own appeal, and to take its right place in the mind of the meeting.

We ought ever to be ready to give unhurried, weighty and truly sympathetic consideration to proposals brought forward from whatever part of the meeting, believing that what is said rises from the depths of a Friend's experience, and is sincerely offered for the guidance of the meeting, and the forwarding of the work of the Church. We should neither be hindered from making experiments by fear or undue caution, nor prompted by novel suggestions to ill-considered courses.

Neither a majority nor a minority should allow itself in any way to overbear or to obstruct a meeting for church affairs in its course towards a decision. We are unlikely to reach either truth or wisdom if one section imposes its will on another. We deprecate division in our meetings and desire unanimity. It is in the unity of common fellowship, we believe, that we shall most surely learn the will of God. We cherish, therefore, the tradition which excludes voting from our meetings, and trust that clerks and Friends generally will observe the spirit of it, not permitting themselves to be influenced in their judgment either by mere numbers or by persistence. The clerks should be content to wait upon God with the meeting, as long as may be necessary for the emergence of a decision which clearly commends itself to the heart and mind of the meeting as the right one.

Let us remember continually in prayer the clerks at the table, whose duty it is to gather up the sense of the meeting and, with the guidance of God, to find the words in which to record a right decision. It is the privilege of all present to continue in an attitude of worship towards God, and of sympathetic fellowship with each other, until the business has been rightly dealt with. And those who are inevitably prevented from attending, may well turn in thought and prayer to the matters before the meeting, remembering that they too share responsibility for the promotion of the work of the Church.

1925

354 Being orderly come together, ⟨you are⟩ not to spend time with needless, unnecessary and fruitless discourses; but to proceed in the wisdom of God not in the way of the world, as a worldly assembly

of men, by hot contests, by seeking to outspeak and over-reach one another in discourse as if it were controversy between party and party of men, or two sides violently striving for dominion, not deciding affairs by the greater vote. But in the wisdom, love and fellowship of God, in gravity, patience, meekness, in unity and concord, submitting one to another in lowliness of heart, and in the holy Spirit of truth and righteousness, all things ⟨are⟩ to be carried on; by hearing, and determining every matter coming before you, in love, coolness, gentleness and dear unity;—I say, as one only party, all for the truth of Christ, and for the carrying on the work of the Lord, and assisting one another in whatsoever ability God hath given; and to determine of things by a general mutual concord, in assenting together as one man in the spirit of truth and equity, and by the authority thereof. In this way and spirit all things are to be amongst you, and without perverseness, in any self-separation, in discord and partiality; this way and spirit is wholly excepted, as not worthy to enter into the assembly of God's servants, in any case pertaining to the service of the Church of Christ; in which his Spirit of love and unity must rule.   *Edward Burrough, 1662*

355 The central committees of the Society exist to carry out the work and to forward the concerns of Friends. They are, with our business meetings, local and national, part of our discipline, a discipline not of legal code or delegated authority, but a method which has grown out of the experience of men and women working and worshipping together, and together seeking to follow the guidance of Christ. They can rightly fulfil their purpose only as they continue to reflect the concerns of·Friends, and have our faithful support and interest.
1959

356 In considering the financial claims of the Society, the maintenance of the local meeting will probably take first place. Monthly and Quarterly Meeting needs must also be met, and the Yearly Meeting Fund, and the various committees appointed by Yearly Meeting and Meeting for Sufferings have also a claim upon all our members, and must receive the support which will enable them to carry out the Society's concerns.   *1959*

357 In the multiplicity of details and in the pressure of business, a committee may lose the keen sense of mission to attempt and achieve great tasks. The committee, like the individual, needs time to think and it needs an attitude of mind and soul which can make it able to receive increasingly what is of God about its work. We cannot be too clear that it is nothing less than 'a new thing' which will meet the situation. Individually the faith of most of us is too weak sufficiently to grasp the promise 'Behold I will do a new thing' (Isaiah 43. 19)* but a committee which grasps with corporate faith such a promise is the committee which will have a spirit of adventure in attempting the humanly impossible. And those who thus trust God discover God. *Friends Prayer League, 1914*

358 To follow the highest purpose always involves the setting aside of many things which in themselves are good, whether by individuals or by the Yearly Meeting as a whole. To find the purpose of God in a gathering such as this involves the bringing together of every one of our differing points of view to that place where they may be united in the power of God. If in our hearts as individuals we maintain barriers between ourselves and other Friends, we cannot be finders; and if we maintain such barriers between ourselves and our fellow men we shall not find our part in working out God's will in the world.

It has been the experience of this Yearly Meeting in the past to know that Friends have met in division and uncertainty, and that then guidance has come, and light has been given to us, and we have become finders of God's purpose. This gives us ground for confidence. We shall not be held back by the magnitude of the questions which are to come before us, nor by a sense of our own unworthiness. *Yearly Meeting, 1936*

The individual in the meeting

359 The promise of the Holy Spirit was to a group. We need one another to strengthen each other's will to goodness. The concern

* Mgr R. A. Knox translates Isaiah 43. 19 'I mean to perform new wonders'.

of an individual should be laid before the worshipping group, so that corporate guidance may be given by an expression of unity or disunity. The life and teachings of Jesus, seen not so much in detail as in totality, provide another check which should be employed in seeking guidance. *Friends World Conference, 1952*

360 It is with individuals rather than with communities that new truth originates...While corporate guidance is of great value in controlling individual extravagance, it is a source of great danger to the church if it is opposed to a genuine individual concern...⟨The church⟩ should be concerned not with its privileges but with its duties; not with its limitations but with its life; not with its methods but with its message. The living church has a prophetic function— the duty of using its faculty of spiritual vision so as to penetrate below the surface of life to its inner meaning...Is it possible then to suggest how the corporate guidance of the community can be applied so as to conserve its wonderful helpfulness and avoid as far as possible the dangers that attend it? The line of safety lies, I think, in maintaining our churches as fellowships rather than as institutions. ..It is the business of the church to foster open-hearted intercourse, united prayer and study, loyal comradeship, communion in worship and in service—all those human channels along which education and illumination come. Chiefly does it need to promote leadership and comradeship—leadership strong in teaching and in high example, comradeship rich in study and in service.
William Charles Braithwaite (1909)

361 It is necessary to have individual freedom and corporate organisation in a meeting so that each may be able to give the service for which he is most fitted, for there is always some personal service a member may give, however shy, young, inexperienced or humble he may be, and so that no one may be overlooked.
Kathleen M. Slack, 1952

362 Are there not different states, different degrees, different growths, different places?..What wisdom and spirit is that, which doth not

acknowledge this, but would make all equal?..Therefore, watch
every one to feel and know his own place and service in the body,
and to be sensible of the gifts, places, and services of others, that
the Lord may be honoured in all, and every one owned and honoured in the Lord, and no otherwise.   *Isaac Penington, 1667*

363 'Concern' is a word which has tended to become debased by
excessively common usage among Friends, so that too often it is
used to cover merely a strong desire. The true 'concern' ⟨emerges as⟩
a gift from God, a leading of his Spirit which may not be denied. Its
sanction is not that on investigation it proves an intelligent thing
to do—though it usually is; it is that the individual (and if his
concern is shared and adopted by the meeting, then the meeting)
knows, as a matter of inward experience, that here is something
which the Lord would have done, however obscure the way,
however uncertain the means to human observation. Often proposals for action are made which have every appearance of good
sense, but as the meeting waits before God, it becomes clear that
the proposition falls short of 'concern'.   *Roger C. Wilson (1949)*

364 We are thankful that so often in our common worship, and in our
experience of joint responsibility for the service of God's kingdom,
as well as in times of private retirement, new impulses are felt
towards wider service. It is our earnest hope that Friends will
always cherish these impulses, and be willing to share their concerns with others in our meetings, seeking united guidance as to the
manner in which the tasks that are laid upon them may be accomplished. It is the privilege of the fellowship to foster the growth of
right concerns, and to encourage and provide for the development
of the service in question. A real concern is a gift from God. We
believe that more and more work will be entrusted to us, as we turn
to Him, and surrender our hearts more completely, becoming
sensitive to His every leading. For the humble as well as the more
conspicuous tasks, we confidently believe that strength will be
given to each one of us, in proportion as we place ourselves at the
disposal of God and respond to the promptings of His spirit. Such
work is not to be entered upon lightly.   *1925*

The spiritual basis of membership

365 The Society ⟨of Friends⟩ from first to last has affirmed that the spirit of man is the place of all others in which the spirit of God can shine...It has always insisted that each individual is responsible for obeying this light, and that the whole of life ought to be brought under the dominion of the Spirit.   *William Charles Braithwaite (1909)*

366 We believe that the religion of Jesus Christ is primarily spiritual in its essence, and that every follower of His ought to have, and can have, direct personal intercourse with God through the operation of His Holy Spirit in the human heart. Consequently our method of worship, our attitude towards outward rites, our conduct of church meetings, and our whole religious system, are so framed as to keep this aspect of religion ever to the front, and to lead men and women into the full exercise of their privileges as the children of God.
Friends Foreign Mission Association, 1914

367 There are certain broad principles of belief and conduct that afford a basis for an association in and through which living membership can find expression. In the case of our own Society unity is essential upon the spiritual and practical nature of Christianity—the deep and penetrating reality of worship and the claim of Christ to rule our whole life, both inward and outward.   *1931*

368 The test for membership should not be doctrinal agreement, nor adherence to certain testimonies, but evidence of sincere seeking and striving for the Truth, together with an understanding of the lines along which Friends are seeking that Truth.
Friends World Conference, 1952

369 *The experience of Richard Claridge, about 1697:*
This was the way that Friends used with me, when I was convinced of truth, they came oftentimes to visit me; and sate and waited upon the Lord in silence with me; and as the Lord opened our

understandings and mouths, so we had very sweet and comfortable seasons together. They did not ask me questions about this or the other creed, or about this or the other controversie in religion; but they waited to feel that living Power to quicken me, which raised up Jesus from the dead. And it pleased God so in his wisdom to direct, that all the great truths of the Christian religion were occasionally spoken to. Now this was Friends way with me, a way far beyond all rules or methods established by the wisdom of this world, which is foolishness with God: And this is their way with others that are convinced of the truth.

370 Our membership of this, or any other Christian fellowship, is never based upon worthiness... We none of us are members because we have attained a certain standard of goodness, but rather because, in this matter, we still are all humble learners in the school of Christ. Our membership is of no importance whatever unless it signifies that we are committed to something of far greater and more lasting significance than can adequately be conveyed by the closest association with any movement or organisation. Our membership of the Society of Friends should commit us to the discipleship of the living Christ. When we have made that choice and come under that high compulsion, our membership will have endorsed it.

Edgar G. Dunstan (1956)

371 A unity must be sought which is deeper than can be given by mere membership in an organisation professing a common doctrine, whether it be economic or religious: it must be found in the very well-springs of will and aspiration, in our attitude to life, in our way of life itself. In the great Christian society this unity is found in loyalty to Jesus Christ himself as our master and guide. Collectively His disciples share a common experience in fellowship with each other. They naturally and rightly endeavour to express this in terms of thought. From every such endeavour of groups or individuals whether in past ages or in our own day we must seek to learn, but they cannot constitute the ultimate test of discipleship. The binding force which holds the Christian fellowship together is not found in these intellectual formulations of experience, but in the

deepest region of personality, in the fact of discipleship itself, uniting men in the communion of prayer, even though at times that prayer may be but half conscious or imperfectly expressed. The prayer of true discipleship is present in the dedication of man's will to the Highest, in the unspoken cry of his deepest need, as he hungers for goodness and for right, which is to hunger for God himself. Consciously or unconsciously all who put up this prayer share one common life. 'The seekers of the Light are one.'

T. Edmund Harvey (1921)

Responsibilities of membership

372 We are convinced that our distinguishing testimonies arise directly out of the central experience of Friends, but complete agreement with us, whether of formal belief or practice, need not be asked for. .. ⟨Membership implies unity⟩ with the views and practices of Friends not only from an intellectual standpoint but in the realisation that these are based on a sincere and living faith in God as manifested in the life of Jesus Christ and as he is ever manifested as a light in the hearts of men. *1931*

373 Stress should be laid on the importance of regular attendance at our meetings for worship, not only as a joy and privilege to the individual and as a means of growth in grace, but for the sake of the congregation. Each true worshipper in the silent waiting upon God will help his fellow men even if not called to the ministry of the spoken word. *1931*

374 It should be made clear that ⟨a Friend⟩ can neither give nor receive all that true membership offers unless he is a regular attender of our meetings for church affairs and takes his proper share in, and responsibility for, the Society's activities. *1931*

375 Quaker service springs from the roots of our faith. It grows out of the inner experience of that deep compassion and sense of oneness with

all mankind which Jesus Christ revealed as the eternal love of God
for men. We must seek to live our whole lives in the awareness of
this presence of the love of God, giving time gladly to meditation
and worship, to the outreach of preaching from the heart, and to
the compassionate sharing of the burdens of our neighbours.

Friends World Conference, 1952

These extracts have attempted no more than a general survey of some of the responsibilities of membership in our Society, since this subject is in effect the theme of the whole of this book.

Chapter 8: Publishing truth

A universal mission

376 Let all nations hear the word by sound or writing. Spare no place, spare not tongue nor pen, but be obedient to the Lord God and go through the world and be valiant for the Truth upon earth; tread and trample all that is contrary under...Be patterns, be examples in all countries, places, islands, nations, wherever you come, that your carriage and life may preach among all sorts of people, and to them; then you will come to walk cheerfully over the world, answering that of God in every one.   *George Fox, 1656*

377 The Society of Friends is called by its deepest principles, and by the lessons of its own history, to a universal mission. It cannot fulfil its service to humanity unless it responds to this call. The very simple heart of the early Quaker message is needed as much to-day as it ever was...The really universal thing is a living experience. It is reached in varied ways, and expressed in very different language. ..The common bond is in the thing itself, the actual inner knowledge of the grace of God. Quakerism can only have a universal message if it brings men and women into this transforming knowledge. The early Friends certainly had this knowledge, and were the means of bringing many thousands of seekers into the way of discovery. In virtue of this central experience, the Quaker movement can only be true to itself by being a missionary movement.   *Henry T. Hodgkin (1916)*

378 In the fulfilment of our fundamental responsibility of bringing men and women to God there are openings for every Friend. Some have gifts that will help those with spiritual problems; others are better equipped to meet intellectual difficulties; all must strive for a rich and joyous fellowship in the meetings into which we should draw seeking souls. We must go out to those around us in a spirit of love and prayer, letting our lives speak.   *Yearly Meeting, 1953*

379 It is true...that 'our lives should speak' though often if the numbers drawn thereby to our meetings is a legitimate test, our lives do not speak above a whisper! Our lives, of course, do speak, but that does not absolve us from other responsibilities in ⟨proclaiming the Christian message⟩. These responsibilities should be discharged whether or not we are able to trace any result.

Edgar G. Dunstan (1956)

380 The early Friends were fully assured that they had a message for all men—not merely that one or other of their testimonies was specially relevant to their own time, but that their message in its totality, in its wholeness, was God's good news for all sorts and conditions of men...'Have you anything to declare?' is a vital challenge to which every one of us is personally called to respond and is also a challenge that every meeting should consider of primary importance. It should lead us to define, with such clarity as we can reach, precisely what it is that Friends of this generation have to say that is not, as we believe, being said effectively by others. What, indeed, have we to declare to this generation that is of sufficient importance to justify our separate existence as part of the Christian fellowship? If we regard the Society of Friends merely as an ethical society we have no message for a world that is bursting with sin and sorrow and suffering. It is insufficient merely to offer palliatives to physical suffering, important and necessary as they are. There are those whose needs are on a different level and we should covet to have for these others at least an equal concern. Have we 'good news' for them?

Edgar G. Dunstan (1956)

381 Whatever else Jesus was, he was a preacher. He had a message to give and he gave it. His last command to his disciples was that they should preach the Gospel to the whole world. Jesus saw the truth that men needed and he thought it urgent that that truth should be proclaimed. That trust is handed on to us, but it is a responsibility from which we shrink. We feel that we have a very imperfect grasp of the meaning of the Gospel. Perhaps, after all the earnest seeking of the Church, we are only beginning to see the tremendous implications of it. We dimly see that this Gospel, before it has finished with us, will turn our lives upside down and inside out. Our favourite Quaker vice of caution holds us back. We have much more to learn before we are ready to teach. It is right that we have much to learn; it is right to recognise the heavy responsibility of teaching; but to suppose that we must know everything before we can teach anything is to condemn ourselves to perpetual futility.   *George B. Jeffery (1934)*

382 The world needs deliverance from the bondage of fear, a fear which makes men selfish, cruel and callous. Everywhere significance and security have faded out of the lives of men. Our Society should be witnessing, from its own particular angle of approach, to a God who delivers from fear, and in whom men may find strength and abiding peace. We recognise that our ability to give this witness will depend upon the quality of the spiritual life in our meetings for worship. It will also depend upon whether we have sought to fit ourselves both spiritually and intellectually to speak to the condition of men and women in the modern world. The witness should be expressed in the language of today   *Yearly Meeting, 1938*

383 Early Friends spoke a great deal and men were changed as they responded to the leadings of God to whom they were directed. Sometimes we fail to speak when we might, and sometimes when we speak our words are without power. They fail to communicate what we have tested in experience...We do not deserve a hearing until we have tried to understand the ground of our own faith and its relevance to life in the world to-day; which does not mean that we should expect to claim that we know all the answers...

We complicate the service of communication if we imagine that we have to unload on any enquirer all that we have learned about the ways of God through, perhaps, many years of Christian experience. .. As we seek to serve people and their condition and circumstances become known to us, we shall find straightforward openings for us to share a very little of what has been given to us. If we can offer simply a single hint which can now be used, this may open the way to further unforced communication...Is not this the way in which Jesus drew men towards their true life? *Friends World Conference, 1952*

384 We need to be alive with concern for the spiritual welfare of our fellow men, and set on fire for God, so that by the intensity of the convictions by which we live, and with renewed dedication to the life of prayer, we may be enabled to give, faithfully and with power, clear and deliberate spoken witness. In the service of Christ all ... should feel the sense of responsibility to talk of the things that are personal and eternal with the members of their meetings, and with those with whom they meet in daily life.

Friends Home Service Committee, 1950

385 To whom and when shall we go? The answer is very simple—we must go, and only go, when we are sent, and go where people are and especially 'where there are no Friends'—maybe into an emperor's parlour to talk and pray with him as Stephen Grellet did; into a war-stricken area as in Shanghai; with those in flight as from Barcelona; or into a miner's kitchen. The Lord has a great and wide service for Friends to do, and never more than now. The market crosses still stand for us to occupy, the friendly pulpit, the disused meeting house, the town or country Friend's living-room... It has well been said that 'we have hardly grasped the effectiveness of the home for pastoral purposes in a settled congregation or for propaganda work'. The truth of this is daily becoming clearer. We must begin again, where people are, seeking them out, confident in the divine power of our Gospel to lift men out of disillusionment, despair, dishonour and inhumanity into the new day of truth, mutual trust, decency and hope. *John A. Hughes (1940)*

For further extracts on the publishing of truth through international service see §659-669.

The life of the meeting

386 Our congregations and our members individually need, above all things, to manifest a spiritual fellowship vitally in touch with the needs of men...⟨We should⟩ bear in mind that it will be the warmth of fellowship and of brotherhood in our congregations that will attract and speak of the love of God. *Yearly Meeting, 1906*

387 All should be welcome at our meetings for worship, which are public. It is surprising that there are many who assume that these meetings are 'closed'... What experience has led to this unfortunate conclusion it is impossible to say, but it surely places upon Friends a greater local responsibility to ensure that members of the public are left in no doubt that worship with us is not for a privileged few only but for all who wish to join us. *Edgar G. Dunstan (1956)*

388 We should like to see a greater unity between the religious service of our meetings and the social service of Friends, each being complementary to the other, since they are rooted in the same life and spirit; and to see this expressed in meeting houses which act as centres for varied activities of the surrounding neighbourhood... Several of our meeting houses have been brought into increasing use in this way, greatly to the increase of the depth of the religious life of the meeting and of the sense of fellowship between its members.
'The Society of Friends & social service' (1944)

The written word

389 Take heed of printing anything more than ye are required of the Lord God.
Nor none stop writing or speaking when ye are moved with the Spirit of the Lord God. *George Fox, 1656, 1655*

390 Friends have always laid stress on the importance of the printed word, for we must be able to present the truths of our faith to each succeeding generation. More than other religious bodies we need to have literature that will attract thoughtful seekers. ⟨Our committees⟩ are performing a valuable service to the whole Society; it is important that more Friends should be concerned for this work, and we hope that more may be done to appeal to a wider circle of readers, through additional literature in public libraries, and possibly through publications in a more popular form. We have been reminded also of the opportunities that may be open to us in the columns of local newspapers, and of the valuable work that has been done in the way of relations with the press generally.

Yearly Meeting, 1950

391 Only such writings as spring from a living experience will reach the life in others, only those which embody genuine thought in clear and effective form will minister to the needs of the human mind. A faith like Quakerism should find expression in creative writing born of imagination and spirit, and speaking in universal tones that will be understood by many who fail to understand the common presentations of Christianity. It is no disrespect to truth to present it in forms that will be readily understood.   *1925*

Personal witness

392 How little could those of whom we read in the Gospels suppose that the Jesus of Nazareth who moved amongst them was organising a vast Ecclesia. Nor is that our task. He who, on however small a scale, would imitate the Master in bringing in the Kingdom of Heaven, will find his life filled with humbler and simpler duties. Walk with men in the garden or in the grove. Meditate in the desert, and return to feed the hungry. Talk with the reaper in the field, or with the woman at the wayside well. Join the tramp on the road, or discuss with the learned in their long robes. Gather with your friends in an upper room to break bread in the evening. If you are filled with the spirit of the Master, all these little acts of human converse are contributions towards the building up of the Church of Christ. You may not thus reconstruct a theology; you may be doing something far more vital for religion, pure and undefiled. For in the economy of Christ's teaching the vision of God is not reserved for the accomplished theologian; it is accorded to the pure in heart.

Silvanus P. Thompson, 1916

393 If but one man or woman were raised up by his power, to stand and live in the same spirit, that the Prophets and Apostles were in, who gave forth the Scriptures, that man or woman should shake all the country in their profession for ten miles around.   *George Fox, 1652*

Chapter 9: The art of living

'Quakerism, in the light of its great original truth, is "exceeding broad". As interpreted by Penn and Barclay it is the most liberal and catholic of faiths. If we are not free, generous, tolerant, if we are not up to or above the level of the age in good works, in culture and love of beauty, order and fitness, if we are not the ready recipients of the truths of science and philosophy, in a word, if we are not full-grown men and Christians, the fault is not in Quakerism, but in ourselves.'

John Greenleaf Whittier, 1870

Personal character

394 The art of living must be studied, as must every art. It calls for imagination, so that every advance, every change, is not merely a difference, but a creative act. Achievement, at any level above the lowest, calls for courage to hold on, in spite of current moods, and for exacting self-discipline. The art of Christian living calls for the same self-preparation; but its reward is not merely aesthetic satisfactions. The soul, hungry for God, is fed. Life itself takes on new meaning. Thus it is that we break from the confines of the prisons we have built about ourselves. Thus it is we are brought into the freedom of the Kingdom of God which, every day, through the wide world, is being realised in the hearts of men.

Horace B. Pointing (1946)

395 True godliness don't turn men out of the world, but enables them to live better in it, and excites their endeavours to mend it: not hide their candle under a bushel, but set it upon a table in a candlestick...

Whoever they are that would come to Christ, and be right Christians, must readily abandon every delight that would steal away the affections of the mind, and exercise it from the divine principle of life, and freely write a bill of divorce for every beloved vanity; and all, under the Sun of Righteousness, is so. *William Penn (1682)*

396 If we would indeed take a place in God's larger work, more is required of us than the ordinary virtues of respectability. The old law of 'thou shalt not' is superseded by Christ's command 'be ye perfect'. The basis of Christianity is laid deeper than in the maintenance of a certain moral minimum. Yet it would be foolish to ignore the difficulties which beset us, as from day to day we face afresh the task of living cleanly. To none is a life of sincerity, integrity, purity and industry easy. But for the grace of God, it is impossible. We do well, then, to give special time and energy to seeking spiritual support in these matters both for ourselves and for others. The resources in sympathy and intercession of the whole Church should be available for each one as he meets temptation. But personal loyalty to Christ will always be the strongest anchorage in treacherous waters. It is through this allegiance that power for life is received. *1925*

397 While seeking to interpret our Christian faith in the language of today, we must remember that there is one worse thing than failure to practise what we profess, and that is to water down our professions to match our practice. It is a slow task to re-establish men's confidence in Christianity and in Jesus Himself; but we have faith that men can respond to sheer goodness and to genuine loving fellowship. We believe that responsibility is laid upon each individual Friend in our world family, to make a new 'holy experiment' in practical living. *Friends World Conference, 1952*

398 Our forefathers did not talk about the implications of a way of life which they were not already striving to follow; neither dare we let our words outrun our striving, nor our plans our readiness to implement them. The world desperately needs men and women whose yea is yea and whose nay is nay. The testimony of our daily life still matters most. We pray that this may be our sure witness: that of us it may be said that our lives make it easier for men to believe in God. *Yearly Meeting, 1943*

399 It is not necessary that we should know all mysteries before we begin to follow Christ. To some of us much that is taught of His person and His work may not yet be clear, but so it was with the early disciples. They did not understand at first the mystic union with their Master to which they were called, but they followed Him, and as they followed, there was gradually unfolded to them the fulness of His love and life. If we begin where they began, and follow as they followed, we shall end where they ended, in adoring love.   *Yearly Meeting, 1909*

400 Seek on in patience and in hope. Be earnest in prayer. Do not fall back into selfish indifference, but do whatever thou canst truthfully do, for the help, socially and spiritually, of those around thee. Take comfort from the thought that others have passed through as great a strift, and have come forth into peace and happy trustfulness. If thy soul be walking but in twilight, look towards that quarter of the sky from which light seems to be dawning...Thou wilt yet hear His words as a personal message to thy soul, 'I am the light of the world: he that followeth me shall not walk in darkness, but shall have the light of life.'   *Yearly Meeting, 1893*

401 *In her late eighties, Margaret Fox became anxious about the scruples which were growing amongst Friends about wearing any but 'plain' clothes, or attending the christening feasts or funerals of their non-Quaker neighbours. In 1700 she wrote a letter begging them to 'stand fast in that liberty wherewith Christ hath made us free':*
Let us beware of this, of separating or looking upon ourselves to be more holy than in deed and in truth we are; for what are we but what we have received from God, and God is all sufficient to bring in thousands into the same Spirit and Light, to lead and to guide them, as he doth us: and let us frame and fashion ourselves unto the Apostle's doctrine and practice, who was in a glorious shining Light (read 1 Cor. 9. 19 and so to the end). Let the Spirit of God which he hath given us ⟨make⟩ us free, and not be entangled again into bondage, in observing prescriptions in outward things, which will not profit nor cleanse the inward man.

We are now coming into that which Christ cried Woe against, minding altogether outward things, neglecting the inward work of

Almighty God in our hearts, if we can but frame according to outward prescriptions and orders, and deny eating and drinking with our neighbours, in so much that poor Friends is mangled in their minds, that they know not what to do, for one Friend says one way, and another another, but Christ Jesus saith, that we must take no thought what we shall eat, or what we shall drink, or what we shall put on, but bids us consider the lilies how they grow, in more royalty than Solomon. But contrary to this, we must look at no colours, nor make anything that is changeable colours as the hills are, nor sell them, nor wear them: but we must be all in one dress and one colour: this is a silly poor Gospel. It is more fit for us, to be covered with God's Eternal Spirit, and clothed with his Eternal Light, which leads us and guides us into Righteousness. Now I have set before you life and death, and desires you to choose life, and God and his Truth.

402 If we seek first the kingdom of God and his righteousness, we shall be instructed by the example of pious men, but not blind to their infirmities; comforted by their society, but not dependent upon it; helped by religious conversation, but not disposed to enter into it hastily or superficially. If we are concerned aright for the cultivation and cleansing of our own hearts, impressed with the importance of our own stewardship unto God, and duly sensible of our own sins and great need of forgiveness from Him, we shall become very cautious how we converse on the failings of others, and anxious not to violate that charity which is enjoined upon all; that love which is the true badge of discipleship. *Yearly Meeting, 1829*

403 And all Friends take heed of Jars and Strife, for that is it, which will eat out the Seed in you; therefore let not that harbour in your bosoms, lest it eat out the Good in you, and ye come to suffer in your own particulars. Therefore dwell in love and life, and in the Power and Seed of God, which is the honourable, royal state.
George Fox, 1656

404 Our life is love, and peace, and tenderness; and bearing one with another, and forgiving one another, and not laying accusations one

against another; but praying one for another, and helping one another up with a tender hand. *Isaac Penington, 1667*

405 To be made perfect in love is a high state of Christian excellence, and not attainable but by the sacrifice of selfish passions. No degree of resentment can consist with this state. Some persons are apt to profess that they can forgive those whom they suppose to have injured them, when such are brought to know and acknowledge their fault. But that is little else than a disguised pride, seeking for superiority. The love which Christ commanded to his church, goes further than that. 'This is my commandment, that ye love one another, as I have loved you.' *Yearly Meeting, 1806*

The experience of the early Friends is described in §184; for extracts on the need for forgiveness and understanding in the life of the Meeting see §320-324.

The Source of our strength

406 Friends, whatever ye are addicted to, the tempter will come in that thing; and when he can trouble you, then he gets advantage over you, and then you are gone. Stand still in that which is pure, after ye see yourselves; and then mercy comes in. After thou seest thy thoughts, and the temptations, do not think, but submit; and then power comes. Stand still in that which shows and discovers; and then doth strength immediately come. And stand still in the Light, and submit to it, and the other will be hush'd and gone; and then content comes. *George Fox, 1652*

Another letter of George Fox on the source of our strength in time of difficulty is given in §303. Some verses on the subject by Thomas Story will be found in §43.

407 We would remind ⟨Friends⟩ that temptation is common to all and that temptation in itself is not sin. On the contrary, Christian character cannot be developed save as we pass through and over-come temptation. If any are tempted to despair, let them remember

that others have been in like condition before, and that the exceeding grace of our Lord Jesus Christ is able to deliver from the lowest depth to which the human heart can sink. He gives us the right to turn our back upon the past, however dark, and to face forward to a bright future, made possible for us through His death and glorious resurrection. *1911*

408 Our strength or help is only in God; but then it is near us, it is *in us*—a force superior to all possible opposition—a force that never was, nor can be, foiled. We are free to stand in this unconquerable ability, and defeat the powers of darkness; or to turn from it, and be foiled and overcome. When we stand, we know it is God alone upholds us; and when we fall, we feel that our fall or destruction is of ourselves. *Journal of Job Scott (1751-1793)*

409 When work does not turn out as was expected or intended, do not let it depress you. If you are working from a right motive, and doing your best under the guidance of a loving Father in heaven, your work cannot be and is not failure...Remember that the Lord never lays work upon His people that He does not give them strength or ability to perform, and if it please Him in the working out of His great purposes that life shall be sacrificed or cut short in the midst of the work, be assured that the work will not permanently suffer from such a cause. *Joseph John Armistead (1913)*

410 It is necessary that we have a spiritual assistance, to distinguish times and seasons as they are in the hand of God; when we abound, not to be lifted up; when in poverty and want, not to repine too much; when afflicted, that we pray first for the spirit of prayer and supplication, that we may be directed how, and in what manner, to pray, for it is not always consistent that we should have what we most desire as creatures, but that which is most profitable for us as Christians, believers, and followers of Christ...We therefore have great need to distinguish aright, that in all things we may be preserved: by watching in stillness, to be renewed in strength; by virtue of the holy anointing to know what to ask, and temper our

longings by a perfect submission; sometimes to ask no more than
to be endued with patience and strength to bear the present
affliction, that it may terminate to our advantage, and acceptance
with Almighty God. *Letter of John Woolman, c. 1765*

411 *Pierre Ceresole wrote in 1925 when undertaking an uncongenial office job:*
Never to ask for easier circumstances, but for greater strength;
and to accept gladly (when they come) rest and ease along the road.

412 *James Nayler, whose temptation and sufferings are described in §23-24,
wrote the following in 1659 'in the day when my God lift my feet out of
the Pit':*

It is in my heart to praise thee, O my God;
    Let me never forget thee,
    what thou has been to me:

In the night, by thy presence in the
    day of trial when I was beset in darkness,
    when I was cast out as a wandring bird,
    and when I was assaulted with strong temptations,
    Then thy presence in secret did preserve me,
    and in a low estate I felt thee near me.

When the floods sought to sweep me away
    Thou set a compass for them,
    how far they should pass over;

When my way was through the sea,
    and when I passed under the mountains
    there was thou present with me;

When the weight of the hills was upon me
    thou upheld me, else had I sunk
    under the earth;

When I was as one altogether helpless,
    when tribulation and anguish was upon me
    day and night, and the earth
    without foundation;

When I went on the way of wrath,
    and passed by the gates of hell,
    when all comforts stood afar off,
    and he that is mine enemy had dominion;
    when I was cast into the pit,
    and was as one appointed to death;
    when I was between the millstones,
    and as one crushed with the weight
    of his adversary,

As a Father thou was with me,
    and the Rock of thy Presence.

413 *George Fox wrote to Friends in November 1663, during a time of much persecution:* Sing and rejoice, ye children of the Day and of the Light, for the Lord is at work in this thick night of Darkness that may be felt: and Truth doth flourish as the rose, and the lilies do grow among the thorns, and the plants atop of the hills, and upon them the lambs do skip and play. And never heed the tempests nor the storms, floods nor rains, for the Seed Christ is over all and doth reign.

Careers

'Where you have a choice of employment, whether for yourselves or for your children, think first of the service that you may render to God and to your fellow-men. In your relations with others in your daily work, manifest the spirit of justice and understanding, and thus give a living witness to the Truth.'

General Advices, 1928

414 These talents that were given to the Lord's servants, and to every one according to their several abilities, was the Lord's heavenly treasure, and was not their own but the Lord's; and they were, and are, to improve this heavenly treasure for the Lord, and to put it forth...but the wicked and sloathful servant (he is called a servant too) hideth the Lord's talent in his earthly napkin, and did not improve the Lord's heavenly treasure; and he was cast into utter darkness; and therefore all are to consider, whom the Lord hath given more or less of his heavenly treasure to, how you do, and how you have put the Lord's heavenly treasure forth and have improved it. *George Fox (1687)*

415 To be one of the agents of the world's life, enjoying his work and the ordinary contacts of men, with gaiety and humour amongst his fellows, cultivating his skill, loving beauty and contributing thereto —but achieving discipline and mastery for the sake of freedom and service—is this not what each desires for himself and his children and I hope his neighbours? *Francis E. Pollard (1932)*

416 A man's work is perhaps the most important contribution he makes to society. It should therefore offer good possibilities of spiritual contentment. And it happens quite often that people find satisfaction, joy and meaning in their work. But, of course, it is not always the person who looks for the job; often the job looks for the person. Many jobs, especially in industry, are mechanised and humdrum, and offer the worker few possibilities of deeper satisfaction. It is especially bad if the social contacts at the place of work are also unsatisfying. It is an obvious task for Friends and others, to help to produce such an atmosphere in the work place that people can meet in mutual understanding. *Wilhelm Aarek (1954)*

417 For some it is right to give their whole lives explicitly to concrete forms of service, but for most their service will lie 'in the sheer quality of the soul displayed in ordinary occupations'. Such ordinary occupations are sometimes an essential contribution to the liberation of another person for wider service, and in any case, the inspiration of a dedicated life lived in simple surroundings, though often untraceable, may be profound in its reach. *Gerald Littleboy (1945)*

The experience of Luke Cock in business life is described in §42, that of John Woolman in §48. For further extracts on the subject of work see §550-554.

Sources and use of income

418 As Christians, all we possess are the gifts of God. Now in distributing it to others we act as his steward, and it becomes our station to act agreeable to that divine wisdom which he graciously gives to his servants. If the steward of a great family, from a selfish attachment to particulars, takes that with which he is entrusted, and bestows it too lavishly on some, to the injury of others, and to the damage of him who employs him, he disunites himself, and becomes unworthy of the office. *John Woolman, 1763*

419 The guiding principle which a Friend should keep in mind in making an income, whether by work or by investment, should be the good of others and of the community at large, and not simply of himself and his family. He should, even at the risk of loss, strive to be strictly honest and truthful in his dealings; should refuse to manufacture or deal in commodities that are hurtful to society; and should be on his guard against obtaining an undue profit at the cost of the community. If he is an investor he should think not only of security and of the rate of interest, but of the conditions under which his income is produced and the effect which investment in a particular field may have on the welfare of his fellow men, whether at home or in less well developed countries of the world. *1925; 1959*

420 In spending his income a Friend should consider how his actions affect society and whether his expenditure upon himself and his family is to the advantage of the community as a whole. He should also consider whether there is a reasonable relation between the labour expended on producing the things he buys and the real satisfaction yielded by their use. Friends should know their income and live within it; they should beware of incurring debts and avoid entangling themselves in heavy commitments by the unwise obtaining of goods on the hire purchase system. Anxiety for the future, however, should not lead to withholding what should rightly be expended for the needs of the family or devoted to the service of others. That they may be well acquainted with their annual income and expenditure, Friends are advised to keep clear and correct accounts. In times of difficulty, consultation with other Friends may save much trouble. *1925; 1959*

421 Encourage a spirit of Christian bountifulness. Let all... cultivate from early years a true liberality according to their means; it should be a joy to the Christian to support wise efforts to promote the good of others. *1925*

422 We counsel less mystery and more openness towards those who are worthy of confidence. If men conceal from their nearest connections in life a knowledge of the actual state of their affairs, they may deprive themselves of helpful advice, and kind participation in trouble; expenses may be incurred, and subsequent distress may ensue, which might have been avoided. *Yearly Meeting, 1826; 1911*

423 The love of money is apt to increase almost imperceptibly. That which was at first laboured after under pressure of necessary duty, may, without great watchfulness, steal upon the affections, and gradually withdraw the heart from God. The danger depends not upon how much a man has, but upon how much his heart is set upon what he has, and upon accumulating more. *Yearly Meeting, 1858*

Conduct in business

424 From its earliest days our Society has laid great stress on honesty in business and the payment in full of debts justly incurred. Though social conditions have undergone great changes over the years of our Society's history, so that much of the advice given in the past may seem out of date, it is well to remind ourselves that the principles underlying the advice have not changed. Since we believe that all men are the children of God, we cannot take advantage of our fellows by any form of dishonesty, whether in buying or selling goods, in business or privately, or as employees by failing to give an honest return in labour for the pay we receive. When we have received goods or services, we shall be punctual in making payment of the price agreed on, and we shall not attempt to evade our proper obligations to the community by way of rates or taxes. Friends in business are advised to adopt and keep up a clear and methodical system of accounts. They are recommended to inspect the state of their affairs frequently and balance their books at least once in the year. *1959*

425 We caution Friends against hastily starting in business. Time spent in wise enquiry is well spent. This warning is especially to be borne in mind by those contemplating partnership. Let Friends, before entering into relationships involving such far-reaching consequences, not only assure themselves of the solvency and credit of the other parties, but also consider that the happiness and success of this intimate relation depend upon mutual confidence, unselfishness and forbearance; and also upon the partners holding similar standards of business conduct.

We further caution our members against verbal understandings, whether in the formation of partnerships or in other business transactions. Serious trouble has often arisen from the absence of clear and well drawn agreements. Even in the case of near relatives or close friends, equal caution should be observed; for the closer the friendship the more serious is the injury caused by misunderstandings, such as are only too common when important matters are settled by verbal arrangement. *1911*

426 We believe that the secret paying or giving of money or presents to persons employed or trusted by others, to induce them to act otherwise than they would have done without such inducement, in no way differs from the giving and receiving of bribes, and is morally wrong on the part of both the offerer and the receiver... We earnestly advise Friends to adhere to a true standard of integrity in all their transactions, and to accept cheerfully what this may involve. *1911*

The making of Wills

427 Knowing the uncertainty of life, it is strongly recommended that Friends make their wills in time of health and strength of judgment, to prevent the inconvenience, loss and trouble that may fall upon their relatives and friends through their dying intestate. We counsel that none postpone this duty to a sick bed, an improper time to settle our outward affairs. Even if we should be favoured with a clear understanding, this ought not to be diverted from a grave consideration of the approaching solemn change. Making his will in due time can shorten no man's days, but omission and delay have proved very injurious to many. *1782; 1911*

428 Friends are reminded that marriage revokes a will, and that, after marriage, a fresh will should be made without delay. Friends are also urged to keep in mind the need for revising their wills from time to time as circumstances alter. *1911; 1959*

429 Recommended that Friends who have young children do in their wills appoint faithful Friends to be guardians to them, till they come to the age of twenty-one years. *Yearly Meeting, 1706*

430 Let Friends in making their wills have a strict regard to justice and equity, and not be actuated by caprice and prejudice, to the injury of those who may have a reasonable expectation from their kindred and near connections. Let none (although occasion may have been given or taken) carry any resentment to the grave, remembering that we all stand in need of mercy and forgiveness. Friends are advised not to make large bequests to relatives or others who do not need them; and to remember the pressing claims of religious and social concerns. *1782; 1911*

431 Friends are earnestly recommended to employ persons skilful in law and of good repute to make their wills, and to see that those whom they appoint to act as their executors or trustees are suitable and willing to undertake the responsibilities placed upon them.

Great inconvenience and loss, and sometimes the ruin of families, have happened through the unskilfulness of some who have taken upon them to make wills. Friends are advised, on the one hand, to make their wills as simple as possible, avoiding complicated provisions; and, on the other hand, to consider carefully circumstances which may arise after their decease, so that due provision may be made for all who ought to benefit under the will, even should births, marriages or deaths occur, which the testator had not anticipated.   *1782; 1911; 1959*

Care of money held for others

432 Friends who hold moneys on behalf of others should have regard to the importance of the proper safeguarding and wise administration of such moneys. It is desirable that a separate bank account be used which is not in the name of a single individual. Particular care should be taken to keep proper accounts which should be audited once a year.   *1959*

Simplicity

'*Carefully maintain in your own conduct and encourage in your families truthfulness and sincerity. In your style of living, in your dress and in the furniture of your houses, choose what is simple and beautiful. Encourage the reading of good books, so that the taste thus formed may instinctively reject the trivial and the base.*'
General Advices, 1928

433 It is our tender and Christian advice that Friends take care to keep to truth and plainness, in language, habit, deportment and behaviour; that the simplicity of truth in these things may not wear out nor be lost in our days, nor in our posterity's; and to avoid pride and immodesty in apparel, and all vain and superfluous fashions of the world.   *Yearly Meeting, 1691*

434 Simplicity does not mean that all conform to uniform standards. Each must determine in the light that is given him what promotes

and what hinders his compelling search for the Kingdom. The call to each is to abandon those things that clutter his life and to press toward the goal unhampered. This is true simplicity.

Friends are watchful to keep themselves free from self-indulgent habits, luxurious ways of living and the bondage of fashion. This freedom is the first condition of vigour in all kinds of effort, whether spiritual, intellectual or physical. Undue luxury often creates a false sense of superiority, causes unnecessary burdens upon both ourselves and others and leads to the neglect of the spiritual life. By observing and encouraging simple tastes in apparel, furniture, buildings and manner of living, we help to do away with rivalry and we learn to value self-denial.

But this does not mean that life is to be poor and bare, destitute of joy and beauty. All that promotes fullness of life and aids in service for Christ is to be accepted with thanksgiving. Simplicity, when it removes encumbering details, makes for beauty in music, in art and in living. It clears the springs of life and permits wholesome mirth and gladness to bubble up; it cleans the windows of life and lets joy radiate. It requires the avoidance of artificial or harmful social customs and conventions but it opens wide the door to cultivate and express to all sincere cordiality, kindness and friendliness. This sort of simplicity removes barriers and eases tensions. In its presence all can be at ease.

'Faith & practice' of Philadelphia Y.M. (1955)

435 William Penn said of George Fox that he was 'civil beyond all forms of breeding'. Courtesy, considered not as a formal code of good manners, but as a supple and sensitive pattern of response to other people's needs, moods and desires, has marked the lives of many Friends. Even in his last illness John Woolman (as Esther Tuke wrote) was 'exceedingly afraid from the first of giving needless trouble to any'; and Justine Dalencourt, forced by the German invasion of France in 1914 to leave her villa at Fontaine-Lavaganne, first planted her garden with salads, saying 'I had rather they found something to eat at my house, than that they should have to steal from others'.

Like Justine Dalencourt on that occasion, we may never meet those who are the objects of our courtesy. They may be people who enjoy a beach or beauty spot because we have left it clear of litter; or those with whose papers we have dealt expeditiously in an office; or those whose safety has depended on our consideration while driving on the road. Of such details is courtesy made, but though often it may seem to be occupied with trivial things, yet happiness or even life may sometimes depend upon the grace of courtesy. *1959*

436 It is easy to let ourselves slip into 'action for action's sake'. Without noticing it, we unconsciously seek to enlarge our sphere of activity; our social work confronts us with such heart-breaking realities, with such urgent needs, that we should like to...run from this one to that, lengthening our working hours to the detriment of our health, both physical and spiritual...Unconsciously neglecting day after day to restore our spiritual strength, we find ourselves eventually at the bottom of a dry well, with nothing but our wretched little human powers. Yet we had begun our work of brotherhood with the highest motives, we even had the intimate sense of response to the divine call; yes, it was with a following wind that we launched out, God filling the sails, and Christ at the helm.

Even so, bit by bit, we have transformed what was a divinely appointed task into work on a merely human level, with all its pettiness, jealousies, resentments and shortcomings. And why did things end up like that? Because we neglected our inner life, because we were taken up with action, because we were *too tired* to pray, *too tired* to take part in meetings for worship, *too tired* to refresh our spiritual strength by reading...We must be able to stop in the midst of our urgent task for something even more urgent; prayer, self-composure, meditation in silence, worship.

Henry van Etten, 1942

Education

'*Seek for your children that full development of God's gifts which true education can bring. Remember that the service to which we are called needs healthy bodies, well-trained minds, high ideals and an understanding of the laws and purposes of God. Give of your best to the study of the Bible, and the understanding of the Christian faith. Be open minded, ready constantly to receive new light. Be zealous that education may be continued throughout life, and that its privileges may be shared by all.'*   *General Advices, 1928*

437 We shall never thrive upon ignorance. Our Creator would have us cultivate our understandings in matters of a religious as well as civil nature. The great rule is, that all should be subordinate to the highest object, all...'for the glory of God'.

Joseph John Gurney, 1831

438 *As early as 1668 George Fox urged the foundation of schools not only for boys, but also for girls:* Then I came to Waltham and established a school there for teaching of boys, and ordered a women's school to be set up at Shacklewell to instruct young lasses and maidens in whatsoever things were civil and useful in the creation.

439 *The advice of Bristol Yearly Meeting 1695:*
This meeting do desire that, where Friends can, they would get such schools and schoolmasters for their children, as may bring them up in the fear of the Lord and love of his truth, that so they may not only learn to be scholars, but Christians also; and that all parents will take the same care at home that such reproof, instruction, counsel, and example may be constantly continued in their respective families, that so from the oldest to the youngest, Truth may show itself in its beauty and comeliness to God's glory and all his people's comfort.

440 *The advice of London Yearly Meeting 1695:*
See that schools and schoolmasters who are faithful Friends, and well qualified, be placed and encouraged in all counties, cities, great towns, or places where there may be need. And that such schoolmasters (as much as may be) sometimes correspond with one another, for their help and improvement in such good and

easy methods as are most agreeable to the Truth, and the children's advantage and benefit.

441 To watch the spirit of children, to nurture them in Gospel Love, and labour to help them against that which would mar the beauty of their minds, is a debt we owe them; and a faithful performance of our duty not only tends to their lasting benefit and our own peace, but also to render their company agreeable to us. A care hath lived on my mind, that more time might be employed by parents at home, and by tutors at school, in weightily attending to the spirit and inclinations of children, and that we may so lead, instruct and govern them, in this tender part of life, that nothing may be omitted in our power, to help them on their way to become the children of our Father who is in Heaven. *John Woolman, 1758*

442 The attitude of the Society of Friends towards education has been determined by their belief in the Inner Light. Holding as they do that there is something of the divine in every man, they have regarded education (in the broadest sense) as the developing of that Divine Seed, or the fanning into a flame of that Divine Spark... To Friends, therefore, education is an intensely religious thing; it means the training and development of the spiritual life, the liberating of the Divine that is within us.

Gerald K. Hibbert, 1930

443 If we are to educate people *for* democracy we must educate people *in* democracy. And this is not so much a matter of encouraging self-government in schools, and substituting self-discipline for external authority and punishments, valuable as such experiments may be. It is primarily a matter of developing and training those qualities— at once intellectual and moral—which make for a democratic attitude to life. The capacity to weigh up facts and theories in the kind of temper that is impartial without being indifferent, the capacity to argue without scoring off opponents and to listen sympathetically without contempt, the capacity to get beneath the skin of the other man and to appreciate other points of view—

these qualities, so simple, so obvious and yet so rare, are the fruits of a democratic education.   *A. Barratt Brown (1938)*

444   I may reach God through Keats, you by Beethoven, and a third through Einstein. Should not education to the Christian mean just this—enlarging and cultivating the country of God; and the subjects on any school time-table be thought of as avenues to an increasingly fuller life in God, or, to change the metaphor, windows, each of which gives a new view of the Kingdom of Heaven?.. This may seem a fantastically idealised view of what happens in a school, especially in these days of examinations, but is there any other open to the religiously-minded teacher? Is the commercial side of school and college life, the exchange of intellectual wares for examination results, so many facts and opinions for so many marks, which is so terribly dominating nowadays, to be allowed to weaken the allegiance of the young to knowledge and beauty as bringers of God to mortal men? No examination has yet been devised the passing of which will guarantee wisdom or culture. For these are slow-growing breeds, matters of character as well as of intellect and sentiment, the outcome of long exposure to the influences of truth and beauty.
Caroline C. Graveson (1937)

445   We cannot teach ⟨children⟩ 'to glorify God and enjoy him for ever', because no man can teach another this ultimate thing that he must experience for himself, but it has been our experience that we can set our children in the way to be found by him in their own lives... There is no end to the religious education of our children, no standard of illumination which we may say is enough. The only difference between the child's search and the adult's search is that the child depends on his teachers for the initial guidance and stimulus, while the adult must assume responsibility himself. But the adult, like the child, has the same choice: his eyes are either open or closed, his ears either listening or deaf, his mind active or idle, his heart reaching out or turning in upon itself, his will constantly bending towards God or standing proud in its own stubborn course. The preparation of mind and heart and will for the knowledge and love and service of God is a task that can never end: it is what our life is for.   *'The nurture of our spiritual resources' (1954)*

446 *The teaching of history:*

Every child ought to be made to understand not only something of the world in which he lives, but something of the inheritance from the past to which he is born. He cannot take his place worthily as a citizen unless he realises that his life is part of a great stream of national life that has been running for a thousand years, and that this national life is part of a slow-won civilisation that has been many millenniums in the making. To get a child to feel the organic relation of life today with the life of the past is a much greater thing than to fill him full of the dry facts of history. A much greater thing, because the facts may only bury his faculties under a heap of stones; but the historic sense, if once born in him, is a permanent enlargement of his life, kindling imagination, enriching experience, inspiring character. *William Charles Braithwaite, 1909*

447 *Religious instruction:*

We should look upon our specifically 'religious' instruction as a part of this attempt to bring our children to an understanding of the way in which God has hitherto worked among men…The closer and the more sympathetic their study of Hebrew literature, the more clearly will they see in Hebrew history the struggle of a primitive people towards a lofty conception of the divine nature and a noble understanding of the worth of man. The great succession of the Hebrew prophets, the men who spoke on behalf of God to mankind, marks a wonderful period of religious discovery… To this day the conception of a nation as the servant of God, bringing help to the other peoples of the world, and the recognition of a man's duty even towards those who oppose or hate him, are among the foremost achievements of the human spirit, in response to the divine leading.

This literature must be studied in such a way that something of the freshness of the Hebrew discoveries is understood by the children, something of the barely illumined paganism out of which these bold and inspired thinkers tried to lead their people. The great truths of religion cannot be handed down like a material legacy from one generation to another; they have to be experienced anew by each one who receives them; and for this purpose great help can be obtained from a truly sympathetic understanding of the difficulties and achievements of their first discoverers.

If the Old Testament is studied in this spirit, the history and literature of the Hebrews will make it easier for the child to approach with understanding the New Testament story of the life and teachings of Jesus, and also to follow the doings of his followers, and the subsequent growth and development of the Christian Church. The central fact in the religious history of mankind is the life and personality of Jesus Christ. Earlier conceptions of God and of human duty are found inadequate or misleading in the light of his revelation of the universality and the depth and intensity of divine love, and the subsequent progress of civilisation is bound up with the realisation of his aims and ideas in the world. Our teaching, to be fruitful, must give Jesus this central place. *1925; 1959*

For extracts on religious instruction in the home, see §504-508

448 *The teaching of science:*
The power of the human mind when used methodically in the pursuit of truth is seen in the great advances of pure and applied science. Our necessary training in this discipline must not lead us to mistake the means for the end and to forget that in its practice we are engaged in discovering the truths of God's creation, and that it is His will that we should do so.

Science starts from wonder and the unceasing questioning of the free human spirit. The study of it enriches the mind through the fascinating and ever-widening picture of the universe that it provides, and through the understanding of its method. The enrichment is greatest to the person who is most aware of the great variety of man's approaches to his environment. Science means most, not to the person who thinks it means everything, but to the one who is most keenly aware also of man's search for beauty, his urge to create, his capacity for enjoyment of life, and his desire for personal fulfilment. The implications of this in teaching, and the quality that should be sought in teachers, must be obvious. Given a deeper understanding of the functions of education, the increasingly large place taken by scientific instruction should be welcomed. *1959*

For extracts on Science and Religion see §144-147.

449 *The place of the arts:*
Music and drama, painting and sculpture all help to develop our perception, our enjoyment of life and the search for truth and fulfilment. We must recognise that the inner and outer world must be made one; this involves the creation and enjoyment of beauty, in the things that are nearest to us, in our homes and schools and as far afield as we care to go. Understanding cannot come through a narrow approach to knowledge but the emphasis will vary from person to person. It must not be thought of as necessarily only intellectual. For some it will come through a feeling for imaginative and artistic expression; for some through the inheritance of a traditional standard of craftsmanship. For others, and perhaps in a measure for all, it should come through training in the knowledge and skills necessary for home-making and the care of children. *1959*

450 *Diversities of gifts:*
There are among us children who are gifted with high intellectual power, others who have less. Their fundamental needs are the same and all equally deserve our time and attention. Some children who do not distinguish themselves in the class-room may, for instance, be nonetheless able to develop a sensitiveness to others, an awareness of personal and social needs, a spiritual insight, that will enable them to make an outstanding contribution to the life of the community. There are many other qualities of which an observant teacher will be aware, qualities which make a rich and varied experience possible. Let us make sure that these gifts are not wasted for lack of encouragement or of right schooling. *1959*

Friends and their schools

451 The justification of our schools must be that they commend the way of life for which we believe our Society stands, commend it directly and also indirectly, explicitly and also inexplicitly, using such means as are best fitted for the purpose. No more, but also no less, than that. This separateness can only be justified if we *have* something distinctive to offer, and are determined to give it both to Friend and non-Friend pupils. If they are to continue, they must not merely be schools run by Friends, but schools that witness to what is distinctive in the Quaker interpretation of Christianity.

John W. Harvey (1947)

452 The fundamental principle which Friends stress, that in every person there is something of God capable of receiving direct illumination from God, must apply equally to children as to adults, and must therefore set the tone for the whole life of the school. Teachers and scholars make a community living and working together under discipline in friendship and mutual respect...The whole community should live together in friendship, each one recognising the special position held by the others and the contribution required from each for the perfection of the common life.

'*The Society of Friends & its schools*' (*1946*)

Adult education

453 Many Friends find great opportunities for Christian service as teachers; the responsibilities are heavy but the work can be deeply satisfying and at times exhilarating, calling as it does on all the resources of the intellect, skill, understanding, personality and spirit. There are many Friends serving on the staffs of schools, colleges and universities provided and maintained by public funds, in the administrative service which is ancillary to these, in various forms of adult education and in the many fields of social work which bear on education. As citizens, Friends should strive to secure for all children the educational opportunities which they desire for their own children. They should, and do, serve on parent-teacher associations, on the boards of governors and managers of educational institutions, on divisional and county education committees, as magistrates in children's courts and in many other voluntary capacities. Those involved in these and all other like endeavours should be supported by the interest and prayers of Friends. *1959*

454 The cause of God demands keen, devoted, and well-equipped minds that can meet new experiences, new problems and new duties with wisdom and courage. It demands that the young have every opportunity of growth in breadth of mind, strength of purpose and tenderness of heart, and that as years go on there shall come no stagnation or sterility, but rather fresh vision and fresh power.

Our Society has a particular ground for urging this. We have no special training for the vocal ministry. The standard therefore must be high throughout our whole membership. We must see to it that all have that training which ministers to large views, just judgments and wide sympathies.   *1911; 1925*

455 We must place within the reach of all our adult members advanced religious teaching similar in aim to that which we have seen to be needful for our children. We seek to secure such a general condition of church life that spiritual growth shall be fostered, and a high standard of spiritual intelligence shall be maintained. We are but seeking a rich and well-tilled soil from which every type of ministry shall spring with a robuster growth.   *John Wilhelm Rowntree, 1899*

456 The real contest for the soul of man is between the world of temporal values and that world whose values are intrinsic and eternal: whether man shall be the puppet of an hour, or whether he shall manifest in his life those qualities which time does not corrupt. On the issue of this struggle, the future of civilisation waits expectant. Will the world of time become so materialistic as to stifle the faint flickerings of the human spirit, or will it become infused with those qualities of beauty, truth, and goodness which alone can make life worth while? Whether the Society of Friends can aid man to qualify for this higher citizenship depends upon their concept of and passion for adult education, and upon whether their efforts can be made worthy of their aims.   *Horace Fleming (1929)*

457 We have to see education as a whole beginning in early youth and carried forward into the years of maturity as an unbroken develop-

ment. There may be a danger under new conditions of adult education becoming stereotyped and losing the spirit of freedom and concern which voluntary effort has given to it in the past. Residential communities offer special opportunities for wider forms of education than the mere acquiring of knowledge. In this sphere, as in that of the education of children, we believe that the truest development of the human mind and spirit can only be attained on a basis of worship. *Yearly Meeting, 1946*

Leisure

458 There is, it sometimes seems, an excess of religious and social busyness these days, a round of committees and conferences and journeyings, of which the cost in 'peaceable wisdom' is not sufficiently counted. Sometimes we appear overmuch to count as merit our participation in these things...At least we ought to make sure that we sacrifice our leisure for something worthy. True leisureliness is a beautiful thing and may not lightly be given away. Indeed, it is one of the outstanding and most wonderful features of the life of Christ that, with all his work in preaching and healing and planning for the Kingdom, he leaves behind this sense of leisure, of time in which to pray and meditate, to stand and stare at the cornfields and fishing boats, and to listen to the confidences of neighbours and passers-by...

Most of us need from time to time the experience of something spacious or space-making, when Time ceases to be the enemy, goad-in-hand, and becomes our friend. To read good literature, gaze on natural beauty, to follow cultivated pursuits until our spirits are refreshed and expanded, will not unfit us for the up and doing of life, whether of personal or church affairs. Rather will it help us to separate the essential from the unessential, to know where we are really needed and get a sense of proportion. We shall find ourselves giving the effect of leisure even in the midst of a full and busy life. People do not pour their joys or sorrows into the ears of those with an eye on the clock.

Caroline C. Graveson (1937)

459 Recreation is essential to physical, mental and spiritual health; it brings a needed balance into life and promotes wholeness of personality. The strain of modern life and the fears and tensions that frustrate worthy purposes demand the relaxation that recreation affords...In these days a vast amount of time is spent by many in listening to radio or in looking at television and professional sports. While such entertainments may have a proper place if kept in moderation, recreations in which we are participants rather than mere spectators are usually more beneficial and are much needed. Recreation is relief and restoration; the ultimate basis of inward peace and security is trust in God, consciousness of His love and guidance, and whole-souled commitment to Him in work and play.

'Faith & practice' of Philadelphia Y.M. (1955)

460 Love silence, even in the mind...Much speaking, as much thinking, spends; and in many thoughts, as well as words, there is sin. True silence is the rest of the mind; and is to the spirit, what sleep is to the body, nourishment and refreshment. *William Penn (1699)*

The arts

461 While Friends have been among the pioneers of modern science, they have, until recent years, repressed all taste for the fine arts. These, at their greatest, always contain some revelation of the spirit of God, which is in the fullest harmony with our spiritual faith. In the fields of music, art, and literature, as in others, Friends may witness to the glory of God and advance that glory by their service. 'The fulness of the whole earth is his glory', and we mar the beauty of this message by every limitation we set upon it.

William Charles Braithwaite, 1895

462 *A hesitation about the traditional policy of the Society had been expressed by Elizabeth Fry in 1833 in a letter to her brother Joseph John Gurney:*
It appears to me to be one important means of helping the human mind in a healthy state, that in recreations which are needful for it,

it should be trained as much as possible to look to those things that bring profit as well as pleasure with them. My observation of human nature and the different things that affect it frequently leads me to regret that we as a Society so wholly give up delighting the ear by sound. Surely He who formed the ear and the heart would not have given these tastes and powers without some purpose for them.

463 While the study of virtue and sin has engrossed the Church down the ages, that of aesthetics has had scant attention. Hence we tend to draw an over-sharp line between sin and bad taste. We rightly think sin the more urgent and important of the two because its effect immediately passes over to other people. A human being cannot sin even against his own body without weakening his power for active goodness and so indirectly injuring his fellows. Bad taste we regard as more purely personal, less controllable, less important and less standardized than sin. We dismiss an aesthetic judgment as a 'mere matter of taste', usually with the implication that the perpetrator cannot help himself, that it's his own business, that tastes differ incalculably and irrationally, and that it doesn't much matter anyhow. It remains, however, to question whether aesthetic taste would have come to be regarded as an element in life so unimportant and so incapable of discipline and definition if it had received a tithe as much positive attention from the Church as has virtue, and whether...the wider distribution of possessions and the growth of scientific inventiveness in the world are not making this neglect more apparent. For the world becomes increasingly 'full of a number of things', and therefore of opportunities for choice, and therefore occasions for bad taste as well as good taste, for vulgarity and philistinism as well as refinement and culture...So we return to our conviction that, unless matters of culture are more clearly shown to be vitally related to religion, an increasing element in life will stand outside of the religious sphere, and life become either more and more disintegrated or wholly secularized.

Caroline C. Graveson (*1937*)

464 Whatever the medium in which he works, the artist performs a service of social and spiritual value. For he helps us to see with him

the beauty of the world and to share his emotions, sometimes by reminding us of things we have already felt, sometimes by bringing home to us for the first time their beauty and significance. In the words of Browning:

> Art was given for that;
> God uses us to help each other so,
> Lending our minds out...   *1925*

465 The conventional distinction between 'sacred' and 'secular' art is indeed misleading and harmful to both art and religion. Men have come to speak of sacred music, sacred pictures, or sacred verse merely because the subject matter is connected with a world of religion which they have previously separated from the world of ordinary life. But the more fruitful distinction is between inspired art and uninspired art. The former may be, whatever its ostensible occasion or subject, essentially religious; the latter cannot be made so by any selection of a (so-called) 'religious' subject...It is men and women in the first instance who are inspired and who are thus able to produce inspired speech and writing, music and painting; and because the springs of inspiration are never dry the book of revelation is not closed...It may be suggested that the test of the quality of such deliverances—whether in art or in religious speech or writing—will be found in their capacity in turn to inspire, to find an answering echo in the minds and lives of others, and to become a perpetual fount of inspiration. This is the immortality of the great inspirations of the prophets and artists—they continue to inspire because they have in them eternal life. 'The words that I speak unto you they are spirit and they are life.' These are the undying words—inspired and inspiring still.

A. Barratt Brown & John W. Harvey (1929)

466 The truth which the artist seeks and which he expresses through his art is part of the universal truth, just as the truth sought and expressed by the philosopher and the scientist and the theologian is part of the universal truth. 'The judgment of beauty is not, I believe, anything set apart from the rest of spiritual life', wrote Lascelles Abercrombie. 'There is but one faculty of judgment;

and according to the sphere in which it operates, its final verdicts are given as truth, morality, and beauty.' The man who can only see the significance of his own specialised field of vision may not mar his own contribution, but inevitably he will impoverish it. Happy is the artist, the philosopher, the scientist, or the theologian who recognises that all Truth is one.   *Elfrida Vipont Foulds (1955)*

467   *A carpenter ponders on the nature of craftsmanship:*
It is in the workshop and at the bench that an insight into the soul of wood craftsmanship can be truly gained. There are tools, there is the wood—rude planks, ungarnished, their surface scored with the saw. Between them, and without which each is useless, must come the soul and spirit of the designer and craftsman; the deft hands prompted by an alert mind; the knowledge attained only through years of study and service; the creative instinct and ability that will, by the correct use of the tools, transform the mere plank into a thing of usefulness and beauty—possibly a joy for ever... It was at the lathe, when a youth, that I first realised the charm of line, the contour that flows continuously on, diminishing and enlarging, though separated by ornamental members...Those who have studied woodcraft for half a century find themselves still learning and quite unable to pack all their knowledge into a nutshell for the convenience of a beginner. The training is not that of the university; it is, however, quite as exacting in its own way and so merits equal recognition and respect, and it is encouraging to note that this idea is slowly gaining ground. The woodworkers of a century ago added to their carpentry the dignity of craft; this is why the examples of their handiwork that remain are treasured. Let it not be assumed that it is merely because such work is old that it is appreciated so highly. Even a slight study will reveal the artist mind that prompted the hands, the perception that had grasped the principles of design, the certain knowledge in its decisive finish. There is the secret of its permanent inspiration, its power to soothe and charm.   *Walter Rose (1938)*

468   Friends in former times have no doubt erred—a very noble error—in too sternly refusing to give any place to the seductive delights of

the eye and the ear; and in too rigidly excluding from their own and their children's lives much that was innocent and beautiful. Nature and commonsense have been too strong for the policy of exclusion, and the danger now seems to be that in the reaction from it we may forget the supreme and unchanging necessity of a right subordination. So great and overwhelming has been the rush of increasing interest and excitement in the outer life of action, of discovery, of enjoyment and amusement, that even our religion is in danger of becoming an outward thing...It is the central root of obedience alone which can give to outward activity any value or beauty. This is the ancient Quaker principle, and unless we hold firmly to it both in thought and in action our Society will assuredly become as salt that has lost its savour.   *Caroline E. Stephen (1908)*

469 There is a daily round for beauty as well as for goodness, a world of flowers and books and cinemas and clothes and manners as well as of mountains and masterpieces...God is in *all* beauty, not only in the natural beauty of earth and sky, but in all fitness of language and rhythm, whether it describe a heavenly vision or a street fight, a Hamlet or a Falstaff, a philosophy or a joke: in all fitness of line and colour and shade, whether seen in the Sistine Madonna or a child's knitted frock: in all fitness of sound and beat and measure, whether the result be Bach's Passion music or a nursery jingle. The quantity of God, so to speak, varies in the different examples, but His quality of beauty in fitness remains the same.
Caroline C. Graveson (1937)

Wholeness and health

470 *The experience of George Fox, 1652:*
And when they had led me to the common moss, and a multitude of people following, the constables took me and gave me a wisk over the shoulders with their willow rods, and so thrust me amongst the rude multitude which then fell upon me with their hedge stakes and clubs and staves and beat me as hard as ever they could strike on my head and arms and shoulders, and it was a great while before

they beat me down and mazed me, and at last I fell down upon the wet common. There I lay a pretty space, and when I recovered myself again, and saw myself lying on a watery common and all the people standing about me, I lay a little still, and the power of the Lord sprang through me, and the eternal refreshings refreshed me, that I stood up again in the eternal power of God and stretched out my arms amongst them all, and said again with a loud voice, 'Strike again, here is my arms and my head and my cheeks'. And there was a mason, a rude fellow, a professor called, he gave me a blow with all his might just a-top of my hand, as it was stretched out, with his walking rule-staff. And my hand and arm was so numbed and bruised that I could not draw it in unto me again, but it stood out as it was. Then the people cried out, 'He hath spoiled his hand, for ever having any use of it more'. The skin was struck off my hand and a little blood came, and I looked at it in the love of God, and I was in the love of God to them all that had persecuted me. And after a while the Lord's power sprang through me again, and through my hand and arm, that in a minute I recovered my hand and arm and strength in the face and sight of them all, and it was as well as it was before, and I never had another blow afterward.

471 *The experience of George Fox, 1659:*
I was sent for to many sick people: and at one time I was sent for to Whitechapel about three o'clock in the morning to a woman that was dying and her child, and the people was weeping about her; and after a while I was moved to speak to the woman, and she and her child was raised up; and she got up, to the astonishment of the people, and her child also was healed.

And when I came to Gerard Roberts's house about 8 in the morning, there came in Sarah Blackbury to complain to me of the poor, and how many poor Friends was in want; and the Lord had showed me what I should do, in his eternal power and wisdom. So I spoke to her, to bid about sixty women to meet me at the 1st hour in the afternoon at the sign of the Helmet, at a Friend's house, and they did so accordingly, such as were sensible women of the Lord's truth and fearing God. And what the Lord had opened unto me

I declared unto them concerning their having a meeting once a week every second-day; that they might see and enquire into the necessity of all Friends who was sick and weak, and who was in wants, or widows and fatherless, in the City and suburbs... And that they in visiting the sick in the Lord's power and word, through which they would have the wisdom of the Lord and of his creation, and how to administer his creatures, and by the same power to heal and strengthen, with the outward things, and without them; which they have felt prosperous to this day: and great things has been done in their meetings by the Lord's power.

472   *The experience of John Wilhelm Rowntree, 1894:*

Just as he was entering young manhood and was beginning to feel the dawning sense of a great mission before him, he discovered that he was slowly losing his sight. He was told that before middle life he would become totally blind. Dazed and overwhelmed he staggered from the doctor's office to the street and stood there in silence. Suddenly he felt the love of God wrap him about as though a visible presence enfolded him, and a joy filled him, such as he had never known before. From that time... he was a gloriously joyous and happy man. His physical limitations have all along been turned into inward profit. His long, hard battle with a stubborn disease which was attacking the very citadel of his powers—his sight, his hearing and his memory—has only made him more heroic and gentle.   *Rufus M. Jones, 1905*

473   *The experience of Rebecca Beard, 1945:*

There came a time in my life when science and the love of scientific knowledge did not seem to answer the need... We must be able to leap the gap from facts which are known to those facts which are but yet dimly discerned. But so often we do not see or feel this thing until we are forced to our knees and have come to the place where we can no longer go under our own limited human power and strength. I came to that place, and my colleagues who knew me well and loved me, said, 'You must put your affairs in order, for you cannot live through another heart-attack'.

When faced by that ultimatum you realise that you have nothing within yourself with which to meet it. For the first time in my life, literally and figuratively, I went down on my knees. It was only then that God became real and I began to sense the great power that was outside of myself, and yet was part of me, and I cried, 'If it is possible, take this from me or take me. I have gone as far as I can.' A wonderful revelation came: a great spiritual illumination. I knew then that I was healed, and I knew that the rest of my life would be given to helping others find that healing.

The experience of Stephen Grellet during the Philadelphia yellow fever epidemic of 1798 is described in §59; the reflections of Hilda Clark on her sister-in-law's illness and death in childbirth in 1908 are given in §108.

474 Health is a process, not a single and unique event. Health is a becoming; it is not a state of being. The price of health is an eternal vigilance, a constant adaptation to the creative Word of God... During each life period, a new measure of the Word of God must be built, living stone by stone, into the very structure of the growing personality, just as the energy of the sun is built into the plants of the earth. Childhood, adolescence, maturity, middle age and old age, each and every phase of life calls for the discovery of new potentialities within the eternal self... Thus, by a process of growth, the healthy spirit is prepared for the last crisis, death, when the body returns to the earth, and the spirit to God who gave it. If the spirit be in health, the fate of its tabernacle becomes of slight concern...

Experiences of spiritual health produce, I am satisfied, evident, often radical changes within the personality, they produce obvious enhancements of intellectual skill and mental ability; they produce actual increases in physical health and vitality—especially perhaps among those who are young. I have never felt it necessary to suppose either that spiritual health necessarily guaranteed physical health, or that poor physical health was necessarily the consequence of spiritual disorder. What is necessary is that we should first seek the Kingdom and then be prepared to wait in hope and patience for whatever may be added unto us. But it remains true... ⟨that⟩ to seek

health in the spirit and in measure to find it, is as sound a guarantee
of ordinary bodily and mental fitness as any I know.

Howard E. Collier (1945)

475 Although in some cases we may feel impelled through the very
acuteness of the suffering to pray definitely for its removal, in general
what we should aim at is that the sufferer should have such a sense
of the love of God that he is brought to know the true and deep
healing of the spirit which will result in the removal of any obstacles
to the flow of the Divine Life.

Intercession should be a daily practice in ⟨our⟩ lives...It is not
necessary to be in perfect health ourselves in order to pray effectively; nor should we wait till we feel like it. The most powerful
intercessors are those who make it a regular habit. It is helpful
to think that God is waiting for us to offer ourselves to him in the
ministry of healing. Just as the remedies for many diseases had to
wait on the development of medical science (through which we must
believe that his Spirit is working), so in this service of intercession,
results are waiting upon our obedience and readiness to do our
part. Thus we shall come to know what it is to share in the fellowship
of the Spirit, and become 'workers together with God'.

Frederick J. Tritton, 1958

476 *Robert Fortescue Fox (1858-1940) came of a family which had produced
physicians, surgeons, and dentists since the eighteenth century; he was one
of six brothers who 'went into medicine as the obvious family career'. In
1929 he addressed Syria & Palestine Yearly Meeting on 'The place of
medicine in the Society of Friends':*
The calling of medicine seems to approach what I conceive to be
a chief purpose of Friends, to work for the restoration of harmony
in the world...Medical education, which was ⟨once⟩ almost a
priestly office, has become a very long and arduous training in exact
science. But I think that the old sense of obligation survives in all
branches of medical activity. We see it not only in the hospital
and in the daily and nightly routine of the practitioner, but in those
who give up their lives in tropical swamps, or in laboratories almost

as deadly, in an effort, which has become one long instinctive endeavour, for the prevention and cure of disease. I sometimes wonder whether the Society of Friends has appreciated at its real value knowledge that has been gained at such a price and which is informed by such a steadfast spirit of service...At its best and highest it is like the gifts of Heaven, for they are shared by the evil and by the good, that mortals may have life and have it more abundantly.

477 In the final analysis the springs of positive health and the roots of preventive medicine are deeply buried in the life of the spirit and of religion. To me, at least, it is clear that there is no other source from which a sufficiency of steady enduring motive and power can be derived. Therefore the doctor must say to everyone that positive health requires the co-ordinated and balanced culture of body, mind, and spirit. *Howard E. Collier, 1952*

The animal creation

'Let the law of kindness know no limits. Show a loving consideration for all God's creatures.' *General Advices, 1928*

478 I believe that where the love of God is verily perfected, and the true spirit of government watchfully attended to, a tenderness toward all creatures made subject to us will be experienced, and a care felt in us that we do not lessen that sweetness of life in the animal creation which the Great Creator intends for them under our government. *John Woolman, 1772*

479 Animals...are still menaced by fear and pain much of which might be alleviated by succour and comfort. The greater welfare of these creatures, so dependent on us, is based upon the fact that they are part of our earthly life. Is not all life one? In his thirst for knowledge, in his want of thought and want of heart, man is not always kind to animals. *Croydon & Southwark M.M., 1957*

480 Kindness to animals should be explicitly proclaimed as a Christian duty. Suffering can be caused through callousness and carelessness based often upon ignorance, and we must testify against such cruelty wherever we find it. Kindness therefore requires knowledge and understanding as well as good will; the most recent knowledge should continually be sought to help us to comprehend the needs of animals and what circumstances are likely to cause them pain. All our dealings with them should be guided by a sensitive, intelligent understanding of their nature and needs. In recognising the wonder and mystery of God's animal kingdom we increase our reverence for Him. We need to show a humble acknowledgement of the responsibility for animals with which God has entrusted us. We need both to wrestle individually with the implications of this, and to be tolerant of each other's findings, seeking unity in spite of differences in interpretation.   *1959*

Chapter 10: Marriage and the home

'*In looking forward to marriage, remember that happiness depends on the presence of a reverent and understanding love. Consider the serious responsibilities of parenthood, and do not forget the help you may draw from the loving counsel of your own parents. Seek to be joined in a common discipleship of Jesus Christ. Ask guidance of God, desiring, above all temporal considerations, that your union may be owned and blest of Him.*'   *General Advices, 1928*

Preparation for marriage

481 We earnestly advise and exhort Friends that, in the first place, all seriously wait upon the Lord for counsel and clearness in this weighty concern before they make any procedure with any, in order to marriage...that they may not be led by any forward, brittle, or uncertain affections in this weighty concern, to their own hurt, with grief of their friends, and the dishonour of Truth.

Yearly Meeting, 1690

482 Marriage is an ordinance of God, appointed for the help and blessing of both man and woman, and for the right upbringing of the next generation. Our Lord, in His teaching, drew very close the bonds of marriage; and the well-being of any people depends, in large measure, on the purity, strength and love that mark its family life.

The union of husband and wife is fraught with momentous issues, and is not to be thought of lightly. Happiness and blessing in marriage depend first on the presence of devoted love, a love which is not the outcome of a merely passing attraction, but which includes a real respect by each for the personality of the other. Every such union should be undertaken in the fear of the Lord, and with a reverent attention to His counsel and guidance. It will be owned and blessed by Him if the healthy love that draws two human souls together is sanctified by the larger love of Christ and of His brethren; it will yield its fairest fruit as it is chastened by the discipline of care and trial bravely borne, and ripened into self-forgetting devotion by the mutual influence of parents and children. The family is the standing witness that man is not intended to live alone: that he becomes what he is meant to be as his character is trained in unselfishness by responsibility for others, and by the claims and duties of a common life. *1911; 1925*

483 The difficulties in the way of early marriage are real and hard to overcome. Every couple has to decide whether to wait for an added degree of financial security, or whether to marry without much security, often in difficult circumstances and often with the wife continuing to earn her living. It is a problem which can only be decided by each individual couple according to their own scale of values... The early struggles faced in a spirit of adventure can do much to unite husband and wife, and to lay a sure foundation on which to build up the family life of the future. For all young couples the task is fundamentally the same—to follow the light as they see it, and to be prepared to work and sacrifice for the attainment of an ideal. *'Marriage & parenthood' (1954)*

484 An opportunity for consideration of various aspects of marriage in to-day's setting can be of real value to those embarking on this adventure. There is much to be gained if the couple can understand beforehand the physical and emotional factors inherent in the sex relationship, and help can also be obtained by considering such subjects as financial arrangements, practical home-making, and the relative claims of individual and mutual interests and activities.

1959

485 *Job Scott writes to Eunice Anthony in 1780, shortly before their marriage:* Having felt thee abundantly near this evening, I am free to write what revives for thy perusal, hoping it may be useful towards our rightly stepping along through time together. First, dearly beloved, let me tell thee, that however short I may be of strict adherence to the Light of Life; yet it is my crown, my chief joy, to feel the holy

harmonious influences and inshinings of the love of Jesus my Saviour upon my soul; and I feel that without this I must be miserable indeed. I also believe that the true enjoyment of the marriage union consists eminently in *both* being engaged to draw near to the Lord, and act in his counsel; which I not only wish, but in a good degree expect, may be our happy case. If it should, though we have as it were a dry morsel to partake of, as to the things of this life; yet we may joy in the Lord, and rejoice in the God of our salvation. Thou knowest I have no great things to invite thee to. If we are joined together (the which I trust we already measurably are) we must not expect the paths of affluence, no, no:

> This day be bread and peace our lot;
> All else beneath the sun,
> Thou know'st if best bestow'd or not,
> And let thy will be done.

May we, the remainder of our lives, earnestly press after resignation to the Lord's will, and above all things, strive to please him who only can give peace, in whatever circumstances we may be. Then, I trust, the guardian angel of his holy presence will encamp around us, and his everlasting arms be underneath to support.

Solemnisation of marriage

486 Marriage has always been regarded by Friends as a religious, not a mere civil compact. *1833*

487 The simple Quaker wedding, when the two concerned join together with their friends in worship, is the most natural expression of the way of life in which we believe. In the presence of God they take each other freely and equally as life-long partners, asking His blessing on their union and dedicating their new life to His service. From the start also they feel that they are partners with God in the new undertaking. They believe that, while Christian faith remains, there can be no disagreement or difficulty which cannot be resolved by the grace which is theirs in their new and deepening relationship illumined by the love of God.   '*The marriage relationship*' (*1949*)

488 *The experience of Thomas and Mary Ellwood at their marriage on 28 October 1669:*

We sensibly felt the Lord with us and joining us, the sense whereof remained with us all our lifetime, and was of good service and very comfortable to us on all occasions.

For a further extract on the solemnisation of marriage see §272.

The married life

489 Since God is the author of love, no couple can without Him make good their promise to love one another for the rest of their lives. By nature, we cannot love for ever with the same tempo of love the young man or woman we married in our twenties—because we fell in love, not only with all that they then were, but also with all that was potential in them, and in ourselves through them. Love must inevitably change and mature, and every relationship has its times of stress as well as its times of renewal. But there are periods in some married lives when all that can be done is to go on trying to love and to continue to believe in the elusive and unique quality for which we gave ourselves to our partner until death should part us. Should one fail to change, develop and grow, the other may well feel cheated, but we have to remember the fault is generally on both sides, for a couple belong together. One's fault often grows out of the other's carelessness in affection or leading, and one's grief is rightly the other's sorrow too.

True love is proven when the loved one begins to be not only the mysterious beckoner of destiny, but becomes also the occasion of dull indubitable duty. At a frontier of life when one partner begins to say to him or herself: 'How can I love any longer? but I must love', then sometimes steadfastness and faith have power to nurse into existence the new being needed as companion and lover. What a triumph when old love is transformed into a deeper surer new love which can accept more fully what each has, and the pair find a rebirth together in those things which are eternal, and through this a renewal of their every-day living. This is part of the pattern of the cross which leads to creative resurrection in married lives, and it is a path not a few Christian people have to follow. For a couple deeply rooted in the wide charity of Christ, marriage is safe and spiritually fruitful.   *1959*

490   *Barrow Cadbury, after forty years of marriage, wrote in 1933 some notes 'gathered from personal experience and from observation' for the help of young people in the Bournville works:* Start out together on a fifty-fifty basis, each sharing with the other, and thereby doubly enriching both. Recognise the equality of the service each performs, even though the work differs…The wider your interests outside your regular occupation, the more companionship you will enjoy together, and the happier and more fruitful life will be. After all, if two people are going to live together for thirty, forty, or sixty years they must have interesting things to talk about, or they will get cruelly on one another's nerves. It needs a real effort to cultivate new interests, but the effort is well repaid…The foregoing suggestions are dictated by a *common-sense* view of life, and common sense is one of God's best gifts, which is not always used. But for the full enjoyment of all that God gives us in marriage and home life we need spiritual union. Underlying all must be the spiritual union and communion which bring into married life the power and grace which can carry a couple through the most difficult times of testing. The fellowship of fellow Christians which many of us enjoy when worshipping with them is of real spiritual help in life. Much in life goes by precedents, and the habit of attending a place of worship has proved of real value to many parents and children, together helping to create the spiritual bond which unites them and should unite us all.

491   In setting out in life, let there be a prudent and Christian care to avoid a scale of living which may minister to luxury or pride, or tend to an increase of worldly care, and thus diminish the power to devote time and money to the service of others for the Lord's sake.
                                                      Yearly Meeting, 1872

492 Children change and enrich the relationship of husband and wife. Together they must enter upon a new phase of life which will bring them hard work, many anxieties, but also much joy, fun and laughter. For many years their personal pleasures and conveniences will take second place to the needs and demands of the growing family. But husband and wife will be brought closer together by the shared tasks of parenthood and will grow in wisdom and maturity through self-sacrifice and the exercise of patience and understanding.

'Marriage & parenthood' (*1954*)

493 Marriage is to be taken seriously, but not always in grim earnest; its problems take perspective from fun, adventure and fulfilment, and joy and sorrow are mingled together. We rejoice in success, but we must also be glad that we can console each other in failure. 'With my body I thee worship' is to many a blessed phrase: but while some find a perfect physical relationship easily, others reach it the hard way, and it is not less precious for that. It is wonderful never to quarrel, but it means missing the dear delight of making it up. Children bring joy and grief; some will have none and will miss both the grief and the joy. For some, there is a monogamy so entire that no other love ever touches it; but others 'fall in love' time and time again, and must learn to make riches of their affection without destroying their marriage or their friends. Let us thank God for what we share, which enables us to understand; and for the infinite variety in which each marriage stands alone.

We thank God, then, for the pleasures, joys and triumphs of marriage; for the cups of tea we bring each other, and the seedlings in the garden frame; for the domestic drama of meetings and partings, sickness and recovery; for the grace of occasional extravagance, flowers on birthdays and unexpected presents; for talk at evenings of the events of the day; for the ecstasy of caresses; for gay mockery at each other's follies; for plans and projects, fun and struggle; praying that we may neither neglect nor undervalue these things, nor be tempted to think of them as self-contained and self-sufficient.

1959

Difficulties and failures

494 We would counsel Friends to take timely advice in periods of difficulty. The early sharing of problems with sympathetic Friends or marriage counsellors can often bring release from misunderstandings and give positive help towards new joy together. Friends ought to be able to do this, but much will depend on the quality of our life together in the Society. If marriages among us fail, we are all part of that failure. We need to be more sensitive to each other's needs, knowing one another in the things which are material as in the things which are eternal.

Marriage & Parenthood Committee, 1956

495 We believe that those who are involved in marriage difficulties should be able to look for sympathy and understanding to the group where they normally find fellowship in worship. We hope that any who feel drawn to a Friends' meeting will always be welcomed, and that they may there discover the guiding and healing power of God's love. *'The marriage relationship' (1949)*

496 Our particular attention has been given to the difficult problem of the re-marriage, according to Friends' usage, of those who may, one or other, have been divorced. We respect and enter most sympathetically into the deep feelings of those among us who believe that our corporate testimony to the sanctity and life-long nature of marriage, with the promises therein made, would be seriously weakened if we allowed such re-marriages. Nevertheless... we do not feel it would be right indiscriminately to forbid all such re-marriages. In exercising their discretion Monthly Meetings should consider their procedure most carefully. In general they should be fully satisfied that the parties seeking re-marriage are well known to and associated with the meeting...

We ask all our Monthly Meetings very seriously to consider whether everything possible is being done to give timely, wise, sensitive and continuing help and guidance both before and throughout marriage, not only to prevent breakdowns but to build up and maintain the unity and happiness of enduring marriage. We would, yet again, express our profound belief in the sacred and life-long nature of marriage and, notwithstanding our recognition of the failure of some to keep the solemn promises made to each other, we do not accept the view that there should be any modification of the declarations made in our meetings for worship on the occasion of the solemnisation of marriage. They remain, with God's blessing and guidance, as the true basis of marriage. *Yearly Meeting, 1957*

The ideal restated

497 Never marry but for love; but see that thou lovest what is lovely. He that minds a body and not a soul has not the better part of that relation, and will consequently want the noblest comfort of a married life.

Between a man and his wife nothing ought to rule but love... As love ought to bring them together, so it is the best way to keep them well together.

A husband and wife that love and value one another show their children and servants that they should do so too. Others visibly lose their authority in their families by their contempt of one another; and teach their children to be unnatural by their own examples.

Let not enjoyment lessen, but augment, affection; it being the basest of passions to like when we have not, what we slight when we possess.

Here it is we ought to search out our pleasure, where the field is large and full of variety, and of an enduring nature; sickness, poverty, or disgrace being not able to shake it, because it is not under the moving influences of worldly contingencies.

Nothing can be more entire and without reserve; nothing more zealous, affectionate and sincere; nothing more contented and constant than such a couple, nor no greater temporal felicity than to be one of them.

William Penn (1693)

Parents and the family

498   A high ideal of family life, maintained in practice as well as in theory, is an important part of the inheritance which parents are in duty bound to leave to their children; and, so far as they fail to do this, they are depriving them of their just rights, and inflicting on them what may prove an irreparable injury. This ideal is inevitably lowered when love and sympathy and mutual confidence are absent.   *1911*

499   The Quaker home offers a supreme opportunity for the expression of the Quaker way of life. Outward circumstances have varied with the times: from abundance of domestic help to none at all; from leisure, which could be sacrificed for service, to overburdened lives calling for simplification; from individual thrift to dependence upon a welfare state. Nothing has changed the basic spiritual experience of Quaker home-making. Husband and wife are partners with God; and though inevitably young children are more dependent upon the mother for physical care and training in the early years, and though a child will often respond more readily to one parent than to the other, the parental responsibility is a joint one at every stage. As the children grow up they should share actively with their parents in the concerns of the home, the performance of domestic tasks and the interchange of ideas; there should be perfect freedom of expression for all, but no forcing of expression for any. The atmosphere of such a home will give young people a basic security which will remain with them even in periods of rebellion and assertiveness. In some cases a breakaway is essential to growth.

In the busy years of home life the parents are upheld and strengthened by their dependence upon God and upon one another; the efficient running of the home, the simple hospitality, the happy atmosphere, are all outward signs of this three-fold inner relationship. Home-making is a Quaker service in its own right. It should be recognised as such and a proper balance preserved, so that other activities—even the claims of Quaker service in other fields—should not be allowed to hinder its growth.   *1959*

500 Early training in habits of obedience is of the utmost importance in the home. Even young children may unconsciously learn discipline through observing the lives of their parents; later they will come to understand the need for self-discipline. In the home, at school, and progressively as they enter adult life, they will thus develop into good citizens and obedient children of our heavenly Father accepting and doing His will with reverence and joy, 'so from the oldest to the youngest, Truth may show itself in its beauty and comeliness to God's glory and all His people's comfort' (§*439*).   *1959*

501 Many who are shy of attending meetings for an avowedly religious purpose will respond to a loving concern which springs from simple friendship. There is therefore great value in small gatherings or individual talks in the homes of Friends, where people, not only members and attenders, can meet to exchange ideas and theories, doubts and preoccupations, and to discuss projects and careers. It has been our experience that such gatherings have had a profound effect upon the lives of men and women, both those who give and those who receive such hospitality.   *1959*

502 *The following passage describes such a home, that of Warren and Amy Lewis:* In 1920 they joined the Society of Friends and some years later moved to Eccles to establish the home which is inseparable from Amy Lewis's life and work. She did not allow her outside activities to impoverish her home, but rather enriched all her service with the generous warmth of her family life. She and her husband have shown us that under the exacting conditions of the modern world it is possible to build a new kind of Swarthmoor Hall; the outward circumstances may be different but the spirit is the same... Things were never easy materially, and faith and works, conjoined to prayer, were their principal resources. As the years went by, countless men and women, young and old, came to this home to talk out their problems and share in its blessings. *Testimony of Hardshaw East Monthly Meeting concerning Amy Lewis, 1951.*

The life of the Swarthmoor Household in seventeenth-century England is described in §17 and 18; that of a home in nineteenth-century New England in §91.

503   We recognise the new freedom and equality of those marriages in which both parents are able to pursue careers and to share the duties of the home. We are proud to think that in the past, by liberating women in the ministry and encouraging them in service, we have helped to create this pattern. But we know, too, that it brings its own tensions and dangers. If parents pursue their own interests and vocations (however worthy) without consideration for their families, the children will suffer. There are times when family calls must be put before all others, even those of our Society. We do not believe that rules of conduct can be strictly laid down, but we beg parents to be ready, in this as in other ways, to sacrifice monetary advantage, the pleasure of liberty, or the interests of their professional life, in order to preserve and build the family. The institution of marriage has survived many revolutions, social changes, and altered moral codes; we believe that it will survive others. Our task is to apply eternal principles in changing circumstances, and to make homes that are secure and lasting.   *1959·*

504   From the earliest age the child in the truly Christian home will have the tremendous advantage of being born into a family where daily dependence upon God is part of the air he breathes. He will be surrounded by an atmosphere of worship, in which God is glorified not only in times set apart for prayer, when the mother and sometimes the father pray with their child; not only in the quietness of grace before meals, in the Bible reading together...but in all the work and play of the home. So, long before he comes to any conscious realisation of the fact, he knows in his whole being that worship and work are parts of the same life, and that all this is done 'as unto the Lord and not unto men' in confidence and trust in God.   *'Growing up in Quaker worship' (1952)*

505   I have seen much advantage to children, and indeed to whole families, from the practice of a solemn pause at meals. It learns children stillness, decency, and reverence; and where it is done in a feeling manner, with minds rightly turned to feel after God, and experience his blessing, and is not practised in a slight formal manner, it tends to season and solemnize the minds of young and old...I am

morally certain, that I have many a day gone through the cares and concerns of life, with much more composure, stability, satisfaction and propriety, for the strength and assistance I have found in drawing near to God in solemn silence in my family; and I wish the practice of reverently adoring him in this way, may increase more and more.   *Journal of Job Scott (1751-1793)*

506 Parents should not shirk the duty of helping their children to have a right idea of God, and to grow up into a living experience of His power and love. Some will feel acutely the weakness of their own religious experience, and the dangers of suggesting crude beliefs that will afterwards have to be unlearnt. We must never introduce ideas of God that are inconsistent with His perfect love. The essential truths are simple. The scriptural figures of the Father and the Good Shepherd are easily understood by children and will not need to be outgrown.   *1925; 1959*

507 Children should be taught early to pray, and as soon as possible they should be encouraged to speak to God in their own way; the natural difficulties that occur when prayer seems to bring no result should be handled with understanding and sympathy.   *1925*

508 Parents can do much to help their children understand Friends' approach to the principles of Christian truth. It is of value both to the meeting and to the family when parents and children come regularly together to meeting for worship. Even young children, who do not usually stay to the whole of the meeting, can respond to the atmosphere of silence. The habit of quiet waiting may be the starting-point of the child's spiritual development.   *1959*

509 It is the responsibility of parents to see that their children are reliably informed about the formation and functions of their own bodies, and concerning their manner of coming into the world. There must be the fullest confidence between parents and children in this matter, and the responsibility should be shared by both

parents. Information about sex which is naturally sought for by the enquiring mind should be given gradually, in a simple and informal way, according to the growth of the child towards maturity.

1911; 1925; 1959

510 As the boy or girl grows towards adolescence parents often have to stand back, for other people can frequently give better help at this stage. If the parents' way of life continues to make them acceptable partners in adventures of the spirit, and if they are willing to be called upon when needed, they still have opportunities to help the adolescent, but these opportunities come only now and then in actual words. The parents, however, must hold firmly to their own religious faith and principles, and can help the adolescent best by doing so. Trust, a sense of humour, a ready forgiveness, and the ability to 'speak the truth in love' are other elements of the good home background for this age. Parents, too, should be ready to share experiences that they have found precious—not only specifically religious experiences, but experiences of people, art, music, poetry and nature. *'Growing up in Quaker worship'* (*1952*)

Chapter 11: Stages of life

Youth

511 There is no generation of young minds that finds the truths and realities of religion easy of apprehension. Faith is never ready made; it must always be *built*. The building process is easier in some epochs than in others, but the structure of the spirit must be reared in every case in the face of real difficulties.   *Rufus M. Jones (1929)*

512 *By the end of the seventeenth century there was growing up a generation born into the Society and in danger of becoming 'traditional Quakers'. Two years before the experience of Samuel Bownas, recounted in §45, William Penn thus addressed them:*
O! you young men and women, let it not suffice you, that you are the children of the people of the Lord; you must also be born again, if you will inherit the kingdom of God. For you have had line upon line, and precept upon precept, and not only good doctrine but good example; and which is more, you have been turned to, and acquainted with, a principle in yourselves, which others too generally have been ignorant of; and you know you may be as good as you please, without fear of frowns and blows, or being turned out of doors, and forsaken of father and mother, for God's sake and his holy religion; as has been the case of some of your fathers in the day they first entered into this holy path.

Wherefore, O ye young men and women, look to the rock of your fathers: there is no other God but him, no other Light but his, no other grace but his, nor Spirit but his, to convince you, quicken, and comfort you; to lead, guide, and preserve you to God's everlasting kingdom. So will you be possessors as well as professors of the truth, embracing it, not only by education, but judgment and conviction; from a sense begotten in your souls, through the operation of the eternal Spirit and power of God in your hearts... that, as I said before, a generation you may be to God, holding up the profession of the blessed truth in the life and power of it.
                                                        William Penn (1694)

513 And you, young convinced ones, be you entreated and exhorted
to a diligent and chaste waiting upon God, in the way of his blessed
manifestation and appearance of himself to you. Look not out, but
within...Remember it is a still voice that speaks to us in this day,
and that it is not to be heard in the noises and hurries of the mind;
but it is distinctly understood in a retired frame. Jesus loved and
chose solitudes, often going to mountains, to gardens, and sea-sides
to avoid crowds and hurries; to show his disciples it was good to be
solitary, and sit loose to the world. Two enemies lie near your
states, imagination and liberty; but the plain, practical, living,
holy truth, that has convinced you, will preserve you, if you mind
it in yourselves...And when you are converted, as well as convinced, then confirm your brethren; and be ready to every good word
and work, that the Lord shall call you to.   *William Penn (1694)*

514 ⟨Our⟩ work is based on the thought that 'What you have inherited
from your forefathers you must acquire for yourselves to possess it'.
That is to say that each generation of young Friends by its experiments must discover for itself the truths on which the Society is built
if it is to use those truths and to continue and enlarge the work of
the Society. Hence the occasional separate meetings of younger
Friends and our desire to have means of expressing corporately
our own experience.   *Young Friends Committee, 1926*

515 *An incident at Durham Women's Quarterly Meeting in 1795, when representatives to Yearly Meeting were being appointed, illustrates how by imaginative
insight a girl of 18 was first drawn into the larger concerns of the Society:*
A Friend, of Newcastle, whose powerful intellect and strength of
will gave her great influence in the meeting, pointed to Isabel
Richardson and said, 'I do not know the name of that young Friend,
but I should wish her to be one of our representatives to the Yearly
Meeting'. The timid girl sat in speechless terror, equally unable to
raise her voice in refusal, or to endure the thought of what was
involved by acceptance. No sound came from her lips. The clerk,
who knew her name, wrote it down and Isabel went, as the narrative
proceeds to tell, to London Yearly Meeting as one of its representatives; and to the end of her days, after a life of great journeyings,

even as far as America, in the ministry of the Gospel, she loved to tell of the spiritual benefit received from this her 'first Yearly Meeting, the attendance of which she had anticipated with so much fear'.

Later years

516 We must be confident that there is still more 'life' to be 'lived' and yet more heights to be scaled. The tragedy of middle age is that, so often, men and women cease to press 'towards the goal of their high calling'. They cease learning, cease growing; they give up and resign from life. As wisdom dawns with age, we begin to measure our experiences not by what life gives to us, not by the things withheld from us, but by their power to help us to grow in spiritual wisdom. *Evelyn Sturge, 1949*

517 Those of you who are kept by age or sickness from more active work, who are living retired lives, may in your very separation have the opportunity of liberating power for others. Your prayers and thoughts go out further than you think, and as you wait in patience and in communion with God, you may be made ministers of peace and healing and be kept young in soul. *Yearly Meeting, 1923*

518 Perhaps our other powers are being taken from us to teach us to trust more to our prayer-wings, and to pray, pray for the needs of the whole world with an urgency unknown in earlier days, when our longings were more circumscribed by our own immediate horizon. We can pray now, or rather we can try to let prayer stream through us, knowing that our prayer is not ours alone, not only ours. 'It is the Saviour in our hearts that makes us bear all these burdens.' *L. Violet Holdsworth (1940)*

519 I am convinced it is a great art to know how to grow old gracefully, and I am determined to practise it...I always thought I should love to grow old, and I find it is even more delightful than I thought.

It is so delicious to be *done* with things, and to feel no need any longer
to concern myself much about earthly affairs...I am tremendously
content to let one activity after another go, and to await quietly
and happily the opening of the door at the end of the passage way,
that will let me in to my real abiding place.

Hannah Whitall Smith, 1903

Further reflections of Hannah Whitall Smith in old age are given in §79.

520   *The old age of William Penn (1644-1718):*
His memory was almost quite lost, and the use of his understanding
suspended; so that he was not so conversible as formerly; and yet
as near the Truth, in the love of it, as before...His mind was in an
innocent state, as appeared by his very loving deportment to all
that came near him: and that he still had a good sense of Truth
was plain, by some very clear sentences he spoke in the Life and
Power of Truth, in an evening meeting we had together there;
wherein we were greatly comforted; so that I was ready to think
this was a sort of sequestration of him from all the concerns of this
life which so much oppress'd him; not in judgment, but in mercy,
that he might have rest, and not be oppress'd thereby to the end.

Thomas Story, 1714

521   *The old age of Edith J. Wilson (1869-1953):*
During the years of the second world war, Edith Wilson's memory
began to fail, but her ready smile and pleasant response to anyone
who spoke to her never failed. Nor was the hospitality of her home
less than it had been formerly. Young and old were still made welcome and enjoyed the fellowship extended and the real interest
taken in their various circumstances. Till almost the end, Edith
Wilson was keen to do any service possible to her. She typed the
Bible notes for the study group she attended, and addressed en-
velopes when needed; these tasks were a labour of love and were
done competently and gladly. Her circle of friends went far beyond
the Quaker group, and neighbours who met her on walks, or sitting
in the lovely gardens of the Suburb, would stop for a little talk...Her
serenity was apparent to all. She was a great lover of beauty and

often spoke of the beauty of the world, of the sunshine and flowers, and God's goodness in providing all this loveliness for our enjoyment...Her short utterances in meeting or study circle revealed a shining sincerity which made them acceptable to young and old alike. It was as though the words of St Paul were exemplified in her case: 'Though our outward man perish, our inward man is renewed day by day.'   *Testimony of Hampstead M.M., 1954*

522   *That old age may be a time of great activity, even when health is precarious, is shown by the experience of Isaac Sharp (1806-1897), who did not cease from the missionary travels which had occupied a large part of his life until he returned from Syria in his ninetieth year. The following experience took place when he was returning at the age of 87 with Leonard Wigham as his companion on a junk down the Yangtse from Chungking, confined to bed with a bronchial cold and rheumatic pains on the 582-mile journey to Ichang:*

Jan. 19, 1893. More snow on the mountains. The cough was on the verge of intensity for straining... We were now fast approaching the Ching-tan or rapid. It was judged best for about half-a-dozen of our company to land and walk along the shore, and re-embark at the lower end. I was in bed; it was well, for the like exposure might have brought on a very serious relapse. As I lay, the surging of the water was very suggestive. Its swell and tumult I could not see but its effect was very manifest. The bow of the junk was more than once under the water, the vehemence of which rapidly increased. The junk rose and fell by the violence of the water. I shut my eyes to lessen the giddiness which came over me. We passed a stranded wreck laden with oranges. I was sensible of a tremor passing through me, stern in its reality, but very brief. A blessed assurance came to the rescue. The environment of the love of God was around me with a calm and quiet rest in the sealed assurance that, through the love of God and the redemption which is in Christ Jesus, at that moment all was well.

523   *The old age of Sarah Jane Lury (1847-1946):*
With prayer, meditation and the Bible she began her day. Even when over ninety she would leave her home at 6.30 in order to be

present at a Monthly or Quarterly Meeting, willing, if necessary, to wait quietly for the meeting, unless some kindly Friend, knowing her habit, persuaded her to come in and rest. She never lost her gay sense of humour and was a charming raconteur of the events of a full and varied life. Of all her ministries her chief was in the home. She had a world-wide correspondence. It was rightly said of her... when her passing was announced that Sarah Jane Lury could be counted amongst those that are 'planted in the house of the Lord' who 'still bring forth fruit in old age'.

Testimony of North Somerset & Wilts M.M., 1946

Living alone

524 The amount of solitude which is attainable or would be wholesome in the case of any individual life is a matter which each of us must judge for himself... A due proportion of solitude is one of the most important conditions of mental health. Therefore if it be our lot to stand apart from those close natural ties by which life is for most people shaped and filled, let us not be in haste to fill the gap; let us not carelessly or rashly throw away the opportunity of entering into that deeper and more continual acquaintance with the unseen and eternal things which is the natural and great compensation for the loss of easier joys. The loneliness which we rightly dread is not the absence of human faces and voices—it is the absence of love... Our wisdom therefore must lie in learning not to shrink from anything that may lie in store for us, but so to grasp the master key of life as to be able to turn everything to good and fruitful account.

Caroline E. Stephen (1908)

Attitude towards death

525 Every man knows in his heart that there is no greater thing in the world than pure unselfish love. Death cannot conquer, nay he teaches ever that love is supreme. Good men do not die. Their lives are as the tearing of the veil, they show us something of that which is eternal, for if here love is greatest in the heart of man, must it not be greatest in God himself? And if greatest in Himself,

then let the mystery of His will be never so dark, we may gird ourselves each to his life's work with something more than courage. Love bridges death. We are comrades of those who are gone; though death separate us, their work, their fortitude, their love shall be ours, and we will adventure with hope, and in the spirit and strength of our great comrade of Galilee, who was acquainted with grief and knew the shadows of Gethsemane, to fight the good fight of faith.   *John Wilhelm Rowntree, 1905*

526 There are lives so rounded and crowned that death seems to have appeared in the fulness of their prime only to consecrate them for ever; others stand apart from human ties in a solitude which makes time seem of little consequence, and the grave a not unfamiliar country... We do not know to what unfathomable necessities the times and seasons of life and death may correspond; and as little do we know, in looking at each other's lives, what may be unfolding or what may be concluded, as seen from within. That which seems to others a cutting short of activity, may be to ourselves the laying down of arms no longer needed; our eyes may see the haven, where our friends can see only the storm; or if we cannot *see* a fitness in the time of our death, is that a strange thing in such a life as this?   *Caroline E. Stephen (1908)*

527 *From the last letter of Joan Mary Fry to her friends, 1955:*
I believe it is of real value to our earthly life to have the next life in mind, because if we shut it out of our thoughts we are starving part of our spiritual nature—we are like children who fail to grow up—none the finer children for that. Not only do we miss much joy in the earth life if we imagine it to be the whole of our existence, but we arrive on the further shore with no knowledge of the language of the new country where we shall find ourselves unfitted for the larger life of the spirit. George Fox urged Friends to 'take care of God's glory'. That is a motto for all spheres known and unknown.

528 The faith of Christ teaches more than courage in the face of death. Our attitude to death is transformed. As we come to a more intimate experience of the reality of God, we may enter into the overcoming

power and strength of the great words of Christ, 'I am the Resurrection and the Life'. Death is swallowed up in victory. For those
we love it is no longer a dark place of shadows but an entrance into
the fuller light of God. Though we naturally grieve at the withdrawal of loved friends from our physical sight, we may still rejoice
in their new freedom. The dead are not lost to us; they are still our
friends in the service of the Eternal.   *1925*

529 Thinking in this way of death, we feel that therefrom arises a practice
of reverent simplicity in respect to the outward practices attending
death, which simplicity we earnestly commend to Friends everywhere.

The funerals of Friends should be held in a spirit of quiet peace and
trust. Natural sorrow there will be, especially for friends taken
away in youth and in the strength of their days, but often our
thought may be one of great thankfulness for lives which have
borne witness to the upholding power of Christ.   *1925*

*For further extracts on Funerals see §273-274. For a section on 'Life beyond
Death' see §188-195.*

530 Death is not an end, but a beginning. It is but an incident in the
'life of the ages', which is God's gift to us *now*. It is the escape of the
spirit from its old limitations and its freeing for a larger and more
glorious career. We stand around the grave, and as we take our last,
lingering look, too often our thoughts are *there*; and we return to the
desolate home feeling that all that made life lovely has been left
behind on the bleak hillside...Yet the spirit now is *free*, and the
unseen angel at our side points upwards from the grave and whispers,
'He is not here, but is risen'. The dear one returns with us to our
home, ready and able, as never before, to comfort, encourage, and
beckon us onward.   *William Littleboy (1917)*

531
*The following passage was composed by Thomas Wilkinson of Yanwath, and
included in the Yearly Meeting epistle of 1799. In several editions of the Book of*

Discipline it formed the concluding extract. Now restored, it may fitly end this chapter by reminding us that though the expression of our experience in personal life and in our testimonies may change from age to age, there is something permanent which abides:

Finally, friends, collectively and individually, farewell! May all our meetings be held, with weight, as in the immediate presence of the heavenly President. May the aged among us be examples of every Christian virtue; and evince, by the calmness of their evening, that their day has been blest. May the middle-aged not faint in their allotted stations; but, together with their older and younger brethren, firmly support, yea, exalt the several testimonies which we are called to maintain. And O! may the beloved youth, the tender objects of our care, and of our hope, bend early and cheerfully under the forming power of truth: that thus, each standing in his allotment, the harmony of the building may be preserved, and we may truly grow up into an holy temple for the Lord.

Chapter 12: Social responsibilities

Social justice

532 The Creator of the earth is the owner of it. He gave us being thereon, and our nature requires nourishment, which is the produce of it. As he is kind and merciful, we as his creatures, while we live answerable to the design of our creation, are so far entitled to a convenient subsistence that no man may justly deprive us of it. By the agreements and contracts of our fathers and predecessors, and by doings and proceedings of our own, some claim a much greater share of this world than others: and while those possessions are faithfully improved to the good of the whole, it consists with equity. But he who, with a view to self-exaltation, causeth some with their domestic animals to labour immoderately, and with the monies arising to him therefrom, employs others in the luxuries of life, acts contrary to the gracious designs of him who is the owner of the earth; nor can any possessions, either acquired or derived from ancestors, justify such conduct...

Were all superfluities and the desire of outward greatness laid aside, and the right use of things universally attended to, such a number of people might be employed in things useful, as that moderate labour with the blessing of Heaven would answer all good purposes relating to people and their animals, and a sufficient number have time to attend to proper affairs of civil society...

Our gracious Creator cares and provides for all his creatures. His tender mercies are over all his works; and so far as his love influences our minds, so far we become interested in his workmanship and feel a desire to take hold of every opportunity to lessen the distresses of the afflicted and increase the happiness of the creation. Here we have a prospect of one common interest from which our own is inseparable, that to turn all the treasures we possess into the channel of universal love becomes the business of our lives...

Oppression in the extreme appears terrible: but oppression in more refined appearances remains to be oppression; and where the smallest degree of it is cherished it grows stronger and more extensive. To labour for a perfect redemption from this spirit of oppression is the great business of the whole family of Christ Jesus in this world. *John Woolman, 1763*

533 The important thing about worldly possessions, in fact, is whether or not we are tied to them. Some, by an undue love of the things of this world, have so dulled their hearing that a divine call to a different way of life would pass unheard. Others are unduly self-conscious about things which are of no eternal significance, and because they worry too much about them, fail to give of their best. The essence of worldliness is to judge of things by an outward and temporary, and not an inward and eternal standard, to care more about appearances than about reality, to let the senses prevail over the reason and the affections.
'Christian responsibility & material possessions' (1958)

534 A socially reformed life, which rejects all that is inseparably linked with injury to others, will necessarily involve self sacrifice, but this is not an end in itself and is only demanded when some useful purpose is served. The limitation of personal expenditure on clothes to an irreducible minimum does not release clothing for another. It may, as things are, impoverish the tailor or the dressmaker. The effort should be to promote the participation of all in the abundance of the age rather than the extension to all of the privations of the past. *Shipley N. Brayshaw (1933)*

535 As to our own planet which God has given us for a dwelling place, we must be mindful that it is given in stewardship. The power over nature that scientific knowledge has put into our hands, if used in lust or greed, fear or hatred, can bring us to utter destruction. Now as never before we have the choice between life and death. If we choose life we may now feed the hungry, clothe the naked, and heal the sick on a world scale, thus creating new conditions for spiritual advancement so often till now prevented by want. Many of our resources—of oil, of coal and of uranium—are limited. If by condon-

ing waste and luxury we overspend the allowance God has given us, our children's children will be cheated of their inheritance. Limited too is the annual bounty of nature. The material foundation of our life is the tilling of the earth and the growing of food...We must conserve the goodness of the soil and not exploit it.

We must guard, too, the abundance and variety of untamed nature, and not forget the spiritual resources available to us in the continued existence of unoccupied lands. Modern civilisation perpetually threatens our awareness of the true nature of our being which in the presence of the wild we can more easily retain or at length recapture. Year by year silence and solitude are growing more needful, yet harder to obtain, and contacts, by this means, with the mind of the Creator more tenuous. To conserve nature is thus again a contribution to the fuller life of mankind.

Norfolk, Cambs & Hunts Q.M., 1957

536 There is a ⟨particular⟩ element in Quaker faith which is relevant when we talk of social justice and a better social order. We believe in the continued revelation of God, that is to say, we believe the world is in the process of making. Creation continues. It is a continuous process. From a practical point of view, this is of the utmost importance. It teaches us humility and the understanding that whatever we may do, we are not going to establish a perfect, final, ideal order in a finite world. It saves us from all kinds of 'isms' and all the false hopes and all the intolerance which goes with them. We believe in God, in man, but we do not believe in men like gods. Thus we find the strength to keep on struggling for better economic conditions, for the rule of justice, though we know that all the truth has not yet been revealed to us, that we are not going to usher in the millennium. *Friends World Conference, 1937*

537 Fellowship in the life eternal brings a sensitiveness to all wrong and oppression and a desire to identify ourselves with our fellows and to take our share of the burden of the world's suffering. How hard it is to put ourselves in other men's shoes! During our Yearly Meeting we have tried to realise something of what it means to be a refugee,

an unemployed man, a prisoner, a juvenile offender. We have had brought before us the privations of the underpaid and underfed at home and abroad, the disabilities laid on people of other colour and race, the failure of men to distribute equitably the abundant produce that the earth can supply. As followers of Jesus we are called to strive to remedy these injustices, not clinging to exclusive privileges for ourselves or for our nation, but remembering that the earth is the Lord's and that the fulness of it should be used for the well-being of all his children.

We have longed that in this time of world crisis the Society of Friends everywhere may be faithful in its witness to truth, as truth has been and is being revealed to us. Peace and righteousness are inseparable. Outward peace maintained by the conscious surrender of truth and justice can never be lasting. We may never desert the victims of oppression, but we must endeavour to realise the conditions and needs both of the oppressor and of the oppressed. While we hate wrong, we must love our fellow wrong-doers. There is no place for self-righteous indignation, since the roots of evil are in our own hearts. Only by action that flows from penitence and love can hatred and tyranny be overcome.

Yearly Meeting, 1938

538 The population of this country enjoys impartial law courts, an incorrupt administration and tolerable social and economic conditions; we trust all this will survive the crisis of the coming years. Most members of our Society are not exposed to acute misery in which one does not know, from day to day, from where the bare necessities of life are to come, nor to systems under which people, deprived of freedom and human dignity, are little better than slaves. We have time to think and discuss, to read and learn, and for contemplation and worship. This privileged position must not mislead us into assuming an easy victory of brotherly love over the powers of evil on earth. Enormous is the amount of wrong in the world. To innumerable human beings life means poverty and disease, exploitation and oppression, ignorance and indolence, vice and squalor, physical and spiritual hunger which has little or no hope of ever being satisfied. Love, mercy and pity command us to do

our best to right these wrongs, to oppose iniquity and to see more justice done to those who suffer from injustice.

Like the prophets of Israel, like Fox, Penn and Woolman, those who want to establish the realm of peace and love must work for justice too, indeed for justice first. If we regard peace not as a negative and stagnant posture, the absence of war, but as a constructive and dynamic process, then social justice, international justice, and inter-racial justice are indispensable as impelling forces to carry it forward. If love is to regenerate and inspire social, international and inter-racial relations, justice must first promote that freedom of personality, without which there can be no love.

Whoever wishes to see the world moving towards these great ideals, must begin with himself. Justice and love, as a way of life, must be translated into the spirit of living persons, put into action in the trivial round, the common task, in family and society, business and factory, church and state, national and international bodies. Beginning in his small circle, he must trust that he is working with God and for that 'spirit which delights to do no evil nor to revenge any wrong, but delights to endure all things, in hope to enjoy its own in the end'. *Konrad Braun (1950)*

Friends and the social order

'*Do you manifest the spirit of justice and understanding in your relations with your fellows in industry and trade and in all your daily life? Do you as disciples of the Lord Jesus take a living interest in the social conditions of those around you? What place do you give to personal service, and do you undertake this in the spirit of friendship? Do you seek to understand the causes of social evils and to take your right share in the endeavour to remove them?*' *Queries 14 and 15, 1928*

539 The social testimony of the Society of Friends did not arise out of any doctrinaire theory of human rights or of the nature of a just society. As the living experience of the inward light of Christ became a reality to the first followers of George Fox, a force moulding character and making all things new, they found that... the many forms of social injustice witnessed round them, 'struck at their life' and could no longer be tolerated. It was from this central experience that they sought a new order of human relationships in the humdrum tasks of earning a living and in their contacts with their workpeople and customers... In their own business relationships they sought to maintain a simple and steadfast integrity, determining to make or sell only things of good quality. The apprentice in the shop, the serving girl in the home, the labourer at the plough, each was a human personality, lit with a spark of the divine light, and, therefore, demanding respect... The earliest social testimony was eminently practical, setting a new standard to be followed by Friends in all their business activities— a standard of quality in the goods handled, a standard of fairness and consideration in their dealings with all men.

'Friends & the industrial & social order' (*1958*)

540 *The war of 1914-18 made Friends more vividly aware of the close con-*
nection between war and the social order. Nine months after the outbreak
of war Yearly Meeting was impressed by the words of John Woolman,
'May we look upon our treasures, the furniture of our houses, and our garments,
and try whether the seeds of war have nourishment in these our possessions.'
After three years' exercise of mind eight Foundations of a True Social Order
were adopted, which were 'not intended as rules of life but ⟨as⟩ an attempt
to set forth ideals that are aspects of eternal Truth and the direct outcome
of our Quaker testimony to the individual worth of the human soul.'

1. The Fatherhood of God, as revealed by Jesus Christ, should lead us toward a brotherhood which knows no restriction of race, sex or social class.

2. This brotherhood should express itself in a social order which is directed, beyond all material ends, to the growth of personality truly related to God and man.

3. The opportunity of full development, physical, moral and spiritual, should be assured to every member of the community, man, woman and child. The development of man's full personality should not be hampered by unjust conditions nor crushed by economic pressure.

4. We should seek for a way of living that will free us from the bondage of material things and mere conventions, that will raise no barrier between man and man, and will put no excessive burden of labour upon any by reason of our superfluous demands.

5. The spiritual force of righteousness, loving-kindness and trust is mighty because of the appeal it makes to the best in every man, and when applied to industrial relations achieves great things.

6. Our rejection of the methods of outward domination, and of the appeal to force, applies not only to international affairs, but to the whole problem of industrial control. Not through antagonism but through co-operation and good-will can the best be attained for each and all.

7. Mutual service should be the principle upon which life is organised. Service, not private gain, should be the motive of all work.

8. The ownership of material things, such as land and capital, should be so regulated as best to minister to the need and development of man.

541 In your daily work, and in your social and other activities, be concerned for the establishment of the Kingdom of Heaven upon earth. Live not for yourselves but for others. Remember your responsibility as citizens for the government of your own town and country. Study the causes of social evils. Work for an order of society based on mutual service and directed beyond all material ends to the true enrichment of human lives. *General Advices, 1928*

542 The modern man, in his search for the religion of the Kingdom, is faced by certain big problems that cannot be separated, on the one hand from religion, and on the other from politics. The problems of social existence are ever raising great moral issues where the roots of any true solution are religious, and the expression in the act of reform, of reconstruction, economic and political. We cannot touch the drink curse, nor the sex evil, nor the war trade, nor industrial domination, nor slavery, nor the corruption of the opium traffic, nor penal reform, nor the problem of backward races, nor

education, nor free government, but we touch the vitalities of our religion... But we have been told that if the Church... really sought to make application of the Christian ethic to the things that are real in the lives of men, 'it would inevitably divide and destroy itself'. It may be. Christ before Caiaphas and Pilate did not seek to escape division but for the way, the truth and the life's sake went to the cross. 'And they all forsook Him and fled.' And until the Church has a corporate word of eternal life to give, for which it is willing to suffer even destruction in time, and lose the support of the unthinking and of the mighty: until it is possessed of a social thought more powerful than ⟨that of⟩ paganism, it must grow weaker, and less and less important in the eyes of many multitudes of earnest men. And this growing indifference of men to the Church is not a turning away from the light as some suppose, but exactly the reverse. It is the cry for a straight lead, a turning to living things, a turning to live things, to a society of the new spirit, which like Lloyd Garrison* in another crisis of human history, says with authority, 'I am in earnest and will be heard'.   *Carl Heath (1922)*

543 We do not believe that all the ills of men spring from economic causes but many are in fact so caused, and a lack of understanding of economic laws hinders our service. There is need for competent heads, as well as good hearts, and we must guard against the danger that our thinking may be hindered by our material standards of living.   *Friends World Conference, 1952*

544 In practice we find that divine leading is inseparable from a righteous adjustment of our lives to our mundane surroundings, and especially to the lives of others. Experience has shown that we cannot draw a line between religious and secular affairs. The service of God may be found in seeking work for the workless and in search-ing for the underlying causes of poverty and unemployment as much as in preaching the Gospel in England or abroad, indeed there is no division of opinion amongst us as to the unity of life.
                                   Shipley N. Brayshaw (1933)

* Lloyd Garrison (1805-1879) was an American journalist and one of the leaders in the campaign for the abolition of slavery, particularly in the United States.

545 Deep in each human soul lies the seed of the eternal divine life. Its flowering to the glory of God is the aim and purpose of man's being. To this end the resources of the world have been given to all men individually and for their corporate life. To all men they are given, to all men in common ownership they belong. And although these resources may be administered by particular individuals, groups or nations, any system which limits their availability for all men and women, regardless of colour or creed, is hindering Christian fellowship and the divine order.

All men are of the family of God. No man is a 'hand' to be kept in or thrown out of the economic life of the community as suits the needs of any system. The community is a fellowship wherein each man and woman should find a place of significant service and creative living. All are members, all share the duty and should enjoy the right of helping to determine its policies, whether political or economic, industrial or social. For its foundations rest on a democracy based on the brotherhood of man and drawing its reality from the Fatherhood of God.   '*A social testimony*', *1944*

546 We know that Jesus identified himself with the suffering and the sinful, the poor and the oppressed. We know that he went out of his way to befriend social outcasts. We know that he warned us against the deceitfulness of riches, that wealth and great possessions so easily come between us and God, and divide us from our neighbours. The worship of middle-class comfort is surely a side-chapel in the temple of Mammon. It attracts large congregations, and Friends have been known to frequent it. We know that Jesus had compassion on the multitude and taught them many things concerning the Kingdom. He respected the common folk, appealed to them and was more hopeful of a response from them than from the well-to-do, the clever and the learned. Yet he never flattered the workers, never fostered in them feelings of envy and hatred, and never urged them to press for their own interests ruthlessly and fight the class-war to a finish. He called them to love their enemies and to pray for them that despitefully use them.

Yet the very fact that he appealed to the humble and meek leads up to…'the discovery that the blessing and upraising of the masses are the fundamental interest of society'. In brief, he makes us all ashamed that we are not all out in caring for our fellow-men.

There is no doubt…as to the nature of the upward calling of God to us in Christ Jesus. Yet to live in the light of it in the industrial and social order of today is no easy matter; and this is the case not necessarily because the organisation of industry and of society is fundamentally un-Christian, but because the organisation is complex and difficult to control, and seems to involve some relations between men, particularly between groups and classes, which are apparently necessary, and yet difficult to Christianise.   *H. G. Wood, 1958*

In 1958, forty years after the adoption of the Eight Foundations (§540), a Conference on Industry and the Social Order reminded Friends that these were 'not a creed but a continuing challenge'. Although the Conference produced 'no blue prints, nor even ground plans, of the structure of a human society that would be a perfect exemplar of that City of God of which we have had occasional glimpses', it gave Friends 'the opportunity of considering together what this inheritance requires of us in our everyday living'. Extracts from the minutes are given in §547-549:

547 This country is not predominantly Christian and it is in this setting that our Christian witness is called for. For this we need the insights, but not the practical solutions of our forebears, for the world we know has changed beyond all recognition in comparison with theirs…

⟨The issues of⟩ status, dignity, security, remain problems to which material progress does not automatically bring solutions, problems much more difficult to solve than those of providing adequate wages and reasonable working conditions.

Everything is done to stimulate the idea that a high level of material possessions is the greatest good life has to offer and judging by their addiction to gambling more than half the population of the country approves the idea of the legitimacy of wealth obtained by chance rather than as remuneration for service rendered. In this atmosphere serious political thought is at a discount and that this is so comparatively few seem to care. We cannot escape responsibility for this state of affairs and our task should be to try to restore to men the sense of dignity that arises not from the power to purchase goods but from devotion to the Christian values that we profess to accept...

As members of a religious body we have to ask ourselves to what extent the various underlying features of our social and industrial life, for which we ourselves have some responsibility, lead to contentment, happiness and a knowledge of God.

548 The structure of the society in which we live is not something fixed and immutable that determines our courses of action without choice in ourselves, it is the product of human activity in the past, a compound of both success and failure. Far from encouraging us to despair this should drive us rather to renew our efforts to use our own capacities to influence the future direction of the change that is continuously taking place. To seek to withdraw ourselves from this struggle is to turn our backs on the responsibility our Christian discipleship demands of us.

549 As partakers of the marked prosperity of our country in the world of to-day few of us could claim to be outside the category of those rich in material possessions, and all our attempts in the deliberations of the conference to find ways of infusing industry and the social order with Christian principles have served to emphasise how hard it is for those who have riches to enter the Kingdom of God.

The extremity of our sense of difficulty and difference, however, has brought us not to a feeling of despair of accomplishing anything at all, but to a new sense of dependence on and challenge from God to use our individual aptitudes and versatilities in situations that now as in the past are subject to change as a result of dedicated human lives. Indeed, our consciousness of the extremity of our plight serves to underline our affirmation that with God all things are possible.

550 Led by the Holy Spirit, we shall be enabled to show to those around us that the Christian faith is no mere theoretical belief, but a living realisation of the abiding presence of Christ. In all the details of daily life—not only in the meeting house, but in the schoolroom, the workshop, the office or the council chamber—wherever in God's providence our duty calls us, we may know the joy of being guided by His counsel and may find a sanctuary in the midst of our busy occupations. Lives thus consecrated to His service are amongst the most convincing evidences of the truth of Christianity.

Yearly Meeting, 1894

551 The sanctity of labour means...that men should come to see in the very work itself something that is of value because it is part of the whole attitude to life which gives the universe its value. Work can never for all people be done 'for the fun of it' nor 'for the love of it' if by love is meant liking, pleasure, delight. But all men can work for the love of God, and take their 'reward' not as reward at all, but as the means to a life that is full of love and service and joy in work and play.   *Harold Loukes (1954)*

552 A certain amount of routine and repetitiveness is part of the most creative life. Even a genius cannot be creative twenty-four hours a day. What determines the creativity of our life is the degree to which creative or noncreative activities are dominant, as manifested both in the amount of time we devote to meaningful activity and the spirit in which we carry through these activities. The machine as such has not destroyed creative self-expression and self-realisation for the large number of people. Quite to the contrary, it has made them possible by enabling us to do away with the drudgery of manual labour and the low standard of living of pre-industrialism. It is the *use* of the machine, the subordination of human values to the machine in the *organisation* of the work process which has destroyed creative self-expression in industry because it has allowed the machine to set the pattern for our whole life.

Fred H. Blum (1953)

553 It remains to speak of the Way of Service, as it concerns the conduct of our ordinary work and business. Nowhere is the practical working of our faith put to a severer test, yet nowhere is there a nobler and more fruitful witness to be borne. Business in its essence is no mere selfish struggle for the necessities and luxuries of life, but 'a vast and complex movement of social service'. However some may abuse its methods for private ends, its true function is not to rob the community but to serve it. But, in the fierce competition which is so marked a feature of the present day, it has become very difficult, some would say impossible, for those engaged in business to be wholly faithful to Christ. Christianity is challenged in the shop and in the office.

We have been touched with keen sympathy for our friends, whether employers or employed, who find themselves in this strait. We cannot here deal fully with this question, but we are sure there is an answer to the challenge, and that the light which shines upon the Way of Life, and gives us the distinction of things inwardly, will guide us to the answer...

Christianity is tested, not only in the shop and in the office, but also in the home. In the standard of living adopted by the home-makers, in the portion of income devoted to comforts, recreations and luxuries, in willingness to be content with simplicity, the members of a household, both older and younger, may bear witness that there is a Way of Life that does not depend on the abundance of the things possessed.   *Yearly Meeting, 1911*

554 We recognise that modern conditions of business and industry have brought to both workers and employers, their unions or federations. We urge Friends who may be members of such bodies to realise their individual responsibility for action taken by their organisation. A Christian is right in combining with others to obtain justice for himself and his fellows, but he should set his face against oppression and violence as being inconsistent with the example and teaching of our Lord.   *1925*

555 We ask Friends to be very considerate as to the extent to which they make use of the labour of others on the first day of the week. The general cessation of ordinary business gives opportunities for refreshment of body and mind, for united family life, for religious service and for public worship. Friends highly value these privileges for themselves, and we urge them so to regulate their conduct as not needlessly to hinder others from the enjoyment of the same privileges. *1911; 1925*

556 Remember the special opportunities for refreshment of spirit and for service which the first day of the week affords; use them faithfully as befits the friends of the Master whose name we bear.

General Advices, 1928

Moderation and temperance

This title stood for many years in earlier editions of this book: it is now restored because, though many of the extracts in this section refer specifically to the question of alcohol, they have been placed in the wider context of counsel on our responsible use of the fruits of the earth.

557 Every degree of luxury of what kind soever, and every demand for money inconsistent with Divine order, hath some connection with unnecessary labour…To labour too hard or cause others to do so that we may live conformably to customs which Christ our Redeemer contradicted by His example in the days of His flesh, and which are contrary to Divine order, is to manure a soil for propagating an evil seed in the earth. Such who enter deep into these considerations and live under the weight of them, will feel these things so heavy and their ill effects so extensive, that the necessity of attending singly to Divine wisdom will be evident, thereby to be directed and supported in the right use of things in opposition to the customs of the times, and supported to bear patiently the reproaches attending singularity. To conform a little to a wrong way strengthens the hands of such who carry wrong customs to their utmost extent;

and the more a person appears to be virtuous and heavenly-minded, the more powerfully does his conformity operate in favour of evil-doers...While we profess in all cases to live in constant opposition to that which is contrary to universal righteousness... what language is sufficient to set forth the strength of those obligations we are under to beware lest by our example we lead others wrong?   *John Woolman, 1763*

558   *George Fox, 1643*:
When I came towards nineteen years of age, I being upon business at a fair, one of my cousins, whose name was Bradford, being a professor, and having another professor with him, came to me and asked me to drink part of a jug of beer with them, and I, being thirsty, went in with them, for I loved any that had a sense of good, or that did seek after the Lord. And when we had drunk a glass apiece, they began to drink healths and called for more drink, agreeing together that he that would not drink should pay all. I was grieved that any that made profession of religion should offer to do so. They grieved me very much, having never had such a thing put to me before by any sort of people; wherefore I rose up to be gone, and putting my hand into my pocket I took out a groat and laid it down upon the table before them and said 'If it be so, I'll leave you'.

559   *Yearly Meeting 1751:*
As temperance and moderation are virtues proceeding from true religion, and are of great benefit and advantage in many respects, we beseech all to be careful of their conduct and behaviour, 'abstaining from every appearance of evil'; and as an excess in drinking has been too prevalent among many of the inhabitants of these nations, we recommend to all friends a watchful care over themselves, attended with a religious and prudent zeal against a practice so dishonourable and pernicious.

560   *Yearly Meeting 1857:*
This meeting has been brought under deep concern in view of the fearful amount of sin and misery existing in our land through the

prevailing use of intoxicating liquors...Whilst we would carefully avoid interfering in any way with the Christian liberty of our dear Friends we would encourage them seriously to consider what may be their individual duty in relation to this important subject.

561 *Yearly Meeting 1893:*
We feel it right to express the very general sentiment of the body, that it would conduce in no small measure to the usefulness of Friends as individuals, and to the well-being of the Society at large, if all could see their way to give up the use of intoxicating beverages. The experience of many years warrants us in saying that this course would involve no sacrifice of health; but even if it did call for some self-sacrifice, surely it is not too much to ask of those for whom Christ died that they should be willing, for the sake of their weaker brethren and sisters, to deny themselves this indulgence, in order to set before their households and those around them an example which all may safely follow.

562 *Yearly Meeting 1928—General Advices:*
In view of the evils arising from the use of intoxicating drinks, consider whether you should not abstain from using them yourselves, from offering them to others, and from having any share in their manufacture or sale. Do not let the claims of good fellowship, or the fear of seeming peculiar, prevent you from standing by principles which you have conscientiously adopted.

563 Because we would have our countrymen free, we would have them choose the life that is best, and find freedom through abstinence. Yet those of us who take this decision need all the while to remember that abstinence is a means to an end, not an end in itself. By the mere fact of abstinence we may be physically stronger, but not morally or spiritually better. It is a means to an end, and that end is fulness of life. The leisure and the money and strength that are saved by abstinence have too often been regarded selfishly or frittered away unworthily. They must be spent joyfully and un-grudgingly. The freedom of the Kingdom of God is the freedom of perfect service, in which is realised the meaning of membership

of that great family in which Christ Himself is the elder brother and in which the youngest child bears the imprint of His likeness.

The world is a dark enough place still for too many. It can ill spare even the poorest rushlight candle of cheerfulness or the smallest fire of fellowship. We must not put out the glimmer of that light which shines for many still to-day through the tavern windows, unless we can put a better in its place. We need the light of a brighter cheerfulness, and the glow of a warmer fellowship, and if we have them not, our house may be swept and garnished, but may yet become a dwelling-place fitter for evil spirits than for kindly angels of the Kingdom of God. For when all is done we have but made our house of life a little cleaner and more serviceable by our abstinence; for the rest, all depends upon the use it is put to and who it is that dwells there. *T. Edmund Harvey (1931)*

564 God, the creator of the fruits of the earth, trusts us to share His gifts with one another and to use them aright; we betray this trust if we use them wastefully or selfishly.

It is wrong in eating or drinking to be over-indulgent, to do any-thing that blunts the edge of our sensitivity and responsibility towards God or man. Practices to be avoided as evil, because they stand between us and God, may be different for different people, or even for the same person at different times. Moreover, 'none of us lives to himself' and our example may without our knowing it help or hurt someone else in perplexity. Things may be used for good or evil, and the resulting moral dilemma is one which each of us has to solve for himself.

At the present time many Friends, convinced that even the moderate use of alcoholic drinks is fraught with dangers to many, believe that they should totally abstain from them. Others, however, hold that 'temperance' implies their moderate use; they do not believe that alcoholic drinks are evil in themselves and consider that they have a rightful place in their lives. We recognise that in this matter 'it is not for any one of us to specify for another what may or may not be his duty; each one, in the light that is given, must decide'.

We are united in deploring excessive drinking and the miseries it brings in its train. We all desire to restrict the growth of habitual drinking, particularly among young people, which is encouraged both by large-scale advertising campaigns of brewery companies and by the unthinking acceptance of social convention. We are all concerned at the number of road accidents in which alcohol undoubtedly plays a part. Against these things we protest; we urge Friends to work together, determined to make themselves acquainted with the facts and to find constructive solutions to these problems.

Whatever our personal convictions, we need to beware of self righteousness. Those who believe that it is right to drink in moderation must beware of the danger of a false 'good fellowship'; those who believe that they should totally abstain from alcoholic drinks must remember that a merely negative rejection is not enough. If we follow Christ faithfully, it will leave room for no judging spirit but we shall exercise that charity and respect for each other which is required of 'humble learners in the school of Christ'. *1959*

Betting and gambling

565 We believe that all forms of betting and gambling and all merely speculative means of obtaining money, are contrary to the spirit of Christ. Through addiction to such practices the mind becomes set upon quick ways of getting riches, and the sense of the true values of things is often lost, so that the judgment is disordered, the moral faculties are sapped, and life is lived in the excitement of the moment. This state of mind is destructive of the larger life of the soul and the habitual communion with Christ, which are the privileges of His followers.

In addition to the material ruin both of individuals and of families in all sections of the community, the moral and religious fibre of the people is seriously affected. The prevalence of sweepstakes and of lotteries for charities, however disguised, is a disquieting symptom at the present time. *1911*

566 We encourage our members to inform themselves and others as
to the extent of the evil ⟨of gambling⟩, and the distress and sin that
follow in its train, and to promote legislation for its suppression.
Above all, we ask them, by strenuous effort, by personal example and
by earnest prayer, to help those around them to come into the true
relationship with our Lord Jesus Christ, which will satisfy the soul's
longings, and teach the secret of victory over every kind of temptation.   *1911; 1925*

567 Gambling by risking money haphazardly disregards our belief that
possessions are a trust. The persistent appeal to covetousness evident,
for example, in football pool propaganda is fundamentally opposed
to the unselfishness which was taught by Jesus Christ and by the
New Testament as a whole. The attempt, which is inseparable
from gambling, to make profit out of the inevitable loss and possible
suffering of others is the antithesis of that love of one's neighbour
on which our Lord insisted. Moreover, we must consider the moral
and spiritual plight of those who by indulgence in gambling become
suddenly possessed of large financial resources for which they have
rendered no service to the community.   *1959*

568 In our 'Advices' we are warned against commercial speculations
of a gambling character, and we are told to 'remember how widespread and diverse are the temptations to grow rich at the expense
of others'. The faithful observance of this advice points the way
to an issue greater than personal rectitude with regard to gambling.
It should lead to an examination of the system which permits or
encourages these abuses, and to a demand for drastic changes.
                                              Shipley N. Brayshaw (1933)

Sexual morality

569 Security in childhood, and understanding parental guidance and
instruction ensure for very many people a right attitude to sexual relationships. Personal acquaintance with a happy home helps others

growing up in less fortunate conditions: a free united family life is a nation's best guarantee of moral health. The Christian attitude to sex is based on a total view of man's nature, comprising body, mind and spirit; no relationship can be a right one that in any way casts a cloud over the Light within a person. Those who ignore, or are unaware of it, may see no wrong or danger in illicit acts, and experience no shame in regard to them—but harm is done, the dignity and personality of the man or woman are diminished.

The evils of prostitution and perversion flourish where unhealthy living conditions, ignorance and unstable family life are found; these are some of the root causes that need to be understood and then combated if we are to purify our social life. Wise laws, fair to both men and women, are also important and it should be our care, as good citizens, to encourage study of the social problems involved, and to help create a better informed and more enlightened public opinion. The unworthy appeal to sexual instincts for commercial gain in entertainment, pornographic literature and advertising is a stumbling block to the spiritual progress of individuals and a source of corroding weakness in the nation as a whole. We should speak out plainly about this danger so blatantly apparent in our midst and encourage a truer appreciation of the things of real value. *1959*

Administration of justice

Taking of oaths

570 Advised, that our Christian testimony be faithfully maintained against the burden and imposition of oaths, according to the express prohibition of Christ, and also of the apostle James: 'Ye have heard that it hath been said by them of old time, thou shalt not forswear thyself, but shalt perform unto the Lord thine oaths; but I say unto you, Swear not at all; neither by heaven, for it is God's throne; nor by the earth, for it is His footstool; neither by Jerusalem, for it is the city of the great King; neither shalt thou swear by thine head, because thou canst not make one hair white or black; but let your communication be, Yea, yea; Nay, nay; for whatsoever is more than these cometh of evil.' 'But above all things, my brethren, swear not; neither by heaven, neither by the earth, neither by any other oath; but let your yea be yea; and your nay, nay; lest ye fall into condemnation.' *1782*

571 The law permits all those who object to the taking of an oath on religious grounds, or because they have no religious faith, to affirm. We encourage Friends to spread a knowledge of the law so that all those who share either of these objections may take advantage of its provisions. We regard the taking of oaths as contrary to the teaching of Christ, and as setting up a double standard of truthfulness, whereas sincerity and truth should be practised in all dealings of life. *1911; 1959*

572 We believe the oath as at present enforced is undesirable and suggest that a simple promise to tell the truth should be required of all persons giving evidence in a Juvenile Court. To 'swear by Almighty God' is merely to recite the oath children hear day by day from the mouth of the 'man in the street' if not from their own parents. To a large extent it is meaningless. To be required 'to speak the truth' is straightforward and meaningful and the promise to speak the truth would be adequate to deal with the giving of false evidence.
Meeting for Sufferings, 1957

The penal system

573 The terrible sufferings of our forefathers in the prisons of the seventeenth century have given us as a people a special interest in the management of prisons and the treatment of crime. George Fox protested to the judges of his day 'concerning their putting men to death for cattle and money and small matters'; and laid before them 'what a hurtful thing it was that prisoners should lie so long in jail'; showing how 'they learned wickedness from one another in talking of their bad deeds'.

In a later day Elizabeth Fry was the means of introducing urgently needed reforms in the administration of English prisons, particularly those for women. During the two world wars the imprisonment of many on grounds of conscience has made Friends more aware of prison conditions and has deepened the concern of many for more enlightened treatment of the offender. We gratefully recognise the reforms which have already been effected.

There is, however, much work still to be done, in creating a right understanding of the nature and causes of crime, and in emphasising the need for redemptive treatment rather than retributive punishment. Inherited tendency and evil environment are both causes of crime. Society is in measure responsible for the criminal, a fact which emphasises the duty of meeting moral failure by redemptive care. Evil can only be finally overcome by good.

To attain this end there is need, not only, as is now widely recognised, for a more enlightened scientific study of the problems concerning crime and its treatment but also for the personal touch of those who have the good of the individual at heart. We are thankful for the varied practical service and exploratory work of many individual Friends and of concerned groups: their experience strengthens our conviction that there should be a more imaginative exploration of alternatives to traditional modes of punishment; a strengthening of the probation and after-care services; a further development of the Approved Schools for juvenile delinquents in their character of educational rather than penal institutions; and more help available to discharged prisoners to enable them to resume their lives as normal citizens. Prison visiting also is still an indispensable need, and those concerned and qualified to undertake it can find in it opportunities for helpful educational work. Throughout the whole field there is a great need for those who can give concerned service, whether voluntary or vocational, and we would encourage Friends to consider whether they should take advantage of the many openings that are available, and use their talents in working for an improvement of our penal system.

1911; 1925; 1959

Some reflections of Elizabeth Fry on her work are given in §68. Among Friends of her time who shared her concern was Thomas Shillitoe, and an experience of his is recounted in §55.

Capital punishment

574 *Yearly Meeting 1818:*
The awful subject of the punishment of death has at this time deeply impressed our minds. We believe that where the precepts and spirit of our great Lord and Lawgiver have a complete ascendency, they will lead to the abolition of this practice.

575 *Yearly Meeting 1847:*
The subject of the legal punishment of death has at this time obtained our very serious attention. This punishment, to a very great extent, fails to produce the effect of deterring others from the commission of crime; and we believe that it is even the means of hardening in sin many who witness public executions. But a far more serious objection to it is, that man thus undertakes to determine the period at which his fellow men shall cease to exist in this world…We therefore recommend this solemn subject to the very serious attention of our members, and would encourage them to seek…to promote that close examination of the matter by our countrymen and our rulers, which may so enlighten their understandings as to hasten the day when the punishment of death shall be wholly abolished.

576 *John Bright, 1868:*
The real security for human life is to be found in a reverence for it. If the law regarded it as inviolable, then the people would begin also so to regard it. A deep reverence for human life is worth more than a thousand executions in the prevention of murder; and is, in fact, the great security for human life. The law of capital punishment while pretending to support this reverence, does in fact tend to destroy it.

577 *Yearly Meeting 1956, at a time when a Bill was before Parliament for the abolition of the death penalty for murder:*
We feel that we should at this time declare once again our unwavering opposition to capital punishment. The sanctity of human life

is one of the fundamentals of a Christian society and can in no circumstances be set aside. Our concern, therefore, is for all victims of violence, not only the murderer but also those who suffer by his act.

The sanctioning by the State of the taking of human life has a debasing effect on the community, and tends to produce the very brutality which it seeks to prevent. We realise that many are sincerely afraid of the consequences if the death penalty is abolished, but we are convinced that their fears are unjustified.

578

Readers of this book will doubtless be able to supply further examples of practical issues about which Friends should feel concern, and might have a testimony to express. If these receive little or no mention in these pages it is likely to be for one of two reasons.

First the matter may be one which calls for the direct application of some general principle of Christian practice to which attention has already been drawn. Thus the toll of the roads in England today in terms of death and injury is rightly thought to be a challenge which no Christian can ignore. But this raises no new issue of principle; it is a particularly striking illustration of the consequences of persistent selfishness, callousness and carelessness in subordinating the deeper claims of others to one's own convenience or enjoyment. We may well hope that education, with the better provision and wiser regulation of transport, together with greater care on the part of all road users, may mitigate the urgency of this social and moral challenge.

Secondly there are practical issues which rightly exercise the Christian conscience, but upon which the Society of Friends has formed no corporate judgment. Such questions may be so complex, and collective action upon them may involve such intricate and unforeseeable consequences, that no forthright policy of action can be found which could be endorsed by a Christian society. Thus it is easier to see that we must all work and pray for an increasing recognition of world brotherhood, to be expressed in appropriate methods of organisation, than it is to agree upon the extent of authority, and its sanctions, to be accorded to any specific international institution. Or again, within the boundaries of our own national community, it is easier to see the evils of some aspect of the economic or political order than to discover what better alternatives could be introduced without bringing about effects equally harmful in other ways. A third example is our system of justice, so far as it is concerned with the maintenance of rights and the righting of wrongs as distinct from the punishment of offences. Some injustices there must be in a changing society such as ours; but the inexpert may well shrink from presuming to assert the right method for rectifying them.

Confronting all such perplexities we should beware of putting forward our corporate findings too dogmatically. It is our faith that, with changing circumstances and the fresh insights that new experience may make possible, light will be given us to see together the will of God more clearly. It does not lessen our responsibility to press the urgency of a question, if we cannot as yet unite upon the answer to it. Until we can, we may have to refrain from statements implying a corporate decision, not in evasive hesitancy but in resolute patience. It is no service to the Kingdom of God if those who pray for its coming exaggerate the present clarity of their judgment or the present sufficiency of their understanding. *1959*

Chapter 13: National responsibilities

Introductory

579 We are not for names, nor men, nor titles of Government, nor are we for this party nor against the other... but we are for justice and mercy and truth and peace and true freedom, that these may be exalted in our nation, and that goodness, righteousness, meekness, temperance, peace and unity with God, and with one another, that these things may abound. *Edward Burrough (1659)*

580 That if any be called to serve the commonwealth in any public service, which is for the public wealth and good, that with cheerfulness it be undertaken, and in faithfulness discharged unto God.
Meeting of Elders at Balby, 1656

581 He is the truest patriot who benefits his own country without diminishing the welfare of another. For which reason those who induce improvements in the administration of justice, in the maxims of governing, in the political constitution of the state, or those who extend and rectify the education, or in any other manner amend the moral or social condition of a people, possess incomparably higher claims to the praise of patriotism than multitudes of those who receive it from the popular voice.
Jonathan Dymond (1829)

582 The free institutions under which we live give many of our members a direct share in the responsibilities of government and in forming the healthy public opinion that will lead to purity of administration and righteousness of policy. This responsibility belongs to them by virtue of their citizenship, and our members can no more rightly remain indifferent to it, than to the duties which they owe to their parents and near relatives. Men and women of alertness, intelligence and high principle are needed today, to combat the indifference, ignorance and self-interest which are continually impeding the wise solution of great national questions. *1911*

The State's authority and the individual

583 We have...in our Quaker history a lesson for our own lives of the meaning of Christian citizenship. You can see there a two-fold strand constantly interwoven: one, respect for the state as representing authority in the community: and the other, desire to serve the community through the state and in other ways, but along with that, the desire above all to serve the Kingdom of God: this means that we must be willing when loyalty to the Kingdom of God demands it to refuse the demands of the state and show the highest loyalty to the state and the best citizenship by refusing demands that are wrong, because it is only in that way that the conscience of our fellow citizens can be reached, and in the end a better law come into being. *T. Edmund Harvey, 1937*

584 Before deciding on a course which involves disobedience to the command of the State, the good citizen will seek the best guidance he can obtain; he will above all need a vision strengthened by prayer and communion, but he should also be willing to seek counsel with someone whose judgment he can trust, who has sympathy with his sense of duty. Still more will this be needful if he should feel any hesitation about his position. Fresh light may come through such consultation with others, but even if this be not the case, the very act of consultation gives proof of a sense of obligation to the community which is itself significant. *T. Edmund Harvey (1939)*

585 For conscience' sake to God, we are bound by His just law in our hearts to yield obedience to ⟨Authority⟩ in all matters and cases actively or passively: that is to say, in all just and good commands of the King and the good laws of the land relating to our outward man, we must be obedient by doing...but...if anything be

commanded of us by the present Authority, which is not according to equity, justice and a good conscience towards God...we must in such cases obey God only and deny active obedience for conscience' sake, and patiently suffer what is inflicted upon us for such our disobedience to men...And this is our principle, and hath ever been our practice, to obey Authority by doing or suffering, not disputing whether the Authority in itself be absolute of God or not, yet being an Authority over us we are to obey it, either by doing or suffering, because it is an Authority, and not to plot, rebel or rise up with carnal weapons against it: and thus must our obedience be to the King and his Government.   *Edward Burrough (1661)*

586   Christ demands of us that we adhere, without swerving, to the methods of love, and therefore, if a seeming conflict should arise between the claims of His service and those of the State, it is to Christ that our supreme loyalty must be given, whatever the consequences. We would, however, remember that whatever is our highest loyalty to God and humanity is at the same time the highest loyalty that we can render to our nation. *From a statement presented to Yearly Meeting by a committee appointed by the young men of enlistment age present at Yearly Meeting, 1915.*

587   *Statement issued by the Meeting for Sufferings in 1917, after the issue of a regulation requiring the submission of pamphlets to the Censor during the World War:*
The Executive body of the Society of Friends after serious consideration, desires to place on record its conviction that the portion of the recent regulation requiring the submission to the censor of all leaflets dealing with the present war and the making of peace is a grave danger to the national welfare. The duty of every good citizen to express his thoughts on the affairs of his country is hereby endangered, and further we believe that Christianity requires the toleration of opinions not our own, lest we should unwittingly hinder the workings of the Spirit of God.

Beyond this there is a deeper issue involved. It is for Christians a paramount duty to be free to obey, and to act and speak in accord with the law of God, a law higher than that of any state, and no Government official can release men from this duty.

We realise the rarity of the occasions on which a body of citizens find their sense of duty to be in conflict with the law, and it is with a sense of the gravity of this decision, that the Society of Friends must on this occasion act contrary to the regulation, and continue to issue literature on war and peace, without submitting it to the censor. It is convinced that in thus standing firm for spiritual liberty it is acting in the best interests of the nation.

588　The glory of Almighty God and the good of mankind is the reason and end of government, and therefore government in itself is a venerable ordinance of God. *Preamble of the Great Law enacted at Chester, Pennsylvania, by William Penn, 1682.*

589　Not as partisans of a certain type of government, nor as those who despair altogether of the state as of something inherently evil and necessarily immoral shall we make our contribution, but as those who, while recognising as realists the tensions of life, give priority to the spiritual values. We shall acknowledge the legitimacy of social organisation and control. We may even agree with William Penn that government is 'a part of religion itself, a thing sacred in its institution and end', and engage more earnestly in its labours and responsibilities. We shall believe that... peace on earth is possible to men of goodwill, and that the individual and the group may mutually assist each other to their highest self-realisation. We shall apply to the nation as to the individual the searching question, What shall it profit a man if he gain the whole world and lose his soul?
Henry J. Cadbury, 1937

590　Spiritual forces are at work in the modern world but too often lead to faith in false gods. Men crave for certainty and dictators promise a better social order, yet they have merely replaced individual selfishness by a group egoism. Their methods of coercion deny the essential goodness in man and ruin the social changes they have initiated. Their ideas are ephemeral, not eternal.

Friends, whose faith is in the true God, know His is the absolute authority, to which we may surrender ourselves. His is the all-inclusive love: His service is the development of the spiritual in man, not its destruction. Further, we believe in the continued revelation of God, and in humility realise we cannot achieve a perfect order. Let us seek to know the facts of economic conditions and then with intelligence serve our fellow men.   *Friends World Conference, 1937*

Social service in the community

591 The love of God in Christ is creative because it bears the fruits of the Spirit. The ancient words about God's love, about Christ and the cross, about the Holy Spirit and the Church have lost for many their primitive power. They are only sure of a vocation to share humanity's suffering, and enlist others in a like calling. Are we to rebuke such as these? The love of God in Christ calls for disciplined, selfless service. Our service must have roots deep enough to hold when evil is apparently not overcome by good. It may be that such service will be the pathway to worship and faith, as worship and faith issue in service. The two are one in Christ.   *Alexander C. Purdy, 1952*

592 He who desires thus to become the servant of good, the worker in the harvest field of God, will know the need of self-denial. He has seen the vision of the highest, and all lesser goods will take a lower place. For him the call may be for the sacrifice of many legitimate pursuits, many lines of happy activity, in devotion to some imperative service. Principle speaks, and comfort and culture and reputation must be laid aside. The summons comes to give himself to a great cause, to bring liberty to the captive, or light to those that sit in darkness; and the true life, even the abundant life, will be found in obedience to the uttermost. Sacrifice is no end in itself, but it is the test of what we value most, it shows whether we have come out of the narrow circle of self into the great world of human service and divine truth; it is the measure of our devotion to the supreme purpose. It is the stamp of whole-hearted dedication, and thus carries with it an inspiring and uplifting power that appeals to all men and may win its way where all else fails.   *1925*

593 To identify religious practice with social reform may easily prove disastrous, for we may drive out the devils of inequality and un-employment and war, and yet suffer the fate of the tenant of the 'empty, swept and garnished house'. The arts of peace must be guarded meanwhile by each of us. For to all those in the full stream of social or religious work there may come the temptation to under-value the cultural activities which they have given up. The tone in which the often-heard words 'Oh, we haven't time for that', are said sometimes betrays an underground censor, a suggestion that such interests, if not actually frivolous, are certainly inferior. ...Yet the zealous worker in a social campaign has peculiar need of the recreation and refreshment which cultural interests may bring. Fanaticism, as well as indifference, may defeat its own end.

Caroline C. Graveson (*1937*)

594 Service is not a department of life, something outside the main current of personal living. It is sometimes deliberate, but more often is involved unconsciously in the sheer quality of the soul dis-played in ordinary occupations. In our social and recreational activities our gladness and peace of mind will influence others. Special gifts will bring special opportunities and duties. These we shall not think of as tasks to be performed; they will be the natural outcome of a love of men. But we shall seek also to do our part towards the building of an order of society, in which all may be free to enjoy those wholesome pleasures which imply the right exercise of instinct, and that happiness which comes from successful activity of body and mind. *1925*

595 Incomparably the most important thing is that each one of us should be sensitive to the call of God to ourselves and not spend time in passing judgment on the lives of others. To some the call will be to adopt the witness of great simplicity, perhaps to live in an Indian village or in a London slum. To others the most important thing will be to maintain our ancient testimony against 'fightings with outward weapons, for any end, or under any pretence whatever'. But perhaps most will be called to the humdrum tasks of serving an employer supremely well, or running a house, bringing up a family, keeping

the peace with difficult neighbours, serving the community in little things—the tasks which, because they are simple, are in fact most difficult to do with dedication...Our duty is to be sensitive to what God is asking us to do, and not to dissipate our energies trying to be absolutists in several directions at once.

'Christian responsibility & material possessions' (1958)

596 We are sometimes told that the only way to change society is to change its members individually. But this is not only unduly pessimistic; it involves a disregard of man's nature as a social being and what is implied by our membership one of another. Because man is a social being the spiritual level of a whole society can be lifted permanently by a few dedicated individuals, and a great reform such as the abolition of slavery can be brought about even though in other respects the ethical development of the mass of its members remains substantially unchanged. This fact is at the same time an encouragement and a challenge to all who are working for human progress. *W. Russell Brain* (1944)

597 In its history the Society of Friends has produced many people whose lives of conspicuous service have profoundly influenced their times. John Woolman, Elizabeth Fry, Joseph Sturge, and many others would have made for themselves no claim to a special dedication to service, but they were none the less able, out of the depth of their love for their fellows, to take great opportunities that came to them. Their service sprang directly out of their religious faith, but this faith was itself stimulated and fostered by the religious atmosphere in which they lived. To this atmosphere the lives of many Friends, now nameless and unknown, contributed by their faithfulness in inconspicuous service, and so made it possible for the greater spirits to grow to their full stature. *Gerald Littleboy (1945)*

598 The social service of today may not require the fortitude of our forerunners, but it must show an equal grasp of principles and thoroughness of application to be worthy of the past. The economists of the last century failed to give the human factor its proper place.

Much study may still be thrown away if the ethical and spiritual life of man are not kept in the ascendant...All enlargements of the circle of man's life bring their fresh difficulties...The early Friends worked ever from the centre of life to the circumference. Their work came out splendidly true, and it was never shallow.

At the close of the Fourth Gospel comes the supreme inclusiveness, embracing alike diversities of sex, race or condition, 'that they also may be one in us, that the world may believe that Thou hast sent me'. This putting aside of any double standard of Christian levels, whether religious or secular, lay or clerical, or any other dualism, lies at the root of our contention that social service is an integral part of the Christian life and cannot be separated without grave loss on either side. *Joshua Rowntree (1913)*

599 The Christian should...recognise a responsibility for the material welfare of others and may be grateful that in Britain society as a whole has to some extent accepted this responsibility. In so far as this has been done he is relieved from much of the need for direct material gifts to people in this country which there was in the past. There is, however, still the same need that there always was in the manner in which help is given. The spirit of Jesus needs to inspire the ⟨social services⟩ whether...carried out in the name of the state or in the name of a private organisation, and one hopes that some Christians will find their vocations in the paid service of the welfare state...

Besides the need for right material conditions there is the at least equally vital need of right personal relationships, of all that is involved in loving one's neighbour. It is particularly important that this should be emphasised in connection with the satisfaction of material needs, because it is so often the effort to produce material results which generates wrong relationships. How often, indeed, does one hear a ruthless, or unscrupulous or hard man excused on the grounds that at any rate he produces results. There may therefore be a special Christian responsibility in those services which deal with the provision of material things.

'Individual responsibility in a changing society' (1958)

600 Our fathers were pioneers, sharing the outlook of their time, and yet impelled to move forward, devoting themselves to new forms of service as they were prompted by the Spirit within them. We can only share their labours by building on their foundations, by exploring beyond their furthest posts, by taking advantage of new machinery. Our fathers have made possible the new developments which are coming and which we must have a part in.

The new outlook has made obsolete the old lines of separation between philanthropy and politics, between religious and secular. 'Politics' cannot be relegated to some outer place, but must be recognised as one side of life, which is as much the concern of religious people and of a religious body as any other part of life. Nay, more than this, the ordering of the life of man in a community, so that he may have the chance of a full development, is and always has been one of the main concerns of Quakerism.

Lucy Fryer Morland (1918)

601 It is the place of the Christian citizen, whether in legislatures or in municipal bodies, to try to appeal to the best in all men, to the best in his colleagues, not only in his own party, but in other parties, and in that way he may sometimes be able to bring about an agreement which would otherwise never have been achieved.

T. Edmund Harvey, 1937

602 Social problems, like religious, when we do our best and earnestly desire the highest, are often seen in wrong perspective due to limited horizon, lack of essential knowledge, the impossibility of dealing with them in any genuinely detached sense, or of seeing the wood for the trees. Such conditions present no case for a stern refusal to look at compromise. We can but arrive at the relatively higher, and that is reached more often by a spirit of co-operative search for the best, a readiness to give and take and understand another view with a clear sense that none will show absolute wisdom. It is not, I am persuaded, political compromise that is the enemy of religion, but the method by which such compromise is reached, the method, that is falsely called democratic, of reaching an agreed end by immoral surrender of principle, and by voting down and coercing one another. There is a wide difference between Quaker method, which includes but transcends compromise, and the method of a party deal and a political coercion.　　　　*Carl Heath (1922)*

603　There has always been in the Society of Friends a group of persons pledged unswervingly to the ideal... If there comes a collision between allegiance to the ideal and the holding of public office, then the office must be deserted. If obedience to the soul's vision involves eye or hand, houses or lands or life, they must be immediately surrendered. But there has always been as well another group who have held it to be equally imperative to work out their principles of life in the complex affairs of the community and the state, where to gain an end one must yield something; where to get on one must submit to existing conditions; and where to achieve ultimate triumph one must risk his ideals to the tender mercies of a world not yet ripe for them.　　　　*Rufus M. Jones (1911)*

604　If a concerned Quaker (or any man or woman committed to an absolute religious ethic) decides to enter practical politics in order to translate his principles into actuality, he may achieve a relative success: he may be able to raise the level of political life in his time, as John Bright did, or maintain a comparatively happy and just and peaceful society, as the Quaker legislators of Pennsylvania did. But he can apparently do it only at a price—the price of compromise, of the partial betrayal of his ideals. If, on the other hand, he decides to preserve his ideals intact, to maintain his religious testimonies unsullied and pure, he may be able to do that, but again at a price—the price of isolation, of withdrawal from the main stream of life in his time, of renouncing the opportunity directly and immediately to influence history. Let me call the two positions the relativist and the absolutist. And let me suggest that perhaps each one needs the other. The relativist needs the absolutist to keep alive and clear the vision of the City of God while he struggles in some measure to realise it in the City of Earth. And conversely, the absolutist needs the relativist, lest the vision remain the possession of a few only, untranslated into any degree of reality for the world as a whole. *Frederick B. Tolles (1956)*

The experience of John Bright in public life is described in §72.

Chapter 14: International responsibilities

The Peace testimony

605 In considering the character and basis of our testimony for peace
we have felt strongly that its deepest foundation lies in the nature
of God, and that its character must be inclusive of the whole of
life. There is urgent need for a fuller recognition that God's essential
nature is love, that the Cross of Jesus represents the highest point
in the revelation of the character of God, and that there is a seed
of God in every man, that spiritual forces are the mightiest, and
that we must be prepared to rely upon them and to give expression
to them in daily work and character as well as in what we call the
great crises of life. We must set before us the highest ideal, that
which ought to be, rather than that which is, believing that God
is not alone the God of things as they are but the God of things as
they are meant to be.   *All Friends Conference, 1920*

606 The Quaker testimony concerning war does not set up as its standard
of value the attainment of individual or national safety, neither
is it based primarily on the iniquity of taking human life, profoundly
important as that aspect of the question is. It is based ultimately
on the conception of 'that of God in every man' to which the
Christian in the presence of evil is called on to make appeal, following out a line of thought and conduct which, involving suffering
as it may do, is, in the long run, the most likely to reach to the
inward witness and so change the evil mind into the right mind.
This result is not achieved by war.   *A. Neave Brayshaw (1921)*

607 A word of peace and healing can only be spoken by those who
have entered deeply into a sense of the sin as well as the suffering
of the world and have themselves been brought to the place of
penitence. Repentance involves the humble acceptance of the
overwhelming obligation to do better, whatever the cost. Each one
who has entered into such a renewed spiritual experience will be

enabled to minister to the world's need in response to an irresistible divine call. It is not for us to pledge our members: it is for each individual Friend to dedicate himself with a devotion that is more personal and more abiding than any printed document; the life of each one of us should testify with a decisiveness that is proof, against all temporal argument.   *Yearly Meeting, 1942*

608 Aggressive tyranny is an evil to be undone by right constructive act, but the first and immediate demand is that it be *opposed* and opposed with a virile acceptance of all the danger that that may involve... Hence the call to Christian peacemakers for non-violent resistance to violence... Whilst massed might resists and kills, and aggression is hurled back *perhaps*, there is in it no redemption. But the other has a deeper purpose of conversion whilst it resists.   *Carl Heath (1939)*

609 It requires great self denial and resignation of ourselves to God to attain that state wherein we can freely cease from fighting when wrongfully invaded, if by our fighting there were a probability of overcoming the invaders. Whoever rightly attains to it does in some degree feel that spirit in which our Redeemer gave his life for us, and through divine goodness many of our predecessors, and many now living, have learned this blessed lesson; but many others having their religion chiefly by education, and not being enough acquainted with that Cross which crucifies to the world, do manifest a temper distinguishable from that of an entire trust in God.
John Woolman, 1757

610 We had been talking for an hour and a half with a clergyman neighbour, and afterwards I sat by the fire and thought. He had maintained that war has not as yet been grown out of, and that God still uses it as a means of training His children. As I thought over this, old thoughts and memories awoke from sleep. I remembered the familiar words about William Penn's sword—'Wear it as long as thou canst': and it seemed clear to me that if William Penn had given it up from self-interest or cowardice, or for any reason short of the 'witness of God in his own Soul', he would have been wrong. And then the thought extended itself from the life of one man to the life of mankind, and I remembered a sentence in the Epistle to Diognetus 'What the soul is in the body, that Christians are in the world'. Then I seemed to see that war cannot rightly come to an end from self-interest or cowardice or any worldly reason but only because men and women, by one and one, without waiting for the others, have become loyal to the spirit of Christ.   *Marion Fox, 1914*

611 In the present situation persuasive methods and peaceful adjustment should be tried as sincerely and consistently as possible. What if they fail, as well they may, and aggression is imminent? A tragic moral dilemma seems to arise: shall we set violence against violence and defend the society to which we feel bound by duty and affection, the lives and the future of those we love—or shall we reject violence and allow the aggressor to do his worst? This looks like the choice between two equally monstrous evils. But essentially they are not equal. According to all moral standards, and seen in the light both of love and justice, the bearing of evil is diametrically opposed to the inflicting of evil. 'It is better, if the will of God be so, that ye suffer for well doing than for evil doing' (1 Pet. 3. 17). By fighting for civilisation and precious lives we may not save but destroy them, and would most probably destroy all moral and spiritual standards of our world through the use of the weapons of mass-destruction. And on the other hand refusal to fight need not be surrender. Nevertheless, nothing can be harder than that choice.

Those who proclaim non-violence as a political technique often suggest that, if carried through with utter self-denial and self-control, it may force the hand of an aggressor. We must be prepared for the possibility of it having no such positive effect and of it leading to outward defeat. Whether successful or not it will bring suffering, martyrdom and death to many. And we must accept the way of the Cross not only for ourselves. If we believe in non-violence as the true way of peace and love, we must make it a principle not only of individual but of national and universal conduct. It would be too easy to take the position of people who are specially called for an absolute obedience to the law of love and to be content with remaining a small and ineffective group, while the majority of our fellow men defend themselves and, in fact, us too. Whilst respecting those who decide to fight, because they equally follow the voice of their conscience, we must endeavour to win them, or as many of them as possible, to the way of non-violence, whatever the consequences. Certainly we shall try to do so without any feeling of moral superiority. For not by proclaiming the way of love can we prove it to be right and applicable, but only by following it to the bitter end—and we know how soon we may stumble when put to the test.   *Konrad Braun (1950)*

612 The whole world is drawn into common suffering. Is there no way out of its evils but by waging war yet more ruthlessly? War is evil and wrong; military victory will not bring true peace. Cannot our common suffering make us aware of our common brotherhood? Let us turn from the terrible deeds we do to one another and seek one another's forgiveness. The way of friendship can overcome evil. We see it perfectly in Jesus Christ. Its cost was the Cross. The loyal spirit which faced the Cross showed us the triumphant power of God. For us as children of a common Father it is time to follow His lead.   *Yearly Meeting, 1942*

Friends' historic testimony

613 *George Fox, 1651:*
I told ⟨the Commonwealth Commissioners⟩ I lived in the virtue of that life and power that took away the occasion of all wars and I knew from whence all wars did rise, from the lust, according to James's doctrine... I told them I was come into the covenant of peace which was before wars and strifes were.

614 *Declaration to Charles II, 1661:*
We utterly deny all outward wars and strife and fightings with outward weapons, for any end or under any pretence whatsoever. And this is our testimony to the whole world. The spirit of Christ, by which we are guided, is not changeable, so as once to command us from a thing as evil and again to move unto it; and we do

certainly know, and so testify to the world, that the spirit of Christ, which leads us into all Truth, will never move us to fight and war against any man with outward weapons, neither for the kingdom of Christ, nor for the kingdoms of this world.

615 *Robert Barclay, 1678:*
Whoever can reconcile this, 'Resist not evil', with 'Resist violence by force', again, 'Give also thy other cheek', with 'Strike again'; also, 'Love thine enemies', with 'Spoil them, make a prey of them, pursue them with fire and the sword', or, 'Pray for those that persecute you, and those that calumniate you', with 'Persecute them by fines, imprisonments and death itself', whoever, I say, can find a means to reconcile these things may be supposed also to have found a way to reconcile God with the Devil, Christ with Antichrist, Light with Darkness, and good with evil. But if this be impossible, as indeed it is impossible, so will also the other be impossible, and men do but deceive both themselves and others, while they boldly adventure to establish such absurd and impossible things.

616 *Issued by Yearly Meeting 1744, during the War of the Austrian Succession:*
We entreat all who profess themselves members of our Society to be faithful to that ancient testimony, borne by us ever since we were a people, against bearing arms and fighting, that by a conduct agreeable to our profession we may demonstrate ourselves to be real followers of the Messiah, the peaceable Saviour, of the increase of whose government and peace there shall be no end.

617 *Issued by Yearly Meeting 1804, 1805, during the Napoleonic Wars:*
Most, if not all, people admit the transcendent excellency of peace. All who adopt the petition, 'Thy kingdom come', pray for its universal establishment. Some people then must begin to fulfil the evangelical promise, and cease to learn war any more. Now, friends, seeing these things cannot be controverted, how do we long that your whole conversation be as becometh the Gospel; and that while any of us are professing to scruple war, they may not in some parts of their conduct be inconsistent with that profession!... Friends

it is an awful thing to stand forth to the nation as the advocates of inviolable peace; and our testimony loses its efficacy in proportion to the want of consistency in any...And we can serve our country in no way more availingly, nor more acceptably to him who holds its prosperity at his disposal, than by contributing, all that in us lies, to increase the number of meek, humble, and self-denying Christians.

Guard against placing your dependence on fleets and armies; be peaceable yourselves, in words and actions, and pray to the Father of the Universe that he would breathe the spirit of reconciliation into the hearts of his erring and contending creatures.

618 *Issued by Yearly Meeting 1854, during the Crimean War:*
We feel bound explicitly to avow our continued unshaken per suasion that all war is utterly incompatible with the plain precepts of our Divine Lord and Lawgiver, and with the whole spirit and tenor of His Gospel; and that no plea of necessity or of policy, however urgent or peculiar, can avail to release either individuals or nations from the paramount allegiance which they owe unto Him who hath said 'Love your enemies'.

619 *Issued by Yearly Meeting 1900, during the South African War:*
We believe that the Spirit of Christ will ultimately redeem national as well as individual life. We believe further that, as all church history shows, the human means will be the faithful witness borne by Christ's disciples. It has been well said 'It seems to be the will of Him, who is infinite in wisdom, that light upon great subjects should first arise and be gradually spread through the faithfulness of *individuals* in acting up to their own convictions'. This was the secret of the power of the early Church. The blood of the Christians proved a fruitful seed. In like manner the staunchness of early Friends and others to their conscientious convictions in the seventeenth century won the battle of religious freedom for England. We covet a like faithful witness against war from Christians today.

620 *Issued by Yearly Meeting 1915, during the First World War:*
Meeting at a time when the nations of Europe are engaged in a war

of unparalleled magnitude, we have been led to recall the basis of the peace testimony of our religious Society. It is not enough to be satisfied with a barren negative witness, a mere proclamation of non-resistance. We must search for a positive, vital, constructive message. Such a message, a message of supreme love, we find in the life and death of our Lord Jesus Christ. We find it in the doctrine of the indwelling Christ, that re-discovery of the early Friends, leading as it does to a recognition of the brotherhood of all men. Of this doctrine our testimony as to war and peace is a necessary outcome, and if we understand the doctrine aright, and follow it in its wide implications, we shall find that it calls to the peaceable spirit and the rule of love in all the broad and manifold relations of life.

Thus while love, joy, peace, gentleness and holiness are the teaching of the life and death of our Lord, it is to these that we are also impelled by the indwelling of the Divine in men. As this spirit grows within us, we shall realise increasingly what it is to live in the virtue of that life and power which takes away the occasion of all wars.

621 *Issued by Yearly Meeting 1943, during the Second World War:*
All thoughtful men and women are torn at heart by the present situation. The savage momentum of war drags us all in its wake. We desire a righteous peace. Yet to attain peace it is claimed that, as Chungking, Rotterdam and Coventry were devastated, so the Eder and Moehne dams must needs be destroyed and whole districts of Hamburg obliterated. The people of Milan and Turin demonstrate for peace but the bombing continues. War is hardening our hearts. To preserve our sanity, we become apathetic. In such an atmosphere no true peace can be framed; yet before us we see months of increasing terror. Can those who pay heed to moral laws, can those who follow Christ submit to the plea that the only way is that demanded by military necessity?

True peace involves freedom from tyranny and a generous tolerance; conditions that are denied over a large part of Europe and are not fulfilled in other parts of the world. But true Peace cannot be dictated, it can only be built in co-operation between all peoples. None of us, no nation, no citizen, is free from some responsibility for this situation with its conflicting difficulties.

To the world in its confusion Christ came. Through him we know that God dwells with men and that by turning from evil and living in his spirit we may be led into his way of peace. That way of peace is not to be found in any policy of 'unconditional surrender' by whomsoever demanded. It requires that men and nations should recognise their common brotherhood, using the weapons of integrity, reason, patience and love, never acquiescing in the ways of the oppressor, always ready to suffer with the oppressed. In every country there is a longing for freedom from domination and war which men are striving to express. Now is the time to issue an open invitation to co-operate in creative peacemaking, to declare our willingness to make sacrifices of national prestige, wealth and standards of living for the common good of men.

The way of Christ is followed not by those who would be mighty and powerful, but by those who would serve. His peace for the world will be won by those who follow him in repentance and willingness to forgive.

622 *During the American War of Independence, the Quaker whaling community on the island of Nantucket suffered heavily from both sides for their neutrality. William Rotch (1734-1828), one of their leaders, had in a disused warehouse a consignment of bayonets which had been taken from muskets which he had accepted twelve years earlier in quittance of a debt, and sold as fowling pieces. In 1776 the bayonets were demanded from him by the Americans:*

The time was now come to endeavour to support our Testimony against War, or abandon it, as this very instrument was a severe test. I could not hesitate which to choose, and therefore denied the applicant. My reason for not furnishing them was demanded, to which I readily answered, 'As this instrument is purposely made and used for the destruction of mankind, I can put no weapon into a man's hand to destroy another, that I cannot use myself in the same way.' The person left me much dissatisfied. Others came, and received the same denial. It made a great noise in the Country, and my life was threatened. I would gladly have beaten them into 'pruning hooks', but I took an early opportunity of throwing them into the sea.

A short time after I was called before a Committee appointed by the Court then held at Watertown near Boston, and questioned amongst other things respecting my bayonets.

I gave a full account of my proceedings, and closed it with saying, 'I sunk them in the bottom of the sea, I did it from principle, I have ever been glad that I had done it, and if I am wrong I am to be pitied.' The chairman of the Committee Major Hawley (a worthy character) then addressed the Committee, and said 'I believe Mr. Rotch has given us a candid account, and every man has a right to act consistently with his religious principles, but I am sorry that we could not have the bayonets, for we want them very much.' The Major was desirous of knowing more of our principles on which I informed him as far as he enquired. One of the Committee in a pert manner observed 'then your principles are passive Obedience and non-resistance'. I replied, 'No, my friend, our principles are active Obedience or passive suffering.'

Memorandum written by William Rotch in the
eightieth year of his age, 1814

623 We are deeply convinced that the testimony for Peace, which we believe has been entrusted to us as a Society, is not an artificial appendage to our faith, which can be dropped without injuring the whole, but rather an organic out-growth of our belief as Christians and as Friends, which cannot be abandoned without mutilating our whole message for the world.

We believe in common with other Christians, that in Jesus Christ, the Divine Word, which in all ages had been the 'Light' of men, took human form. We have seen in him the revelation of the priceless worth of manhood in the sight of God, and know that in virtue of his 'Light' shed abroad in every human soul, all men, of whatever race or nation, are brothers. Upon this sacred human personality, war rudely tramples, virtually regarding men as *things*, as obstacles to be got rid of, if they are enemies; or, if they are our own soldiers, as military instruments whose consciences may be disregarded. As Christians we cannot be parties to putting ourselves or others in such a position. Further, since the Divine Light within us is the Light of Christ, we cannot separate it from the spirit of his teaching, when he was here on earth. We cannot claim his authority for impulses within us which lead us to act in opposition to that teaching, which he summed up in love to God and love to all men.

In so far as we have grasped and been obedient to these leadings, we have been enabled to see a splendid vision of what human unity is, and of what human fellowship may be, and have of necessity been filled with a profound sense of the evil of violating this fellowship. This vision has brought us a renewed faith in the power of spiritual forces to build the structure of humanity, and to redeem it from error and wrong. It is only spiritual forces that can do this, the powers that touch men's hearts, that convince their minds and win their loyalty and set free the uniting forces of humanity. The very refusal of all violence, if it springs evidently and sincerely from a deep reverence and love for 'that of God' in an opponent's nature, will be potent to reach and win his soul. Those who see this, even if dimly and amid much perplexity, must hold it fast.

We have so valued this vision and recognised its authority that war— 'the arbitrament of self-assertion and passion', with all its abrogation of moral restraint, its denial of discriminating justice, its responsibility for atrocities, its destruction of all the divine possibilities of human life—is for us an impossibility.

Backed by these convictions, we hold the moral law of gentleness and forgiveness and love to be unconditionally binding upon us now. It seems a poor and pitiful thing to believe in principles except when they may have to be applied, in forgiveness only when there is nothing to forgive, in love only for those who love us. It is our present sinning and stricken world that needs these redeeming messages in word and life. May we be faithful to the vision! It bears with it a grave but splendid responsibility.

Yearly Meeting, 1912; 1925

624 Our peace testimony is much more than our special attitude to world affairs; it expresses our vision of the whole Christian way of life; it is our way of living in this world, of looking at this world and of changing this world. Only when the seeds of war—pride, prestige, and lust for power and possessions—have been purged from our personal and corporate ways of living; only when we can meet all men as friends in a spirit of sharing and caring, can we call upon others to tread the same path.

Our Christian Pacifism, expressed in lives dedicated to the service of God and all his family, should be an experience from which we may speak to peoples and rulers and which transforms a negative refusal to take part in war into a positive witness to the better way. We must by study, by group discussion, and by experience of active peace work equip ourselves with reliable knowledge to enable us not only to expound but also to apply our peace testimony.

Friends World Conference, 1952

Conscription

625 *Issued by Yearly Meeting, on the passing of the Military Service Act, 1916:*
We take this, the earliest opportunity, of re-affirming our entire opposition to compulsory military service and our desire for the repeal of the Act.

War, in our view, involves the surrender of the Christian ideal and a denial of human brotherhood; it is an evil for the destruction of which the world is longing; but freedom from the scourge of war will only be brought about through the faithfulness of individuals to their inmost convictions, under the guidance of the spirit of Christ.

Our position is based upon our interpretation of the teaching of Jesus Christ. We regard the central conception of the Act as imperilling the liberty of the individual conscience—which is the main hope of human progress—and as entrenching more deeply that militarism from which we all desire the world to be freed. It follows that our opposition is not removed by the provisions with regard to conscience, welcome as these are. We have in mind not only conscientious objectors, but also a large number hitherto held back from military service from no unworthy motive, but by a restraining influence to which they would find it impossible to give expression...

Young men may do important service by going before the tribunals claiming exemption and making clear their reasons for doing so. At the same time we cannot admit that a human tribunal is an adequate judge of any man's conscience. The final appeal can only be to the source from which the conscientious convictions themselves spring.

Our lives should prove that compulsion is both unnecessary and impolitic. They should manifest a sense of duty not less strong than that which has driven many whom we respect (and some even of our own members) into the fighting forces. We can identify ourselves to the full with the griefs of our nation in which few hearts are not torn by suffering or harrowed by suspense. We pray that in steadfast conformity to the path of duty we may be set free to serve—to give to the community the fullest service of which we are capable—each one in the way of God's appointing.

626 *Issued by Yearly Meeting 1939, at the time of the Military Training Bill:* We recognise that it is not in our power to define or determine another's attitude. We should not urge anyone to be either more or less uncompromising than his own conscience compels. The duty is laid upon us to help each man to make a right decision and then to help him to be faithful to it when made.

627 *Issued by Meeting for Sufferings, 1945:* Compulsory military service is sometimes claimed as a duty attaching to citizenship. But it is not true social service. On the one hand it is part of the attempt to maintain peace by force, and on the other it is training in methods that are contrary to the highest moral standards recognised by man...The training of men to kill each other is a violation of the sacredness of personality for it is a crime against that of God in every man. It requires an inhumanity and a blind obedience that is a negation of responsible service to our fellow men. It demands much that in private life is recognised as anti-social and criminal... Christ bids us love our enemies; governments bid us kill them... The conscript is, in effect, required to endorse war in advance.

628 *Issued by Meeting for Sufferings, 1948, in a statement presented to the British Council of Churches:*
We believe that the training of youth for war does a flagrant wrong to the young man on whom it is imposed. At a time of life when young men should be learning the joy of freely given service on behalf of their fellows they are subjected to a compulsory negative service which will lead in many cases to a hatred or ignoring of the word 'service' and its claims in later life... It may be suggested that our opposition is only part of our wider testimony against war. That is not altogether true. We believe that conscription for military training would still be wrong even if war were never to come... The existence of a conscience clause does not minimise this evil, for it is only the exceptional lad who is able to form a moral judgment on such an issue at this age, and to express it convincingly in public.

Disarmament

629 Our conviction is that Christianity has this to say to the world. 'Your reliance upon armaments is both wrong and futile. Armaments are the weapons of organised violence and outrage. Their use is a denial of the true laws of good living. They involve the perpetuation of strife. They stand in the way of the true fellowship of men. They impoverish the peoples. They tempt men to evil, and they breed suspicion and fear and the tragic results thereof. They are therefore not legitimate weapons in the Christian armoury, nor are they sources of security.' You cannot foster harmony by the apparatus of discord, nor cherish good will by the equipment of hate. But it is by harmony and goodwill that human security can be obtained. Armaments aim at a security in isolation; but such would at best be utterly precarious and is, as a matter of fact, illusory. The only true safety is the safety of all, and unless your weapon of defence achieves this work, or works towards this, it is a source of antagonism and therefore of increased peril.

All Friends Conference, 1920

630 Under a deep sense of the need for constructive service for international peace, ⟨we⟩ have united in a concern that Friends should realise more fully the fundamental character of our peace testimony and the essential importance of removing enmity and suspicion between countries. We have been led more clearly than ever to regard total disarmament as the Christian solution of the problem before Europe, and to see that it is especially the work of the Society of Friends to put forward this solution. *Service Committee, 1917*

631 While hatred and fear are growing everywhere, the treasure of the world and the technical skills of men are being dissipated in rearmament, and schemes for the welfare of mankind in the underdeveloped countries are in danger of breaking down. In face of the longing of men and women for peace we must impress on our countrymen and on our Government the need for such hopeful and constructive alternatives to the policies which seem all too likely to lead the world into destruction. There is good will in many hearts which will respond to a spiritual appeal, and we must seek to convince others that 'only the unarmed have inexhaustible resources'. *Yearly Meeting, 1952*

632 We in Great Britain have decided to make hydrogen bombs. If a major war breaks out the temptation to use them will be very great. We are warned by our scientists that their use will involve not only the most terrible suffering now, but unknown consequences for succeeding generations who will pay the penalty for our sin. We believe that no one has the right to use these weapons in his defence or to ask another person to use them on his behalf. To

rely on the possession of nuclear weapons as a deterrent is faithless; to use them is a sin.   *Meeting for Sufferings, 1955*

International tensions

633 If war is to be prevented, the spirit from which war proceeds must be excluded. As with individuals so with nations, the beginnings of strife must be watchfully guarded against. To give occasions of offence or jealousy to the governments or to the inhabitants of other countries, whether by imputing evil motives, by needless alarms of invasion, or by anything approaching to a hostile attitude, is inconsistent alike with Christian duty and with true patriotism.

Yearly Meeting, 1859

634 *At a time of tense feeling, following the outbreak of the Crimean War in 1854, Meeting for Sufferings issued 'A Christian appeal':*
Although it may be admitted that the precepts and example of our Lord have a primary reference to the conduct of individuals, they can surely be no less binding upon a nation professing allegiance to Christ the Supreme Ruler, than upon the individuals of whom it is composed...To affirm that they are impracticable, or not to be practised, is to set at naught their supreme authority, and to put dishonour upon their Divine Author. To postpone their application until all shall act upon them, is, in scarcely a less degree, to deny His present authority; and involves the practical contradiction of supposing that He has prescribed a series of duties for a state of things, in which the occasion for their exercise shall have ceased to exist. It is *now*, in this still tossed and conflicted world, that the Christian is called upon to act out these lessons. It is *now* that he is bound to prove his allegiance to his Divine Master; and, so far as his influence may extend, to promote the spreading of His kingdom upon the earth. That kingdom is one of righteousness and peace.

635 *After the bombardment of Alexandria in 1882, John Bright, in explaining his resignation from the Government, said to the Commons:*

The House knows that for forty years at least I have endeavoured to teach my countrymen an opinion and doctrine which I hold, namely, that the moral law is intended not for individual life only, but for the life and practice of States in their dealing with one another. I think that in the present case there has been a manifest violation both of International Law and of the moral law, and therefore it is impossible for me to give my support to it.

636 *The following minute was issued by Yearly Meeting 1930, at a time of widespread rioting during India's long struggle for political freedom, which was achieved in 1947:*
The situation in India has drawn out our deep sympathy towards those upon whom the weight of responsibility rests from day to day. We are thankful to know that both the Viceroy and the Secretary of State desire the extension of political freedom to India on constitutional lines and we pray that they may steadily persevere in this aim in spite of discouragements. We rejoice that the Indian nationalists have among their leaders of thought men like Tagore and Gandhi, who combine with their burning sense of India's wrongs the conviction that the remedy must be sought through the extension of sympathetic understanding.

The Society of Friends believes that God reveals Himself in the hearts of all men. This belief makes us advocates of freedom and inspires us to take the risks of freedom rather than maintain a system of tutelage, however beneficent it may have been both in purpose and results, which is now felt to be galling to an awakened and developed India.

We know that nothing can be gained by violence on one side or coercion on the other, which inevitably interfere with the workings of God's spirit, and we earnestly pray that it may be possible for the leaders on both sides to take some definite step towards reconciliation and thus release all the latent forces of goodwill which are now failing of expression.

637 *Characteristic of Yearly Meeting's growing concern for economic justice among the nations is the following extract from the Epistle of 1937:*

We have thought of the widespread exploitation of economically underdeveloped peoples, and of those industrial and other workers who are also exploited and heavily burdened. We must therefore work for a larger measure of liberty in political and economic life. For not only is this at the heart of the Christian message, but we have seen that peace stands on a precarious footing so long as there is unrelieved poverty and subjection. Subjection, poverty, injustice and war are closely allied. This situation demands sweeping political and economic changes; and we are convinced that the hope of freedom does not lie in violence, which is at its root immoral, but in such changes as may be brought about by fellowship and mutual service.

638 *The following extract is taken from an address in 1958 entitled 'Christians in a divided world' by Margarethe Lachmund, a German Friend with intimate knowledge of conditions in both East and West Germany. In discussing the problem of Communism for Christians, she can truly state 'I therefore do not speak on this subject theoretically, but from insight gained through personal experience and personal contact with people and conditions on both sides':*

Is Christianity capable of contributing to the overcoming of tensions and showing a way to their solution? I am convinced that we can find a clear, positive answer by investigating how Christ himself met the tensions of his time; for him tensions which separate people simply do not exist. Jesus knows no fear, nothing holds him apart from other people. His fearlessness, however, flows from his communion with God. But this communion with God can be achieved by all men. Thus he sees in the other man only his brother, his neighbour. Next to the love of God, the commandment 'Love thy neighbour as thyself' is for Jesus the most essential of all commandments.

Such a concept does not mean that opposite views are abolished... On the contrary, they ⟨remain distinct and⟩ must not be veiled— that would be untruthful. The courage for clarity and the strength to stand up for truth are repeatedly demanded of us. However, the secret lies in the way in which truth is spoken. If it is spoken with contempt, bitterness or hatred, it results in bitterness; if, however, truth is spoken in love, the door to the other's heart can slowly open so that the truth can perhaps have some effect.

In the fourth chapter of John's Gospel, Jesus talks with the Samaritan woman about her life, and she is able to listen to him, although he speaks openly with her. I was deeply touched when, for the first time, I noticed a word in the story of Christ's passion as told by Matthew. For forty years I had simply overlooked it. When Judas comes to take Jesus prisoner, Jesus says to him: 'My friend, wherefore art thou come?' Jesus knows what is to happen, but even in this moment he addresses Judas with the words, 'my friend'. By doing this, he does not break the bridges of communication between them.

In order to understand Communism, I believe it is absolutely necessary to study it more seriously than people in the Western world usually do. We tend to react emotionally toward the unknown and sinister; we lose self-control and this creates the basis for fear. Today, it is a striking fact that often those people who are the furthest away from Communism and who have no clear knowledge of it, fear it the most.

A more thorough knowledge of Communism also creates a different atmosphere in personal contacts with Communists. Time and again we noticed that Communists were open-minded with people in whom they saw a readiness to take them and their teaching seriously. Regardless of the fact that they may have rejected Communism, the people who had at least thought about it, also gained the respect of the Communists. After all, it is human nature to wish to be taken seriously. Our intellectual and spiritual struggle with the issues of Communism also help us reach greater clarity about ourselves. Such clarity is sometimes full of bitter truth. We are opposed, and rightly so, to the Communist dogma that there is no final moral basis—only that which serves the working class is good. This appears to us to be a complete relativisation of ethics and absolute moral disintegration, which necessarily leads to the principle: 'The end justifies the means'. However, how does this apply to the political and economic life of Christian people? Is spying, the activities of agents, and all the rest in politics that uses lying and deceit rejected?

Does the principle of Christian charity rule in the division and use of goods? Does it look like anything but hypocrisy to the Communist when we constantly talk about our Christianity, without realising ourselves that our practice is something quite different? It should be our concern to create a basis of ⟨inner⟩ parity between us and the Communists so that we may speak truthfully to one another. Those who are unafraid and want to do justice to the opponent prove how much one may actually say on the basis of one's convictions. We repeatedly experienced the subtle sensitivity of the Russians with regard to whether they were being lied to or told the truth. Often they reacted in a surprisingly positive way when one had to say what was for them an unpleasant truth and did so in a quiet way. Isn't there a natural feeling alive in every person against being lied to which should be respected? If we are unable to tell the truth there is something wrong within us, too; our relation to another lacks inner freedom because we simply do not meet him as another human being, but with bitterness, hate or contempt in our hearts.

We can help to ease the tensions and live within them in the right way if we fulfil simultaneously Christ's two commandments—the commandment to love and the commandment to speak truth. A synthesis of these two must be found. Out of fear, we may betray truth; out of bitterness or self-righteousness we may betray love. A desire for peace without truthfulness is worthless and does not bring about peace; without love truth has no effect because it is not heard.

639 Whilst conscious of inadequacies ⟨in our western civilisation⟩ in which we share, we must reaffirm our fundamental differences from Communists. These differences lie on three planes: that of belief (for we believe in God); of attitude to man (for we cherish his individuality); and of social action (for we forswear violence). We differ from Communism in believing that, since there is the 'seed of God' in the heart of every man, there are ways open, to those who honestly desire rightful change, to overcome opposition by conversion, not compulsion. We differ from them in believing that there is a dynamism in human affairs, such that violence and

mendacity, even when employed with good intentions, have insidious results unforeseen by those who use them. We believe that such qualities as humility and loving kindness are good in themselves, and that their growth in individuals has a powerful effect in shaping society. *'Practical implications of our faith'* (*1953*)

640 What are the particular responsibilities which this 'East-West' situation imposes on us as Friends? We shall not over-estimate what inter-governmental negotiation, even at a high level, can do to resolve the complexities of the East-West problem and to make possible a genuine peaceful co-operation between the two sides. We shall certainly not exaggerate the role of Friends in areas and in actions that are essentially political... Meanwhile we can continue to take and to make opportunities of personal inter-visitation and contact with the peoples of Communist countries, putting ourselves alongside them on their own ground and on ours in a spirit of goodwill and seeking to develop a greater mutual understanding at each and every level of the East-West relationship. *East-West Relations Committee, 1958*

Reconciliation and co-operation

641 We appeal to all men to recognise the great spiritual force of love which is found in all and which makes us all one common brotherhood. In spite of sacrifice and devotion there is dissatisfaction and unrest in all lands. Consciously or unconsciously, men are seeking for a new way of life. They cry for a bond that shall unite the world in freedom, righteousness and love; that shall liberate it from its suffering, its hatreds, its disunion. They cry for a religion of life, for an active spirit of peace on earth, of goodwill to men.

Through the dark clouds of selfishness and materialism, shines the Eternal Light of the Christ in man. It can never perish. This light of Christ in the heart of every man is the ground of our hope, the basis of our faith in the spiritual unity of all races and nations. Because we have been blind to this essential fact of life we have failed in social and international relations and are now in confusion. The profound need of our time is to realise the everlasting truth of the common Fatherhood of God—the Spirit of Love—and the oneness of the human race.

We have used the words of Christ, but we have not acted upon them. We have called ourselves by his name but we have not lived in his spirit. Nevertheless, the Divine Seed is in all men. As men realise its presence, and follow the light of Christ in their hearts, they enter upon the right way of life and receive power to overcome evil by good. Thus will be built the City of God. We stretch out our hands in fellowship, sympathy and love across frontiers, lands and seas. We call upon all men everywhere to unite in the service of healing the broken world, to bear one another's burdens, and so fulfil the law of Christ. *Meeting for Sufferings, 1919*

642 There are many separate problems in the life of humanity to be faced and resolved by the religious community. Our desire is that we may faithfully consider each such problem in the full light of the life and teaching of Jesus Christ... Each clear testimony upon right human relations, springing out of a faithful study of such problems as war, disarmament, patriotism, the treatment of weaker peoples, and co-operation between nations, is but another effort to express the inward oneness and harmony of the Community of the Spirit. We are not working for individual reforms alone. We are seeking a new and unified way of life for the Society of Man, and finding it in the reality of the Kingdom set before us in vision by Christ Jesus.

The Spirit of God works in the world in every creative act that liberates and lifts the human race. The eternal purpose is wrought out daily before us in slow ways, and by hard experience men learn, as they struggle towards the light, that God and the Power of God is what they truly seek. For with him is the secret of effective action: the vision, the driving force and the power to build a city of God and a Realm of Right. And with him, too, is the willingness to share with us the mighty corporate life of the Spirit. Have we knowledge of this life, and having it, are we ready individually and as a community, to take our place in this great fellowship of the Spirit, and to find ourselves builders together with the living God? *1925*

643 In face of deepening fear and mutual distrust throughout the world, the Society of Friends (Quakers) is moved to declare good will to all men everywhere. Friends appeal for the avoidance of words and deeds that increase suspicion and ill-feeling, for renewed efforts at understanding and for positive attempts to build a true peace. They are convinced that reconciliation is possible. They hope that this simple word, translated into many tongues, may itself help to create the new spirit in which the resources of the world will be diverted from war-like purposes and applied to the welfare of mankind. *'A message of goodwill to all men', issued by Yearly Meeting, 1950.*

644 We call upon peoples everywhere... to behave as nations with the same decency as they would behave as men and brothers, to substitute the institutions of peace for the institutions of war. Let us join together throughout the world to grow more food, to heal and prevent disease, to conserve and develop the resources of the good earth to the glory of God and the comfort of man's distress. These are among the tasks to which, in humility for our share in the world's shame, and in faith in the power of love, we call our own Society and all men and nations everywhere. *Friends World Conference, 1952*

645 It is the experience of the Society of Friends in its relief and reconciliation work that it is not enough to do good to others. One must work not for them so much as alongside of them. They must be brought into a common undertaking. In the forefront of any general international organisation must stand the machinery for effective economic and cultural collaboration. The hope of peace lies in mutual co-operation in international reconstruction and public works, in concerted measures against poverty and disease, in educational collaboration and in the establishment together of the freedoms and responsibilities essential for the common man.
Meeting for Sufferings, 1945

646 *In 1925, the following questions were included in a section of our Book of Discipline on the League of Nations as showing some of the tests by which Friends might judge the League and its actions. These questions still remain cogent, as they indicate the criteria by which the international organisations of today may be assessed:*

Has it promise of becoming a League of all nations? Does it reflect the aspirations towards human brotherhood that are growing up among men and women in all nations? Does it stand for justice and mercy? Is it relying upon intelligent public opinion and on the consent of its members, rather than on fear or on threats of coercion? Does its moral authority increase or diminish? Is it working for the welfare, material and spiritual, of men and women, and not in the interests of powerful groups or tyrannical authorities? Is it bringing the light of day into places of deceit and corruption? Is it helping to succour the needy, to release those who are in bonds, to give light to those who are in darkness? Is it fostering co-operation? Does it show by its deeds a recognition of the truth that all men, whatever their colour or creed or class may be, are children of one Father?

647 Though rejecting on principle the provisions for coercion incorporated in the charter ⟨of the United Nations⟩, we must support the present organisation, the only peaceful meeting place for West and East, in its positive work of negotiation and functional co-operation, knowing well how imperfect and provisional its machinery still is. As citizens in a democracy we must urge our Government to do everything for the improvement of that machinery, and we may well take the idea of a world federation as a guiding principle for such improvement.

It is most important to use and develop the provisions of the charter for peaceful change of the *status quo*, so that fair and just conditions are created, which the nations are prepared to uphold. It is true that this is more a matter of will than of machinery; our aim must be to strengthen both the good will of nations and international machinery. *Konrad Braun (1950)*

648 *Yearly Meeting 1727:*
It is the sense of this meeting, that the importing of negroes from their native country and relations by Friends, is not a commendable nor allowed practice, and is therefore censured by this meeting.

649 *Yearly Meeting 1772:*
It appears that the practice of holding negroes in oppressive and unnatural bondage, hath been so successfully discouraged by Friends in some of the colonies, as to be considerably lessened. We cannot but approve of these salutary endeavours, and earnestly intreat they may be continued, that, through the favour of Divine Providence, a traffic so unmerciful and unjust in its nature to a part of our own species made equally with ourselves for immortality, may come to be considered by all in its proper light, and be utterly abolished, as a reproach to the Christian profession.

John Woolman was present at this Yearly Meeting: the experience which, sixteen years earlier, led to his concern in this matter, is described in §49.

650 *Yearly Meeting 1795:*
A feeling hath been witnessed amongst us at this time, which directs the mind in pity towards the deplorable state of those men who promote, procure, and execute the tearing away of the Africans from their parent-soil...let us seek for and cherish that disposition of mind, which can pray for these enemies of humanity, and fervently breathe for their restoration to soundness of judgment, and purity of principle.

651 *Yearly Meeting 1822 adopted 'An Address to the Inhabitants of Europe on the Iniquities of the Slave Trade, issued by the Religious Society of Friends':*
The arguments of the Christian, like the religion from which they are derived, are plain and simple, but they are in themselves invincible. The gospel of our Lord Jesus Christ is a system of peace, of love, of mercy, and of good-will. The slave trade is a system of

fraud and rapine, of violence and cruelty...That which is morally
wrong cannot be politically right.

652 *Yearly Meeting 1875:*
A deep concern was laid upon the minds of Friends of a past
generation for the abolition of the slave trade and slavery. In that
cause they laboured faithfully, and in the end with much success.
These great evils still prevail under various names. In Africa and
elsewhere indentured labour is secured and maintained by professedly Christian nations, under conditions similar to those of the
slave trade and slavery; whilst slavery itself with its cruelty and
immorality still exists in various parts of the world. We desire that
the interest of Friends in the cause of the helpless and oppressed
may be maintained, and that they may still labour and pray for the
removal of these great iniquities.

653 *Yearly Meeting 1958:*
It has probably come as a shock to many Friends to learn that
slavery still exists in many parts of the world, either in its usually
understood form or as forced labour which is akin to slavery...
The prime need, as a preliminary to action, is the gathering together
of accurate information on all aspects of this important problem...
Though the powers of the British Government to deal with potential
slavery or slave trading are now much more circumscribed, we
would encourage any efforts they are able to make through
international channels to bring to an end this deplorable traffic in
the lives of members of the world family.

Race relations

654 The roots of racial prejudice lie deep within us, and in seeking a
solution to the evil results of racial tensions we need to search our
own hearts. Our belief in the significance of every individual in
the sight of God and his need for an abundant life can guide us
even when we shrink before the vastness of the problem.

Yearly Meeting, 1952

655 *During the Mau Mau disturbances, a Quaker deputation visited East Africa in 1954, and on their return they wrote:*

To enter the troubled areas of Kenya to-day having a white face is naturally enough an act inviting prejudgment and prejudice on the part of many of those whom one is attempting to serve; one is a European, a 'White', and the association is inevitable. It is a situation in some ways akin to that confronting Quaker relief work in Germany immediately after the war when the association with 'the occupation' was inescapable, and our workers were confronted with tensions of another kind. Completely overcome they never can be; absolute identification is impossible. But they can be resolved as much by a willingness to listen as to speak, to learn as to teach, and to receive as to give.

656 Emergent Africa presents an inescapable moral challenge to the Christian conscience, and there is grave danger that African distrust of white politicians may extend to a distrust of the whole Christian Church. We face perhaps the greatest ethnological problem of all time and we have to confess that our understanding of the situation is lamentably weak. We are uneasy at the privileges of white people, and are disturbed at the conditions brought about by rapid industrial development. We must face realities, good as well as bad, and remember how we are linked with Friends in Africa, particularly with that small company of Friends in South Africa who are facing the issues at much closer quarters, and who need our prayerful support in all their efforts towards reconciliation. *Yearly Meeting, 1953*

657 Racial discrimination arises because fundamentally it is easier to see a man as a stranger rather than as a brother if his skin is of a different colour. The stranger tends to be feared rather than loved, and it must be remembered that fears engendered by such differences are not always imaginary. They can be resolved only in so far as relationships between man and man, of whatever race, are conceived in terms of a constant realisation that the members of one race are the children not of the members of another race but the children of God. Against this, imperialism, exploitation and even paternalism cannot stand. *Race Relations Conference, 1954*

658 We are faced today with the tremendous challenge of rapid growth in Africa, but although on the one hand natural resources, industries and communications are being developed at a great rate, there is still a vast amount of poverty and illiteracy in that continent. Independence and hoped-for independence are accompanied by some very disquieting problems, not only of relations between white and black but between Africans themselves, and of distrust and violence. The creation of real nationhood is no easy task.

Africa is no longer a remote continent to which we send Christian missionaries in the old sense, but is a very near neighbour demanding our concerned understanding and personal service of a new kind. The need is not for sympathy only, though that is essential, but for men—men prepared to serve in humility alongside or under Africans in educational or other developments there—and for the support of movements for the improvement of race relations. We must practise right relationships wherever our lives touch those of Africans, guarding against any feelings of superiority, showing respect for one another's point of view and finding our way into the heart and mind of others. *Yearly Meeting, 1959*

Publishing truth

Extracts relating to the publishing of truth in general will be found in Chapter 8, especially §376-385.

659 The international service of Friends has a common purpose, at once personal and social. All the activities of our centres, whether in Europe or the East, have this double end in view, the redemption of the individual lives of men, and the establishment of the kingdom of God on earth. We are convinced that the international service cannot be considered by the Society simply as a number of external activities, in which groups of Friends may, if they are so concerned, take part. Prophecy, missionary effort, personal, social and international redemption and reconstruction, touching the whole process of human existence, belong of essence to the life of the whole

Church. That *whole* way of life for *all* mankind is ignored by the Church at its own most deadly peril.

Kingsmead Conference on International Service, 1922

660 We are deeply impressed...by the thought that this world service and widespread missionary effort ⟨are⟩ of the very essence of the life of a religious community following in the path of Christ. No humility of spirit or sense of inadequacy for the task can excuse the Church for a failure of sustained effort in this respect. Hence we feel justified in striving to bring home to Friends the responsibility of every member of every Meeting for this world venture in which modern Quakerism is engaged.

It was John Wilhelm Rowntree who told us that 'the Gospel must be social', and who prayed that Christ would 'lay on us the burden of the world's suffering and drive us forth with the apostolic fervour of the early Church'. The going forth in that spirit was common to the early Friends, and whether we picture the need of to-day as chiefly that of a ministry of preaching, teaching, healing, social service, the care of children, or of prison work, relief, committee work at home, or of prayer, financial support, or whatever it may be, the call is strong to all Friends to share in this great ministry of reconciliation throughout the world. *Letter to all Friends from Friends Foreign Mission Association and Council for International Service, 1926.*

661 *In 1917 Carl Heath wrote a significant pamphlet entitled 'Quaker embassies', which led to the founding of the Council for International Service. Looking back after ten years in this work, he wrote:*
The conception of the Quaker Embassy...was an embassy of the City of God to every great city of man. To preach the gospel, yes, but not to preach only. An integral life was to be demonstrated which in its freedom, joy and intelligence would draw men and women of good will everywhere. At the heart of each embassy was worship, that loving cultivation of the presence of God; and in its activism, be it relief, reconstruction work, educational service, medical and sanitary aid, peace activity, prison service, clubs, lectures, research and what not, the embassies would set forth Christ anew, in the

largeness and strength of that applied mysticism which is characteristic of the Quaker Society.

662 All Friends who live abroad may have a share in this international service, whether they are called especially to such work, or are engaged in other occupations. In every sphere a life lived in obedience to the spirit of Christ will have its part in breaking down racial and national barriers, and bringing together in one the whole family of mankind. We thankfully recognise the fact that many of our members have been working towards this end in employment abroad; and it may be that in the future many others may find it their duty and privilege to seek such employment, in order that they may become pioneers in the development of true international relationships.   *1911; 1925*

Relief work

663 Most relief work begins with some obvious physical need. But almost always there is, behind the physical need, something much less concrete, a damaged or lonely or hopeless or hungry spirit, and relief work which does not penetrate to this level, directly or indirectly, consciously or unconsciously, and make some contribution to healing is a job only partially done... Inspired relief workers cease to be external agents; like Woolman they have a sense of 'being mixed in with' suffering mankind: unselfconsciously they become part of the chaos, the misery and the perplexity in which they move, and yet they neither accept nor are degraded by the situation. Because of their certainty of the will of God for them they are not frightened to find themselves in the centre of the world's evil, and because of their experience of the love of God, they have the patience and the understanding to speak to the condition of their fellows. They do not go about looking for a job to do. They are drawn by their divinely-rooted imagination to the service of God and their fellows in the way that the Lord wills. A relief organisation, then, ought to be a corporate body capable of both common-sense and imaginative action, combined with a natural ability to convey to others a sense of inner peace and stability, surviving outward chaos and yet not divorced from it.   *Roger C. Wilson (1949)*

664 There are no barriers of race, national feeling, custom, climate or culture which cannot be broken down by the method of Woolman and St Francis—the method of self-identification with the need of the poorest, even in distant lands, by means of hard manual work done at his side for his benefit. It remains to apply this method, and this idealism, to the international situation in Europe to-day...The influence of such work will no doubt be entirely negligible as regards the international situation, as the influence of Woolman seemed to be in his own lifetime, or as the influence of Francis seemed to be in his lifetime...But failure does not matter. All that matters is that the right way should be tried; and if the Christian religion means anything at all, the right way is the way of self-identification with the poorest, the way of appeal to the friendliness in others by means of active and practical friendliness in ourselves, the way of unostentatious service... The original international fellowship of Christianity was founded in this way, as barriers of every kind—language, nationality, race, sex, class—were broken down through the literal following of the command for this august sacrament of menial service, as instituted by Christ at his last supper with his disciples.

John S. Hoyland (1936)

665 The discovery is, in the first place, of the unique value of *action*, even humble, menial and manual action—indeed, perhaps especially action that is of the nature of labour—not merely as means to express a belief or conviction, but in order to confirm, even to create our faith in its validity. Not: 'Bring your belief to the proof of action, testify to it by practising it', but 'Bring your half-belief into the power-house of co-action that it may become full belief, creative and compelling'. No doubt the saints and the humble Christian disciples down the ages have known this well, but I do not think any collective expression has been found for the truth in our times more significant than this unpretentious movement of Pierre Ceresole's inspiration.   *John W. Harvey (1947)*

The work of Pierre Ceresole in founding Service Civil International is referred to in a note preceding §103.

666 I do not wish to exaggerate the peculiar importance of *labouring* together in the most literal physical sense of the word. Other forms of co-operation are, of course, indispensable. Men must often come together to confer, and sometimes even to unite in a common demonstration and it is well that they should learn to share enjoyments and even jokes. Yet we know how easily conferences may breed disputation, how easily the co-operative demonstration becomes the mere mass meeting in which numbers are all important, judgement in abeyance, and how easily the shared hilarity expresses the lowest common factor in appreciation among those who join in it. But persons, whether two or ten or twenty or fifty, who have been working together on a disinterested job in whose value they severally believe can confer with less probability of quarrel, and their enjoyment of each other's company (and jokes) will be more likely to be rooted in mutual respect. *John W. Harvey (1947)*

A universal message

667 In the early days of the Society the first publishers of Truth went forth from the British Isles proclaiming in various parts of the world the message of the Indwelling Christ. They did so in the firm belief that it was a universal message for all mankind. In these latter days we are realising again, as we look out upon a stricken and restless world, that there is an urgent call to proclaim that message, and to show to others that the fellowship of Christ is a living reality, and only in this fellowship can nations and classes reconcile their antagonism. It is fully recognised that the service required can only be rendered by those who feel a deep inward call to undertake it, and who are bound together, as were the pioneers of early Quakerism, by a fundamental unity of conviction, based on some experience of the Light of Christ in their own souls, and of the presence of that Light even though it be as yet unrecognised and not responded to, in the souls of all men. It is this that breaks down the barriers of race and nation and religion, and binds men together in the one Divine life. *Council for International Service, 1919*

668 *Henry T. Hodgkin, from 1910 until 1920 secretary of the Friends Foreign Mission Association, wrote in 1916:*

We are coming to recognise on all hands today the need for a growth of indigenous Christianity. Our task is not the reproduction of exact forms, however valuable these may have proved in the West; still less of elaborate credal statements...almost impossible of translation into a simple language. It is clearly to give the fundamental and permanent essence of the Christian message in its very simplest form, and let it work. We are to lead men into a living experience, and to believe that the Holy Spirit will fall on them 'as on us at the beginning'.

Is not much of the failure of missionary work due to the fact that we have overloaded the message with non-essentials? We have expected those to whom we go to receive the message just in the form in which we found it most suited for ourselves, and we have toiled and spent ourselves in trying to reproduce a fully-developed Western product in Eastern soil.

Quakerism, in its essence, is not a system; it is a spirit. If we could get back to the living experience of the early days, all that would be needed would be to go out and communicate it, and leave the results with God. This is exactly the point of view from which we ought to work in a mission field, planting a seed, not setting up a system. The creed, the ritual, the organisation, if needed at all, would develop normally in order to clothe the living organism, to give stability or coherence, a totally different thing from their being superimposed as part of the essence of a 'foreign religion'... The task is not to be measured by the numbers who are in religious fellowship with Friends. Let us rather measure it by the greatness of the truths for which they stand.

669 We believe profoundly in the divine initiative. We believe that, long before we begin our missionary effort, God has visited the heart of every man and woman whom we may approach, preparing the way, calling, wooing, pleading. Our message of His actual presence already in every soul gives us wondrous hope and inspiration. This thought of the Divine Indwelling, so far from cutting the nerve of missionary effort in the case of the early Friends, was the chief message which sent them forth. 'They gave their message with confidence, assured that God had visited the soul in advance to prepare the way for His truth. The word of God to Pascal: "Thou wouldst not seek Me, if thou hadst not already found Me", was in substance their philosophy of the conversion of any person.' This fundamental belief gives the whole atmosphere of our missionary activity...It follows that we regard our missionary service as a working out *together* of a fuller and deeper conception of the nature and the life of God. It is a co-operative search and a co-operative finding—in a double sense. We co-operate with our fellows in seeking and finding God, and all the while we are all co-operating with Him.   *Gerald K. Hibbert (1933)*

Chapter 15: The world family of Friends

Two years after the memorable Whitsun fortnight of 1652 the first of the Valiant Sixty had begun their work in the south of England. In July 1654 Anthony Pearson in an interview with Oliver Cromwell 'showed him what great things the Lord had done in the north, which was going over England, and should pass over the whole earth' and within a year John Audland was writing back to Swarthmoor Hall that 'many are raised up and moved for several parts; here are four from hereaway moved to go for New England, two men and two women; some are gone for France and some for Holland'.

This is not the place to tell of the adventures of those who set forth, carrying letters to the Great Turk and the Grand Cham of Tartary, to Prester John and the Emperor of China, to 'all the nations under the whole heavens'. Not everywhere did they find response to their message, but many communities of Friends were established, and epistles were sent back to London from Rhode Island, Maryland, Virginia, from Antigua and Jamaica, Bermuda and Nevis, from the meeting in Amsterdam where Friends gathered from Holland, Germany and Danzig.

670 By the opening of the eighteenth century the Friends were *one* people throughout the world, though there was absolutely no *bond* but love and fellowship. There was no visible head to the Society, no official creed, no ecclesiastical body which held sway and authority. But instead of being an aggregation of separate units the Society was in an extraordinary measure *a living group*. Friends had suffered together and they were baptised into one spirit. Wherever any Friend was in trouble the world over, all Friends, however remote, were concerned and were ready to help share the trouble if it could be shared... The greatest and the best of the entire Society made their way from meeting to meeting, and from house to house —even into the cabin of the settler on the frontier—and they wove an invisible bond, stronger than the infallible decrees of Councils, which held the whole body together as an integral unit. Hospitality with the Quaker was not a virtue, it was **an** unconscious habit. His house was wide open to every Friend who passed that way, and...there were practically no limits to the hospitality of board or bed. *Rufus M. Jones (1911)*

671 The prayer of our Lord 'that they may all be one' is the one sure ground for world community, and must be central to all our prayer, thought and service...As intervisitation between Yearly Meetings and groups of Friends becomes more possible there will be many openings, not only for Friends travelling with specific concerns, but for those who will make their ordinary journeys abroad in other lands...There is almost unlimited scope for the development of Friendly contacts by means of personal correspondence, which can mean so much to Friends living in isolation and small groups...A special responsibility to help the smaller and more scattered groups, and to learn from them, rests upon us in the older and larger Yearly Meetings. *Yearly Meeting, 1945*

672 A necessary condition of closer union is that we should get to know and understand one another better, and find out how much we have in common...A most vital need is the widening of our sympathy, and the deepening of the spirit of love and brotherhood that seeks, not our own good, but the good of all. We do not want the invertebrate good-fellowship that has no grasp of essential principles, no sense of the difference between truth and error; we need to be built up together on the strong foundation of the love of God revealed in Jesus Christ. *Edward Grubb (1914)*

673 The Friends World Conference in 1937 saw a vision of creating the Friends World Committee for Consultation. Its aims and purposes are to foster mutual understanding and a sense of interdependence between all the groups of Friends through channels of communication, and by the exchange of ideas of fellowship and searchings after truth. This is being achieved through intervisitation, the written word, and gatherings together both large and small, in regional groups and on a world scale. *European Friends Conference, 1947*

674 *Carl Heath, speaking at the All Friends Conference, 1920:*
It is for us to conceive of the international service of the Society of
Friends as one service throughout the world. The internal difficulties are obvious...Before we can bring the message of reconciliation to the world, with the power and the conviction that God
is ever ready to forgive us, we must all be reconciled one to another.
We are all Friends. But that is only a sentimental term in face of the
catastrophic war conditions and revolutionary surging of the world,
unless we can bring order into the House of Love; and, having
studied our testimony in all its aspects, leave the things wherein
we differ for further consideration, after the manner of Friends, and
apply ourselves with all the capacity we possess to uniting and
concentrating our efforts to set forth the way of Christ anew in a
great and common international order of service...In this gathering
of all who bear the name of Friend, whether American, British,
Irish, French, German, Austrian, Norwegian, Danish, Indian,
Chinese, Japanese, or other race, can we not rise to the thought and
the practice of a great Quaker brotherhood, organised, not to
promote the Society of Friends in the world, but to serve the world
of God's children by changing the unnatural anger and aversion
which makes them enemies into that loving co-operation which will
turn the whole world into a society of friends?

675 *Minute of the Friends World Conference, 1952:*
This conference believes that the Lord has work for us in 1952.
From the moment that this vision has become real to us we must
needs be missionaries, and our purpose will be to bring men to
Christ, their teacher, and leave them there. If this purpose is upper-
most in our minds it will be our object to convey our fundamental
convictions and in doing so to avoid raising obstacles in the minds
of hearers. There are some to whom the use of familiar Christian
vocabulary, the association of organised Christianity and the lack
of Christian practice are hindrances in their approach to Christ.
We shall need to put ourselves alongside our hearers, to use active
imagination in the use of words...We must always be willing to
learn from others; particularly from the experience of God which is

being revealed in Asia and Africa, and elsewhere; in trusting always the Spirit of God, in the belief that he is still speaking both to ourselves and to those whom we would reach.

676 *Letter of Greeting from the Conference of European Friends 1957:*
In a divided world and among suffering and rootless men our task is not to recreate the Quakerism of the 17th century...It is for us to penetrate anew to the roots of our faith and draw thence the strength which will issue in a Quaker witness for today and in words and actions that will find an echo in the hearts of men... Our service everywhere is one, and we hope to find ways of sharing its responsibilities more widely with each other...We have been made to realise the vast range of concerns and ideas which move Friends over the wide area which was represented. Our times together have been blessed indeed, and we have been deeply and continually aware of the loving prayers of Friends everywhere supporting us.

As we seek to know the tasks to which God calls us we should remember that 'it would be unrealistic to think that unity as a religious community means uniformity of outlook. We have to learn how to hold together a variety of elements in a living harmony. Our personal responsibilities will not therefore be alike, for our circumstances, temperaments and experience are different. Nor should we dwell too much on our part, but rather remember always that it is the grace of God that works through us'. Learning this in experience we may come again to know the freshness and wonder of a great common life, giving God the glory as we re-echo the rhythmical prose of the Elders and faithful Brethren of Philadelphia, writing in the spring of 1683 to their friends three thousand miles across the ocean:

677   Oh, remember us, for we cannot forget you:
            Many waters cannot quench our love,
            Nor distance wear out the deep remembrance
            of you in the heavenly Truth:

        We pray God preserve you in faithfulness,
            That, discharging your places and stewardships,
            You may be honoured and crowned
            with the reward of them that endure to the end.

And though the Lord has been pleased
   to remove us far away from you,
   as to the other end of the earth,
   Yet are we present with you,
   Your exercises are ours;
   Our hearts are dissolved
   in the remembrance of you,
   Dear brethren and sisters in this heavenly love.

And the Lord of heaven and earth
   who is the father of our family,
   Keep us in His love and power,
   and unite, comfort and build us all,
   More and more,
   To His eternal praise, and our rejoicing.

Sources and references

In this book the extracts have been printed with the minimum of information judged necessary for an adequate understanding of them. The author's name or that of the corporate body responsible has been given, together with some indication as to when, and if relevant in what circumstances, the passage was written. This information has usually been given at the end of each extract. The date normally is that of the first separate publication of a work within the author's lifetime and is enclosed in brackets: this may, or may not, be the exact year in which the work in question was written. Where an extract is from a work not separately published in the author's lifetime or not separately published at all, every effort has been made to ascertain the date of composition, and in such cases the date is separated from the author's name by a comma. This usage is modified in some places, notably several Journals of Friends, where the date given is that of the incident recounted, irrespective of whether the passage was written at that time or later in the author's life. Where dates only are given, it indicates approval by Yearly Meeting in the year shown as a part of a revision of the Book of Discipline: this principle does not apply in Chapter 1. Some extracts are compiled from two or more sources and in such cases two references are given, separated by a semi-colon, unless the passage from the secondary source is inconsequential in length, in which case a note to the effect is given in the following references.

In the text of the book the aim has been to give a faithful and accurate representation of the author's intention. Spelling is, in general, modernized, save in some instances where the original spelling was felt to help the reader to place the extract in its historical setting, and to pave the way for his fuller acquaintance with the works from which quotations have been made. Punctuation and capitalization have been altered where necessary, but in words relating to God the usage of the original author has been followed. For the rest, the use of capital letters or italic is justified only when their omission would not give the full weight to what is believed to have been the author's intention. Words not in the original are included in angle brackets ⟨ ⟩ and omissions are indicated by three dots (...) unless the omission is of a single word or short phrase making no material alteration to the purport of the text. Dots of omission have not been shown where the passage has a large number of such omissions: in such a case a note to this effect is given in the following references.

The detailed references which follow are intended to guide readers to the sources, and if this list leads to a fuller study of the works from which the extracts have been taken, it will have achieved one of its purposes. Biographical introductions, preambles and notes in italics have been drafted by the 1959 Revision Committee and are not listed, except where they contain quotations. In such cases, a preamble to an extract is shown by an asterisk (1*). The three extracts 'To the reader' are lettered A-C; the preface to Chapter 1, D.

¶A   WILLIAM CHARLES BRAITHWAITE: *Beginnings of Quakerism*, 1912, p. 311; cf. A. R. Barclay: *Letters, &c., of early Friends*, 1841, p. 282. Postscript to the Letter from the meeting of elders at Balby, 1656.

¶B   ISAAC PENINGTON: *The life of a Christian*, 1653, first page (unnumbered). Not reprinted in his *Works*.

¶C   WILLIAM PENN: *A collection of the works*, 1726, vol. 2, p. 781; 3rd ed., 1782, vol. 5, pp. 9-10. 'A key opening a way to every common understanding' printed 1692.

¶D   Drafted by 1959 Revision Committee. The quotation is from a note written by John Woolman at the foot of a list of ministers and elders of Burlington, N.J., and is printed in *The journal and essays*, ed. A. M. Gummere, 1922, p. 332.

1*   Quotation from *Journal of George Fox*, ed. J. L. Nickalls, 1952, pp. 1, 517.

1   GEORGE FOX: *Journal*, ed. J. L. Nickalls, 1952, pp. 2-3. Entry for 1643. An explanation of Old Style Quaker dating is given *op. cit.*, pp. xiii-xiv.

2   *ibid.*, p. 6. Entry for 1646.

3   *ibid.*, p. 5. Entry for 1646.

4   *ibid.*, pp. 9-10. Entry for 1647.

5   *ibid.*, p. 11. Entry for 1647.

6   *ibid.*, pp. 11-12. Entry for 1647.

7   *ibid.*, p. 19. Entry for 1647.

8   *ibid.*, p. 27. Entry for 1647.

9   *ibid.*, p. 21. Entry for 1647.

10   *ibid.*, pp. 34-5. Entry for 1648.

11   *ibid.*, pp. 759-60. Entry for 1691.

12   GEORGE FOX: *Journal*, 1694, p. xvi; bicent. ed., 1891, vol. 2, p. 526; not in Nickalls ed. 'Testimony of Thomas Ellwood concerning George Fox.'

13   GEORGE FOX: *Journal*, ed. J. L. Nickalls, 1952, pp. xlvii, xliii, xliv. William Penn's 'Preface' issued also as *A brief account of the rise and progress...of the Quakers*, 1694.

14   Quoted from *British Friend*, vol. 25 (1867), p. 103, on the authority of J.A.H., New York, 23.x.1848.

15   EDWARD BURROUGH: *The memorable works of a son of thunder*, 1672, prelim. leaves b2, b3, c1.

16 GEORGE FOX: *Journal*, 1694, prelim. leaf F2; bicent. ed., 1891, vol. 1, p. xxxvii; not in Nickalls ed. William Penn's 'Preface'; see note to extract 13.

17 ABRAM RAWLINSON BARCLAY, ed.: *Letters, &c., of early Friends*, 1841, p. 11. Letter of Anthony Pearson, dated 9 May 1653.

18 WILLIAM CATON: *A journal of the life of... Will. Caton*, 1689, p. 8; cf. *Journals of... William Caton and John Burnyeat*, ed. A. R. Barclay, 1839, pp. 9-10. Entry for 1652.

19 MARGARET FOX: *A brief collection of remarkable passages relating to... Margaret Fell*, 1710, p. 2.

20 GEORGE FOX: *Journal*, 1694, p. ii; bicent. ed., 1891, vol. 2, pp. 512-14; not in Nickalls ed. 'The testimony of Margaret Fox concerning her late husband.'

21 MARGARET FOX: *A brief collection of remarkable passages relating to... Margaret Fell*, 1710, p. 8.

22 JAMES NAYLER: *A collection of sundry books, epistles and papers*, 1716, pp. 12-12. 'The examination of James Nayler at Appleby,' 1652.

23 *ibid.*, pp. 438, 440. 'What the possession of the living faith is' printed 1659.

24 *ibid.*, p. xxviii.

25 ¶1 *ibid.*, p. 696. 'To all the dearly beloved people of God' printed 1660, p. 8.
    ¶2 ROBERT RICH: *Hidden things brought to light*, 1678, pp. 21-2.

26 ISAAC PENINGTON: *The works*, 1681, prelim. leaves c2, c3; 1761 ed., vol. 1, pp. xxxv-xxxvi; 1784 ed., vol. 1, pp. xlii-xliii. 'An account of his spiritual travel' (1667), quoted in 'Testimony by Thomas Ellwood'.

27 *ibid.*, pt. 2, p. 379; 1761 ed., vol. 2, p. 512; 1784 ed., vol. 4, pp. 295-6. 'A treatise concerning God's teachings' written probably about 1670.

28 *ibid.*, prelim. leaves c3, c4; 1761 ed., vol. 1, pp. xxxvii-xxxix; 1784 ed., vol. 1, pp. xliv-xlvii. 'An account of his spiritual travel' (1667), quoted in 'Testimony by Thomas Ellwood'.

29* Quotation from *Experiences... of Mary Penington*, 1911, p. 44.

29 MARY PENINGTON: *Experiences in the life of Mary Penington*, 1911, pp. 44-5. This autobiography was edited by Norman Penney from various MS. sources, notably Penington MSS., vol. 4, and Row MSS., vol. 6, in the Library of the Society of Friends.

30 WILLIAM DEWSBURY: *The faithful testimony of that antient servant of the Lord... in his books, epistles and writings*, 1689, pp. 44-54. 'The discovery of the great enmity of the serpent' printed 1655.

31 ¶1 *ibid.*, preliminary unnumbered page.
    ¶2 NORMAN PENNEY, ed.: *First publishers of truth*, 1907, p. 199.

32 JOSEPH BESSE: *A collection of the sufferings of the people called Quakers*, 1753, vol. 2, pp. 201-2.

33 *ibid.*, vol. 2, pp. 206-7.

34 *ibid.*, vol. 2, pp. 217-8.

35 THOMAS ELLWOOD: *History of the life*, 1714, pp. 21-5; ed. C. G. Crump, 1900, pp. 14-16. Entry for 1659.

36 *ibid.*, pp. 33-4; ed. C. G. Crump, 1900, pp. 23-4. Entry for 1659.

37* Quotation from *Second period of Quakerism*, by W. C. Braithwaite, 1919, p. 211.

37 WILLIAM PENN: *A collection of the works*, 1726, vol. 1, pp. 80-1; 3rd ed., 1782, vol. 3, pp. 438-40. Letter from William Penn to the Countess of Falkenstein, 1677.

38   GEORGE FOX: *Journal*, 1694, prelim. leaves I2, K1; bicent. ed., 1891, vol. 1, pp. li-lii; not in Nickalls ed. William Penn's 'Preface'; see note to extract 13.

39   SAMUEL M. JANNEY: *Life of William Penn*, 1852, p. 166; 6th ed., 1882, p. 175. Letter from William Penn to James Harrison, 25 August 1681.

40   *ibid.*, pp. 42-3; 6th ed., 1882, pp. 50-1. The story derives from an oral tradition through James Simpson (1743-1811).

41*   The words 'In stillness...' are quoted from *Memoirs of the rise, progress and persecutions of the Quakers in the north of Scotland*, by John Barclay, which is printed in *Diary of Alexander Jaffray*, 1833, p. 271.

41   ROBERT BARCLAY: *Apology*, prop. 11, sect. 7. 1678 Lond. ed., p. 240; Glasgow ed., 1886, p. 255.

42   WILLIAM CHARLES BRAITHWAITE: *Second period of Quakerism*, 1919, pp. 552-3. Luke Cock's Weeping Cross sermon at York. The text printed in the extract is slightly modified after consultation of various MSS. in the Library of the Society of Friends.

43   THOMAS STORY: *Journal*, 1747, pp. 20-2. Poem written 1690.

44   *ibid.*, pp. 32-3. Entry for 1691.

45*   Quotation from Joseph Besse's preface to *Life and travels of Samuel Bownas*.

45   SAMUEL BOWNAS: *Life and travels*, 1756, pp. 4-7. Entry for 1696.

46   JOHN WOOLMAN: *Journal and essays*, ed. A. M. Gummere, 1922, p. 151.

47   *ibid.*, pp. 156-7. Entry for 1740.

48   *ibid.*, p. 164. Entry for 1743.

49   *ibid.*, pp. 180-1. Entry for 1756.

50   *ibid.*, p. 254. Entry for 1763. 'Happily' corrected to 'haply'.

51   *ibid.*, pp. 308-9. Entry for 1772.

52   JOB SCOTT: *Journal*, N.Y., 1797, pp. 13-15; 1843 ed., pp. 12-13. Entry for *c.* 1765.

53   *ibid.*, pp. 37-8; 1843 ed., pp. 35-6.

54   JOHN TOMKINS et al.: *Piety promoted*, Phila. ed., 1854, vol. 3, p. 189. Job Scott's dying words.

55   THOMAS SHILLITOE: *Journal*, 1839, vol. 2, pp. 45-8. Entry for 1824.

56   DANIEL WHEELER: *Memoirs*, 1842, pp. 70-1.

57   SARAH LYNES GRUBB: *Letters*, 1864, pp. 3, 4, 6, 7, 12-14. 'Address to her children' written 1832.

58   STEPHEN GRELLET: *Memoirs*, ed. Benjamin Seebohm, 1860, vol. 1, pp. 24-5; 1862 ed., vol. 1, pp. 20-1. Entry for 1795.

59   *ibid.*, vol. 1, pp. 51-2; 1862 ed., vol. 1, pp. 41-4. Entry for 1798.

60   *ibid.*, vol. 1, p. 290; 1862 ed., vol. 1, p. 223. Entry for 1814.

61   JOHN S. ROWNTREE: *The Society of Friends, its faith and practice*, 1901, p. 41; 1919 ed., p. 54. No earlier record of these words of Grellet has, at the time of going to press, been traced.

62   HANNAH KILHAM: *Memoir*, 1837, p. 119.

63   *ibid.*, p. 386.

64*   Quotation from 'Testimony of Yorkshire Q.M.'. In *Y.M. Proc.*, 1862, pp. 78-9.

64   JOSHUA ROWNTREE: *Social service, its place in the Society of Friends* (*Swarthmore lecture*), 1913, pp. 78-9.

65*   Quotations from *Memoir of the life of Elizabeth Fry*, 1847, vol. 1, p. 34; 2nd ed., 1848, vol. 1, pp. 34-5.

65   This extract is taken from the MS. Journal of Elizabeth Fry (Library of the
       Society of Friends, MS. vol. S256). Cf. text in *Memoir of the life of Elizabeth Fry*,
       1847, vol. I, pp. 34-5, 39; 2nd ed., 1848, vol. I, pp. 35-6, 40; and as quoted in
       Elizabeth Fry, by Janet Whitney, 1937, pp. 49, 64.

66   ELIZABETH FRY· *Memoir of the life*, 1847, vol. I, p. 41; 2nd ed., 1848, vol. I,
       pp. 42-3.

67   *ibid.*, vol. 2, p. 470; 2nd ed., 1848, vol. 2, p. 481.

68   ELIZABETH FRY: *Observations on the visiting of female prisoners*, 1827, pp. 21-2.

69   ELIZABETH FRY: *Memoir of the life*, 2nd ed., 1848, vol. 2, p. 509. The extract
       appears in the *Annual monitor for 1846*, pp. 129-30, but is not printed in the 1st ed.
       of the *Memoir*.

70   JOHN GREENLEAF WHITTIER: *The writings*, 1888-1889, vol. 7, p. 313. Letter to
       The Friends review, 1870.

71   *ibid.*, vol. 2, p. 242. 'First-day thoughts' written 1852.

72*   Quotation from an address of John Bright at a public meeting in Birmingham
       Town Hall, 13 December 1865, printed in *The life and times of John Bright*, by
       William Robertson, [1892], vol. 2, p. 379.

72   Testimony of Marsden M.M. concerning John Bright. In *Y.M. Proc.*, 1889
       pp. xii-xiv.

73   Testimony of Westminster and Longford M.M. concerning Joseph Bevan
       Braithwaite. In *Y.M. Proc.*, 1906, pp. 215-16. The public avowal referred to in
       the last paragraph of the extract was, in fact, made at Y.M., 1841. See *J. Bevan
       Braithwaite, a Friend of the nineteenth century*, by Anna Braithwaite Thomas et al.,
       1909, p. 86.

74*   Quotation from *J. Bevan Braithwaite, a Friend of the 19th century*, 1909, pp. 136-7.

74   ANNA BRAITHWAITE THOMAS et al.: *J. Bevan Braithwaite, a Friend of the 19th century*,
       1909, p. 183.

75   CAROLINE FOX: *Memories of old friends*, ed. H. N. Pym, 4th ed., 1882, vol. I,
       pp. xxi-xxii, xxiv. Entry for 1841.

76   *ibid.*, vol. 2, p. 52. Entry for 1846.

77   HANNAH WHITALL SMITH: *The unselfishness of God*, 1903, pp. 14, 18-19.

78   *ibid.*, pp. 289-90.

79   HANNAH WHITALL SMITH: *A religious rebel, the letters of H. W. Smith*, ed. Logan
       Pearsall Smith, 1949, p. 228. Letter dated 28 April 1911.

80   CAROLINE E. STEPHEN: *Quaker strongholds*, 1890, pp. 11-13; 1911 ed., pp. 2-5.

81   WILLIAM LITTLEBOY: *The appeal of Quakerism to the non-mystic*, [1916], pp. 4, 6-7
       1945 ed., pp. 4-7.

82   *ibid.*, p. 10; 1945 ed., p. 10. Quotation from letter by Helen M. Sturge in *British
       Friend*, n.s. vol. 21 (1912), p. 197.

83   WILLIAM LITTLEBOY: *The day of our visitation (Swarthmore lecture)*, 1917, p. 55.

84*   Quotation from *Life of Edward Grubb*, by James Dudley, 1946, p. 11.

84   EDWARD GRUBB: *Flowers of the inner life*, 1933, pp. 2-3.

85   JOHN WILLIAM GRAHAM: *The faith of a Quaker*, 1920, pp. 245-6.

86*   Quotation from Testimony of Ratcliff & Barking M.M. In *Y.M. Proc.*, 1941,
       p. 295.

86   ROSA HOBHOUSE: *Mary Hughes, her life for the dispossessed*, 1949, pp. 4-7. Foreword
       by Howard Spring.

87 A. NEAVE BRAYSHAW: *Memoir and selected writings*, [1941], pp. 38-9. 'Life that is life indeed' written 1911.

88 WILLIAM CHARLES BRAITHWAITE: *Memoir and papers*, 1931, pp. 153-4. 'The spiritual need of England' written 1914. Quotation from *The excursion*, by William Wordsworth, book 1, lines 215-16, corrected.

89 INAZO NITOBE: *A Japanese view of Quakerism*, 1926, pp. 5, 7, 9.

90 INAZO NITOBE: *Selection from Inazo Nitobe's writings*, 1936, p. 159. 'A supplication.'

91 RUFUS M. JONES: *Finding the trail of life*, 1926, pp. 21-2. The extract is an amplification of a passage from his *A boy's religion from memory*, 1903, p. 16.

92 RUFUS M. JONES: *The luminous trail*, 1947, pp. 163-4.

93 MARY HOXIE JONES: *Rufus M. Jones*, 1955, p. 68. Letter to Sallie Coutant.

94* Quotation from *A Quaker business man*, by Anne Vernon, 1958, p. 106, from which other biographical material is also taken.

94 JOHN WILHELM ROWNTREE: *Essays and addresses*, 1905, pp. 397-405. 'Man's relation to God, V: Faith and life' written 1905.

95 MANCHESTER CONFERENCE, 1895: *Report of the proceedings*, 1896, p. 83. 'Has Quakerism a message to the world today?' by John Wilhelm Rowntree.

96 'Testimony of Ratcliff and Barking M.M. concerning Mary Ann Stokeley.' In *Y.M. Proc.*, 1955, p. 161.

97 ELIZABETH FOX HOWARD: *Midstream, a record of many years*, 1943, p. 1.

98 'What does Quakerism mean to me?' by J. Rowntree Gillett. In *Friends quart. exam.*, vol. 71 (1937), pp. 136-8. Cf. reprinted version in *J. Rowntree Gillett a memoir*, by G. M. Ll. Davies, 1942, pp. 18-20.

99 G. M. LL. DAVIES: *J. Rowntree Gillett, a memoir*, 1942, p. 35.

100 T. EDMUND HARVEY: *Workaday saints*, 1949, pp. 124-5.

101 T. EDMUND HARVEY: *A wayfarer's faith*, 1913, pp. 131-2.

102 H. G. WOOD: *Henry T. Hodgkin, a memoir*, 1937, pp. 275-7. Letter of H. T. Hodgkin to Ronald Hodgkin, 1933.

103 Printed from the MS. translation of Pierre Ceresole's application for membership to the Friends Service Council. F.S.C. Foreign Membership files 6/237.
¶1 Letter of 9. ix. 1936 pp. 2, 7-8.
¶2 Letter of 7. x. 1936 p. 3.
¶3 Letter of 9. ix. 1936 pp. 8-9.

104 Prayer of Pierre Ceresole in his last note-book while in prison in 1945 for refusing payment of war-taxes. Translation in *The Friend*, vol. 104 (1946), p. 2. An alternative translation is given in *For peace and truth: from the note-books of Pierre Ceresole*, 1954, pp. 182-3.

105* Quotation from obituary notice by Ernest E Taylor, in *Friends fellowship papers*, vol. 10 (1918), pp. 145, 147.

105 L. VIOLET HOLDSWORTH: *George Lloyd Hodgkin*, [a memoir], 1921, p. 119.

106 *ibid.*, p. 129.

107 'The faith of a sceptic', by Francis H. Knight. In *Wayfarer*, vol. 24 (1945), pp. 110-11.

108* Quotation from Edith M. Pye in *The Friend*, vol. 113 (1955), p. 257.

108 HILDA CLARK: *War and its aftermath, letters*, ed. E. M. Pye, [1957], pp. 6-7

109* Quotation from *Indomitable Friend*, by William R. Hughes, 1956, p. 17

109 WILLIAM R. HUGHES: *Indomitable Friend*, 1956, p. 205.

110 *ibid.*, pp. 218-19.

111*   Quotation from Testimony of Worcester and Salop M.M. In *Y.M. Proc.*, 1953, p. 221.

111   HOWARD E. COLLIER: *Experiment with a life*, 1953, p. 11.

112   *ibid.*, pp. 17-19, 30

113   THOMAS R. KELLY: *A testament of devotion*, 1941, pp. 18-19; 1949 ed., pp. 19-20. From a lecture delivered January 1938, except the last sentence which is from a letter to Rufus Jones, April 1938.

114   *ibid.*, p. 92; 1949 ed., p. 72. 'The eternal now and social concern' written 1938.

115*   Quotation from Testimony of Warwickshire M.M. In *Y.M. Proc.*, 1958, p. 145.

115   JOHN S. HOYLAND: *A book of prayers written for an Indian college*, [1920], p. 6; Lond., 1921, p. 16.

116*   WILLIAM PENN: *A collection of the works*, 1726, vol. 1, p. 840; 1782 ed., vol. 5, p. 159. 'Some fruits of solitude', printed 1693 (maxim 468).

116   Statement presented to Yearly Meeting, 1920, by the Faith and Order Commission. In *Y.M. Proc.*, 1920, pp. 116-17.

117   WILLIAM DEWSBURY: *The faithful testimony of that antient servant of the Lord...in his books, epistles and writings*, 1689, p. 121. 'Christ exalted' printed 1656.

118   WILLIAM PENN: *A collection of the works*, 1726, vol. 2, p. 881; 3rd ed., 1782, vol. 5, p. 344. 'A testimony to the truth of God' printed 1698.

119   Drafted by the 1911 and amended by 1925 Revision Committee.

120   Drafted by the 1925 Revision Committee.

121   EDWARD GRUBB: *Christianity as truth*, 1928, p. 58.

122   *ibid.*, pp. 33-4.

123   JOHN W. HARVEY: *The salt and the leaven* (*Swarthmore lecture*), 1947, p. 76.

124   ARTHUR S. EDDINGTON: *Science and the unseen world* (*Swarthmore lecture*), 1929, pp. 53-6.

125   Letter from Ole Olden. In *The Friend*, vol. 113 (1955), p. 1026.

126   Article by Herbert G. Wood. In *Birmingham post*, 26 November 1955.

127   ISAAC PENINGTON: *The works*, 1681, pt. 1, p. 116; 1761 ed., vol. 1. p. 189; 1784 ed., vol. 1, p. 274. 'The axe laid to the root of the old corrupt tree' printed 1659.

128   RUFUS M. JONES: *Religious foundations*, 1923, p. 11.

129   ISAAC PENINGTON: *The works*, 1681, pt. 1, pp. 381-2, 384; 1761 ed., vol. 1, pp. 539-40, 544; 1784 ed., vol. 2, pp. 321-2, 328. 'Some questions and answers shewing mankind his duty' printed in the 1662 ed. of 'To all such as complain that they want power'.

130   GEORGE FOX: *A collection of...epistles*, 1698, p. 39. Epistle 43, written 1653.

131   WILLIAM PENN: *A collection of the works*, 1726, vol. 2, p. 783; 1782 ed., vol. 5, pp. 14-15. 'A key opening a way to every common understanding' printed 1692.

132   ISAAC PENINGTON: *The works*, 1681, pt. 2, p. 452; 1761 ed., vol. 2, p. 615; 1784 ed., vol. 4, p. 450. 'An epistle to all serious professors' undated and not known to have been separately printed. The heading to this extract is taken from the entry in the Index to the 1761 ed. of Penington's Works.

133   JOHN WILLIAM GRAHAM: *The faith of a Quaker*, 1920, p. 52.

134   GEORGE FOX: *Journal*, ed. J. L. Nickalls, 1952, p. 25. Entry for 1648.

135   GEORGE FOX: *A collection of...epistles*, 1698, pp. 325-6. Epistle 292, written 1672.

136   'Where the beyond breaks through' by Rufus M. Jones. In *The Friend*, n.s. vol. 60 (1920), p. 26.

137   Epistle of Yearly Meeting, 1912. In *Y.M. Proc.*, 1912, p. 169.

138   H. G. WOOD: *Belief and unbelief since 1850*, 1955, p. 59.

139   JOHN E. HOARE: *The warrant for youth's search (Swarthmore lecture)*, 1946, pp. 20-1.

140   ARTHUR S. EDDINGTON: *Science and the unseen world (Swarthmore lecture)*, 1929, p. 50.

141   W. RUSSELL BRAIN: *Man, society and religion (Swarthmore lecture)*, 1944, p. 15.

142   'Psychology and religious experience,' by Horace B. Pointing. In *Friends quart. exam.*, vol. 79 (1945), p. 126.

143   Drafted by 1959 Revision Committee. Quotation from *The castle and the field (Swarthmore lecture)*, by Harold Loukes, 1959, pp. 8-9, quoting in turn from *God and the unconscious*, by Victor White, 1952, p. 57. Scriptural quotation from Eph. 3.15.

144   JOHN WILHELM ROWNTREE: *Essays and addresses*, 1905, p. 388. 'Man's relation to God, V: Faith and life' written 1905.

145   SILVANUS P. THOMPSON: *The quest for truth (Swarthmore lecture)*, 1915, pp. 47-8.

146   Drafted by 1959 Revision Committee. The quotation in para. 6 is from the 12th query, 1928.

147   HOWARD H. BRINTON: *Creative worship (Swarthmore lecture)*, 1931, p. 13.

148   Epistle of Yearly Meeting, 1915. In *Y.M. Proc.*, 1915, pp. 277-9.

149   GEORGE FOX: *A collection of...epistles*, 1698, p. 97. Epistle 128, written 1656.

150   YEARLY MEETING: *Epistles...1681 to 1857*, 1858, vol. 2, pp. 365-6. Epistle of Yearly Meeting, 1852. The scriptural quotations are from Heb. 3. 1; John 1. 1, 14, 18; Phil. 2. 7; Heb. 4. 15; Heb. 6. 20; Heb. 4. 15; I Pet. 3. 22; Heb. 9. 24.

151   JOB SCOTT: *The works*, 1831, vol. 1, pp. 517-18. 'Some openings of truth', appended to 'Salvation by Christ', believed to have been written shortly before Job Scott set sail in 1792 for Europe.

152   Epistle of Yearly Meeting, 1920. In *Y.M. Proc.*, 1920, p. 205

153   JOHN WILHELM ROWNTREE: *Essays and addresses*, 1905, pp. 361-2. 'Man's relation to God, III: What has Jesus to say to the individual?' written 1905.

154   WILLIAM PENN: *A collection of the works*, 1726, vol. 1, pp. 286-7; 3rd ed., 1782, vol. 2, pp. 33-4. 'No cross, no crown' 2nd ed., 1682.

155   JOB SCOTT: *Works*, 1831, vol. 1, p. 518. 'Some openings of truth'; see note to extract 150.

156   *ibid.*, vol. 1, p. 520. 'Some openings of truth'; see note to extract 151.

157   Yorkshire Q.M.'s Memorandum on the Book of Discipline, section III: The divinity and humanity of Christ. In *Y.M. Proc.*, 1919, pp. 182-3.

158   EDGAR G. DUNSTAN: *Quakers and the religious quest (Swarthmore lecture)*, 1956, pp. 41-2.

159   CHRISTIAN RELATIONSHIPS COMMITTEE: *The nature of the church according to the witness of the Society of Friends*, 1945, p. 19; 1950 ed., p. 29. Also printed in *Y.M. Proc.*, 1946, p. 96. (Quotation from the Y.M. epistle of 1906). This document was written in response to a desire expressed by the Continuation Committee of the World Conference on Faith and Order in 1939. The statement is printed in abridged form, together with those of other churches, in *The nature of the church, papers presented to the Theological Commission appointed by the Continuation Committee of the World Conference on Faith and Order*, ed. R. N. Flew, 1952.

160   JOHN GREENLEAF WHITTIER: *The writings*, 1888-89, vol. 2, pp. 274, 276. 'Our master' written 1866.

161   GEORGE FOX: *Journal*, ed. J. L. Nickalls, 1952, p. 312. 'An epistle to Friends' written 1657.

162   ISAAC PENINGTON: *The works*, 1681, pt. 1, pp. 420-1; 1761 ed., vol. 1, p. 603; 1784 ed., vol. 2, p. 417. 'Some of the mysteries of God's kingdom glanced at' printed 1663.

163   GEORGE FOX: *Journal*, ed. J. L. Nickalls, 1952, p 33; 1694, p. 22; bicent. ed., 1891, vol. 1, pp. 34-5. Entry for 1648.

164   ISAAC PENINGTON: *The works*, 1681, pt. 2, p. 148; 1761 ed., vol. 2, p. 202; 1784 ed., vol. 3, p. 332. 'Naked truth', printed 1674.

165   WILLIAM DEWSBURY: *The faithful testimony of that antient servant of the Lord...in his books, epistles and writings*, 1689, p 54. 'The discovery of the great enmity' printed 1655.

166   GEORGE FOX: *Journal*, ed. J. L. Nickalls, 1952, pp. 108-9; 1694, pp. 74-5; bicent. ed., 1891, vol. 1, p. 113 Entry for 1652.

167   GEORGE FOX: *George Fox, an autobiography, [being his Journal]*, ed. Rufus M. Jones, 1903, pp. 526-7; cf. *Journal*, ed. J. L. Nickalls, 1952, p. 642.

168   JOHN WILLIAM GRAHAM: *The faith of a Quaker*, 1920, p. 66.

169   Minute of the Friends Foreign Mission Association. 6.iii.1919. In *Y.M. Proc.*, 1919, p. 148.

170   Epistle of Yearly Meeting, 1879. In *Y.M. Proc.*, 1879, pp. 38-9. The scriptural quotations are from I John 2. 2; Rev. 22. 17; Ps. 89. 15.

171   H. G. WOOD: *Theology and prayer*, 1951, p. 9. Reprinted from *Friends quart*.

172   EDWARD GRUBB: *Christianity as truth*, 1928, pp. 87-8. Quotation from Acts 14. 17.

173   WILLIAM PENN: *A collection of the works*, 1726, vol. 2, p. 863; 3rd ed., 1782, vol. 5, p. 300. 'Primitive Christianity revived' printed 1696 (ch. 6, para. 2).

174   FRANCIS HOWGILL: *The dawnings of the gospel day (Works)*, 1676, p. 46. 'The inheritance of Jacob discovered' printed 1656.

175   A. NEAVE BRAYSHAW: *Memoir and selected writings*, [1941], p. 67. 'Friends and the inner light' written 1915.

176   FRANCIS HOWGILL: *The dawnings of the gospel day (Works)*, 1676, pp. 70-1. 'A lamentation for the scattered tribes' printed 1656.

177   EDWARD BURROUGH: *The memorable works of a son of thunder*, 1672, p. 698. 'To the beloved and chosen of God' printed 1660.

178   ROBERT BARCLAY: *Apology*, prop. 5 and 6, sect. 24. 1678 Lond. ed., p. 116; Glasgow ed., 1886, pp. 125-6.

179   YEARLY MEETING: *Epistles...1681 to 1857*, 1858, vol. 2, pp. 393-4. Epistle of Yearly Meeting, 1857. The theme of the extract is built upon Jer. 31. 31-4 Heb. 8. 7-13; Heb. 10. 15-22.

180   ROBERT BARCLAY: *Apology*, ¶1: Prop. 2, sect. 10; ¶2: Prop. 2, sect. 10; ¶3: Prop. 2, sect. 10. 1678 Lond. ed., pp. 19, 21-24; Glasgow ed., 1886, pp. 26-7, 29-32.

181   T. EDMUND HARVEY: *Authority and freedom in the experience of the Quakers*, 1935, pp. 43-4.

182   ELLEN S. BOSANQUET: *The inward light*, 1927, p. 6.

183   GEORGE FOX: *Journal*, 1694, prelim. leaf M2; bicent. ed., 1891, vol. 1, pp. lx-lxi; not printed in Nickalls ed. William Penn's 'Preface'. See note to extract 13.

184   EDWARD BURROUGH: *The memorable works of a son of thunder*, 1672, prelim. leaf e3. 'Testimony of Francis Howgill concerning Edward Burrough.' The extract as printed is considerably abridged and omissions are not indicated in the text.

185 ROBERT BARCLAY: *Apology*, prop. 10, sect. 3. 1678 Lond. ed., p. 183; Glasgow ed., 1886, pp. 195-6.

186 Epistle of Yearly Meeting, 1899. In *Y.M. Proc.*, *1899*, pp. 76-7. The scriptural references are from I Pet. 2. 5; Rom. 12. 1.

187 Drafted by the Committee appointed to consider Children's Membership. In *Y.M. Proc.*, 1940, p. 55. Based on a text approved in the 1931 revision of *Church Government* which in its turn was based on a draft submitted to Yearly Meeting, 1930, by Hertford and Hitchin M.M. (see *Y.M. Proc.*, 1930, pp 60-2).

188 GEORGE FOX: *Gospel truth demonstrated*, 1706, pp. 947-8. 'A distinction betwixt the two suppers' printed 1685.

189 WILLIAM PENN: *A collection of the works*, 1726, vol. 2, p. 787; 3rd ed., 1782, vol. 5, pp. 24-5. 'A key opening a way to every common understanding' printed 1692 (sect. 11).

190 *ibid.*, vol. 1, pp. 841, 850-1; 3rd ed., 1782, vol. 5, pp. 162-3, 183. 'Some fruits of solitude' printed 1693 (maxims 489-90, 498-503, 505; More fruits, maxims, 127-34).

191 LOUISE CREIGHTON: *Life and letters of Thomas Hodgkin*, 1917, p. 429. 'Emori nolo' written 1868.

192 THOMAS R. KELLY: *Reality of the spiritual world (Pendle Hill pamphlet)*, 1942, p. 40. Paper written 1940-41.

193 RUFUS M. JONES: *The luminous trail*, 1947, p. 165.

194 Letter of Carl Heath, 2.vii.1940, printed from a manuscript in private hands.

195 J. RENDEL HARRIS: *The guiding hand of God*, 1905, pp. 125-6. The extract as printed is abridged and omissions are not indicated in the text.

196 WORLD CONFERENCE, 1937: *Report of Commission I*, p. 18. 'The spiritual message of the Religious Society of Friends', by T. Edmund Harvey.

197 WORLD CONFERENCE, 1952: *Friends face their fourth century (official report)*, p. 54. Report of group in 'Friends and the ecumenical movement'.

198 H. G. WOOD: *Quakerism and the future of the church (Swarthmore lecture)*, 1920, pp. 69-70.

199 GEORGE FOX: *Journal*, ed. J. L. Nickalls, 1952, pp. 604-5; 1694, pp. 359-360; bicent. ed., 1891, pp. 156-8. Epistle to the Governor of Barbadoes, written 1671.

200 ROBERT BARCLAY: *Apology*, prop. 3. 1678 Lond. ed., p. 38; Glasgow ed., 1886, p. 46.

201 MEETING FOR SUFFERINGS: *Statement about the Bible*, 1956. This document is not included in *Y.M. Proc.*, but for reference to the concern see *Y.M. Proc.*, 1955, pp. 89-91, 223; 1956, p. 2.

202 Yorkshire Q.M.'s Memorandum on the Book of Discipline, section V: The Scriptures. In *Y.M. Proc.*, 1919, p. 188. Quotation based on a phrase in 'Confessions of an inquiring spirit', by S. T. Coleridge, 1853, p. 47.

203 RICHARD HUBBERTHORNE: *A collection of the several books and writings*, 1663, p. 271. 'Something that lately passed in discourse between the king and R.H.' printed 1660.

204 ISAAC PENINGTON: *Letters*, ed. John Barclay, 1828, pp. 39-40; 3rd ed., 1844, pp. 39-40. Letter XVI, undated.

205 *The true basis of Christian unity*, prepared by the Commission on Faith and Order and presented to Yearly Meeting, 1917. In *Y.M. Proc.*, 1917, pp. 158-9. This document was prepared as a result of a statement *Towards Christian unity*, issued

in 1916 by a group of Anglicans and Free Churchmen and considered by Friends unsatisfactory because it implied that unity was to be sought along a line of agreement in doctrine and practice without sufficiently emphasizing 'the essential basis of Christian experience and the Christian spirit and way of life'. The calling of the World Conference on Faith and Order at Lausanne in 1927 led to a revision of the statement as *The basis of Christian unity*, and a further .evision under this title was issued in 1937.

206   WORLD CONFERENCE, 1937: *Report of Commission I*, pp. 10-11. 'The spiritual message of the Religious Society of Friends', by Rufus M. Jones.

207   WILLIAM CHARLES BRAITHWAITE: *The second period of Quakerism*, 1919, p. 641.

208   WORLD CONFERENCE, 1937: *Official report*, p. 71. Report of Commission I.

209   GERALD K. HIBBERT: *Quaker fundamentals*, 1941, pp. 7-8.

210   MAURICE A. CREASEY: *Sacraments, a Quaker approach*, 1956, pp. 6-8.

211   T. EDMUND HARVEY: *A wayfarer's faith*, 1913, pp. 67-8.

212   EDGAR G. DUNSTAN: *Quakers and the religious quest (Swarthmore lecture)*, 1956, p. 36.

213   ELIZABETH B. EMMOTT: *The story of Quakerism*, 1908, p. 96.

214   JOHN WILHELM ROWNTREE: *Essays and addresses*, 1905, pp. 100, 92. 'The basis of the Quaker faith' written 1902.

215   A. BARRATT BROWN: *Wayside sacraments*, 1932, pp. 9, 10.

216   Minute 13 of Yearly Meeting, 1916. In *Y.M. Proc.*, 1916, p. 9.

217   COMMISSION ON FAITH AND ORDER: *The basis of true Christian unity*, 1937 ed., p. 3. The extract follows the general lines of the 1917 draft: see note to extract 205.

218   Minute of Faith and Order Commission 1/2.iv.1935. In *Y.M. Proc.*, 1936, p. 110.

219   Report of Christian Relationships Committee to Yearly Meeting, 1957. In *Y.M. Proc.*, 1957, p. 61.

220   Report of Christian Relationships Committee to Yearly Meeting, 1954. In *Y.M. Proc.*, 1954, p. 123.

221   THOMAS STORY: *Discourse at Horslydown*, 1737, title-page.

222   ISAAC PENINGTON: *The works*, 1681, pt. 1, pp. 240-2; 1761 ed., vol. 1, pp. 320-4; 1784 ed., vol. 1, pp. 446-9. 'An examination of the grounds and causes which are said to induce the Court of Boston, in New England, to make that order or law of banishment upon pain of death against the Quakers' printed 1659.

223   WORLD CONFERENCE, 1952: *Friends face their fourth century (official report)*, p. 41. 'What is our faith? report of groups 1-4.'

224   ROBERT BARCLAY: *Apology*, prop. 10, sect. 2. 1678 Lond. ed., p. 181-2; Glasgow ed., 1886, pp. 194-5.

225   MARGARET B. HOBLING: *The concrete and the universal (Swarthmore lecture)*, 1958, p. 17.

226   FRIENDS WORLD COMMITTEE: *Sharing our Quaker faith*, 1959, pp. 104-5. 'Friends and world religions' by Marjorie Sykes. Paper written 1957.

227   WILLIAM PENN: *A collection of the works*, 1726, vol. 1, p. 842; 3rd ed., 1782, vol. 5, pp. 164-5, 163. 'Some fruits of solitude', printed 1693 (maxims 519, 507).

228* Quotations from Yearly Meeting epistles 1947, 1857. (*Y.M. Proc.*, 1947, p. 274 *Epistles... 1681 to 1857*, 1858, vol. 2, p. 394.)

228   GERALD K. HIBBERT, ed.: *Studies in Quaker thought and practice*, pt. 2, 1933, p. 49. 'Worship and ministry', by Robert Davis.

229   THOMAS R. KELLY: *A testament of devotion*, 1941, pp. 29-30; 1949 ed., p. 27. 'The light within.'

230   THOMAS F. GREEN: *Preparation for worship (Swarthmore lecture)*, 1952, p. 17.

231   *ibid.*, pp. 18-19.

232   JOHN W. HARVEY: *The salt and the leaven (Swarthmore lecture)*, 1947, p. 79.

233   BERKS AND OXON Q.M.: *A message to seekers*, [1919], pp. 1, 4. The last sentence does not appear in the document and is perhaps drafted by the 1925 Revision Committee.

234   Drafted by 1925 Revision Committee. Quotation from *Gospel truth demonstrated* by George Fox, 1706, p. 103. 'Something further concerning silent meetings' printed 1657.

235   EDGAR G. DUNSTAN: *Quakers and the religious quest (Swarthmore lecture)*, 1956, pp. 32-3.

236   JOHN KENDALL, ed.: *Letters of Isaac Penington...and others*, 1796, p. 100. Letter from Stephen Crisp, dated Amsterdam, 10.ii.1663 (O.S.).

237   Drafted by 1925 Revision Committee Quotation from *A collection of...epistles*, by George Fox, 1698, p. 115, Epistle 149, 1657.

238   EDWARD GRUBB: *What is Quakerism?*, [1917], pp. 57-8.

239   THOMAS F. GREEN: *Preparation for worship (Swarthmore lecture)*, 1952, pp. 29-30.

240   A. NEAVE BRAYSHAW: *The things that are before us (Swarthmore lecture)*, 1926, pp. 29-30.

241   Epistle of Yearly Meeting, 1928. In *Y.M. Proc.*, 1928, p. 330.

242   Epistle of Yearly Meeting, 1884. In *Y.M. Proc.*, 1884, p. 38. The last sentence is from the Epistle of Y.M., 1886 (see *Y.M. Proc.*, 1886, p. 33).

243   JOHN BELLERS: ¶1: *Epistle to the Quarterly Meeting of London and Middlesex*, 1718. p. 14.
       ¶2: *Watch unto prayer*, 1703, p. 7.

244   WORLD CONFERENCE, 1937: *Report of Commission I*, p. 13. 'The spiritual message of the Religious Society of Friends', by Rufus M. Jones.

245   THOMAS R. KELLY: *The gathered meeting*, 1944 ed., pp. 11-12. This paper was written in 1940 and printed in *The Friend* (Phila.), vol. 114 (1940-41), pp. 201-5.

246   CAROLINE E. STEPHEN: *Light arising*, 1908, pp. 68-9.

247   'Worship and ministry, a letter from London Y.M. on Ministry and Oversight 1899.' In *Y.M. Proc.*, 1900, p. 123.

248   Epistle of Yearly Meeting, 1929. In *Y.M. Proc.*, 1929, p. 300.

249   THOMAS R. KELLY: *The gathered meeting*, 1944 ed., pp. 5-7. See note to extract 245.

250   THOMAS F. GREEN: *Preparation for worship (Swarthmore lecture)*, 1952, pp. 20-21.

251   *ibid*, pp. 30-1.

252   Epistle of Yearly Meeting, 1912. In *Y.M. Proc.*, 1912, pp. 167-8.

253   Drafted by 1925 Revision Committee.

254   YEARLY MEETING: *Extracts from the minutes and advices*, 1783, p. 125. The extract is taken from the written advices of Yearly Meeting, 1675 (see MS. *Y.M. Minutes*, vol. 1, p. 17).

255   YEARLY MEETING: *Epistles...1681 to 1857*, 1858, vol. 1, p. 338. Epistle of Yearly Meeting, 1765.

256   Minute of Berks and Oxon Q.M. Ministry and Extension Committee, 20.iii.1958. The extract is taken direct from the MS. minute book.

257   Drafted by 1911 Revision Committee. Quotation from Olive Schreiner.

258   Minute of Berks and Oxon Q.M. Ministry and Extension Committee, 3.v.1947. The extract is taken direct from the MS. minute book.

259   Drafted by 1959 Revision Committee.

260   YEARLY MEETING: *Rules of discipline*, 1834, pp. 155-6. The extract is taken from 'Advice on meetings for discipline' issued by Y.M., 1821 (see MS. *Y.M. Minutes*, vol. 22, pp. 314-15).

261   Drafted by 1911 Revision Committee.

262   ABRAM RAWLINSON BARCLAY, ed.: *Letters, &c., of early Friends*, 1841, pp. 365-6. Letter of Alexander Parker to Friends, dated 14.xi.1659 [i.e. Jan., 1660].

263   DOUGLAS V. STEERE: *Where words come from (Swarthmore lecture)*, 1955, pp. 37-8.

264   W. RUSSELL BRAIN: *Man, society and religion (Swarthmore lecture)*, 1944, p. 54.

265   The story in this extract is recounted by Nathan Kite in 'Thomas Scattergood and his times' and is printed in *The Friend* (Phila.), vol. 21 (1847-48), p. 286. The articles, edited by William Kite, were published as *Biographical sketches and anecdotes*, 1871, the text of this extract being on p. 111: it is printed also in *Select miscellanies*, by Wilson Armistead, 1851, vol. 4, p. 320.

266   YEARLY MEETING: *Epistles...1681 to 1857*, 1858, vol. 1, pp. 142-3. Epistle of Yearly Meeting, 1716.

267   Drafted by 1925 Revision Committee.

268   YEARLY MEETING: *Epistles...1681 to 1857*, 1858, vol. 2, pp. 162-3. Epistle of Yearly Meeting, 1813.

269   Drafted by 1925 Revision Committee.

270   YEARLY MEETING, 1905: *Letter to isolated members*, pp. 3-6. The second and third sentences and the second paragraph are drafted by the 1911 and 1925 Revision Committees. The extract as printed is considerably abridged and omissions are not indicated in the text. The document is not printed in *Y.M. Proc.*, but for reference to the concern see *Y.M. Proc.*, 1905, pp. 30, 71.

271   Drafted by 1925 Revision Committee, except the third sentence which was drafted by the 1883 Revision Committee.

272   Drafted by 1911 and 1925 Revision Committees.

273   Minute of Berks and Oxon Q.M. Ministry and Extension Committee, 29.xi.1951. The extract is taken direct from the MS. Minute book.

274   Document issued by Warwickshire North M.M. Ministry Committee. In *Y.M. Proc.*, 1912, pp. 80-1.

275   T. EDMUND HARVEY: *A wayfarer's faith*, 1913, pp. 100-1.

276   Epistle of Yearly Meeting, 1871. In *Y.M. Proc.*, 1871, p. 33.

277   Additional advice on ministry, approved by Yearly Meeting, 1949. In *Y.M. Proc.*, 1949, p. 32, and amended p. 297. Quotations in preamble to extract are from the report of a committee of Meeting for Sufferings, i.iv.1948 (see *Y.M. Proc.*, 1948, p. 28). For information on the Advices on Ministry themselves see note to extract 296.

278   DOUGLAS V. STEERE: *Where words come from (Swarthmore lecture)*, 1955, pp. 53-5.

279   WORLD CONFERENCE, 1937: *Report of Commission I*, p. 18. 'The spiritual message of the Religious Society of Friends', by T. Edmund Harvey.

280   Drafted by 1931 Revision Committee. Quotation from *A collection of...epistles*, by George Fox, 1698, p. 306, Epistle 275, 1669.

281 YEARLY MEETING: *Extracts from the minutes and advices*, 1783, p. 142. The extract is taken from an 'Epistle of advice to ministering Friends that travel' issue by Y.M., 1731 (see MS. *Y.M. Minutes*, vol. 7, pp. 270-1).

282 Drafted by 1911 Revision Committee.

283 W. RUSSELL BRAIN: *Man, society and religion (Swarthmore lecture)*, 1944, pp. 55-6.

284 Report on ministry and eldership, presented to Yearly Meeting, 1868. In *Y.M. Proc.*, 1868, p. 14.

285 GEORGE FOX: *Journal*, ed. J. L. Nickalls, 1952, p. 282. Entry for 1656.

286 Drafted by 1925 Revision Committee.

287 A. NEAVE BRAYSHAW: *The Quakers, their story and message*, 1921, p. 103; 1953 ed., p. 275.

288 'Worship and ministry, a letter from London Y.M. on Ministry and Oversight, 1899.' In *Y.M. Proc.*, 1900, p. 125. The fourth sentence ('The very fact') was drafted by the 1925 Revision Committee.

289 A. NEAVE BRAYSHAW: *The things that are before us (Swarthmore lecture)*, 1926, pp. 34-6.

290 L. VIOLET HOLDSWORTH: *Silent worship, the way of wonder (Swarthmore lecture)*, 1919, pp. 77-8.

291 Drafted by 1911 Revision Committee.

292 JOHN FOTHERGILL: *An account of the life and travels*, 1753, pp. 17-18, 21.

293 JOHN WOOLMAN: *The journal and essays*, ed. A. M. Gummere, 1922, pp. 159-60. Entry for 1741.

294 GEORGE FOX: *Gospel truth demonstrated*, 1706, p. 103. 'Something concerning silent meetings' printed [1657].

295 JOHN GRIFFITH: *Journal*, 1779 ed., p. 28; 1830 ed., pp. 41-2. Entry for *c.* 1734.

296 Advices on ministry, approved by Yearly Meeting, 1928. The Advices on Ministry are based on 'A memorial of some necessary advices recommended to ministers' (1775) printed in the *Book of extracts*, 1783, pp. 149-50. For an account by T. Edmund Harvey of the 1928 revision see *The Friend*, n.s. vol. 68 (1928), p. 483.

297 GERALD K. HIBBERT, ed.: *Studies in Quaker thought and practice*, pt. 2, 1933, p. 58. 'Worship and ministry', by Robert Davis.

298 'Worship and ministry, a letter from London Y.M. on Ministry and Oversight, 1899.' In *Y.M. Proc.*, 1900, pp. 126-7.

299 Epistle of Yearly Meeting, 1898. In *Y.M. Proc.*, 1898, p. 57.

300 Drafted by 1925 Revision Committee. Quotation from *The faithful testimony of... William Dewsbury in his books*, 1689, p. 185.

301 Report on ministry and eldership, presented to Yearly Meeting, 1868. In *Y.M. Proc.*, 1868, p. 12.

302 Drafted by 1959 Revision Committee. Based on draft submitted to Meeting for Sufferings, 4.ii.1949, by the committee on the Additional Advice on Ministry.

303* 8th query, approved by Yearly Meeting, 1928.

303 GEORGE FOX: *Journal*, ed. J. L. Nickalls, 1952, p. 346. Letter of George Fox to the Lady Claypole, 1658.

304 GERALD K. HIBBERT, ed.: *Studies in Quaker thought and practice*, pt. 2, 2nd ed., 1936, pp. 25-6. 'The place of prayer in life', by Mary F. Smith. This extract is not printed in the 1st ed.

305 THOMAS R. KELLY: *A testament of devotion*, 1941, pp. 38-9; 1949 ed., pp. 33-4. 'The light within.'

306 WILLIAM LITTLEBOY: *The appeal of Quakerism to the non-mystic*, [1916], pp. 15-16; 1949 ed., pp. 19-20.

307 WILLIAM LITTLEBOY: *The meaning and practice of prayer*, 1937, pp. 7-9. This pamphlet was a reprint from *The Friend* of an address found among the papers of William Littleboy after his death: see *The Friend*, vol. 95 (1937), p. 176.

308 T. EDMUND HARVEY: *Along the road of prayer*, 1929, pp. 32-3.

309 R. DUNCAN FAIRN: *Quakerism, a faith for ordinary men (Swarthmore lecture)*, 1951, p. 39.

310 Epistle of Yearly Meeting, 1888. In *Y.M. Proc.*, 1888, p. 60. The last sentence of the extract is from the Epistle of Y.M., 1877 (see *Y.M. Proc.*, 1877, p. 36).

311 DOUGLAS V. STEERE: *Prayer and worship*, 1938, p. 17.

312 Drafted by 1925 Revision Committee.

313 T. EDMUND HARVEY: *Along the road of prayer*, 1929, p. 26.

314 *A little book on prayer*, 1946, pp. 19-21. 'Intercession' [by Edgar G. Dunstan].

315 JOHN WOOLMAN: *The journal and essays*, ed. A. M. Gummere, 1922, pp. 286-7. Entry for 1770.

316 WILLIAM LITTLEBOY: *The meaning and practice of prayer*, 1937, p. 10. See note to extract 307.

317 WILLIAM CHARLES BRAITHWAITE: *Memoir and papers*, 1931, p. 118. 'The widening of the Quaker fellowship' written 1905.

318 WILLIAM CHARLES BRAITHWAITE: *The message and mission of Quakerism*, [1912], p. 21; Phila. ed., 1912, pp. 22-3.

319 WILLIAM CHARLES BRAITHWAITE: *Memoir and papers*, 1931, p. 172. 'Jesus the likeness of God' written 1921.

320 Drafted by 1925 Revision Committee.

321 YEARLY MEETING: *Epistles...1681 to 1857*, 1858, vol. 1, p. 65. Epistle of Yearly Meeting, 1692. The last sentence of the extract is drafted by the 1925 Revision Committee.

322 Epistle of Yearly Meeting, 1872. In *Y.M. Proc.*, 1872, p. 28. The two first sentences are taken from the Epistle of Y.M., 1870 (see *Y.M. Proc.*, 1870, p. 29).

323 YEARLY MEETING: *Epistles...1681 to 1857*, 1858, vol. 2, pp. 258-9. Epistle of Yearly Meeting, 1834.

324 JOHN WOOLMAN: *The journal and essays*, ed. A. M. Gummere, 1922, p. 59. Letter of John Woolman to John Smith, 16.iv.1760.

325 Drafted by 1925 Revision Committee.

326 A. NEAVE BRAYSHAW: *The things that are before us (Swarthmore lecture)*, 1926, pp. 27, 39-41.

327 HOME SERVICE COMMITTEE: *The nurture of our spiritual resources*, 1954, p. 13.

328 Epistle of Yearly Meeting, 1956. In *Y.M. Proc.*, 1956, p. 247.

329 THOMAS ELLWOOD: *History of the life*, 1714, prelim. leaf b2; ed. C. G. Crump, 1900, p. xlii. 'Testimony of Upperside Women's M.M. concerning him.'

330 Testimony of Alton, Southampton and Poole M.M. concerning G. Herbert Grubb, 5.iv.1952. In *Y.M. Proc.*, 1952, p. 184.

331 Drafted by 1911 Revision Committee.

332 'Membership and pastoral care', by Edward H. Milligan. In *Friends quart.*, vol. 5 (1951), p. 156.

333 FRIENDS EDUCATION COUNCIL: *Up to eighteen*, [1949], pp. 6-7.

334 W. RUSSELL BRAIN: *Man, society and religion (Swarthmore lecture)*, 1944, pp. 56-7.

335   FRIENDS EDUCATION COUNCIL: *Growing up in Quaker worship*, [1952], p. 35.

336   FRIENDS EDUCATION COUNCIL: *Up to eighteen*, [1949], pp. 12-14.

337   YEARLY MEETING: *Rules of discipline*, 1834, pp. 105-6. The extract is taken from a minute on apprentices issued by Y.M., 1828 (see MS. *Y.M. minutes*, vol. 23, p. 281).

338   Report to Meeting for Sufferings, Jan. 1949, from the Committee on the Additional Advice on Ministry. In *Y.M. Proc.*, 1949, p. 31.

339   THOMAS F. GREEN: *Preparation for worship (Swarthmore lecture)*, 1952, p. 31.

340   'Membership and pastoral care', by Edward H. Milligan. In *Friends quart.*, vol. 5 (1951), p. 156.

341   YEARLY MEETING: *Epistles...1681 to 1857*, 1858, vol. 2, pp. 360-1. Epistle of Yearly Meeting, 1851. The latter part of the second sentence is as modified by the 1931 Revision Committee, which also drafted the third sentence.

342   'The appointment of elders and overseers', by Edward Grubb. In *The Friend*, vol. 91 (1933), p. 700.

343   GEORGE FOX: *A collection of...epistles*, 1698, p. 284. Epistle 264, 1669.

344   Drafted by 1931 Revision Committee.

345   Drafted by 1931 Revision Committee.

346   Epistle of Yearly Meeting, 1871. In *Y.M. Proc.*, 1871, p. 33.

347   Drafted by 1931 Revision Committee.

348   STEPHEN J. THORNE: *Oversight in our changing Society: an address to overseers*, *Y.M. 1959*, 1959, pp. 19-20.

349   Drafted by 1925 Revision Committee.

350   Drafted by 1959 Revision Committee. Quotations from 7th query, 1928; and *A collection of...epistles*, by George Fox, 1698, p. 290, Epistle 264, 1669.

351   Drafted by 1931 Revision Committee.

352   Drafted by 1925 Revision Committee.

353   Drafted by 1925 Revision Committee.

354   ABRAM RAWLINSON BARCLAY, ed.: *Letters, &c., of early Friends*, 1841, pp. 305-6. 'A testimony concerning the beginning of the work of the Lord', by Edward Burrough, dated 1662. The passage is considerably abridged and omissions are not indicated in the text.

355   Drafted by 1959 Revision Committee.

356   Drafted by 1959 Revision Committee.

357   This extract, displayed by the Friends Prayer League for many years in committee rooms in old Devonshire House and elsewhere, is taken from an addres by Rev. Cyril Bardsley, a leader in the Student Christian Movement.

358   Minute 14 of Yearly Meeting, 1936. In *Y.M. Proc.*, 1936, p. 300.

359   WORLD CONFERENCE, 1952: *Friends face their fourth century (official report)*, p. 43. 'What is our faith? report of groups 1-4.'

360   WILLIAM CHARLES BRAITHWAITE: *Spiritual guidance in the experience of the Society of Friends (Swarthmore lecture)*, 1909, pp. 101-5.

361   WORLD CONFERENCE, 1952: *Friends face their fourth century (official report)*, p. 24. 'The service of the meeting to its members', by Kathleen M. Slack.

362   ISAAC PENINGTON: *Letters*, ed. John Barclay, 1828, pp. 68-9; 3rd ed., 1844, pp.55-6. Postscript to Epistle to Friends of truth in and about the Chalfonts, dated Aylesbury prison, 26.xi.1666 [i.e. Jan. 1666/7].

363   ROGER C. WILSON: *Authority, leadership and concern (Swarthmore lecture)*, 1949 pp. 12-13.

364   Drafted by 1925 Revision Committee.

365   WILLIAM CHARLES BRAITHWAITE: *Spiritual guidance in the experience of the Society of Friends (Swarthmore lecture)*, 1909, p. 81.

366   'Statement of the principles which should guide Friends in their relation with other Christian bodies in the mission field', presented by the Friends Foreign Mission Association to Yearly Meeting, 1914. In *Y.M. Proc.*, 1914, pp. 13-14.

367   Drafted by 1931 Revision Committee.

368   WORLD CONFERENCE, 1952: *Friends face their fourth century (official report)*, p. 39. 'The state of the Society: report of group 2.

369   RICHARD CLARIDGE: *Lux evangelica attestata*, 1701, p. [x].

370   EDGAR G. DUNSTAN: *Quakers and the religious quest (Swarthmore lecture)*, 1956, p. 68.

371   T. EDMUND HARVEY: *The long pilgrimage (Swarthmore lecture)*, 1921, pp. 35-6.

372   Drafted by 1931 Revision Committee.

373   Drafted by 1931 Revision Committee.

374   Drafted by 1931 Revision Committee.

375   WORLD CONFERENCE, 1952: *Friends face their fourth century (official report)*, p. 43. 'What is our service? reports of groups 1 and 2.'

376   GEORGE FOX: *Journal*, ed. J. L. Nickalls, 1952, p. 263. 'Exhortation to Friends in the ministry', from Launceston prison, 1656.

377   HENRY T. HODGKIN: *Friends beyond seas*, 1916, pp. 224-5.

378   Minute 17 of Yearly Meeting, 1953. In *Y.M. Proc.*, 1953, p. 253.

379   EDGAR G. DUNSTAN: *Quakers and the religious quest (Swarthmore lecture)*, 1956, p. 10.

380   *ibid.*, pp. 60-1.

381   GEORGE B. JEFFERY: *Christ yesterday and to-day (Swarthmore lecture)*, 1934, p. 47.

382   Minute 17 of Yearly Meeting, 1938. In *Y.M. Proc.*, 1938, p. 267.

383   WORLD CONFERENCE, 1952: *Friends face their fourth century (official report)*, pp. 33-5. 'Report of worship-fellowship groups.'

384   Minute of Home Service Committee, 2.ii.1950. The extract is taken direct from the official minute book.

385   JOHN A. HUGHES: *The light of Christ in a pagan world (Swarthmore lecture)*, 1940, pp. 95-6. Quotation from *Principles of extension work*, by Ernest E. Taylor.

386   Minute 53 of Yearly Meeting, 1906. In *Y.M. Proc.*, 1906, p. 56.

387   EDGAR G. DUNSTAN: *Quakers and the religious quest (Swarthmore lecture)*, 1956, p. 32.

388   SOCIAL SERVICE INVESTIGATING COMMITTEE: *The Society of Friends and social service*, 1944, p. 16.

389   GEORGE FOX: *A collection of...epistles*, 1698, pp. 104, 85. Epistles 131, 1656; 104, 1655.

390   Minute 32 of Yearly Meeting, 1950. In *Y.M. Proc.*, 1950, p. 267.

391   Drafted by 1925 Revision Committee.

392   SILVANUS P. THOMPSON: *A not impossible religion*, 1918, pp. 39-40.

393   GEORGE FOX: *Journal*, 1694, p. 72; bicent. ed., 1891, vol. 1, p. 109; cf. ed. J. L. Nickalls, 1952, p. 103. Entry for 1652.

394*   JOHN GREENLEAF WHITTIER: *The writings*, 1888-1889, vol. 7, p. 308. Letter to *The Friends review*, 1870.

394   HORACE B. POINTING: *The Society of Friends*, 1946, p. 20.

395 WILLIAM PENN: *A collection of the works*, 1726, vol. 1, pp. 296, 360; 3rd ed., 1782, vol. 2, pp. 53, 191. 'No cross, no crown' 2nd ed. printed 1682 (ch. 5, sect. 12; ch. 16, sect. 3).

396 Drafted by 1925 Revision Committee.

397 WORLD CONFERENCE, 1952: *Friends face their fourth century (official report)*, pp. xvi-xvii. 'A message to all Friends.'

398 Epistle of Yearly Meeting, 1943. In *Y.M. Proc.*, 1943, p. 237.

399 Epistle of Yearly Meeting, 1909. In *Y.M. Proc.*, 1909, p. 167.

400 Epistle of Yearly Meeting, 1893. In *Y.M. Proc.*, 1893, pp. 58-9.

401 This extract is printed from a MS. in the Library of the Society of Friends, Port. 25.(66). The passage is considerably abridged and omissions are not indicated in the text.

402 YEARLY MEETING: *Epistles...1681 to 1857*, 1858, vol. 2, pp. 232-3. Epistle o. Yearly Meeting, 1829.

403 GEORGE FOX: *A collection of...epistles*, 1698, p. 102. Epistle 131, 1656.

404 ISAAC PENINGTON: *Letters*, ed. John Barclay, 1828, p. 139; 3rd ed., 1844, p. 138. Letter LII: To Friends in Amersham, dated Aylesbury, 4.iii.[May] 1667.

405 YEARLY MEETING: *Epistles...1681-1857*, 1858, vol. 2, p. 132. Epistle of Yearly Meeting, 1806.

406 GEORGE FOX: *A collection of...epistles*, 1698, p. 11. Epistle 10, 1652.

407 Drafted by 1911 Revision Committee.

408 JOB SCOTT: *Journal*, N.Y., 1797, p. 8; 1843 ed., p. 7.

409 JOSEPH JOHN ARMISTEAD: *Ten years near the Arctic circle*, 1913, p. 176.

410 Letter of John Woolman to Susanna Lightfoot. In *J. Friends hist. soc.*, vol. 48 (1956-58), p. 154. The letter is undated: it was written at some time after 1764.

411 PIERRE CERESOLE: *Vivre sa vérité*, 1950, p. 162. The extract is translated for this book by Ormerod Greenwood.

412 JAMES NAYLER: *Works*, 1716, p. xlix. 'A psalm or song of praise which he sang in the day of his deliverance.'

413 GEORGE FOX: *A collection of...epistles*, 1698, p. 199. Epistle 227, 1663.

414* General advices, approved by Yearly Meeting, 1928.

414 GEORGE FOX: *Gospel truth demonstrated*, 1706, p. 993. 'A testimony for God's truth' printed 1687.

415 FRANCIS E. POLLARD: *Education and the spirit of man (Swarthmore lecture)*, 1932, p. 79.

416 WILHELM AAREK: *From loneliness to fellowship (Swarthmore lecture)*, 1954, pp. 76-7.

417 'Service, an interpretation for Quakers', by Gerald Littleboy, 1945. In *Y.M. Proc.*, 1946, p. 52. Quotation from §594.

418 JOHN WOOLMAN: *The journal and essays*, ed. A. M. Gummere, 1922, p. 413. 'A plea for the poor' written 1763.

419 Drafted by 1925 and amended by 1959 Revision Committee. This extract and §420, are based on a paper prepared by the Committee on Social Questions and issued by Yearly Meeting 1910 as 'The stewardship of wealth' (see *Y.M. Proc.*, 1910, pp. 158-60).

420 Drafted by 1925 and amended by 1959 Revision Committee.

421 Drafted by 1925 and slightly amended by 1959 Revision Committee: based on an extract of the 1911 Revision Committee and part of the Y.M. Epistle of 1872 (see *Y.M. Proc.*, 1872, p. 28).

422 YEARLY MEETING: *Rules of discipline*, 1834, pp. 277-8. The extract is taken from a written epistle issued by Y.M., 1826 (see MS. *Y.M. Minutes*, vol. 23, p. 120) and was modified by the 1911 Revision Committee.

423 Epistle of Yearly Meeting, 1858. In *Y.M. Proc.*, 1858, pp. 25-6.

424 Drafted by 1959 Revision Committee.

425 Drafted by 1911 Revision Committee.

426 Drafted by 1911 Revision Committee. The extract reflects the treatment of the subject in a minute of Yearly Meeting, 1899 (see *Y.M. Proc.*, 1899, p. 19).

427 Drafted by 1782 and amended by 1911 Revision Committee. The extract is based on Yearly Meeting advices of 1691 and epistles of 1695 and 1703.

428 Drafted by 1911 and modified by 1959 Revision Committee.

429 YEARLY MEETING: *Extracts from the minutes and advices*, 1783, p. 258. The extract is taken from a Yearly Meeting minute of 1706 (see MS. *Y.M. Minutes*, vol. 3, p. 273).

430 Drafted by 1782 and amended by 1911 Revision Committee.

431 Drafted by 1782 and amended by 1911 and 1959 Revision Committees.

432 Drafted by 1959 Revision Committee. This extract is a shortened form of a passage in the 1925 *Christian practice* which reflected the tenor of a memorandum presented to Yearly Meeting, 1905 (see *Y.M. Proc.*, 1905, pp. 36-7).

433* General advices, approved by Yearly Meeting, 1928.

433 YEARLY MEETING: *Epistles...1681-1857*, 1858, vol. 1, p. 55. Epistle of Yearly Meeting, 1691. The passage is considerably abridged and omissions are not indicated in the text.

434 PHILADELPHIA Y.M.: *Faith and practice*, 1955, pp. 22-3.

435 Drafted by 1959 Revision Committee. Quotations from *Journal of George Fox*, ed. J. L. Nickalls, 1952, p. xxix (William Penn's 'Preface'); *Journal and essays of John Woolman*, ed. A. M. Gummere, 1922, p. 145 (Letter of Esther Tuke to Samuel Emlen); *The life and work of Justine Dalencourt*, by Mrs. R. C. Morgan, [1932], p. 85.

436 'Action and the spiritual life', by Henry van Etten, trsl. by Donald Fishlock. In *Wayfarer*, vol. 21 (1942), pp. 147-8.

437 JOSEPH JOHN GURNEY: *Memoirs*, ed. J. B. Braithwaite, 1854, vol. 1, p. 440; 2nd ed., 1855, vol. 1, p. 424. Entry for 1831.

438 GEORGE FOX: *Journal*, ed. J. L. Nickalls, 1952, p. 520.

439 A. NEAVE BRAYSHAW: *The Quakers, their story and message*, 2nd ed., 1927, p. 182; 1953 ed., p. 211. Epistle of Bristol Y.M., 1695: not quoted in 1st ed.

440 YEARLY MEETING: *Epistles...1681 to 1857*, 1858, vol. 1, pp. 83-4. Epistle of Yearly Meeting, 1695.

441 JOHN WOOLMAN: *The journal and essays*, ed. A. M. Gummere, 1922, p. 392. 'On schools' written probably 1758.

442 *Mount Street, 1830-1930, an account of the Society of Friends in Manchester*, 1930, pp. 49-50. 'Friends and education', by Gerald K. Hibbert.

443 A BARRATT BROWN: *Democratic leadership (Swarthmore lecture)*, 1938, pp. 56-7.

444 CAROLINE C. GRAVESON: *Religion and culture (Swarthmore lecture)*, 1937, pp. 21-2.

445 HOME SERVICE COMMITTEE: *The nurture of our spiritual resources*, 1954, p. 8. Quotation from Shorter Catechism, Westminster Confession, 1648, corrected.

446 WILLIAM CHARLES BRAITHWAITE: *Memoir and papers*, 1931, p. 142. 'The teaching of history and historical geography' written 1909.

447 Drafted by 1925 and amended by 1959 Revision Committee.

448 Drafted by 1959 Revision Committee.

449 Drafted by 1959 Revision Committee.

450 Drafted by 1959 Revision Committee.

451 JOHN W. HARVEY: *The salt and the leaven (Swarthmore lecture)*, 1947, pp. 53, 58.

452 *The Society of Friends and its schools*, 1946, p. 5. The second sentence has been modified by the 1959 Revision Committee to cover ground made in subsequent sentences of the original, omitted from this extract.

453 Drafted by 1959 Revision Committee.

454 Drafted by 1911 and amended by 1925 Revision Committee.

455 JOHN WILHELM ROWNTREE: *Essays and addresses*, 1905, pp. 130, 133-4. 'The problem of a free ministry' written 1899. The passage is considerably abridged and omissions are not indicated in the text.

456 HORACE FLEMING: *The lighted mind*, 1929, p. 51.

457 Minute 40 of Yearly Meeting, 1946. In *Y.M. Proc.*, 1946, p. 319.

458 CAROLINE C. GRAVESON: *Religion and culture (Swarthmore lecture)*, 1937, pp. 37-40.

459 PHILADELPHIA Y.M.: *Faith and practice*, 1955, pp. 24-5.

460 WILLIAM PENN: *A collection of the works*, 1726, vol. 1, p. 899; 3rd ed., 1782, vol. 5, p. 448. 'Advice to his children' printed 1699 (ch. 2, para. 27).

461 MANCHESTER CONFERENCE, 1895: *Report of the proceedings*, 1896, p. 44. 'Has Quakerism a message to the world to-day?' by William Charles Braithwaite.

462 Letter from Elizabeth Fry to Joseph John Gurney, 27.ii.1833. In *J. Friends hist. soc.*, vol. 34 (1937), p. 25.

463 CAROLINE C. GRAVESON: *Religion and culture (Swarthmore lecture)*, 1937, pp. 28-30.

464 Drafted by 1925 and slightly amended by 1959 Revision Committee. Quotation from 'Fra Lippo Lippi', by Robert Browning.

465 A. BARRATT BROWN and JOHN W. HARVEY: *The naturalness of religion*, 1929, pp. 160, 163, 172-3.

466 ELFRIDA V. FOULDS: *Living in the Kingdom (William Penn lecture)*, 1955, p. 14.

467 WALTER ROSE: *The village carpenter*, 1938, pp. 43-4, 46, 135-6.

468 CAROLINE E. STEPHEN: *Light arising*, 1908, pp. 51-2.

469 CAROLINE C. GRAVESON: *Religion and culture (Swarthmore lecture)*, 1937, pp. 24-5.

470 GEORGE FOX: *Journal*, ed. J. L. Nickalls, 1952, pp. 127-8. Entry for 1652.

471 GEORGE FOX: *Journal*, ed. N. Penney, 1911, vol. 2, pp. 342-3; not in Nickalls ed. The spelling of this extract has been modernized. The text is printed also, with slight variations, in Fox's epistle 'Concerning the first spreading of the truth' written 1676, printed in *A collection of ...epistles*, 1698, p. 6.

472 JOHN WILHELM ROWNTREE: *Essays and addresses*, 1905, p. 434. Article by Rufus M. Jones, originally printed in *The American Friend*, 16 March 1905.

473 REBECCA BEARD: *Everyman's search*, 1957, pp. 15-16.

474 HOWARD E. COLLIER: *Health and the Quaker way of life*, 1945, pp. 12-14.

475 'Friends and spiritual healing', by Frederick J. Tritton. In *The Friend*, vol. 116 (1958), p. 506.

476 'The place of medicine in the Society of Friends', by R. Fortescue Fox. In *Friends quart. exam.*, vol. 63 (1929), pp. 300-1, 306.

477 JOHN KAVANAUGH, ed.: *The Quaker approach to contemporary problems*, 1952, p. 196. 'Health and healing', by Howard E. Collier.

478* General advices, adopted by Yearly Meeting, 1928.

478 JOHN WOOLMAN: *The journal and essays*, ed. A. M. Gummere, 1922, p. 302. Entry for 1772.

479 Document approved by Croydon and Southwark M.M., 15.v.1957. The extract is taken direct from the official minute book.

480 Drafted by 1959 Revision Committee.

481* General advices, adopted by Yearly Meeting, 1928.

481 YEARLY MEETING: *Epistles...1681 to 1857*, 1858, vol. I, p. 49. Epistle of Yearly Meeting, 1690. As printed here, the text is abbreviated and adapted.

482 Drafted by 1911 and amended by 1925 Revision Committee.

483 MARRIAGE AND PARENTHOOD COMMITTEE: *Marriage and parenthood*, 1954 ed., pp. 4-5.

484 Drafted by 1959 Revision Committee.

485 JOB SCOTT: *Journal*, N.Y., 1797, pp. 74-5; 1843 ed., pp. 69-70. Quotation from 'A universal prayer', by Alexander Pope.

486 Drafted by 1833 Revision Committee, being part of the Introduction 'On the origin and establishment of our Christian discipline', written by Samuel Tuke. (*Rules of discipline*, 1834, p. xx; *Church government*, 1951 ed., p. xxi.)

487 MARRIAGE RELATION COMMISSION: *The marriage relationship*, 1949, p. 19.

488 THOMAS ELLWOOD: *History of his life*, 1714, p. 257; ed. C. G. Crump, 1900, p. 160. Entry for 1669.

489 Drafted by 1959 Revision Committee.

490 JANET WHITNEY: *Geraldine S. Cadbury*, 1948, pp. 46-7. Memorandum written by Barrow Cadbury, 1933.

491 From the revised 'Advices and regulations' on marriage approved by Yearly Meeting, 1872. In *Y.M. Proc.*, 1872, p. 19.

492 MARRIAGE AND PARENTHOOD COMMITTEE: *Marriage and parenthood*, 1954 ed., pp. 8-9.

493 Drafted by 1959 Revision Committee.

494 Report of Marriage and Parenthood Committee to Yearly Meeting, 1956. In *Y.M. Proc.*, 1956, p. 102.

495 MARRIAGE RELATION COMMISSION: *The marriage relationship*, 1949, p. 20.

496 Minute 27 of Yearly Meeting, 1957. In *Y.M. Proc.*, 1957, p. 255.

497 WILLIAM PENN: *A collection of the works*, 1726, vol. I, pp. 825-6; 3rd ed., 1782, vol. 5, pp. 129-32. 'Some fruits of solitude' printed 1693. (Maxims 79, 100, 101, 103, 81, 97, 99.)

498 Drafted by 1911 Revision Committee.

499 Drafted by 1959 Revision Committee.

500 Drafted by 1959 Revision Committee.

501 Drafted by 1959 Revision Committee.

502 Testimony of Hardshaw East M.M. concerning Amy Lewis. In *Y.M. Proc.*, 1952, p. 168.

503 Drafted by 1959 Revision Committee.

504 FRIENDS EDUCATION COUNCIL: *Growing up in Quaker worship*, [1952], pp. 10-11.

505 JOB SCOTT: *Journal*, N.Y., 1797, pp. 89-90; 1843 ed., pp. 83-4.

506 Drafted by 1925 and amended by 1959 Revision Committee.

507 Drafted by 1925 and slightly amended by 1959 Revision Committee.

508 Drafted by 1959 Revision Committee:

509 Drafted by 1911 and amended by 1925 and 1959 Revision Committees.

510 FRIENDS EDUCATION COUNCIL: *Growing up in Quaker worship*, [1952], pp. 14-15.

511 RUFUS M. JONES: *The trail of life in college*, 1929, p. 64.

512 GEORGE FOX: *Journal*, 1694, prelim. leaf L2; bicent. ed., 1891, vol. 1, pp. lxvii, lviii; not in Nickalls ed. William Penn's 'Preface', see note to extract 13.

513 *ibid.*, prelim. leaves L1, L2; bicent. ed., 1891, p. lxvi; not in Nickalls ed. William Penn's 'Preface', see note to extract 13.

514 Report of Young Friends Committee to Yearly Meeting, 1926. In *Y.M. Proc.*, 1926, pp. 98-9.

515 WILLIAM BECK: *The Friends, who they are and what they have done*, 1895, p. 157. The extract is based on an anecdote in *The Richardsons of Cleveland*, by A. O. Boyce, 1889, p. 53.

516 EVELYN STURGE: *The glory of growing old*, 1950 ed., pp. [7-8].

517 Epistle of Yearly Meeting, 1923. In *Y.M. Proc.*, 1923, p. 355.

518 L. VIOLET HOLDSWORTH: *Seas of the moon*, 1940, p. 27.

519 HANNAH WHITALL SMITH: *A religious rebel, the letters of H. W. Smith*, ed. Logan Pearsall Smith, 1949, pp. 156-7.

520 THOMAS STORY: *Journal*, 1747, pp. 463-4. Entry for 1714.

521 Testimony of Hampstead M.M. concerning Edith J. Wilson. In *Y.M. Proc.*, 1954, pp. 197-8.

522 FRANCES ANN BUDGE: *Isaac Sharp*, 1898, pp. 232-3. The text of this extract has been corrected from the Isaac Sharp MS. Journal, vol. 84, in the Library of the Society of Friends.

523 Testimony of North Somerset and Wilts M.M. concerning Sarah Jane Lury. In *Y.M. Proc.*, 1946, p. 212.

524 CAROLINE E. STEPHEN: *Light arising*, 1908, pp. 130-1.

525 JOHN WILHELM ROWNTREE: *Essays and addresses*, 1905, pp. 417-18. 'In memoriam' written 1905.

526 CAROLINE E. STEPHEN: *Light arising*, 1908, pp. 164-5.

527 Last letter of Joan Mary Fry to her friends. This letter is not printed and the extract is taken from the copy in the Library of the Society of Friends. Quotation from *A collection of...epistles*, by George Fox, 1698, p. 553, Epistle 412, 1687.

528 Drafted by 1925 and slightly amended by 1959 Revision Committee.

529 Drafted by 1925 Revision Committee.

530 WILLIAM LITTLEBOY: *Our beloved dead*, [1918], p. 11; 1948 ed., p. 10.

531 YEARLY MEETING: *Epistles...1681 to 1857*, 1858, vol. 2, p. 107. Epistle of Yearly Meeting, 1799.

532 JOHN WOOLMAN: *The journal and essays*, ed. A. M. Gummere, 1922, pp. 403-5, 427. 'A plea for the poor' written 1763.

533 INDUSTRY AND THE SOCIAL ORDER CONFERENCE, 1958: *Preparatory document 5, Christian responsibility and material possessions*, pp. 5-6.

534 SHIPLEY N. BRAYSHAW: *Unemployment and plenty (Swarthmore lecture)*, 1933, pp. 140-1.

535 Minute of Norfolk, Cambs and Hunts Q.M., 20.vii.1957. The extract is taken direct from the official minute book.

536 WORLD CONFERENCE, 1937: *Official report*, p. 86. Report of Commission IIIa, Methods of achieving economic justice.

537 Epistle of Yearly Meeting, 1938. In *Y.M. Proc.*, 1938, p. 287.

538 KONRAD BRAUN: *Justice and the law of love (Swarthmore lecture)*, 1950, pp. 71-2.

539* 14th and 15th queries, adopted by Yearly Meeting, 1928.

539 INDUSTRY AND THE SOCIAL ORDER CONFERENCE, 1958: *Preparatory document 2, Friends and the industrial and social order*, p. 3.

540 'Foundations of a true social order', approved by Yearly Meeting, 1918. In *Y.M. Proc.*, 1918, pp. 80-1. The quotations in the preamble are from John Woolman's 'A plea for the poor' as printed in *The journal and essays*, ed. A. M. Gummere, 1922, p. 419, and from minute 69 of Yearly Meeting, 1918 (*Y.M. Proc.*, 1918, p. 78).

541 General advices, adopted by Yearly Meeting, 1928.

542 CARL HEATH: *Religion and public life (Swarthmore lecture)*, 1922, p. 69.

543 WORLD CONFERENCE, 1952: *Friends face their fourth century (official report)*, p. 87. Minute 12 of the Conference.

544 SHIPLEY N. BRAYSHAW: *Unemployment and plenty (Swarthmore lecture)*, 1933, pp. 118-19.

545 'A social testimony' adopted by the Industrial and Social Order Council, December 1944, and approved by Yearly Meeting, 1945. In *Y.M. Proc.*, 1945, pp. 135, 261.

546 'The nature of Christian responsibility for the industrial and social order', by H. G. Wood. In *Friends quart.*, vol. 13 (1959), pp. 19-20. Quotation from Horace Bushnell.

547* Quotations from minute 4 and from Concluding minute of Conference on Industry and the Social Order, 1958.

547 INDUSTRY AND THE SOCIAL ORDER CONFERENCE, 1958: Minute 5.

548 *ibid.* Minute 8.

549 *ibid.* Concluding minute.

550 Epistle of Yearly Meeting, 1894. In *Y.M. Proc.*, 1894, p. 65.

551 HAROLD LOUKES: *Friends face reality*, 1954, p. 152.

552 FRED H. BLUM: *Towards a democratic work process*, 1953, pp. 189-90.

553 Epistle of Yearly Meeting, 1911. In *Y.M. Proc.*, 1911, pp. 166-7.

554 Drafted by 1925 Revision Committee.

555 Drafted by 1911 and amended by 1925 Revision Committee.

556 General advices, adopted by Yearly Meeting, 1928.

557 JOHN WOOLMAN: *The journal and essays*, ed. A. M. Gummere, 1922, pp. 410-12. 'A plea for the poor' written 1763.

558 GEORGE FOX: *Journal*, ed. J. L. Nickalls, 1952, pp. 2-3. Entry for 1643. This passage has also been printed as extract 1.

559 YEARLY MEETING: *Epistles...1681 to 1857*, 1858, vol. 1, p. 273. Epistle of Yearly Meeting, 1751. Quotation from I Thess. 5. 22.

560 *ibid.*, vol. 2, p. 397. Epistle of Yearly Meeting, 1857.

561 'An appeal by the Yearly Meeting to...its members...on their duty in regard to the temperance question' adopted by Yearly Meeting, 1893. In *Y.M. Proc.*, 1893, p. 52.

562 General advices, adopted by Yearly Meeting, 1928.

563 T. EDMUND HARVEY: *Moderation or abstinence*, 1931, pp. 16-17.

564   Drafted by 1959 Revision Committee. Quotation in para. 2 from Rom. 14.7 in para. 3 from *Alcohol, our personal responsibility*, a statement approved by Meeting for Sufferings, 5.iv.1935 (not reprinted in *Y.M. Proc.*).

565   Drafted by 1911 Revision Committee. Minor alteration made by 1959 Revision Committee.

566   Drafted by 1911 and amended by 1925 Revision Committee.

567   Drafted by 1959 Revision Committee.

568   SHIPLEY N. BRAYSHAW: *Unemployment and plenty (Swarthmore lecture)*, 1933, p. 45.

569   Drafted by 1959 Revision Committee.

570   Drafted by 1782 Revision Committee, the initial phrase (ending at 'of oaths'), being a Yearly Meeting advice of 1693.

571   Drafted by 1911 and amended by 1959 Revision Committee.

572   'Statement regarding the taking of oaths in juvenile courts', adopted by Meeting for Sufferings, 5.iv.1957. Extract taken direct from the official minute book; not reprinted in *Y.M. Proc.*

573   Drafted by 1911 and amended by 1925 and 1959 Revision Committees. Quotation from *Journal of George Fox*, ed. J. L. Nickalls, 1952, p. 66. Entry for 1657.

574   YEARLY MEETING: *Epistles...1681 to 1857*, 1858, vol. 2, p. 185. Epistle of Yearly Meeting, 1818.

575   *ibid.*, vol. 2, p. 340. Epistle of Yearly Meeting, 1847.

576   SELECT COMMITTEE ON CAPITAL PUNISHMENT: *Report*, 1930, para. 283. Letter from John Bright to Martin H. Bovee, Wisconsin, 3 January 1868.

577   'Statement on the death penalty' contained in minute 39 of Yearly Meeting, 1956. In *Y.M. Proc.*, 1956, p. 241.

578   Drafted by 1959 Revision Committee.

579   EDWARD BURROUGH: *The memorable works of a son of thunder*, 1672, p. 604. 'To the present distracted and broken nation' printed 1659.

580   ABRAM RAWLINSON BARCLAY, ed.: *Letters, &c., of early Friends*, 1841, pp. 280-1. Letter from the meeting of elders at Balby, 1656.

581   JONATHAN DYMOND: *Essays on the principles of morality*, 1829, vol. 2, p. 363.

582   Drafted by 1911 Revision Committee.

583   WORLD CONFERENCE, 1937: *Official report*, p. 36. 'The individual Christian and the state', by T. Edmund Harvey.

584   T. EDMUND HARVEY: *The Christian citizen and the state*, 1939, p. 15 note.

585   EDWARD BURROUGH: *The memorable works of a son of thunder*, p. 786 (wrongly numbered 778). 'A just and righteous plea' printed 1661.

586   Statement presented to Yearly Meeting, 1915, by young men of enlistment age. In *Y.M. Proc.*, 1915, p. 193. The committee appointed to give expression to this concern was known as the Service Committee (cf. §630).

587   Statement issued by Meeting for Sufferings, 7.xii.1917. In *Y.M. Proc.*, 1918, p. 9.

588   PENNSYLVANIA: *Charter and laws of Pennsylvania, 1682-1700*, 1879, p. 107. Preamble of the Great Law enacted at Chester, Pa, 1682.

589   WORLD CONFERENCE, 1937: *Official report*, p. 35. 'The individual Christian and the state', by Henry J. Cadbury. Quotation from *The frame of government for Pennsylvania*, by William Penn, 1682.

590   *ibid.*, p. 121. Minute 18 of Conference.

591 WORLD CONFERENCE, 1952: *Friends face their fourth century (official report)*, p. 14. 'Man's condition and the Christian answer', by Alexander C. Purdy.

592 Drafted by 1925 Revision Committee.

593 CAROLINE C. GRAVESON: *Religion and culture (Swarthmore lecture)*, 1937, pp. 36-7.

594 Drafted by 1925 Revision Committee.

595 INDUSTRY AND THE SOCIAL ORDER CONFERENCE, 1958: *Preparatory document 5, Christian responsibility and material possessions*, p. 5. Quotation from §614.

596 W. RUSSELL BRAIN: *Man, society and religion (Swarthmore lecture)*, 1944, p. 26.

597 'Service, an interpretation for Quakers', by Gerald Littleboy, 1945. In *Y.M. Proc.*, 1946, p. 52.

598 JOSHUA ROWNTREE: *Social service in the Society of Friends (Swarthmore lecture)*, 1913, pp. 109-10, 119-20.

599 INDUSTRY AND THE SOCIAL ORDER CONFERENCE, 1958: *Preparatory document 7, Individual responsibility in a changing society*, p. 6.

600 LUCY FRYER MORLAND: *The new social outlook (Swarthmore lecture)*, 1918, p. 44.

601 WORLD CONFERENCE, 1937: *Official report*, p. 38. 'The individual Christian and the state', by T. Edmund Harvey.

602 CARL HEATH: *Religion and public life (Swarthmore lecture)*, 1922, pp. 60-1.

603 RUFUS M. JONES et al.: *The Quakers in the American colonies*, 1911, pp. 175-6.

604 FREDERICK B. TOLLES: *Quakerism and politics (Ward lecture)*, 1956, p. 20.

605 ALL FRIENDS CONFERENCE, 1920: *Official report*, p. 54. Minute 7 of Conference.

606 A. NEAVE BRAYSHAW: *The Quakers, their story and message*, [1921], p. 45; 1953 ed., p. 131.

607 Minute 44 of Yearly Meeting, 1942. In *Y.M. Proc.*, 1942, p. 229.

608 CARL HEATH: *Christians and aggression*, 1939, pp. 2, 4.

609 JOHN WOOLMAN: *The journal and essays*, ed. A. M. Gummere, 1922, p. 207. Entry for 1757.

610 MARION C. FOX: *A selection of her letters*, ed. Hubert Fox, 1951, pp. 33-4.

611 KONRAD BRAUN: *Justice and the law of love (Swarthmore lecture)*, 1950, pp. 46-7.

612 Minute 68 of Yearly Meeting, 1942. In *Y.M. Proc.*, 1942, p. 240.

613 GEORGE FOX: *Journal*, ed. J. L. Nickalls, 1952, p. 65. Entry for 1651.

614 *ibid.*, pp. 399-400. 'A declaration from the harmless and innocent people of God called Quakers' issued 1661, following the Fifth Monarchy rising, to allay fears that Friends might also be prepared to engage in armed combat. The extract as printed is abridged and omissions are not indicated in the text.

615 ROBERT BARCLAY: *Apology*, prop. 15, sect. 13. 1678 Lond. ed., pp. 382-3; Glasgow ed., 1886, pp. 401-2.

616 YEARLY MEETING: *Epistles...1681 to 1857*, 1858, vol. 1, p. 247. Epistle of Yearly Meeting, 1744.

617 *ibid.*, vol. 2, pp. 123-4, 129. Epistles of Yearly Meeting, 1804, 1805.

618 *ibid.*, vol. 2, pp. 379-80. Epistle of Yearly Meeting, 1854.

619 'Christianity and war, an address by the Religious Society of Friends', adopted by Yearly Meeting, 1900. In *Y.M. Proc.*, 1900, pp. 65-6. Quotation from Joseph Sturge, see *Memorial of Joseph Sturge*, by Henry Richard, 1864, p. 415.

620 Minute 13 of Yearly Meeting, 1915. In *Y.M. Proc.*, 1915, pp. 9-10.

621 'To all men everywhere' issued by Yearly Meeting, 1943. In *Y.M. Proc.*, 1943, pp. 236-7.

622 WILLIAM ROTCH: *Memorandum written in the 80th year of his age*, 1916, pp. 3-5.

623 Compiled by 1925 Revision Committee. The first two paragraphs are based on 'Our testimony for peace' approved by Yearly Meeting, 1912 (*Y.M. Proc.*, 1912, pp. 113-14); the fourth paragraph is taken from 'The Society of Friends and the war', issued by the Northern Friends Peace Board, 1914.

624 WORLD CONFERENCE, 1952: *Friends face their fourth century (official report)*, pp. 58-9. 'The peace testimony, report of group.'

625 Minute 157 of Adjourned Yearly Meeting, 1st mo. 1916. In *Y.M. Proc.*, 1916, pp. 241-2.

626 Minute 32 of Yearly Meeting, 1939. In *Y.M. Proc.*, 1939, p. 295.

627 'The Society of Friends and military conscription', adopted by Meeting for Sufferings, 6.iv.1945. In *Y.M. Proc.*, 1945, pp. 34-5.

628 Statement adopted by Meeting for Sufferings, 2.i.1948, for presentation to the British Council of Churches. In *Y.M. Proc.*, 1948, pp. 206-7.

629 ALL FRIENDS CONFERENCE, 1920: *Report of Commission II*, p. 66.

630 Report of Service Committee to Yearly Meeting, 1917. In *Y.M. Proc.*, 1917, p. 33. The Service Committee was appointed in 1915 to give expression to a concern of young men of enlistment age, which is described in §586 (see *Y.M. Proc.*, 1915, p. 193).

631 Minute 23 of Yearly Meeting, 1952. In *Y.M. Proc.*, 1952, p. 229.

632 'An appeal to all men and women', adopted by Meeting for Sufferings, 6.v.1955. In *Y.M. Proc.*, 1956, p. 4.

633 Epistle of Yearly Meeting, 1859. In *Y.M. Proc.*, 1859, p. 27.

634 MEETING FOR SUFFERINGS: *A Christian appeal*, 1854.

635 WILLIAM ROBERTSON: *Life and times of John Bright*, 1892, vol. 2, p. 266. Speech in the House of Commons, 17 July 1882 (see *Hansard*, 3rd ser., vol. 272, col. 722f).

636 Minute 34 of Yearly Meeting, 1930. In *Y.M. Proc.*, 1930, pp. 286-7.

637 Epistle of Yearly Meeting, 1937. In *Y.M. Proc.*, 1937, p. 305.

638 'The attitude of Christians in the tensions between east and west', by Margarethe Lachmund. In *Friends quart.*, vol. 12 (1958), pp. 154-9. Reprinted as *Christians in a divided world*, 1959, pp. 6-12. The passage is considerably abridged and omissions are not indicated in the text.

639 WORLD COMMITTEE FOR CONSULTATION: *The vocation of Friends in the modern world*, pt. 4: *Practical implications of our faith*, 1953, p. 27.

640 Report of East-West Relations Committee to Yearly Meeting, 1958. In *Y.M. Proc.*, 1958, p. 72.

641 'A message to all men', adopted by Meeting for Sufferings, 5.xii.1919. In *Y.M. Proc.*, 1920, pp. 256-7.

642 Drafted by 1925 Revision Committee.

643 'A message of goodwill to all men', adopted by Yearly Meeting, 1950. In *Y.M. Proc.*, 1950, p. 266.

644 WORLD CONFERENCE, 1952: *Friends face their fourth century (official report)*, p. xviii. 'A message to men everywhere.'

645 'Statement on San Francisco Conference', adopted by Meeting for Sufferings, 2.iii.1945. Not reprinted in *Y.M. Proc.* Extracts from the statement are printed in *The Friend*, vol. 103 (1945), pp. 243-4.

646   Drafted by 1925 Revision Committee, the preamble being drafted by the 1959 Revision Committee.

647   KONRAD BRAUN: *Justice and the law of love (Swarthmore lecture)*, 1950, p. 46.

648   YEARLY MEETING: *Extracts from the minutes and advices*, 1783, p. 227. Minute of Yearly Meeting, 1727 (see MS. *Y.M. Minutes*, vol. 6, pp. 457-8). The minute reaffirms the answer given by the Y.M. Correspondents to Friends of Pennsylvania and the Jerseys, 17.vi.[Aug.] 1713, and to Friends of Pennsylvania, 3.viii.[Oct.] 1715.

649   *ibid.*, vol. 2, p. 10. Epistle of Yearly Meeting, 1772.

650   *ibid.*, vol. 2, p. 93. Epistle of Yearly Meeting, 1795.

651   YEARLY MEETING, 1822: *An address to the inhabitants of Europe on the iniquities of the slave trade*, 1822, pp. 8, 10.

652   Epistle of Yearly Meeting, 1875. In *Y.M. Proc.*, 1875, p. 43. The words 'In Africa ...of the world' were drafted by the 1911 Revision Committee to replace the former sentences.

653   Minute 27 of Yearly Meeting, 1958. In *Y.M. Proc.*, 1958, p. 238.
The extracts contained in the section on Slavery (§648-653) are intended to do no more than point to the broad outline of the continuing concern of Friends in this subject, and it is recognized that the passages chosen cannot do justice to all the detailed development of thought. A fuller selection of extracts is provided in *Quaker testimony against slavery and racial discrimination*, by Stella Alexander, 1958.

654   Minute 41 of Yearly Meeting, 1952. In *Y.M. Proc.*, 1952, pp. 233-4.

655   Report presented to the Friends Service Council by Richard S. Rowntree and Eric D. Cleaver on their return from Kenya, 1954. The extract is taken direct from the official minute book.

656   Minute 25 of Yearly Meeting, 1953. In *Y.M. Proc.*, 1953, p. 235.

657   RACE RELATIONS CONFERENCE, 1954: Minute 4.

658   Minute 24 of Yearly Meeting, 1959. In *Y.M. Proc.*, 1959, p. 211.

659   Report of the Kingsmead Conference on International Service, 1922. Reprinted from *Christian practice*, the original not having been traced.

660   Letter to all Friends from F.F.M.A. and C.I.S., 1926. The original has not, at the time of going to press, been traced. The exact words of the first J. W. Rowntree quotation have not been traced, but for the general theme see *Essays and addresses*, 1905, pp. 365-6ff; second quotation from §95.

661   COUNCIL FOR INTERNATIONAL SERVICE: *Supplementary report 1 [to Annual report 1926-27]: The spiritual purpose of the C.I.S.*, [1927], p. 3.

662   Drafted by 1911 and amended by 1925 Revision Committee.

663   ROGER C. WILSON: *Authority, leadership and concern (Swarthmore lecture)*, 1949, pp. 15, 18-19. Quotation from §51.

664   JOHN S. HOYLAND: *Digging for a new England*, 1936, pp. 221-3.

665   JOHN W. HARVEY: *The salt and the leaven (Swarthmore lecture)*, 1947, pp. 37-8.

666   *ibid.*, pp. 38-9.

667   'Friends Council for International Service', a statement dated Tenth mo. 1919. Taken from a copy in the Library of the Society of Friends, CIS Publ. 1.(4).

668   HENRY T. HODGKIN: *Friends beyond seas*, 1916, pp. 226-7, 238.

669   GERALD K. HIBBERT: *The Christian faith and modern missions*, 1933, pp. 27-8. Quotation from *The heart of the Christian message*, by George A. Barton, 1910, p. 99.

670*   Drafted by 1959 Revision Committee. Quotations from Anthony Pearson and John Audland as printed in *The beginnings of Quakerism*, by W. C. Braithwaite, 1912, p. 161; *The Atlantic community of the early Friends*, by Frederick B. Tolles, 1952, p. 20.

670   RUFUS M. JONES et al.: *The Quakers in the American colonies*, 1911, pp. 314-16.

671   Minute 18 of Yearly Meeting, 1945. In *Y.M. Proc.*, 1945, p. 253.

672   EDWARD GRUBB: *Separations, their causes and effects*, 1914, pp. 131, 135.

673   EUROPEAN CONFERENCE, 1947: *The spiritual need of Europe and the responsibility of Friends (official report)*, pp. 25-6.

674   ALL FRIENDS CONFERENCE, 1920: *Official report*, p. 171. Address by Carl Heath.

675   WORLD CONFERENCE, 1952: *Friends face their fourth century (official report)*, p. 171. Minute 14 of Conference.

676   EUROPEAN CONFERENCE, 1957: *Official report*, p. 9. Letter of greeting.

677   WILLIAM CHARLES BRAITHWAITE: *The second period of Quakerism*, 1919, p. 407. Epistle from a select meeting of elders and faithful brethren of Pennsylvania and Jersey, held at Philadelphia, 17 March 1683. W. C. Braithwaite comments, 'I have set it out rhythmically, as, alas, few Church-letters could be printed'. Quotation in preamble from minute of Berks and Oxon Q.M. Ministry and Extension Committee, gathering with a group of continental Friends, 20.vii.1957.

Bibliographical note

Within two generations of the establishment of London Yearly Meeting the need was felt by Friends up and down the country for a digest of the counsel on practice and government which was contained year by year in its epistles and other minutes and documents. In 1738, therefore, the Yearly Meeting approved such a compilation, issued under the title of *Christian and brotherly advices given forth from time to time by the Yearly Meetings in London, alphabetically digested under proper heads*—a manuscript volume made available to the clerks of Quarterly and Monthly Meetings.

Additions were circulated to these Meetings from time to time during the eighteenth century, but the need for a printed volume was increasingly felt, and in 1782 the text of *Christian and brotherly advices* was entirely revised and brought up to date, being printed the following year as *Extracts from the minutes and advices of the Yearly Meeting of Friends held in London from its first institution.* It is pertinent to recall that since that time a revision has been undertaken by the Yearly Meeting almost once in each generation until the present day, the 1782 *Book of extracts* (as it was popularly called) being revised in 1801 and a supplement being approved in 1822.

In 1833 the Yearly Meeting undertook a more substantial revision, printed the following year with the title *Rules of discipline*. Besides substantial alterations in the counsel on practice and government, a long introduction 'On the origin and establishment of our Christian discipline' was written for the occasion by Samuel Tuke, and four extracts were subjoined to the preface 'from approved documents of the Society, issued at different periods, and declaratory of its views, in reference to some of the fundamental doctrines of the Christian faith'. A Supplement to this revision was approved in 1848.

In 1861 a further substantial revision was undertaken. The old alphabetical subject arrangement was abandoned in favour of a more logical order of chapters, which were grouped in three parts, *Christian doctrine*, *Christian practice*, and *Church government*. The doctrinal extracts included as a part of the preface in 1833 were thus supplemented, and the whole incorporated as an integral part of the book.

There was a further revision in 1883 entitled *Book of Christian discipline*, the last occasion on which the book was revised as a whole and issued in a single volume. The history of subsequent revisions and editions of the three parts of the book is complex, and it is beyond the purpose of this note to enter into all the details, or to relate successive revisions to the changing climate of thought within the Society.

It became increasingly clear in the later nineteenth century that, because of the number and frequency of alterations in the detailed regulations, *Church government* would need more frequent re-issue than the other two parts. Apart from any interim revised editions containing incidental alterations, thorough revisions were approved by the Yearly Meeting in 1906, 1917 and 1931. *Christian practice* meanwhile had undergone two revisions approved by Yearly Meeting in 1911 and 1925, while the 1883 Part I, *Christian doctrine*, was substantially revised and re-cast in a form approved by Yearly Meeting, 1921, the title being altered to *Christian life, faith and thought*.

In 1955 Yearly Meeting agreed to the revision of the 1921 *Christian life, faith and thought*, and the 1925 *Christian practice*. The revised text was approved by Yearly Meeting in 1959. It is now printed in one volume entitled *Christian faith and practice in the experience of the Society of Friends* which, with *Church government*, forms the *Book of Christian discipline*.

Index of names

This index comprises in one alphabetical sequence names of persons and corporate bodies and titles of books or reports where these are best known. References are to extract numbers: a preamble to an extract is shown by an asterisk (*). Where the figure is in Roman type it indicates authorship of the entire extract, unless preceded by 'quot'. when it indicates that a quotation from the author is included in an extract by someone else. Italic figures indicate a biographical or other reference to the author rather than any writing by him. Dates of birth and death are given for authors not now living.

Index of subjects

Pastoral care:

 need for a personal interest in one
 another, 325, 326, 328; illustrated in
 the lives of two Friends, 329, 330;
 care for children, 333-6; young
 Friends away from home, 337; for
 the lonely, sick and elderly, 338-40;
 the duties of overseers, 346-8; cannot
 be accomplished in our own strength,
 332

Patriotism, nature of true: 581

Peace:

 Quaker testimony stated, 589, 605-24;
 experience of William Dewsbury, 30;
 and William Penn, 40; peace inseparable from justice, 537, 538

Penal reform: 573-7

Penitence, its place in worship: 231

Personal character: 394-405

Personal relationships: 599

Personal witness: 392, 393

Personality, respect for: 319

Politics:

 a duty of Christian citizenship, 542,
 582, 600, 601; to be cheerfully
 undertaken, 580; idealism and rela-
 tivism, 603, 604; problems of compromise, 602; and indifference, 547;
 the experience of John Bright, 72

Pornography: 569

Possessions: 418, 532-5, 540*, 547

Prayer:

 an exercise of the spirit, 304; a quiet
 persistent practice, 305; a response to
 God's prompting, 306; to bring our
 wills into correspondence with his,
 307; and realize his presence, 308;
 finding time for prayer, 309-11;
 difficulties, 312; times of dryness, 94,
 313; intercession, 314; communion,
 316; 'a precious habitation', 315;
 problem of 'unanswered' prayer, 84,
 304, 306; experience of being 'prayed
 through', 249, 518; children's prayers,
 507; prayer in old age, 517, 518; for
 the sick, 339, 475; for clerks of business meetings, 353; see also Vocal prayer

Prayers:

 of Inazo Nitobe, 90; J. W. Rowntree,
 95; Pierre Ceresole, 104; John S.
 Hoyland, 115

Priesthood: 186, 275; see also Ministry

Printed word, importance of: 389, 390, 391

Prison reform: see Penal reform

Prison visiting: 573

Probation service: 573

Profession of religion without possession:
 1, 15, 26

Prostitution: 569

Psychology and religion: 141, 142, 143

Public office, support of those holding: 325

Quaker embassies: 659, 660, 661, 662

Quaker schools: see Schools; Education

Quakerism (descriptive phrases):

 'protestant and catholic', 197; 'a
 movement not a sect', 197; 'orthodox
 and evangelical', 116; Caroline Fox
 on 'Quaker-catholicism', 76

Race relations: 654-8

Reconciliation:

 between people, 321-3; in international affairs, 641-7

Recreation: 411, 436, 458, 459, 462; see
 also Leisure

Relief work: 663

Religious education: 441, 442, 445, 447;
 see also Education

Resurrection, nature of: 188, 189

Road accidents: 435, 564, 578

Rush of life, guarding against: 91, 309,
 310, 311, 436, 458

Sacraments:

 positive attitude needed, 209, 212,
 213; doctrine of 'real presence', 210;
 meeting as communion, 210; history
 of sacraments, 211; inner meaning
 and outward observance, 213; rites
 not needful, 214; but means of grace
 not to be undervalued, 215; our
 testimony in the ecumenical move-

Anecdotes and quotations

This index gives under Friends' names references to well-known episodes in their lives and anecdotes about them recounted in this book, and to the quotations most frequently sought.